Perspectives on Black America

Perspectives

on

Black America

edited by

Russell Endo / William Strawbridge

University of Washington

Prentice-Hall, Inc.

To Jean and Jane

Prentice-Hall Sociology Series
Neil J. Smelser, Editor

C–13–660738–1
P–13–660720–9

Library of Congress Catalog Card Number 70–118809

Printed in the United States of America

Current printing (last digit):

12 11 10 9 8 7 6 5 4 3 2 1

Prentice-Hall International, Inc., *London*
Prentice-Hall of Australia, Pty. Ltd., *Sydney*
Prentice-Hall of Canada, Ltd., *Toronto*
Prentice-Hall of India Private Limited, *New Delhi*
Prentice-Hall of Japan, Inc., *Tokyo*

Contents

Preface

Perspectives on Black America is an outgrowth of our experience in teaching introductory level courses in sociology. It is one product of our desire to make the course material relevant to an important social issue and problem in American society, yet to do this without sacrificing the traditional presentation of sociological concepts and perspectives. The subject matter of sociology is exciting; this approach to the subject matter should make it even more so for both the student and the instructor.

Each article in this volume deals with the contemporary Black community—an area of intense interest. The readings are organized around those subject areas that are often taught in an introductory course. An instructor using this book may therefore present a certain subject area (such as family) and then examine this same area within the context of the Black community. The book can thus be used throughout the entire period of instruction. This in turn can give some sense of continuity to the often diverse subject matter of an introductory course. Although the book can be used in this manner, the kinds of articles that are included also make it appropriate for use in courses in general social science, race and ethnic relations, and Black studies.

Given the vast amount of literature on Black America, certain things were considered in the selection of the articles. Readings were selected that were felt to be readable, interesting, and appropriate for the subject areas covered in an introductory course. An attempt was made to include a number of descriptive articles; these would allow each instructor to approach the readings in his own manner. Current articles were stressed; historical materials are important but they are readily available elsewhere. Finally, it was decided to ignore the vast and important body of writings on discrimination and prejudice that merely attempts to demonstrate that Blacks are being mistreated. We are taking the existence of such discrimination and prejudice as a given condition, one that does not have to be proven or demonstrated.

The readings are organized into chapters. An introduction before each chapter presents important sociological concepts and perspectives that are both central to the subject matter of that chapter and useful in an analysis of the articles that follow. We have tried, however, not to make these introductions so extensive that they "get in the way" of the frameworks or ideas that might be presented by an instructor or by an introductory textbook. The introductions also allow the instructor to use the chapters in the order he feels is most appropriate.

We would like to thank the editorial staff of Prentice-Hall and the authors and publishers of the included articles for making this book possible. Numerous people provided valuable suggestions, criticisms, and encouragement. We would especially like to express our appreciation to Ernest Barth, Otto Larsen, and Margaret (Penny) O'Neill for their careful and perceptive evaluations and to Jean Endo for her clerical help and moral support. While we would like to share both the advantages and shortcomings of the volume with those who provided assistance, we alone will accept responsibility for the latter.

Russell Endo / William Strawbridge

Culture and Social Organization

one

What does it mean to be Black? How do the meanings that are attached to color get changed? Black Americans are engaged in an active redefinition of their own identity and their place in society. They are forging new values, changing attitudes, and developing new styles of life. But they are also challenging established cultural patterns.

Cultural Patterns

All societies develop rules and procedures that provide general guidelines for appropriate behavior. Such rules and procedures are called norms. Their importance to a society lies in the fact that they are learned and shared by the members. Without some structure of norms, interaction between individuals would be very difficult.

The norms in every society vary in their characteristics. For example, norms differ in their degree of specificity and applicability to various situations. Some are more important than others and become formalized into laws. Many norms, commonly referred to as institutional norms, are arranged in complex networks that specify behavior concerning important societal activities such as the distribution of power or the bearing and care of children.

Societies also develop values and beliefs. These are ideas and attitudes about those things considered to be worthwhile and important. Values and beliefs often define important societal goals. They usually become embodied in legends and traditions. Values and beliefs tend to supplement and support the norms of a society. The values and beliefs of a society, together with the structure of norms, are major ingredients of what is called culture.

The ingredients of a culture can be seen as being interwoven in a consistent and integrated fashion. However, cultural patterns may undergo changes because of the introduction of innovations, or because of the efforts of groups to modify important norms and values, or for a number of other reasons. And within complex societies the ingredients of a culture may exhibit a wide range of variation and diversity. For example, large groups of people may act and think somewhat differently from one another. These groups often have their own partially developed systems of norms, values, and beliefs. Their members follow some of the patterns of the general culture and also some alternative patterns that are peculiar to their own group. Such groups are usually designated as having subcultures.

Racial and ethnic groups often have significant subcultures. In America such groups voluntarily immigrated from other societies. Upon their arrival they established their own communities and followed many of the patterns of their parent culture. Although some groups eventually gave up their distinct way of life, others continue to persist.

Blacks are an outstanding exception to this process. Blacks were brought to this country in bondage and worked as slaves. Such an experience erased almost all of the elements of their former African cultures. It can therefore be felt that Black Americans have never had a distinct subculture, that they have always followed the general cultural patterns of American society.

However, Blacks have endured a unique set of experiences from slavery up through the present forms of discrimination and oppression. Since they have always been segregated from the rest of society, Blacks have shared in these experiences together as a group. Such a process has led to the development of some cultural patterns that differ from those commonly found in American society.

It may be argued that these patterns are not sufficient to receive recognition as a subculture. It might also be argued that they are merely a variation of the subcultural patterns characteristic of impoverished people in the lower class. A further complication is that there are differences in these patterns within the Black community; all Blacks do not follow the same norms, values, and beliefs. However it is clear that distinct cultural elements do characterize at least some portions of the Black community. This milieu may be defined not only by its different styles of living, but also by the significant products that it has developed and contributed to American society, especially in the areas of literature and music. This milieu also provides the base upon which Black Americans are attempting to rediscover their former African heritage.

Members of a subculture often have some sense of group consciousness and identification. They are aware of those things that they share in common and are conscious of the differences between themselves and others. For many Blacks such an awareness is reflected in the meaning of the term "soul." In the early 1950s the term "baby" had many of the same implications as "soul" and may have been its immediate predecessor. In the first article, Ulf Hannerz examines the importance of "soul" to the Black community.

In the second selection Claude Brown relates some of his Harlem experience with both "baby" and "soul." His descriptive account of "Saturday Night" successfully conveys some of the flavor of the life-style in Harlem.

Language often takes on certain distinct forms in a subculture, as it has in portions of the Black community. Vocabulary and speech patterns are described in the third selection by Thomas Kochman. As Kochman points out, there is a heavy reliance upon certain kinds of verbal communication to control and manipulate situations.

All of the selections in this volume touch upon aspects of the Black community.

Perhaps more than the others, two additional selections would be of immediate interest in an examination of cultural patterns: the discussion of the different styles of life in the ghetto by St. Clair Drake and John Horton's description of street life.

GROUP IDENTITY

"The Rhetoric of Soul:
Identification in Negro Society"

by Ulf Hannerz

I

The last few years have witnessed the emergence of a concept of "soul" as signifying what is "essentially Negro" in the black ghettos of the large cities of the Northern United States. In this paper I will attempt to place this concept of "soul" in its social and cultural matrix, in particular with respect to tendencies of social change as experienced by ghetto inhabitants. In doing so, I will emphasise what I believe to be the dominant purpose of a "soul" vocabulary among its users. There will be clear points of convergence between my view of "soul" and that stated by Charles Keil in his book *Urban Blues*.[1] However, I believe that Keil's personal evaluation of some of the features of black ghetto culture tends to obscure the issue in some ways, and I also feel that a clearer picture of the essential social-structural and social-psychological features may be achieved.

This paper is based on field work in a lower-class Negro neighbourhood in Washington, D.C. The field site seems to be in many ways typical of Negro slums in Northern American cities. It is situated at the edge of a large, ethnically homogeneous area. Its inhabitants share the common characteristics of America's lower-class urban Negroes: poverty, a high rate of unemployment, a considerable amount of crime, including juvenile delinquency, and widely varying family role-structures according to which it is relatively common that the adult woman dominates the family while the male is either absent or only temporarily attached—even when he is a permanent member of the household his participation in household affairs may be quite limited. (It should be noted that this is not said to be true of all households—it is only pointed out that unstable family relation-

[1] Charles Keil, *Urban Blues* (Chicago, University of Chicago Press, 1966).

ships and female dominance are much more common among lower-class Negroes than among the American people in general.) Of the adults at the field site—a block-long street lined by two- or three-story row houses— a minority was born in Washington, D.C. The majority are immigrants from the South, particularly from Virginia, North Carolina, and South Carolina. Apart from conducting field work in this area by means of participant observation in the traditional sense, I have paid attention to those impersonal media which have a significant part in ghetto life; these are particularly important in the context of this study. I refer here to media which are specifically intended for a lower-class Negro audience: radio (three stations in Washington, D.C. are clearly aimed at Negroes), the recording industry, and stage shows featuring Negro rock-and-roll artists and comedians. (The term "rhythm and blues" used by whites to denote Negro rock-and-roll is now only infrequently used by the Negroes themselves.) These media have played a prominent part in promoting the vocabulary of "soul." (It may be added, on the other hand, that both the local Negro press such as the Washington *Afro-American,* and the national Negro publications, for example the monthly *Ebony,* are largely middle-class oriented and thus of limited value in the understanding of life in the ghetto where few read them.)

II

What, then, is "soul"? As the concept has come to be used in urban ghettos over the last number of years, it stands for what is "the essence of Negroness" and, it should be added, this "Negroness" refers to the kind of Negro with which the urban slum dweller is most familiar—people like himself. The question whether a middle-class, white-collar suburban Negro also has "soul" is often met with consternation. In fact, "soul" seems to be a folk conception of the lower-class urban Negro's own "national character." Modes of action, personal attributes, and certain artifacts are given the "soul" label. Typically, in conversations, one hears statements such as, "Man, he got a lot of soul." This appreciative opinion may be given concerning anybody in the ghetto, but more often by younger adults or adolescents about others of their own categories. In particular, speaking in terms of "soul" is common among younger men. This sex differentiation of the use of "soul" conceptions, I will suggest below, may be quite important in the understanding of the basis of the use of the "soul" concept.

The choice of the term "soul" for this "Negroness' is in itself noteworthy. First of all, it shows the influence of religion on lower-class Negroes, even those who are not themselves active church members— expressions of religious derivation, such as "God, have mercy!" are frequent in everyday speech among lower-class Negroes of all age and sex categories, and in all contexts. A very great number of people, of course, have been regular church goers at some point or other, at least at the time when they attended Sunday school, and many are actively involved in church activities, perhaps in one of the large Baptist churches but at least as often in small spiritualist storefront churches. Although the people who use the "soul" vocabulary in which we are interested here are seldom themselves regular church-goers, they have certainly been fully (although sometimes indirectly) exposed to the religious idiom; including such phrases as "a soul-stirring revival meeting."

Furthermore, the choice of a term which in church usage has a connotation of "the essentially human" to refer to "the essentially Negro," as the new concept of "soul" does, certainly has strong implications of ethnocentrism. If "soul" is Negro, the non-Negro is "non-soul," and, it appears, somewhat less human. Although I have never heard such a point of view spelled out, it would seem to me that it is implicitly accepted as part of an incipient "soul" ideology. It is very clear that what is "soul" is not only different from what is not "soul" (particularly what is mainstream middle-class American); it is also superior. "Soul" is an appraisive as well as designative concept.[2] If one asks a young man what a "soul brother" is, the answer is usually something like "someone who's hip, someone who knows what he's doing." It may be added here that although both "soul brother" and "soul sister" are used for "soul" personified, the former is more common. Like "soul," "soul brother" and "soul sister" are terms used particularly by younger males.

Let us now note a few fields that are particularly "soul." One area is that of music (where the concept may have originated—see the article on the "soul" movement among jazz musicians by Szwed),[3] particularly the field of progressive jazz and rock-and-roll. This has been seized upon by those actively engaged in these fields. James Brown, a leading rock-and-roll singer, is often referred to as "Soul Brother Number One"; two of the largest record stores in Washington, D.C., with practically only Negro customers, are the "Soul Shack" and the "Soul City." Recently a new magazine named "Soul" appeared; its main outlet seems to be these *de facto* segregated record stores. It contains stories on rock-and-roll artists, disc jockeys, and the like. Excellence in musical expression is indeed a part of the lower-class Negro self-conception, and white rock-and-roll is often viewed with scorn as a poor imitation of the Negro genius. Resentment is frequently aimed at the Beatles who stand as typical of white intrusion into a Negro field. (Occasionally, a Beatle melody has become a hit in the Negro ghetto as well, but only when performed in a local version by a Negro group, such as the recordings of "Day Tripper" by the

[2]Charles Morris, *Signification and Significance* (Cambridge, Mass., The M.I.T. Press, 1964).

[3]John F. Szwed, 'Musical Style and Racial Conflict,' *Phylon* (vol. 27, 1966), pp. 358–66.

Vontastics. In such a case, there is little or no mention of its Beatles origin.)

The commercial side of Negro entertainment is, of course, directly tied to "soul" music. With counterparts in other large Negro ghettos in the United States, the Howard Theater in Washington stages shows of touring rock-and-roll groups and individual performers—each show usually runs a week, with four or five performances every day. Larger shows also make one-night only appearances at the Washington Coliseum. Occasionally, a comedian also takes part; Moms Mabley, Pigmeat Markham, or Red Foxx are among those who draw large Negro audiences but few whites.

The "emcees" of these shows are often celebrities in their own right— some, such as "King" Coleman and "Georgeous George," tour regularly with the shows, others are local disc jockeys from the Negro radio stations. In Washington, such disc jockeys as "The Nighthawk" (Bob Terry), and "Soulfinger" (Fred Correy), make highly appreciated appearances at the Howard. Their station is WOL "Soul Radio": it is clear that the commercial establishments with a vested interest in a separate Negro audience have seized upon the "soul" vocabulary, using it to further their own interests as well as supporting its use among the audience. Thus there is also for instance a WWRL "soul brother radio" in New York. However, one should not view the "soul" vocabulary solely as a commercial creation. It existed before it was commercialized, and the fact that it seems so profitable for commercial establishments to fly the banner of "soul" also indicates that whatever part these establishments have had in promoting it, it has fallen into fertile ground.

A second area of widespread "soul" symbolism is that of food. The dishes that are now "soul food" were once—and still are to some extent —referred to simply as "Southern cooking"; but in the Northern ghettos they increasingly come to stand for race rather than region. In the center of the Washington Negro area, for instance, there is a "Little Harlem Restaurant" advertising "soul food." There are a number of such foods; some of those which are most frequently mentioned as "soul foods" are chitterlings (a part of the intestine of the pig), hog maw (pig tripe), black-eyed peas, collard greens, corn bread, and grits (a kind of porridge). Typically, they were the poor man's food in the rural South—in the urban North, they may still be so to some extent, but in the face of the diversity of the urban environment, they also come to stand as signs of ethnicity. (Thus in some Northern cities there are "soul food" restaurants catering to curious whites, much in the same way as any exotic cuisine.) One may note that references to "soul food" occur frequently in "soul music"; two of the hits of the winter 1966-7 were "Grits and Cornbread" by the Soul Runners and the Joe Cuba Sextet's "Bang! Bang!" with the refrain "corn bread, hog maw and chitterling." Sometimes, the names of "soul foods" may themselves be used as more or less synonymous with "soul"—Negro

entertainers on stage, talking of their experiences while journeying between ghetto shows around the country, sometimes refer to it as "the
chitterling circuit," and this figure of speech usually draws much favoura-
ble audience reaction.

What, then, is "soul" about "soul music" and "soul food"? It may be
wise to be cautious here, since there is little intellectualizing and analyzing on the part of the ghetto's inhabitants on this subject. I believe that
this comparative absence of defining activity may itself be significant, and
I will return to this possibility below. Here, I will only point to a few basic
characteristics of what is "soul" which I feel make it particularly "essentially Negro"—referring again, of course, to urban lower-class Negroes
rather than to any other category of people.

There is, of course, the Southern origin. The "Down Country" connotations are particularly attached to "soul food"; however, although Negro
music has changed more and the contemporary commercial rock-and-roll
is an urban phenomenon, it is certainly seen as the latest stage of an
unfolding musical heritage. Thus the things that are "soul," while taking
on new significance in the urban environment, provide some common
historical tradition for ghetto inhabitants. One might also speculate on the
possibility that the early and from then on constant and intimate exposure
to these foods and to this music—for radios and record players seem to
belong to practically every poor ghetto home—may make them appear
particularly basic to a "Negro way of life."

When it comes to "soul" music, there are a couple of themes in style
and content which I would suggest are pervasive in ghetto life and which
probably make them appear very close to the everyday experience of
ghetto inhabitants.

One of these is the lack of control over the social environment. There
is a very frequent attitude among "soul brothers"—that is, the ghetto's
younger males—that one's environment is somewhat like a jungle where
tough, smart people may survive and where a lot happens to make it
worth while and enjoyable just to "watch the scene" if one does not have
too high hopes of controlling it. Many of the reactions in listening to
"progressive jazz" seem to connect to this view; "Oooh, man, there just
ain't nothing you can do about it but sit there and feel it goin' all the way
into you." Without being able to do much about proving it, I feel that
exposure to experiences—desirable or undesirable—in which one can only
passively perceive events without influencing them is an essential fact of
ghetto life, for better or for worse; thus it is "soul."

Related to this is the experience of unstable personal relationships, in
particular between the sexes. It is a well-known fact that among lower-
class urban Negroes there are many "broken" families (households without a husband and father), many temporary common-law unions, and in
general relatively little consensus on sex roles. Thus, it is not much of an

exaggeration to speak of a constant "battle of the sexes," and the achieve-ment of success with the opposite sex is a focal concern in lower-class Negro life. From this area come most of the lyrics of contemporary rock-and-roll music. It may be objected that this is true of white rock-and-roll as well; to this it may be answered that this is very much to the point. For white rock-and-roll is predominantly adolescent music, thus reaching peo-ple with similar problems of unstable personal relationships. In the case of lower-class urban Negroes, such relationships are characteristic of a much wider age-range, and music on this theme also reaches this wider range. Some titles of recent rock-and-roll hits may show this theme: "I'm losing you" (Temptations), "Are you lonely" (Freddie Scott), "Yours until to-morrow" (Dee Dee Warwick), "Keep me hangin' on" (Supremes). "Soul" stands for a bitter-sweet experience; this often arises from contacts with the other sex, although there are certainly also other sources. This bitter-sweetness, of course, was typical already of the blues.

Turning to style, a common element in everyday social interaction as well as among storefront church preachers, Negro comedians, and rock-and-roll singers is an alternation between aggressive, somewhat boasting behaviour, and plaintive behaviour from an implicit under-dog position.

This may not be the place to give a more detailed account of this style of behaviour. However, as I said, it occurs in many situations and may itself be related to the unstable personal relationships, and the concomi-tant unstable self-conception, which was mentioned above. In any case, it seems that this style is seen as having "soul"; without describing its ele-ments, "soul brothers" tend to describe its occurrences in a variety of contexts.

As I noted above, I have hesitated to try to analyze and define "soul," because what seems to be important in the emergence of the present "soul" concept is the fact that there is felt to be *something* which is "soul" rather than *what* that something is. There is, of course, some logic to this; if "soul" is what is "essentially Negro," it should not be necessary for "soul brothers" to spend too much time analyzing it. Asking about "soul" one often receives answers such as " You know, we don't talk much about it, but we've all been through it, so we know what it is anyway." Probably, this is to some extent true. What the lack of pronounced definition points to, in that case, is that "soul" vocabulary is predominantly for in-group consumption. It is a symbol of solidarity among the people of the ghetto, but not in more than a weak and implicit sense of solidarity *against* anybody else. "Soul" is turned inward; and so everybody who is touched by it is supposed to know what it means. So far there has been little interference with the "soul" vocabulary by outsiders, at least in any way noticeable to the ghetto dwellers. There have been none of the fierce arguments about its meaning which have developed around "black power," a concept which did not really evolve in the ghetto but is largely the creation of white mass media. "Black power" is controversial, and so white people insist on a definition. (And many black people, also depending on white media for news, tend to accept the interpretations of these media.) "Soul" is not equally threatening, and so ghetto dwellers can keep its mystique to themselves.

We may note in this context that the few interpreters of "soul" to the outside world are, in fact, outsiders; a kind of cultural brokers who give interested members of the larger society the "inside stuff" on the ghetto. But serving as such brokers, they hardly affect the uses of "soul" within the ghetto community. LeRoi Jones, the author, a convert to ghetto life who like so many converts seems to have become more militantly partisan than the more authentic ghetto inhabitants, has moved from a position where he rather impartially noted the ethnocentric bias of "soul"[4] to one where he preaches for the complete destruction of the present American society,[5] an activist programme which I am sure is far out of step with the immediate concerns of the average "soul brother." Bennett, an editor of the middle-class *Ebony* magazine, is not particularly interested in "the folk myth of soul" but explains what he feels that "soul" really is.[6] I am not convinced that his conception is entirely correct; it is certainly not expressed in the idiom of the ghetto. Keil, an ethnomusicologist, probably comes closer to the folk conception than anyone else, by giving what amounts to a catalogue of those ghetto values and experiences which its inhabitants recognize as their own.[7] In doing so, of course, one does not get a short and comprehensive definition of "soul" that is acceptable to all and in every situation—one merely lists the fields in which a vocabulary of "soul" is particularly likely to be expressed. This, of course, is what has been done in a partial and parsimonious way above.

Here we end the exposition of the "soul" concept. Summing up what has been said so far, the vocabulary of "soul," which is a relatively recent phenomenon, is used among younger Negro ghetto dwellers, and particularly young men, to designate in a highly approving manner the experiences and characteristics which are "essentially Negro." As such it is not an activist vocabulary for use in inter-group relations but a vocabulary which is employed within the group, although it is clear that by discussing what is "typically Negro" one makes an implicit reference to the non-Negro society. We turn now to an interpretation of the emergence of such a vocabulary in this group at this point of Negro history.

[4]LeRoi Jones, *Blues People* (New York, William Morrow & Co., 1963), p. 219.
[5]LeRoi Jones, *Home: Social Essays* (New York, William Morrow & Co., 1966).
[6]Lerone Bennett, Jr., *The Negro Mood* (New York, Ballantine Books, 1965), p. 89.
[7]Charles Keil, op.cit., pp. 164 et seq.

III

For a long time, the social boundaries which have constituted barriers to educational, economic and other achievement by Negro Americans have been highly impermeable. Although lower-class Negroes have to a considerable degree accepted the values of mainstream American culture in those areas, the very obviousness of the impermeability of social boundaries has probably prevented a more complete commitment to the achievement of those goals which have been out of reach. Instead, there has been an adjustment to the lower-class situation in which goals and values more appropriate to the ascribed social position of the group have been added to, and to some extent substituted for, the mainstream norms. Whether these lower-class concerns, experiences, and values are direct responses to the situation or historically based patterns for which the lower-class niche provides space is not really important here. What is important is that the style of life of the lower class, in this case the Negro lower class, is different from that of the upper classes, and that the impermeability of group boundaries and the unequal distribution of resources between groups have long kept the behavioural characteristics of the groups relatively stable and distinct from one another, although to a great extent, one of the groups—the lower-class Negroes—would have preferred the style of life of the other group—the middle-class whites—had it been available to them. As it has been, they have only been able to do the best with what they have had. In a way, then, they have had two cultures, the mainstream culture with which they are relatively familiar, which has in many ways appeared superior and preferable, and which has been closed to them, and the ghetto culture which is a second choice and based on the circumstances of the ascribed social position. (I will not dwell here on the typical features of the two cultures and the relationship between them; articles by Miller[8] and Rodman[9] are enlightening discussions of these topics.)

This, of course, sounds to some extent like the position of what has often been called "the marginal man." Such a position may cause psychological problems. However, when the position is very clearly defined and where the same situation is shared by many, the situation is perhaps reasonably acceptable—there is a perfectly understandable reason for one's failure to reach one's goal. Nobody of one's own kind is allowed to reach that goal, and the basis of the condition is a social rule rather than a personal failure. There are indications that marginality is more severely felt if the barrier is not absolute but boundary

[8] Walter B. Miller, 'Lower Class Culture as a Generating Milieu of Gang Delinquency,' *Journal of Social Issues* (vol. 14, 1958), pp. 5–19.

[9] Hyman Rodman, 'The Lower-Class Value Stretch,' *Social Forces* (vol. 42, 1963), pp. 205–15.

permeability is possible although uncertain. According to Kerckhoff and McCormick,

> . . . an absolute barrier between the two groups is less conducive to personality problems than "grudging, uncertain and unpredictable acceptance." The impact of the rejection on an individual's personality organization will depend to some extent upon the usual treatment accorded members of his group by the dominant group. If his group as a whole faces a rather permeable barrier and he meets with more serious rejection, the effect on him is likely to be more severe than the same treatment received by a more thoroughly rejected group (one facing an impermeable barrier).[10]

My thesis here is that recent changes in race relations in the United States have indeed made the social barriers to achievement at least seem less impermeable than before to the ghetto population. One often hears people in the ghetto expressing opinions such as, "Yeh, there are so many programs, job-training and things, going on, man, so if you got anything on the ball you can make it." On the other hand, there are also assertions about the impossibility of getting anywhere which contradict the first opinion. Obviously, the clear-cut exclusion from mainstream American culture is gradually being replaced by ambivalence about one's actual chances. This ambivalence, of course, seems to represent an accurate estimate of the situation; the lower-class Negro continues to be disadvantaged, although probably his chances of moving up and out are somewhat better than earlier—people do indeed trickle out of the ghetto.

It is in this situation that the ethnocentric vocabulary of "soul" has emerged, and I want to suggest that it is a response to the uncertainty of the ghetto dweller's situation. This uncertainty is particularly strong for the younger male, the "soul brother." While women have always been able to live closer to mainstream culture norms, as homemakers and possibly with a type of job keeping them in touch with the middle-class world, men have had less chance to become competent in mainstream culture as well as to practice it. Older men tend to feel that current social changes come too late for them but put higher expectations on the following generation. Thus the present generation of young men in the Negro ghettos of the United States are placed in a new situation to which it is making new responses, and much of the unrest in the ghettos today is perhaps the result of these emerging pressures.

I will suggest here that this new situation must be taken into account if we are to understand the basis of the emergence of the "soul" vocabulary. The increasing ambivalence in conceptions of one's opportunities in the changing social structure may be accompanied by doubts about one's own worth. Earlier, the lack of congruence between mainstream culture norms and the lower-class Negro's achievements could easily be explained

---

[10] Alan C. Kerckhoff and Thomas C. McCormick, 'Marginal Status and Marginal Personality,' *Social Forces* (vol. 34, 1955), p. 51.

by referring to the social barriers. Under-achievement with respect to mainstream norms was an ascribed characteristic of lower-class Negroes. However, when as at present the suspicion arises, which may very well be mistaken, that under-achievement is not ascribed but due to one's own failure, self-doubt may be the result. Such doubt can be reduced in different ways. Some, of course, are able to live up to mainstream norms of achievement, thereby reducing the strain on themselves (but at the same time increasing that on others). Higher self-esteem can also be arrived at by affirming that the boundaries are still impermeable. A third possibility is to set new standards for achievement, proclaiming one's own achievements to be the ideals. It is not necessary, of course, that the same way of reducing self-doubt is always applied. In the case of "soul," the method is that of idealizing one's own achievements, proclaiming one's own way of life to be superior. Yet the same "soul brother" may argue at other times that they are what they are because they are not allowed to become anything else.

In any case, "soul" is by native public definition "superior," and the motive of the "soul" vocabulary, I believe, is above all to reduce self-doubt by persuading "soul brothers" that they are successful. Being a "soul brother" is belonging to a select group instead of to a residual category of people who have not succeeded. Thus, the "soul" vocabulary is a device of rhetoric. By talking about people who have "soul," about "soul music" and about "soul food," the "soul brother" attempts to establish himself in an expert and connoisseur role; by talking to others of his group in these terms, he identifies with them and confers the same role on them. Using "soul" rhetoric is a way of convincing others of one's own worth and of their worth; it also serves to persuade the speaker himself. As Burke expresses it,

> A man can be his own audience, insofar as he, even in his secret thoughts, cultivates certain ideas or images for the effect he hopes they may have upon him; he is here what Mead would call 'an "I" addressing its "me" '; and in this respect he is being rhetorical quite as though he were using pleasant imagery to influence an outside audience rather than one within.[11]

The "soul" vocabulary has thus emerged from the social basis of a number of individuals, in effective interaction with one another, with similar problems of adjustment to a new situation. The use of "soul" rhetoric is a way of meeting their needs as long as it occurs in situations where they can mutually support each other. Here is, of course, a clue to the confinement of the rhetoric to in-group situations. If "soul" talk were directed toward outsiders, they might not accept the claims for its excellence—it is not their "folk myth." Viewing "soul" as such a device of rhetoric, it is also

[11]Kenneth Burke, *A Grammar of Motives and a Rhetoric of Motives* (Cleveland, Meridian Books, 1962), p. 562

easier to understand why it is advantageous for its purposes not to have made it the topic of too much intellectualizing. As Geertz makes clear in his paper on "Ideology as a Cultural System,"[12] by analyzing and defining activity, one achieves maximum intellectual clarity at the expense of emotional commitment. It is doubtful that "soul" rhetoric would thrive on too much intellectual clarity; rather, by expressing "soul" ideals in a circumspect manner in terms of emotionally charged symbols such as "soul food" and "soul music," one can avoid the rather sordid realities underlying these emotions. As I pointed out above, the shared lower-class Negro experiences which seem to be the bases of "soul" are hardly in themselves such as to bring out a surge of ethnic pride. That is a psychological reason for keeping the "soul" concept diffuse. There is also, I believe, a sociological basis for the diffuseness. The more exactly a "soul brother" would define "soul," the fewer others would probably agree upon the "essential Negroness" of his definition; and, as we have seen, a basic idea of the rhetoric of "soul" is to cast others into roles which satisfy them and at the same time support one's own position. If people are cast into a role of "soul brother" and then find that there has been a definition established for that role which they cannot accept, the result may be overt disagreement and denial of solidarity rather than mutual deference. As it is, "soul" can be an umbrella concept for a rather wide variety of definitions of one's situation, and the "soul brothers" who are most in need of the ethnocentric core conception can occasionally get at least fleeting allegiance to "soul" from others with whom in reality they share relatively little, for instance individuals who are clearly upwardly mobile. On one occasion I listened to a long conversation about "soul music" in a rather heterogeneous group of young Negro men who all agreed on the "soulfulness" of the singers whose records they were playing, and afterwards I asked one of the men who is clearly upwardly mobile of his conception of "soul." He answered that "soul" is earthy, "there is nothing specifically Negro about it." Yet the very individuals with whom he had just agreed on matters of "soul" had earlier given me the opposite answer—only Negroes have "soul." Thus by avoiding definitions, they had found together an area of agreement and satisfaction in "soul" by merely assuming that there was a shared basis of opinion.

IV

Summing up what has been said, "soul" is a relatively recent concept used in the urban Negro ghetto, in particular by young men, to express what is "essential Negroness" and to convey appreciation for it. The point of view which has been expressed here is that the need for such a concept

[12]Clifford Geertz, 'Ideology as a Cultural System,' in David E. Apter (ed.), *Ideology and Discontent* (New York, The Free Press, 1964).

has arisen at this point because of increasingly ambivalent conceptions of the opportunity structure. While earlier, lack of achievement according to American mainstream ideals could easily be explained in terms of impermeable social barriers, the impression is gaining ground in the ghetto that there are now ways out of the situation. The young men who come under particularly great strain if such a belief is accepted must either achieve some success (which many of them are obviously still unable to do, for various reasons), explain that achievement is impossible (which is probably not as true as it has been), or explain that achievement according to mainstream ideals is not necessarily achievement according to their ideals. The emergence of "soul," it has been stated here, goes some way toward meeting the need of stating alternative ideals and also provides solidarity among those with such a need. In implying or stating explicitly that ghetto culture has a superiority of its own, the users of the "soul" vocabulary seem to take a step beyond devices of established usage which are terms of solidarity but lack or at least have less clear cultural references—for example the use of "brother" as a term of either reference or address for another Negro. That is, it is more in the cultural than in the social dimension that "soul" is an innovation rather than just one more term of a kind. Of course, the two are closely connected. It is advantageous to maintain a diffuse conception of "soul," for if an intellectually clear definition were established, "soul" would probably be both less convincing and less uniting.

The view of "soul" taken here is one of a piecemeal rhetoric attempt to establish a satisfactory self-conception. For the great majority of "soul brothers" I am sure this is the major basis of "soul." It may be added that for instance LeRoi Jones[13] and Charles Keil[14] tend to give the impression of a more social-activist conception of "soul," although Keil tends to make it a prophecy rather than an interpretation. At least at present, I think that there is little basis for connecting the majority of "soul brothers" with militant black nationalism—there is hardly a "soul movement." "Soul" became publicly associated with black militancy as the term "soul brother" made its way to international prominence during recent ghetto uprisings—Negro businessmen posted "soul brother" signs in their windows, it was noted by mass media all over the world. However, it is worth noting that this was an internal appeal to the ghetto moral community by black shopkeepers, not a sign of defiance of the outside world by the participants. It may be said that the outsiders merely caught a glimpse of an internal ghetto dialogue. Yet organized black nationalism may be able to recruit followers by using some kind of transformed "soul" vocabulary, and I think there are obviously attempts on its side to make more of "soul" than it is now. Certainly, there is seldom any hostility to black

[13]LeRoi Jones, *Home: Social Essays.*
[14]Charles Keil, op. cit.

militants among the wider groups of self-defined "soul brothers," although the vocabulary of "soul" has not been extensively employed for political purposes. If it is so used, however, it could possibly increase the ghetto dwellers' identification with political nationalism. Thus, if at present it is not possible to speak of more than a "rhetoric of soul," it may be that in the future we will find a "soul movement." If that happens, of course, "soul" may become a more controversial concept, as "black power" is now.

HARLEM:

"BABY" AND "SATURDAY NIGHT"

Manchild in the Promised Land

by Claude Brown

Baby

The first time I heard the expression "baby" used by one cat to address another was up at Warwick in 1951. Gus Jackson used it. The term had a hip ring to it, a real colored ring. The first time I heard it, I knew right away I had to start using it. It was like saying, "Man, look at me. I've got masculinity to spare." It was saying at the same time to the world, "I'm one of the hippest cats, one of the most uninhibited cats on the scene. I can say 'baby' to another cat, and he can say 'baby' to me, and we can say it with strength in our voices." If you could say it, this meant that you really had to be sure of yourself, sure of your masculinity.

It seemed that everybody in my age group was saying it. The next thing I knew, older guys were saying it. Then just about everybody in Harlem was saying it, even the cats who weren't so hip. It became just one of those things.

The real hip thing about the "baby" term was that it was something that only colored cats could say the way it was supposed to be said. I'd heard gray boys trying it, but they couldn't really do it. Only colored cats could give it the meaning that we all knew it had without ever mentioning it— the meaning of black masculinity.

Before the Muslims, before I'd heard about the Coptic or anything like that, I remember getting high on the corner with a bunch of guys and watching the chicks go by, fine little girls, and saying, "Man, colored people must be somethin' else!"

Somebody'd say, "Yeah. How about that? All those years, man, we was down on the plantation in those shacks, eating just potatoes and fatback and chitterlin's and greens, and look at what happened. We had Joe Louises and Jack Johnsons and Sugar Ray Robinsons and Henry Armstrongs, all that sort of thing."

Sombody'd say, "Yeah, man. Niggers must be some real strong people who just can't be kept down. When you think about it, that's really something great. Fatback, chitterlin's, greens, and Joe Louis. Negroes are some beautiful people. Uh-huh. Fatback, chitterlin's, greens, and Joe Louis . . . and beautiful black bitches."

Cats would come along with this "baby" thing. It was something that went over strong in the fifties with the jazz musicians and the hip set, the boxers, the dancers, the comedians, just about every set in Harlem. I think everybody said it real loud because they liked the way it sounded. It was always, "Hey, baby. How you doin', baby?" in every phase of the Negro hip life. As a matter of fact, I went to a Negro lawyer's office once, and he said, "Hey, baby. How you doin'?" I really felt at ease, really felt that we had something in common. I imagine there were many people in Harlem who didn't feel they had too much in common with the Negro professionals, the doctors and lawyers and dentists and ministers. I know I didn't. But to hear one of these people greet you with the street thing, the "Hey, baby"—and he knew how to say it—you felt as though you had something strong in common.

I suppose it's the same thing that almost all Negroes have in common, the fatback, chitterlings, and greens background. I suppose that regardless of what any Negro in America might do or how high he might rise in social status, he still has something in common with every other Negro. I doubt that they're many, if any, gray people who could ever say "baby" to a Negro and make him feel that "me and this cat have got something going, something strong going."

In the fifties, when "baby" came around, it seemed to be the prelude to a whole new era in Harlem. It was the introduction to the era of black reflection. A fever started spreading. Perhaps the strong rising of the Muslim movement is something that helped to sustain or even usher in this era.

I remember that in the early fifties, cats would stand on the corner and talk, just shooting the stuff, all the street-corner philosophers. Sometimes, it was a common topic—cats talking about gray chicks—and somebody might say something like, "Man, what can anybody see in a gray chick, when colored chicks are so fine; they got so much soul." This was the coming of the "soul" thing too.

"Soul" had started coming out of the churches and the nightclubs into the streets. Everybody started talking about "soul" as though it were something that they could see on people or a distinct characteristic of colored folks.

Cats would say things like, "Man, gray chicks seem so stiff." Many of them would say they couldn't talk to them or would wonder how a cat who was used to being so for real with a chick could see anything in a gray girl. It seemed as though the mood of the day was turning toward the color thing.

Everybody was really digging themselves and thinking and saying in their behavior, in every action, "Wow! Man, it's a beautiful thing to be colored." Everybody was saying, "Oh, the beauty of me! Look at me. I'm colored. And look at us. Aren't we beautiful?" . . .

Saturday Night

Saturday night. I suppose there's a Saturday night in every Negro community throughout the nation just like Saturday night in Harlem. The bars will jump. The precinct station will have a busy night. The hospital's emergency ward will jump.

Cats who have been working all their lives, who've never been in any trouble before, good-doing righteous cats, self-respecting, law-abiding citizens—they'll all come out. Perhaps it'll be their night in the bar, their night in the police station, maybe their night in the emergency ward.

They tell me that young doctors really try hard for a chance to do their internship in Harlem Hospital—it offers such a wide variety of experiences. They say it's the best place in the city where a surgeon can train. They say you get all kinds of experience just working there on Saturday nights.

It's usually the older folks who practice this Saturday night thing, or some of the younger cats who haven't come out of the woods yet, young cats who drink a lot of liquor, who didn't quite finish junior high school, who still have most of the Southern ways . . . the young cats who carry knives, the young cats who want to be bad niggers. It's usually the guys around eighteen to twenty-five, guys who haven't separated themselves yet from the older generation or who just haven't become critical of the older generation. They follow the pattern that has been set by the older generation, the Saturday night pattern of getting drunk, getting a new piece of cunt, and getting real bad—carrying a knife in your pocket and ready to use it, ready to curse, ready to become a Harlem Saturday night statistic, in the hospital, the police station, or the morgue.

The intern who comes to Harlem and starts his internship around April will be ready to go into surgery by June. He's probably already tried to close up windpipes for people who've had their throat slit. Or tried to put intestines back in a stomach. Or somebody has hit somebody in the head with a hatchet. Or somebody has come into his house at the wrong time and caught somebody else going out the window. That's quite a job too, putting a person back together after a four- or five-story fall.

I suppose any policeman who's been in Harlem for a month of Saturday nights has had all the experience he'll ever need, as far as handling violence goes. Some of them will have more experience than they'll ever be able to use.

To me, it always seemed as though Saturday night was the down-home night. In the tales I'd heard about down home—how so-and-so got bad and killed Cousin Joe or knocked out Cousin Willie's eye—everything violent happened on Saturday night. It was the only time for anything to really happen, because people were too tired working all week from sunup to sundown to raise but so much hell on the week nights. Then, comes Saturday, and they take it kind of easy during the day, resting up for another Saturday night.

Down home, when they went to town, all the niggers would just break bad, so it seemed. Everybody just seemed to let out all their hostility on everybody else. Maybe they were hoping that they could get their throat cut. Perhaps if a person was lucky enough to get his throat cut, he'd be free from the fields. On the other hand, if someone was lucky enough to cut somebody else's throat, he'd done the guy a favor, because he'd freed him.

In the tales about down home that I'd heard, everybody was trying to either cash out on Saturday night or cash somebody else out. There was always the good corn liquor that Cy Walker used to make, and there was always that new gun that somebody had bought. The first time they shot the gun at so-and-so, he jumped out of the window and didn't stop running until he got home—and got his gun. You'd sit there and say, "Well, I'll be damned. I never knew they had all those bad niggers in the South. I always thought the baddest cat down there was Charlie." But it seemed as though on Saturday night, the niggers got bad. Of course, they didn't get bad enough to mess with Charlie, but they got bad. They were bad enough to cut each other's throats, shoot each other, hit each other in the head with axes, and all that sort of action. Women were bad enough to throw lye on one another.

Saturday night down home was really something, but, then, Saturday night in Harlem was really something too. There is something happening for everybody on Saturday night: for the cat who works all day long on the railroad, in the garment center, driving a bus, or as a subway conductor. On Saturday night, there is something happening for everybody in Harlem, regardless of what his groove might be. Even the real soul sisters, who go to church and live for Sunday, who live to jump up and clap and call on the Lord, Saturday night means something to them too. Saturday night is the night they start getting ready for Sunday. They have to braid all the kids' hair and get them ready. They have to iron their white usher uniforms and get pretty for Sunday and say a prayer. For the devoted churchgoers, Saturday night means that Sunday will soon be here.

Saturday night is a time to try new things. Maybe that's why so many people in the older generation had to lose their lives on Saturday night. It must be something about a Saturday night with Negroes. . . . Maybe they wanted to die on Saturday night. They'd always associated Sunday with going to heaven, because that was when they went to church and sang all those songs, clapped and shouted and stomped their feet and praised the Lord. Maybe they figured that if they died on Sunday morning, the Lord's day, they'd be well on their way.

Everybody has this thing about Saturday night. I imagine that before pot or horse or any other drugs hit Harlem good and strong, the people just had to try something else, like knifing or shooting somebody, because Saturday night was the night for daring deeds. Since there was no pot out on a large scale then, I suppose one of the most daring deeds anyone could perform was to shoot or stab somebody.

Many of the chicks in the neighborhood took some of their first really big steps on Saturday night. Some cats—or as a girl I knew might say, "no-good niggers"—talked many girls into turning their first tricks on a Saturday night just because the cats needed some money. That's how that thing goes on Saturday night. I recall talking a girl into a trick on a Saturday night. She said it was her first, but I like to tell myself it wasn't. If it was, that was okay. She was a part of Harlem, and Saturday night was a time for first things, even for girls turning their first tricks, pulling their first real John.

Saturday night has also been a traditional night for money to be floating around in places like Harlem. It's a night of temptation, the kind of temptation one might see on Catfish Row at the end of the cotton season on the weekend. Most of the people got paid on Friday night, and Saturday they had some money. If they didn't get paid on Friday, there was a good chance that they'd be around playing the single action on Saturday in the afternoon. By the time the last figure came out, everybody might have some change, even if it was only eight dollars—one dollar on the 0 that afternoon. It was still some money.

Then there were all the crap games floating around. The stickup artists would be out hunting. The Murphy boys would be out strong. In the bars, the tricks would be out strong. All the whores would be out there, and any decent, self-respecting whore could pull at least two hundred dollars on Saturday night in some of the bad-doing bars on 125th Street.

As a matter of fact, Reno used to say, "The cat who can't make no money on Saturday night is in trouble." There was a lot of truth to it, because there was so much money floating around in Harlem on Saturday night, if anyone couldn't get any money then, he just didn't have any business there.

It seemed as though Harlem's history is made on Saturday nights. You hear about the times people have gotten shot—like when two white cops were killed on 146th Street a couple of years ago—on a Saturday night. Just about every time a cop is killed in Harlem, it's on a Saturday night.

People know you shouldn't bother with Negroes on Saturday night, because for some reason or another, Negroes just don't mind dying on Saturday night. They seem ready to die, so they're not going to take but so much stuff. There were some people who were always trying to get themselves killed. Every Saturday night, they'd try it all over again.

One was Big Bill. When I was just a kid on Eighth Avenue in knee pants, this guy was trying to get himself killed. He was always in some fight with a knife. He was always cutting or trying to cut somebody's throat. He was always getting cut or getting stabbed, getting hit in the head, getting shot. Every Saturday night that he was out there, something happened. If you heard on Sunday morning that somebody had gotten shot or stabbed, you didn't usually ask who did it. You'd ask if Big Bill did it. If he did it, no one paid too much attention to it, because he was always doing something like that. They'd say, "Yeah, man. That cat is crazy."

If somebody else had done it, you'd wonder why, and this was something to talk about and discuss. Somebody else might not have been as crazy. In the case of Big Bill, everybody expected that sooner or later somebody would kill him and put him out of his misery and that this was what he was trying for. One time Spanish Joe stabbed him. He just missed his lung, and everybody thought he was going to cool it behind that. But as soon as the cat got back on the street, he was right out there doing it again.

Even now, he's always getting in fights out on the streets on Saturday night. He's always hurting somebody, or somebody's hurting him. He just seems to be hanging on. I think he's just unlucky. Here's a cat who's been trying to get himself killed every Saturday night as far back as I can remember, and he still hasn't made it. I suppose you've got to sympathize with a guy like that, because he's really been trying.

LANGUAGE

" 'Rapping' in the Black Ghetto"

by *Thomas Kochman*

"Rapping," "shucking," "jiving," "running it down," "gripping," "copping a plea," "signifying" and "sounding" are all part of the black ghetto idiom and describe different kinds of talking. Each has its own distinguishing features of form, style, and function; each is influenced by, and influences, the speaker, setting, and audience; and each sheds light on the black perspective and the black condition—on those orienting values and attitudes that will cause a speaker to speak or perform in his own way within the social context of the black community.

I was first introduced to black idiom in New York City, and, as a professional linguist interested in dialects, I began to compile a lexicon of such expressions. My real involvement, however, came in Chicago, while preparing a course on black idiom at the Center for Inner City studies, the southside branch of Northeastern Illinois State College.

Here I began to explore the full cultural significance of this kind of verbal behavior. My students and informants within black Chicago, through their knowledge of these terms, and their ability to recognize and categorize the techniques, and to give examples, gave me much reliable data. When I turned for other or better examples to the literature—such as the writings of Malcolm X, Robert Conot, and Iceberg Slim—my students and informants were able to recognize and confirm their authenticity.

While often used to mean ordinary conversation, rapping is distinctively a fluent and a lively way of talking, always characterized by a high degree of personal style. To one's own group, rapping may be descriptive of an interesting narration, a colorful rundown of some past event. An example of this kind of rap is the answer from a Chicago gang member to a youth worker who asked how his group became organized:

> Now I'm goin tell you how the jive really started. I'm goin to tell you how the club got this big. 'Bout 1956 there used to be a time when the Jackson Park show was open and the Stony show was open. Sixty-six street, Jeff, Gene, all of 'em, little bitty dudes, little bitty . . . Gene wasn't with 'em then. Gene was cribbin (living) over here. Jeff, all of 'em, real little bitty dudes, you dig? All of us were little.

Sixty-six (the gang on sixty-sixth street), they wouldn't allow us in the Jackson Park show. That was when the parky(?) was headin it. Everybody say, If we want to go to the show, we go! One day, who was it? Carl Robinson. He went up to the show . . . and Jeff fired on him. He came back and all this was swelled up 'bout yay big, you know. He come back over to the hood (neighborhood). He told (name unclear) and them dudes went up there. That was when mostly all the main sixty-six boys was over here like Bett Riley. All of 'em was over here. People that quit gang-bangin (fighting, especially as a group), Marvell Gates, people like that.

They went on up there, John, Roy and Skeeter went in there. And they start humbuggin (fighting) in there. That's how it all started. Sixty-six found out they couldn't beat us, at *that* time. They couldn't *whup* seven-o. Am I right Leroy? You was cribbin over here then. Am I right? We were dynamite! Used to be a time, you ain't have a passport, Man, you couldn't walk through here. And if didn't nobody know you it was worse than that. . . . "

Rapping to a woman is a colorful way of "asking for some pussy." "One needs to throw a lively rap when he is 'putting the make' on a broad." (John Horton, "Time and Cool People," *Trans*-action, April, 1967.)

According to one informant the woman is usually someone he has just seen or met, looks good, and might be willing to have sexual intercourse with him. My informant says the term would not be descriptive of talk between a couple "who have had a relationship over any length of time." Rapping then, is used at the beginning of a relationship to create a favorable impression and be persuasive at the same time. The man who has the reputation for excelling at this is the pimp, or mack man. Both terms describe a person of considerable status in the street hierarchy, who, by his lively and persuasive rapping ("macking" is also used in this context) has acquired a stable of girls to hustle for him and give him money. For most street men and many teenagers he is the model whom they try to emulate. Thus, within the community you have a pimp walk, pimp style boots and clothes, and perhaps most of all "pimp talk," is a colorful literary example of a telephone rap. One of my informants regards it as extreme, but agrees that it illustrates the language, style and technique of rapping. "Blood" is rapping to an ex-whore named Christine in an effort to trap her into his stable:

Now try to control yourself baby. I'm the tall stud with the dreamy bedroom eyes across the hall in four-twenty. I'm the guy with the pretty towel wrapped around his sexy hips. I got the same hips on now that you X-rayed. Remember that hump of sugar your peepers feasted on?

She said, "Maybe, but you shouldn't call me. I don't want an incident. What do you want? A lady doesn't accept phone calls from strangers."

I said, "A million dollars and a trip to the moon with a bored, trapped, beautiful bitch, you dig? I'm no stranger. I've been popping the elastic on your panties ever since you saw me in the hall. . . . "

Rapping between men and women often is competitive and leads to a lively repartee with the women becoming as adept as the men. An example follows:

> A man coming from the bathroom forgot to zip his pants. An unescorted party of women kept watching him and laughing among themselves. The man's friends "hip" (inform) him to what's going on. He approaches one woman—"Hey baby, did you see that big black Cadillac with the full tires? ready to roll in action just for you." She answers—"No mother-fucker, but I saw a little gray Volkswagen with two flat tires." Everybody laughs. His rap was "capped" (Excelled, topped).

When "whupping the game" on a "trick" or "lame" (trying to get goods or services for someone who looks like he can be swindled), rapping is often descriptive of the highly stylized verbal part of the maneuver. In well established "con games" the rap is carefully prepared and used with great skill in directing the course of the transaction. An excellent illustration came from an adept hustler who was playing the "murphy" game on a white trick. The "murphy" game is designed to get the *trick* to give his money to the hustler, who in this instance poses as a "steerer" (one who directs or steers customers to a brothel), to keep the whore from stealing it. The hustler then skips with the money.

> Look Buddy, I know a fabulous house not more than two blocks away. Brother you ain't never seen more beautiful, freakier broads than are in that house. One of them, the prettiest one, can do more with a swipe than a monkey can with a banana. She's like a rubber doll; she can take a hundred positions."
>
> At this point the sucker is wild to get to this place of pure joy. He entreats the con player to take him there, not just direct him to it.
>
> The "murphy" player will prat him (pretend rejection) to enhance his desire. He will say, "Man, don't be offended, but Aunt Kate, that runs the house don't have nothing but highclass white men coming to her place. . . . You know, doctors, lawyers, big-shot politicians. You look like a clean-cut white man, but you ain't in that league are you? (Iceberg Slim, *Pimp: The Story of My Life*)

After a few more exchanges of the "murphy" dialogue, "the mark is separated from his scratch."
•An analysis of rapping indicates a number of things.
For instance, it is revealing that one raps *to* rather than *with* a person supporting the impression that rapping is to be regarded more as a performance than verbal exchange. As with other performances, rapping projects the personality, physical appearance and style of the performer. In each of the examples given, the intrusive "I" of the speaker was instrumental in contributing to the total impression of the rap.
•The combination of personality and style is usually best when "asking

for some pussy." It is less when "whupping the game" on someone or "running something down."

In "asking for some pussy" for example, where personality and style might be projected through non-verbal means: stance, clothing, walking, looking, one can speak of a "silent rap." The woman is won here without the use of words, or rather, with words being implied that would generally accompany the non-verbal components.

•As a lively way of "running it down" the verbal element consists of personality and style plus information. To someone *reading* my example of the gang member's narration, the impression might be that the information would be more influential in directing the listener's response. The youth worker might be expected to say "So that's how the gang got so big," instead of "Man, that gang member is *bad* (strong, brave)" in which instance he would be responding to the personality and style of the rapper. However, if the reader would *listen* to the gang member on tape or could have been present when the gang member spoke he more likely would have reacted more to personality and style as my informants did.

Remember that in attendance with the youth worker were members of the gang who *already knew* how the gang got started (e.g. "Am I right Leroy? You was cribbin' over here then") and for whom the information itself would have little interest. Their attention was held by the *way* the information was presented.

•The verbal element in "whupping the game" on someone, in the preceding example, was an integral part of an overall deception in which information and personality-style were skillfully manipulated for the purpose of controlling the "trick's" response. But again, greater weight must be given to personality-style. In the "murphy game" for example, it was this element which got the trick to trust the hustler and leave his money with him for "safekeeping."

The function of rapping in each of these forms is *expressive*. By this I mean that the speaker raps to project his personality onto the scene or to evoke a generally favorable response. When rapping is used to "ask for some pussy" or to "whup the game" on someone its function is *directive*. By this I mean that rapping becomes an instrument to manipulate and control people to get them to give up or to do something. The difference between rapping to a "fox" (pretty girl) for the purpose of "getting inside her pants" and rapping to a "lame" to get something from him is operational rather than functional. The latter rap contains a concealed motivation where the former does not.

"Shucking," "shucking it," "shucking and jiving," "S-ing" and "J-ing" or just "jiving," are terms that refer to language behavior practiced by the black when confronting "the Man" (the white man, the establishment, or *any* authority figure), and to another form of language behavior practiced by blacks with each other on the peer group level.

In the South, and later in the North, the black man learned that American society had assigned to him a restrictive role and status. Among whites his behavior had to conform to this imposed station and he was constantly reminded to "keep his place." He learned that it was not acceptable in the presence of white people to show feelings of indignation, frustration, discontent, pride, ambition, or desire; that real feelings had to be concealed behind a mask of innocence, ignorance, childishness, obedience, humility and deference. The terms used by the black to describe the role he played before white folks in the South was "tomming" or "jeffing." Failure to accommodate the white Southerner in this respect was almost certain to invite psychological and often physical brutality. A description related by a black psychiatrist, Alvin F. Poussaint, is typical and revealing:

> Once last year as I was leaving my office in Jackson, Miss., with my Negro secretary, a white policeman yelled, "Hey, boy! Come here!" Somewhat bothered, I retorted: "I'm no boy!" He then rushed at me, inflamed, and stood towering over me, snorting "What d'ja say, boy?" Quickly he frisked me and demanded, "What's your name boy?" Frightened, I replied, "Dr. Poussaint. I'm a physician." He angrily chuckled and hissed, "What's your first name, boy?" When I hesitated he assumed a threatening stance and clenched his fists. As my heart palpitated, I muttered in profound humiliation, "Alvin."
>
> He continued his psychological brutality, bellowing, "Alvin, the next time I call you, you come right away, you hear? You hear?" I hesitated. "You hear me, boy?" My voice trembling with helplessness, but *following my instincts of self-preservation,* I murmured, "Yes, sir." *Now fully satisfied that I had performed and acquiesced to my "boy" status,* he dismissed me with, "Now, boy, go on and get out of here or next time we'll take you for a little ride down to the station house! (Alvin F. Poussaint, "A Negro Psychiatrist Explains the Negro Psyche," *The New York Times Magazine,* August 20, 1967), (emphasis mine).

In the northern cities the black encountered authority figures equivalent to Southern "crackers": policemen, judges, probation officers, truant officers, teachers and "Mr. Charlies" (bosses), and soon learned that the way to get by and avoid difficulty was to shuck. Thus, he learned to accommodate "the Man," to use the total orchestration of speech, intonation, gesture and facial expression for the purpose of producing whatever appearance would be acceptable. It was a technique and ability that was developed from fear, a respect for power, and a will to survive. This type of accommodation is exemplified by the Uncle Tom with his "Yes sir, Mr. Charlie," or "Anything you say, Mr. Charlie."

Through accommodation, many blacks became adept at concealing and controlling their emotions and at assuming a variety of postures. They became competent actors. Many developed a keen perception of what affected, motivated, appeased or satisfied the authority figures with whom they came into contact. Shucking became an effective way for many blacks to stay out of trouble, and for others a useful artifice for avoiding arrest or getting out of trouble when apprehended. Shucking it with a judge, for example, would be to feign repentance in the hope of receiving a lighter or suspended sentence. Robert Conot reports an example of shucking in his book, *Rivers of Blood, Years of Darkness:* Joe was found guilty of possession of narcotics. But he did an excellent job of shucking it with the probation officer.

The probation officer interceded for Joe with the judge: "His own attitude toward the present offense appears to be serious and responsible and it is believed that the defendant is an excellent subject for probation."

Some field illustrations of shucking to get out of trouble came from some seventh grade children from an inner-city school in Chicago. The children were asked to talk their way out of a troublesome situation.

•You are cursing at this old man and your mother comes walking down the stairs. She hears you.
   To "talk your way out of this":
   "I'd tell her that I was studying a scene in school for a play."
•What if you were in a store stealing something and the manager caught you?
   "I would start stuttering. Then I would say, 'Oh, Oh, I forgot. Here the money is.' "

•A literary example of shucking comes from Iceberg Slim's autobiography. Iceberg, a pimp, shucks before "two red-faced Swede rollers (detectives)" who catch him in a motel room with his whore. My italics identify which elements of the passage constitute the shuck.

I put my shaking hands into the pajama pockets . . .
I hoped I was keeping the fear out of my face. I gave them a wide toothy smile. They came in and stood in the middle of the room. Their eyes were racing about the room. Stacy was open mouthed in the bed.
I said, *"Yes gentlemen, what can I do for you?"*
Lanky said, "We wanta see your I.D."
   I went to the closet and got the phony John Cato Fredrickson I.D. I put it in his palm. I felt cold sweat running down my back. They looked at it, then looked at each other.
   Lanky said, "You are in violation of the law. You signed the motel register improperly. Why didn't you sign your full name? What are you trying to hide? What are you doing here in town? It says you're a dancer. We don't have a club in town that books entertainers."
   I said, *"Officers, my professional name is Johnny Cato. I've got nothing to hide. My full name had always been too long for the marquees. I've fallen into the habit of using the shorter version.*
   "My legs went out last year. I don't dance anymore. My wife and I decided to go into business. We are making a tour of this part of the country. We

think that in your town we've found the ideal site for a Southern fried chicken shack. My wife has a secret recipe that should make us rich up here."
(Iceberg Slim, *Pimp: The Story of My Life*)

Another example of shucking was related to me by a colleague. A black gang member was coming down the stairway from the club room with seven guns on him and encountered some policemen and detectives coming up the same stairs. If they stopped and frisked him he and others would have been arrested. A paraphrase of his shuck follows: "Man, I gotta get away from up there. There's gonna be some trouble and I don't want no part of it." This shuck worked on the minds of the policemen. It anticipated their questions as to why he was leaving the club room, and why he would be in a hurry. He also gave *them* a reason for wanting to get up to the room fast.

It ought to be mentioned at this point that there was not uniform agreement among my informants in characterizing the above examples as shucking. One informant used shucking only in the sense in which it is used among peers, e.g., bull-shitting, and characterized the above examples as jiving or whupping game. Others however, identified the above examples as shucking, and reserved jiving and whupping game for more offensive maneuvers. In fact, one of the apparent features of shucking is that the posture of the black when acting with members of the establishment be a *defensive* one.

Frederick Douglass, in telling how he taught himself to read, would challenge a white boy with whom he was playing, by saying that he could write as well as he. Whereupon he would write down all the letters he knew. The white boy would then write down more letters than Douglass did. In this way, Douglass eventually learned all the letters of the alphabet. Some of my informants regarded the example as whupping game. Others regarded it as shucking. The former were perhaps focusing on the manuever rather than the language used. The latter may have felt that any maneuvers designed to learn to read were justifiably defensive. One of my informants said Douglass was "shucking *in order to* whup the game." This latter response seems to be the most revealing. Just as one can rap to whup the game on someone, so one can shuck or jive for the same purpose; that is, assume a guise or posture or perform some action in a certain way that is designed to work on someone's mind to get him to give up something.

"Whupping Game" to Con Whitey

The following examples from Malcolm X illustrate the shucking and jiving in this context though jive is the term used. Today, whupping game might also be the term used to describe the operation. Whites who came at night got a better reception; the several Harlem nightclubs they patronized were geared to entertain and jive (flatter, cajole) the night white crowd to get their money. (Malcolm X, *The Autobiography of Malcolm X*)

The maneuvers involved here are clearly designed to obtain some benefit or advantage.

> Freddie got on the stand and went to work on his own shoes. Brush, liquid polish, brush, paste wax, shine rag, lacquer sole dressing . . . step by step, Freddie showed me what to do.
>
> "But you got to get a whole lot faster. You can't waste time!" Freddie showed me how fast on my own shoes. Then because business was tapering off, he had time to give me a demonstration of how to make the shine rag pop like a firecracker. "Dig the action?" he asked. He did it in slow motion. I got down and tried it on his shoes. I had the principle of it. "Just got to do it faster," Freddie said. *"It's a jive noise, that's all. Cats tip better, they figure you're knocking yourself out!"* (Malcolm X, *The Autobiography of Malcolm X*)

An eight year old boy whupped the game on me one day this way:

> My colleague and I were sitting in a room listening to a tape. The door to the room was open and outside was a soda machine. Two boys came up in the elevator, stopped at the soda machine, and then came into the room.
>
> "Do you have a dime for two nickels?" Presumably the soda machine would not accept nickels. I took out the change in my pocket, found a dime and gave it to the boy for two nickels.
>
> After accepting the dime, he looked at the change in my hand and asked, "Can I have two cents? I need carfare to get home." I gave him the two cents.

At first I assumed the verbal component of the maneuver was the rather weak, transparently false reason for wanting the two cents. Actually, as was pointed out to me later, the maneuver began with the first question which was designed to get me to show my money. He could then ask me for something he knew I had, making my refusal more difficult. He apparently felt that the reason need not be more than plausible because the amount he wanted was small. Were the amount larger, he would no doubt have elaborated on the verbal element of the game. The form of the verbal element could be in the direction of rapping or shucking and jiving. If he were to rap the eight-year old might say, "Man, you know a cat needs to have a little bread to keep the girls in line." Were he to shuck and jive he might make the reason for needing the money more compelling, look hungry, etc.

The function of shucking and jiving as it refers to blacks and "the Man" is designed to work on the mind and emotions of the authority figure for the purpose of getting him to feel a certain way or give up something that will be to the other's advantage. Iceberg showed a "toothy smile" which said to the detective, "I'm glad to see you" and "Would I be glad to see you if I had something to hide?" When the maneuvers seem to be *defensive* most of my informants regarded the language behavior as shucking. When the maneuvers were *offensive* my informants tended to regard the behavior as 'whupping the game.'

Also significant is that the first form of shucking described, which developed out of accommodation, is becoming less frequently used today by many blacks, because of a new found self-assertiveness and pride, challenging the system. The willingness on the part of many blacks to accept the psychological and physical brutality and general social consequences of not "keeping one's place" is indicative of the changing self-concept of the black man. Ironically, the shocked reaction of some whites to the present militancy of the black is partly due to the fact that the black was so successful at "putting Whitey on" via shucking in the past. This new attitude can be seen from a conversation I recently had with a shoe shine attendant at O'Hare airport in Chicago.

I was having my shoes shined and the black attendant was using a polishing machine instead of the rag that was generally used in the past. I asked whether the machine made his work any easier. He did not answer me until about ten seconds had passed and then responded in a loud voice that he "never had a job that was easy," that he would give me "one hundred dollars for any *easy* job" I could offer him, that the machine made his job "faster" but not "easier." I was startled at the response because it was so unexpected and I realized that here was a new "breed of cat" who was not going to shuck for a big tip or ingratiate himself with "Whitey" anymore. A few years ago his response probably would have been different.

The contrast between this "shoe-shine" scene and the one illustrated earlier from Malcolm X's autobiography, when "shucking Whitey" was the common practice, is striking.

Shucking, jiving, shucking and jiving, or S-ing and J-ing, when referring to language behavior practiced by blacks, is descriptive of the talk and gestures that are appropriate to "putting someone on" by creating a false impression. The terms seem to cover a range from simply telling a lie, to bullshitting, to subtly playing with someone's mind. An important difference between this form of shucking and that described earlier is that the same talk and gestures that are deceptive to "the Man" are often transparent to those members of one's own group who are able practitioners at shucking themselves. As Robert Conot has pointed out, "The Negro who often fools the white officer by 'shucking it' is much less likely to be successful with another Negro. . . . " Also, S-ing and J-ing within the group often has play overtones in which the person being "put on" is aware of the attempts being made and goes along with it for enjoyment or in appreciation of the style.

"Running it down" is the term used by speakers in the ghetto when it is their intention to give information, either by explanation, narrative, or giving advice. In the following literary example, Sweet Mac is "running this Edith broad down" to his friends:

> Edith is the "saved" broad who can't marry out of her religion . . . or do anything else out of her religion for that matter, especially what I wanted her to do. A bogue religion, man! So dig, for the last couple weeks I been quoting the Good Book and all that stuff to her; telling her I am now saved myself, you dig. (Woodie King, Jr., "The Game," *Liberator,* August, 1965)

The following citation from Claude Brown uses the term with the additional sense of giving advice:

> If I saw him (Claude's brother) hanging out with cats I knew were weak, who might be using drugs sooner or later, I'd run it down to him.

It seems clear that running it down has simply an informative function, that of telling somebody something that he doesn't already know.

"Gripping" is of fairly recent vintage, used by black high school students in Chicago to refer to the talk and facial expression that accompanies a *partial* loss of face or self-possession, or showing of fear. Its appearance alongside "copping a plea," which refers to a total loss of face, in which one begs one's adversary for mercy, is a significant new perception. In linking it with the street code which acclaims the ability to "look tough and inviolate, fearless, secure, 'cool,' " it suggests that even the slightest weakening of this posture will be held up to ridicule and contempt. There are always contemptuous overtones attached to the use of the term when applied to the others' behavior. One is tempted to link it with the violence and toughness required to survive on the street. The intensity of both seems to be increasing. As one of my informants noted, "Today, you're *lucky* if you end up in the hospital"—that is, are not killed.

Reaction to Fear and Superior Power

Both gripping and copping a plea refer to behavior produced from fear and a respect for superior power. An example of gripping comes from the record *"Street and Gangland Rhythms"* (Band 4 Dumb Boy). Lennie meets Calvin and asks him what happened to his lip. Calvin says that a boy named Pierre hit him for copying off him in school. Lennie, pretending to be Calvin's brother, goes to confront Pierre. Their dialogue follows:

> Lennie: "Hey you! What you hit my little brother for?"
> Pierre: "Did he tell you what happen man?"
> Lennie: "Yeah, he told me what happened."

Pierre: "But you . . . but you . . . but you should tell your people to teach him to go to school, man." (Pause) I, I know, I know I didn't have a right to hit him."

Pierre, anticipating a fight with Lennie if he continued to justify his hitting of Calvin, tried to avoid it by "gripping" with the last line.

Copping a plea, originally meant "To plead guilty to a lesser charge to save the state the cost of a trial," (with the hope of receiving a lesser or suspended sentence) but is now generally used to mean 'to beg,' 'plead for mercy,' as in the example "Please cop, don't hit me. I give." (*Street and Gangland Rhythms,* Band 1 "Gang Fight"). This change of meaning can be seen from its use by Piri Thomas in *Down These Mean Streets.*

> The night before my hearing, I decided to make a prayer. It had to be on my knees, 'cause if I was gonna cop a plea to God, I couldn't play it cheap.

The function of gripping and copping a plea is obviously to induce pity or to acknowledge the presence of superior strength. In so doing, one evinces noticeable feelings of fear and insecurity which also result in a loss of status among one's peers.

Signifying is the term used to describe the language behavior that, as Abrahams has defined it, attempts to "imply, goad, beg, boast by indirect verbal or gestural means." (Roger D. Abrahams, *Deep Down in the Jungle*) In Chicago it is also used as a synonym to describe language behavior more generally known as "sounding" elsewhere.

Some excellent examples of signifying as well as of other forms of language behavior come from the well known "toast" (narrative form) "The Signifying Monkey and the Lion" which was collected by Abrahams from Negro street corner bards in Philadelphia. In the above toast the monkey is trying to get the lion involved in a fight with the elephant:

> Now the lion came through the jungle one peaceful day,
> When the signifying monkey stopped him, and that is what he started to
>   say:
> He said, "Mr. Lion," he said, "A bad-assed motherfucker down your way,"
> He said, "Yeah! The way he talks about your folks is a certain shame.
> "I even heard him curse when he mentioned your grandmother's name."
> The lion's tail shot back like a forty-four
> When he went down that jungle in all uproar.

Thus the monkey has goaded the lion into a fight with the elephant by "signifying," that is, indicating that the elephant has been "sounding on" (insulting) the lion. When the lion comes back, thoroughly beaten up, the monkey again "signifies" by making fun of the lion:

> . . . lion came back through the jungle more dead than alive,
> When the monkey started some more of that signifying jive.

He said, "Damn, Mr. Lion, you went through here yesterday, the jungle
   rung.
Now you come back today, damn near hung."

The monkey, of course, is delivering this taunt from a safe distance
away on the limb of a tree when his foot slips and he falls to the ground,
at which point,

Like a bolt of lightning, a stripe of white heat,
The lion was on the monkey with all four feet.

In desperation the monkey quickly resorts to "copping a plea":

The monkey looked up with a tear in his eyes,
He said, "Please, Mr. Lion, I apologize."

His "plea" however, fails to move the lion to show any mercy so the
monkey tries another verbal ruse, "shucking":

He said, "You lemme get my head out of the sand,
ass out the grass, I'll fight you like a natural man."

In this he is more successful as,

The lion jumped back and squared for a fight.
The motherfucking monkey jumped clear out of sight.

A safe distance away again, the monkey returns to "signifying":

He said, "Yeah, you had me down, you had me at last,
But you left me free, now you can still kiss my ass."

This example illustrates the methods of provocation, goading and taunt-
ing artfully practiced by a signifier.
   Interestingly, when the *function* of signifying is *directive* the *tactic* employed is *indirection,* i.e., the signifier reports or repeats what someone
else has said about the listener; the "report" is couched in plausible language designed to compel belief and arouse feelings of anger and hostility.
There is also the implication that if the listener fails to do anything about
it—what has to be "done" is usually quite clear—his status will be seriously compromised. Thus the lion is compelled to vindicate the honor of
his family by fighting or else leave the impression that he is afraid, and

that he is not "king" of the jungle. When used for the purpose of directing action, "signifying" is like "shucking" in also being deceptive and subtle in approach and depending for success on the naivete or gullibility of the person being "put on."

When the function of signifying is to arouse feelings of embarrassment, shame, frustration or futility, to diminish someone's status, the tactic employed is direct in the form of a taunt, as in the example where the monkey is making fun of the lion.

"Sounding" to Relieve Tensions

Sounding is the term which is today most widely known for the game of verbal insult known in the past as "Playing the Dozens," "The Dirty Dozens" or just "The Dozens." Other current names for the game have regional distribution: Signifying or "Sigging" (Chicago), Joning (Washington, D.C.), Screaming (Harrisburg), etc. In Chicago, the term "sounding" would be descriptive of the initial remarks which are designed to sound out the other person to see whether he will play the game. The verbal insult is also subdivided, the term "signifying" applying to insults which are hurled directly at the person and the dozens applying to results hurled at your opponent's family, especially, the mother.

Sounding is often catalyzed by signifying remarks referred to earlier such as "Are you going to let him say that about your mama" to spur an exchange between members of the group. It is begun on a relatively low key and built up by verbal exchanges. The game goes like this:

> One insults a member of another's family; others in the group make disapproving sounds to spur on the coming exchange. The one who has been insulted feels at this point that he must reply with a slur on the protagonist's family which is clever enough to defend his honor (And therefore that of his family). This, of course, leads the other (once again, more due to pressure from the crowd than actual insult) to make further jabs. This can proceed until everyone is bored with the whole affair, until one hits the other (fairly rare), or until some other subject comes up that interrupts the proceedings (the usual state of affairs). (Roger D. Abrahams, "Playing the Dozens," *Journal of American Folklore,* July-September, 1962)

Mack McCormick describes the dozens as a verbal contest:

> in which the players strive to bury one another with vituperation. In the play, the opponent's mother is especially slandered . . . Then, in turn fathers are identified as queer and syphilitic. Sisters are whores, brothers are defective, cousins are "funny" and the opponent is himself diseased. (Mack McCormick, "The Dirty Dozens," book jacket in the record album *The Unexpurgated Folksongs of Men,* Arhoolie Records).

An example of the "game" collected by one of my students goes:

> Frank looked up and saw Leroy enter the Outpost. Leroy walked past the

room where Quinton, "Nap," "Pretty Black," "Cunny," Richard, Haywood, "Bull" and Reese sat playing cards. As Leroy neared the T.V. room, Frank shouted to him.

Frank: "Hey Leroy, your mama—calling you man."

Leroy turned and walked toward the room where the sound came from. He stood in the door and looked at Frank.

Leroy: "Look motherfuckers, I don't play that shit."

Frank (signifying): "Man, I told you cats 'bout that mama jive" (as if he were concerned about how Leroy felt)

Leroy: "That's all right Frank; you don't have to tell these funky motherfuckers nothing; I'll fuck me up somebody yet."

Frank's face lit up as if he were ready to burst his side laughing. "Cunny" became pissed at Leroy.

Cunny: "Leroy, you stupid bastard, you let Frank make a fool of you. He said that 'bout your mama."

"Pretty Black": "Aw, fat ass head 'Cunny' shut up."

"Cunny": Ain't that some shit. This black slick head motor flicker got nerve 'nough to call somebody 'fathead.' Boy, you so black, you sweat Permalube Oil."

This eased the tension of the group as they burst into loud laughter.

"Pretty Black": "What 'chu laughing 'bout 'Nap,' with your funky mouth smelling like dog shit."

Even Leroy laughed at this.

"Nap": "Your mama motherfucker."

"Pretty Black": "Your funky mama too."

"Nap": (strongly) "It takes twelve barrels of water to make a steamboat run; it takes an elephant's dick to make your Grandmammy come; she been elephant fucked, camel fucked and hit side the head with your Grandpappy's nuts."

Reese: "Godorr-damn; go on and rap motherfucker."

Reese began slapping each boy in his hand, giving his positive approval of "Naps" comment. "Pretty Black" in an effort not to be undone, but directing his verbal play elsewhere stated:

"Pretty Black": "Reese, what you laughing 'bout? You so square, you shit bricked shit."

Frank: "Whoooowee!"

Reese (sounded back): "Square huh, what about your nappy ass hair before it was stewed; that shit was so bad till, when you went to bed at night, it would leave your head and go on the corner and meddle."

The boys slapped each other in the hand and cracked up.

"Pretty Black": "On the streets meddling, bet Dinky didn't offer me no pussy and I turned it down."

Frank: "Reese scared of pussy."

"Pretty Black": "Hell yeah; the greasy mother rather fuck old ugly, funky cock Sue Willie than get a piece of ass from a decent broad."
Frank: "Godorr-damn! Not Sue Willie."
"Pretty Black": "yeah ol meat-beating Reese rather screw that cross-eyed, clapsy bitch, who when she cry, tears rip down her ass."
Haywood: "Don't be so mean, Black."
Reese: "Aw shut up, you half-white bastard."
Frank: "Wait man, Haywood ain't gonna hear much more of that half-white shit; he's a brother too."
Reese: "Brother, my black ass; that white ass landlord gotta be this motherfucker's paw."
"Cunny": "Man, you better stop foolin with Haywood; he's turning red."
Haywood: "Fuck yall. (as he withdrew from the "sig" game.)
Frank: "Yeah, fuck yall; let's go to the stick hall."
The group left enroute to the billiard hall. (James Maryland, "Signifying at the Outpost," unpublished term paper for the course *Idiom of the Negro Ghettos,* January 1967)

The above example of sounding is an excellent illustration of the "game" as played by 15–17-year-old Negro boys, some of whom have already acquired the verbal skill which for them is often the basis for having a high "rep." Ability with words is apparently as highly valued as physical strength. In the sense that the status of one of the participants in the game is diminished if he has to resort to fighting to answer a verbal attack, verbal ability may be even more highly regarded than physical ability.

The relatively high value placed on verbal ability must be clear to most black boys at early age. Most boys begin their activity in sounding by compiling a repertoire of "one liners." When the game is played the one who has the greatest number of such remarks wins. Here are some examples of "one liners" collected from fifth and sixth grade black boys in Chicago:

Yo mama is so bowlegged, she looks like the bit out of a donut.
Yo mama sent her picture to the lonely hearts club, and they sent it back and said "We ain't that lonely!"
Your family is so poor the rats and roaches eat lunch out.
Your house is so small the roaches walk single file.
I walked in your house and your family was running around the table. I said, "Why you doin that?" Your mama say, "First one drops, we eat."

Real proficiency in the game comes to only a small percentage of those who play it. These players have the special skill in being able to turn around what their opponents have said and attack them with it. Thus, when someone indifferently said "fuck you" to Concho, his retort was immediate and devastating: "Man, you haven't even kissed me yet."

The "best talkers" from this group often become the successful street-corner, barber shop, and pool hall story tellers who deliver the long, rhymed, witty, narrative stories called "toasts." They are, as Roger D. Abrahams has described, the traditional "men of words" and have become on occasion entertainers such as Dick Gregory and Redd Fox, who are virtuosos at repartee, and preachers, whose verbal power has been traditionally esteemed.

The function of the "dozens" or "sounding" is to borrow status from an opponent through an exercise of verbal power. The opponent feels compelled to regain his status by "sounding" back on the speaker or other group member whom he regards as more vulnerable.

The presence of a group seems to be especially important in controlling the game. First of all, one does not "play" with just anyone since the subject matter is concerned with things that in reality one is quite sensitive about. It is precisely *because* "Pretty Black" has a "Black slick head" that makes him vulnerable to "Cunny's" barb, especially now when the Afro-American "natural" hair style is in vogue. Without the control of the group "sounding" will frequently lead to a fight. This was illustrated by a tragic epilogue concerning Haywood, when Haywood was being "sounded" on in the presence of two girls by his best friend (other members of the group were absent), he refused to tolerate it. He went home, got a rifle, came back and shot and killed his friend. In the classroom from about the fourth grade on fights among black boys invariably are caused by someone "sounding" on the other person's mother.

Significantly, the subject matter of sounding is changing with the changing self-concept of the black with regard to those physical characteristics that are characteristically "Negro," and which in the past were vulnerable points in the black psyche: blackness and "nappy" hair. It ought to be said that for many blacks, blackness was always highly esteemed and it might be more accurate to regard the present sentiment of the black community toward skin color as reflecting a shifted attitude for only a *portion* of the black community. This suggests that "sounding" on someone's light skin color is not new. Nevertheless, one can regard the previously favorable attitude toward light skin color and "good hair" as the prevailing one. "Other things being equal, the more closely a woman approached her white counterpart, the more attractive she was considered to be, by both men and women alike. "Good hair" (hair that is long and soft) and light skin were the chief criteria." (Elliot Liebow, *Tally's Corner*).

The dozens has been linked to the over-all psychosocial growth of the black male. McCormick has stated that a "single round of a dozen or so exchanges frees more pent-up aggressions than will a dose of sodium pentothal." The fact that one permits a kind of abuse within the rules of the game and within the confines of the group which would otherwise not be tolerated, is filled with psychological import. It seems also important, however, to view its function from the perspective of the non-participating members of the group. Its function for them may be to incite and prod individual members of the group to combat for the purpose of energizing the elements, of simply relieving the boredom of just "hanging around" and the malaise of living in a static and restrictive environment.

A summary analysis of the different forms of language behavior which have been discussed above permit the following generalizations:

The prestige norms which influence black speech behavior are those which have been successful in manipulating and controlling people and situations. The function of all of the forms of language behavior discussed above, with the exception of "running it down," was to project personality, assert oneself, or arouse emotion, frequently with the additional purpose of getting the person to give up or do something which will be of some benefit to the speaker. Only running it down has as its primary function to communicate information and often here too, the personality and style of the speaker in the form of rapping is projected along with the information.

The purpose for which language is used suggests that the speaker views the social situations into which he moves as consisting of a series of transactions which require that he be continually ready to take advantage of a person or situation or defend himself against being victimized. He has absorbed what Horton has called "street rationality." As one of Horton's respondents put it: "The good hustler . . . conditions his mind and must never put his guard too far down, to relax, or he'll be taken."

I have carefully avoided limiting the group within the black community of whom the language behavior and perspective of their environment is characteristic. While I have no doubt that it is true of those whom are generally called "street people" I am uncertain of the extent to which it is true of a much larger portion of the black community, especially the male segment. My informants consisted of street people, high school students, and blacks, who by their occupation as community and youth workers, possess what has been described as a "sharp sense of the streets." Yet it is difficult to find a black male in the community who has *not* witnessed or participated in the dozens or heard of signifying, or rapping, or shucking and jiving at some time during his growing up. It would be equally difficult to imagine a high school student in a Chicago inner-city school not being touched by what is generally regarded as "street culture."

In conclusion, by blending style and verbal power, through rapping, sounding and running it down, the black in the ghetto establishes his personality; through shucking, gripping and copping a plea, he shows his respect for power; through jiving and signifying he stirs up excitement. With all of the above, he hopes to manipulate and control people and situations to give himself a winning edge.

two

At birth each person, Black or White, is dependent upon others for survival and for the development of personality. Social interaction constitutes the basic fiber of human association. What forms of groups result? What patterns emerge and what purposes are served? Do Blacks have special problems of entry into associational life? How do they respond to the obstacles they confront?

Groups and Associations

There are many different kinds of groups within a community. At one end of the scale are primary groups, such as the family or peer groups. Such groups tend to be small, intimate, and informal. They provide opportunities for interaction and are also a means whereby individuals are socialized into society. Primary groups are usually flexible, allowing members to participate in a wide variety of activities. At the other end of the scale are what are called secondary groups. These groups tend to be large and formally structured. They usually exist for a specific purpose, such as political, social, or recreational activity.

Voluntary associations are a type of secondary group in which members are relatively free to join or abstain if they so wish. Examples would include churches, charitable organizations, service clubs, or recreational groups. Voluntary associations perform various functions within a community. They fill many social needs for members, disseminate information, teach organizational participation, and often provide recreational outlets.

Voluntary associations are potentially important as a basis for community-wide organization. Large numbers of people can be quickly informed, and rapid community action becomes feasible if the community has an efficient network of such groups. Within the Black community such associations may be even more important for organizing community action because Blacks seldom have control of information media; such as television stations or local newspapers. Many movements within the Black community depend upon the strength of such associations for success.

Since Blacks are often denied membership in voluntary associations within the larger society, they must maintain their own associations. Such segregation of course hinders communication flow and inhibits interaction between members of the Black community and the rest of society.

America is often characterized as a nation of joiners, yet many persons do not belong to any voluntary associations. Membership appears to vary by social class: the higher a person's social status, the more likely he is to belong to associations. Since most Blacks are members of the lower class, it would be expected that they would belong to few associations.

Anthony Orum attempts to shed some light on the question of Black participation in community organizations. Some researchers of the Black community have felt that few Blacks participate in associations. Others argue that, in attempting to overcompensate for their lower status, Blacks tend to join as many organizations as possible. Orum's data indicate that the relationship between social class and organizational membership is not as strong for Blacks as it is for the rest of society. In fact, Blacks are more likely to participate actively in organizations. However, the organizations to which these Blacks belonged were largely segregated, probably the reason that non-Black researchers previously underestimated the organizational participation of Blacks. Orum also indicates some differences in the type of organizations to which Blacks belong.

John Howard's article examines membership in one particular all-Black organization, the Black Muslims. Some social scientists feel that associations like the Black Muslims attract a certain type of person who already has the requisite attitudes to join, while others hold that such associations change the new member to their views only after he has become an active member. The Black Muslims interviewed by Howard seem to support the view that they joined to secure organizational support for attitudes which they already held. It is interesting to speculate into the general factors that lead to the joining of such an organization. Most of Howard's informants indicated that they had experienced much tension (stemming from discrimination) in their lives and that they had an outlook that was in sympathy with the stated goals of the Black Muslims prior to actually joining. Most also seem to have had a past history of trying various solutions on their own, none of which was successful. They therefore turned to the Black Muslims, where they had the promise of strong organizational support, only after other solutions had failed.

PARTICIPATION

"A Reappraisal of the Social and Political Participation of Negroes"[1]

by Anthony M. Orum

Social scientists have often pointed to the important role that social and political organizations play in facilitating the assimilation of minority groups into the larger American society. As compared with other immigrants to urban America, Negroes are believed to be particularly lacking in those organizational resources that provide both the means by which group demands are effectively brought to bear in the political and economic spheres and the opportunities to learn the co-operative skills that equip them for life in the metropolis. Without these organizational supports, so the argument goes, the individual Negro migrant is left "naked unto his enemies."

The rapid and effective rise of the civil rights movement and the proliferation of action organizations that display a relatively high degree of sophistication is surprising in light of the general beliefs about the Negroes' low level of organizational experience. While much has been said and written about the movement, very little attention has been given to the social facts upon which it is based—that is, the participation of Negroes in social and political life. In this paper we shall examine critically the evidence on which the belief in the low level of Negro participation rests and present new data indicating that some significant facts have been overlooked in earlier studies.

The most prevalent interpretation of Negro participation is based partly on the observation that people in the lower socioeconomic stratum in American society participate less in voluntary associations and general elections than do those in the middle and upper social strata. In the

[1]*Revision of a paper presented at the annual meeting of the Midwest Sociological Society, April, 1965. This investigation was supported by Public Health Service Special Grant No. MH 09183 from the National Institute of Mental Health to the National Opinion Research Center. The author wishes to express his appreciation to Norman Bradburn for his encouragement and sustained interest in this research. David Caplovitz and Amy Wexler Orum provided helpful suggestions on an earlier version of this paper.*

precursor to many studies on participation in voluntary association, Komarovsky showed that, among people in an urban area, the extent of affiliation varied directly with social class.[2] Axelrod, in a more recent study in Detroit, found that both membership and degree of activity in associations were positively associated with family income.[3]

Since Negroes are found predominantly in the lower socioeconomic groups, one is led to suppose that they are also less likely to be affiliated with and actively participate in formal organizations. At least one piece of evidence directly confirms this supposition. Using a national sample of respondents, Wright and Hyman showed that 60 per cent of Negro families, compared with 46 per cent of white families, did not belong to any organizations, while only 11 per cent of the Negroes and 23 per cent of the whites belonged to two or more organizations.[4] This study, however, failed to control for the previous relationship found between social class and participation, thereby obscuring membership rates of whites and Negroes at comparable socioeconomic levels. This consideration, as we shall see later, is crucial in any investigation of Negro-white differentials in participation.

Research on voting behavior has reached conclusions similar to those found in studies of associational membership. In a study of the 1952 election, Campbell, Gurin, and Miller stated that "Negroes feel more politically impotent than the rest of the population."[5] A later work based on the elections of 1948, 1952, and 1956 confirmed this impression. Campbell *et al.* suggested that while "Negroes . . . are almost unanimous in their belief that the group has a right to further its end by political activity," the motivation for Negroes to vote was lower than in most other groups.[6] Woodward and Roper also came to the same conclusion. They indicated that 38 per cent of the total adult population was politically very inactive, but 60 per cent of the Negroes were very inactive.[7] The voting studies, however, also failed to consider the Negro-white differentials among comparable socioeconomic groups of voters.

An explanation that supports these and similar results is implicit in these findings. It is a two-headed demon: one head may be seen as social

[2]Mirra Komarovsky, "The Voluntary Associations of Urban Dwellers," *American Sociological Review,* XI, No. 6 (December, 1946), 686–98, esp. 689.

[3]Morris Axelrod, "Urban Structure and Social Participation," *American Sociological Review,* XXI, No. 1 (February, 1956), 13–18, esp. 15.

[4]Charles R. Wright and Herbert H. Hyman, "Voluntary Association Memberships of American Adults: Evidence from National Sample Surveys," *American Sociological Review,* XXIII, No. 3 (June, 1958), 284–94, esp. 287.

[5]Angus Campbell, Gerald Gurin, and Warren E. Miller, *The Voter Decides* (Evanston, Ill.: Row, Peterson & Co., 1954), pp. 191–92.

[6]Angus Campbell, Philip E. Converse, Warren E. Miller, and Donald E. Stokes, *The American Voter* (New York: John Wiley & Sons, 1960), p. 316.

[7]Julian L. Woodward and Elmo Roper, "Political Activity of American Citizens," *American Political Science Review,* XLIV, No. 4 (December, 1950), 872–85, esp. 877.

alienation or anomie and the other as political apathy. Perhaps the best way of describing the demon is with the concept of involuntary "isolation" from civic affairs.[8] As Lipset put it: "[The] characteristics [of the lower strata] also reflect the extent to which [they] are *isolated* from the activities, controversies, and organizations of democratic society—an isolation which prevents them from acquiring the sophisticated and complex view of the political structure which makes understandable and necessary the norms of tolerance."[9] Various forms of the prevalent social segregation of Negroes are viewed as conducive to their "isolation" from civic affairs; this isolation, in turn, accounts for both a low level of participation in associations and a low voting turnout.

This view of the Negroes' "isolation" is not universally accepted, however. There is a second point of view that is in direct opposition to it. Myrdal, appearing as its first advocate, suggested that Negroes are "exaggerated Americans" since they organize and are active in *more* voluntary organizations than other Americans.[10] Hunter supported this contention.[11] He found more than 350 organizations within the Negro subcommunity of Atlanta; that, he said "represents the high degree of social organization within the Negro community."[12] Aside from fraternal and other social groups, he stated, "the top associational groupings identified in the subcommunity have a political content not found in the larger community. This is true even in the welfare and recreational associations."[13] A recent and somewhat more systematic investigation has provided evidence to support Myrdal and Hunter. In comparison with the findings on the organizational membership of whites from previous studies, Babchuk and Thompson concluded that Negroes in their sample were more likely to be affiliated with associations than whites.[14]

The explanation for the higher organizational participation of Negroes is most succinctly stated by Babchuk and Thompson. Following the line of argument established by Myrdal, they claim that since Negroes are not allowed to gain prestige and power in most "organized life" in America, for example, in the occupational sphere, they compensate by exaggerated tendencies to create and/or participate in a large number of formal organi-

---

[8]The author recognizes that there has been rather heated controversy about the concept of alienation. Since this paper does not attempt a theoretical excursion into the meanings and nuances of alienation, it was felt that the value-free concept of isolation would be sufficient for our purposes.

[9]Seymour Martin Lipset, *Political Man* (Garden City, N.Y.: Doubleday & Co., 1960), p. 112.

[10]Gunnar Myrdal, Richard Sterner, and Arnold Rose, *An American Dilemma* (New York: Harper & Bros., 1944), p. 952.

[11]Floyd Hunter, *Community Power Structure* (Garden City, N.Y.: Doubleday & Co., 1963), pp. 114 ff.

[12]*Ibid.,* p. 114.

[13]*Ibid.,* p. 125.

[14]Nicholas Babchuk and Ralph V. Thompson, "Voluntary Associations of Negroes," *American Sociological Review,* XXVII (October, 1962), 647–55.

zations. In other words, they contend that the response of Negroes to segregation is quite the opposite of civic indifference and apathy.

The contradiction betwen these two interpretations stands out boldly. The "isolation" point of view supposes that Negroes participate much less in associations and general elections than whites. The "compensatory" point of view claims, on the other hand, that Negroes participate much more than whites. To resolve this contradiction, we shall analyze data on Negro-white differentials in participation in formal organizations and voting turnout obtained from a number of sample surveys conducted during the past few years.

The strategy for the following analysis was guided essentially by three questions: What is the extent of participation—that is, membership and activity—in organizations among comparable socioeconomic groups of Negroes and whites in similar ecological settings? What kinds of organizations do Negroes participate in? And finally, are both the participation in associations and the voting turnout of Negroes so low that we could describe them as isolated from most civic affairs?

Data

A major part of this analysis is based on data gathered for a panel study in mental-health-related behavior currently being conducted by the National Opinion Research Center (NORC).[15] For the purposes of this paper we will be concerned only with questions on membership and activity in organizations. While this study was conducted in several different communities, we shall be concerned primarily with two samples, one Negro and the other white. The Negro sample is located in the inner city area of Detroit. The socioeconomic composition of this sample is predominantly lower class with almost two-thirds of the families earning less than five thousand dollars a year. The white sample is also located in an urban area, the inner city of Chicago. Here, too, many families are in the lower socioeconomic groups, one-third of them earning less than five thousand dollars a year. This sample is drawn from a traditional ethnic area; many of the respondents were either born in eastern Europe or are second-generation Americans of eastern European descent.

Of lesser concern is a third sample located in a suburban county outside Washington, D.C. While most of the sample consists of middle-class whites, there are included in it seventy Negroes who are primarily lower or lower middle class. The Washington suburb will be used for comparisons of differential participation between Negroes and whites in that area, as well as for comparisons with the two other samples.

In addition to the data obtained from these three samples, data on

---

[15]The panel study, financed by grants from the National Institutes of Health, is under the supervision of Professor Norman Bradburn of the National Opinion Research Center.

organizational participation and voting in presidential elections from several unpublished NORC studies and from previously published sources will be used.

Findings

Participation in formal organizations.—There are two facets of participation in formal organizations. The one that has been most commonly studied is membership in an association. Since, in the past, many authors have been concerned with either proving or disproving the thesis of De Tocqueville and the Beards that America is a nation of "joiners," this measure of participation has been quite adequate. Another view, which has gained some recent currency, is found in such works as Barber's "Participation and Mass Apathy in Associations" and those of students of trade unions.[16] This view has been concerned with the apathy prevailing among the members of organizations, a tendency the consequence of which may be the concentration of power among a clique of officials. In order to focus on this issue, authors have studied the kinds of people who participate actively in organizations and who, thus, may be said to exert influence within organizations. To acquire a comprehensive picture of the participation of Negroes in associations, we will look at the characteristics of both those people who are members and those who are active participants.

Organizational membership.—Information about the affiliations of respondents was obtained by asking the following question: "How many organizations such as church and school groups, labor unions, or social, civic, and fraternal clubs do you belong to?" Measures of total membership for each community demonstrate the relationship between race and membership already found without examining membership rates for comparable socioeconomic groups of Negroes and whites. Thus, the white middle-class Washington suburb showed the highest membership rate, while the Detroit Negro community showed the lowest. Within each community, we also find that the relationship between socioeconomic status (SES) and membership was generally sustained; the higher the SES, the more likely a person was to belong to organizations.[17]

Table 1, controlling for SES, presents the membership differences between the two races. Looking first at the Detroit and Chicago data, we find that, among the lowest SES groups, the Detroit Negro respondents

[16] Bernard Barber, "Participation and Mass Apathy in Associations," in Alvin W. Gouldner (ed.), *Studies in Leadership* (New York: Harper & Bros., 1950).

[17] The SES index was constructed by using occupation, education, and income with scores ranging from 0 to 3 assigned to individuals on the basis of percentiles. With each of the three categories scored accordingly, they were combined into an index that yielded scores from 0 to 9. A person with a score of 9, for example, would be a professional or official with some college education or better, earning ten thousand dollars or more a year.

were more likely to belong to organizations than the Chicago white respondents. The importance of this result should not be overlooked; the
community rates by themselves obscure the fact that, among Negroes and
whites at the lower-class level, the Negroes were more likely to be affiliated with organizations. Further evidence of this finding comes from the
Washington suburb, where we observe again that within the lowest SES
group Negroes were more likely to be "joiners" than whites; 71 per cent
of the Negroes in the low SES group compared to 60 per cent of their
white counterparts belonged to at least one organization.

*Table 1. Per Cent of Membership in Organizations by Community, SES,
and Race*

SES	White		Negro	
	Per Cent	*N*	*Per Cent*	*N*
		Detroit		
Low	–	–	66	327
Medium	–	–	70	90
High	–	–	[83]*	12
		Chicago		
Low	58	117	–	–
Medium	79	90	–	–
High	92	40	–	–
		Washington Suburb		
Low	60	137	71	34
Medium	71	455	75	24
High	82	595	[92]	12

*Brackets indicate that the number of cases was less than twenty.
Source: Unpublished data from the National Opinion Research Center panel study of
mental-health-related behavior, No. 485, 1965-66.

The findings for the medium- and high-SES groups are less clear. The
medium-SES respondents in Chicago were more likely than medium-SES
respondents in Detroit to belong to an organization, but there was no
important difference between Negro and white medium-SES respondents
in the Washington suburb. The number of cases in the high-SES Negro
samples was too small to make meaningful comparisons.
    In order to clarify the relationship of race, class, and membership found
in the three communities, we examined similar data from two NORC
studies involving nationwide samples of respondents. The wording of the
membership question was the same in both studies and somewhat differ-

ent from that in the panel study: "Do you belong to any groups or organizations here in the community?" In Table 2 we present data from the 1955 study used by Wright and Hyman. Education is used here as an approximation of SES. We find that the less well-educated Negroes were slightly more likely to belong to organizations than equally educated whites, while the situation was reversed in slight favor of whites in the medium-education stratum. Comparing high-education groups, we find that better educated whites were more likely to belong than their Negro counterparts.

Table 2. Per Cent of Membership in Organizations by Race and Education

Education	White		Negro	
	Per Cent	*N*	*Per Cent*	*N*
Grade school or less	22	720	25	142
Part high school	33	449	30	43
High-school graduate or more	49	954	33	40

Source: National Opinion Research Center study, No. 367, 1955; data used by Wright and Hyman (see n. 4).

The clearest way to view these findings is to observe that for whites there is a strong positive relationship between education and membership but that for Negroes the relationship is not as strong. Table 1 also shows that the relationship for Negroes between SES and membership is not nearly as pronounced as for whites in the Detroit, Chicago, and suburban Washington samples.

There were similar results in a nationwide NORC study conducted in 1962. Table 3 presents these data showing the relationship of race, education, and membership. We find again that Negroes in the lower stratum were more likely to belong to organizations than their white counterparts. In the medium-education group there was no difference between Negroes and whites, while more highly educated whites were more likely to belong than similarly educated Negroes.

The evidence here clearly shows that the relationship between social class and membership in organizations is not nearly as pronounced for Negroes as for whites. These findings help to explain the similarity in the aggregate figures on Negro and white membership in organizations. Since the large majority of Negroes come from the lower socioeconomic strata, the aggregate proportion of Negro membership will tend to be similar to the total lower-class figure. For whites, on the other hand, the aggregate proportion will tend to be similar to the proportion of middle- and upper-class membership. Aggregate figures, then, obscure racial differences because of the strong correlation between social class and race.

Table 3. Per Cent of Membership in Organizations by Race and Education

Education	White		Negro	
	Per Cent	N	Per Cent	N
Grade school or less	30	2,288	45	505
Part high school	36	1,699	36	283
High-school graduate or more	51	4,561	43	330

Source: Unpublished data from the National Opinion Research Center study of adult education, No. 447, 1962. For the report of this study, see John W. Johnstone and Ramon Rivera, *Volunteers for Learning* (NORC Monograph in Social Research series [Chicago: Aldine Publishing Co., 1965]).

Organizational activity.—We learned about the activity of respondents in organizations by asking the following question: "How many [of the organizations to which you belong] do you take an active part in?" As in the case of the membership results, we find that the relationship between SES and activity was not as pronounced among Negroes as among whites.

Following the strategy on membership and controlling for SES, we looked at activity rates within samples by race. Table 4 presents these findings for members of organizations. Comparisons of the Detroit and Chicago respondents clearly show that Negroes in each SES group were more likely than whites to participate actively. Within the Washington-suburb sample, we find further evidence: among the low-SES respondents, almost two-thirds of the Negroes participated actively compared to only one-half of the white respondents.

Again we examined data from the 1955 study used by Wright and Hyman. Table 5 shows the relationship of race, education, and activity. As with SES, the relationship between education and activity was not as pronounced for Negroes as for whites. Nevertheless, Negroes in each educational group were more likely than their white counterparts to be active in organizations.

In the previous section on membership, we found that Negroes apparently were not much less likely than whites to belong to organizations. Lower-class Negroes, in fact, were more likely to be "joiners" than their white counterparts. In contrast to these findings, the activity data from the three communities and a nationwide sample indicate that Negroes, without exception, are more likely to be active in associations than whites.

Kinds of associations.—Thus far we have considered simply the membership and activity of Negroes in associations. Although the evidence suggests that comparatively large proportions of Negroes are participating in organizations, it does not enable us to conclude anything about the

Table 4. *Per Cent Active Members by Community, Race, and SES*

SES	White		Negro	
	Per Cent	N	Per Cent	N
		Detroit		
Low	–	–	66	212
Medium	–	–	84	62
High	–	–	[90]*	10
		Chicago		
Low	38	68	–	–
Medium	60	69	–	–
High	71	35	–	–
		Washington Suburb		
Low	49	72	63	24
Medium	62	322	[89]	18
High	74	489	[82]	11

*Brackets indicate that the number of cases was less than twenty.
Source: Unpublished data from the National Opinion Research Center panel study of mental-health-related behavior, No. 485, 1963-66.

Table 5. *Per Cent of Active Members by Race and Education*

Education	White		Negro	
	Per Cent	N	Per Cent	N
Grade school or less	47	161	71	34
Part high school	55	149	[67]*	12
High-school graduate or less	64	464	[77]	13

*Brackets indicate that the number of cases was less than twenty.
Source: Unpublished data from National Opinion Research Center study, No. 367, 1955; data used by Wright and Hyman (see n. 4).

kinds of organizations and, hence, the kinds of organizational activities that the largest proportions of Negroes pursue. To investigate this matter, we shall consider two studies that obtained information on the types of associations to which Negroes belong.

Table 6. *Per Cent of Membership in Type of Organization by Race and Income (for Individuals)*

Income	Civic	Church	Cultural	Political	N
		White			
Under $4,000	20	32	3	2	237
$4,000-7,499	40	21	4	3	373
$7,500 plus	38	21	4	7	170
Total sample	34	24	4	3	780
		Negro			
Under $4,000	28	32	2	12	50
$4,000-$7,499	[50]*	[42]	[0]	[25]	12
$7,500 plus	–	–	–	–	0
Total sample	32	34	2	15	62

*Brackets indicate that the number of cases was less than twenty.
Source: Unpublished data from National Opinion Research Center study, No. 367, 1955; data used by Wright and Hyman (see n. 4).

The 1955 NORC data used by Wright and Hyman revealed several interesting facets of Negro participation compared with white participation in particular kinds of organizations. Table 6 presents these data; we approximated the class distinction here by controlling for income level. In general, even in 1955 Negroes were more likely than whites to belong to political organizations. Thus, comparing low-income whites with low-income Negroes, we find that 12 per cent of the low-income Negroes compared with 2 per cent of the low-income whites belonged to political organizations. Civic organizations such as the PTA, YMCA, community centers, and others attracted a large proportion of Negroes. Comparison of the total sample measures for Negroes and whites shows that Negroes were as likely to belong to civic associations as were whites, 34 per cent of the whites compared to 32 per cent of the Negroes. And, finally, Negroes in general were more likely to belong to churches and related groups than whites.

To confirm these findings on the participation of Negroes, we then looked at evidence from a study by NORC in 1964 of Negro families in a heavily Negro urban area in the Midwest. In Table 7, we present these data, controlling for income level. Comparing low-income Negroes and the total sample measure with their respective groups in Table 6, we find similar proportions of Negroes belonging to each type of organization. While this evidence is quite tentative because we lack comparative data

*Table 7.   Per Cent of Membership in Type of Organization by Income
(for Negro Families Only)*

Income	Civic	Church	Cultural	Political	N
Under $4,000	35	28	6	15	68
$4,000-$7,999	34	37	4	11	134
$8,000 plus	52	20	11	28	54
Total sample	36	31	6	15	256

Source: Unpublished data from the National Opinion Research Center study of community housing, January-February, 1964.

for whites, it nonetheless appears to confirm the above findings on the particular kinds of organizations to which Negroes predominantly belong, that is, political, civic, and church groups.

Although there are some limitations to the data presented here, two observations seem in order. First, in general Negroes are more likely to participate in political organizations than whites. And second, Negroes are just as likely as whites to participate in civic organizations and tend to be somewhat more likely to participate in church associations.

Voting behavior.—In this section we will examine the voting turnout of Negroes. Although the "compensatory" point of view has little to say about Negro voting behavior, the "isolation" point of view would lead us to expect a comparatively small turnout of Negroes in elections. Results from an intensive nationwide survey of the 1952 presidential election, conducted by the University of Michigan's Survey Research Center, support this expectation.[18] These findings, reported by Janowitz and Marvick, show a positive relationship between voting turnout and social class; 89 per cent of the upper middle class voted in that election compared to 55 per cent of the lower lower class. Among Negroes, however, only one out of every three eligible persons reported voting in 1952. The proportion of voters for the entire sample was 73 per cent.

Despite the paucity of reliable information on Negro voting, two nationwide studies allow us to contrast the above findings with turnout in the 1960 presidential election. Both were conducted by NORC—one in May, 1963, and the other directly after the assassination of President Kennedy in November, 1963.[19] In each study, the following question was

[18]Morris Janowitz and Dwaine Marvick, "Competitive Pressure and Democratic Consent," *Public Opinion Quarterly*, XIX (Winter, 1955–56), 384–85. See tables.
[19]For papers using data from these studies see—May, 1963, study: Herbert H. Hyman and Paul B. Sheatsley, "Attitudes toward Desegregation," *Scientific American*, CCXI, No. 1 (July, 1964), 16–23; Post-Assassination study, November, 1963: Paul B. Sheatsley and Jacob J. Feldman, "The Assassination of President Kennedy: A Preliminary Report on Public Reactions and Behavior," *Public Opinion Quarterly*, Vol. XXVIII, No. 2 (Summer, 1964).

asked of respondents: "Did you happen to vote in that [the 1960 election] or were you unable to for some reason?" Table 8 is a comparison of these findings with those of the 1952 study. Looking first at the proportion of voters in the samples, we observe little change from 1952 to 1960. By contrast, the proportions of Negro voters show a dramatic positive trend. Indeed, the NORC figures indicate that Negroes were almost twice as likely to vote in 1960 as in 1952.[20]

More adequate information on trends in Negro voting behavior is available for urban areas. The presence of political machines in these areas encourages voter registration and turnout in general, and among Negroes in particular. In fact, there seems to have been consistently high turnout among urban Negroes in the North—despite fluctuations in some cities— for the past several presidential elections.[21] Glantz's examination of census data for predominantly Negro areas in several Northern cities shows, for example, that about three-fourths of the registered Negroes voted in Chicago and St. Louis in the elections of 1948, 1952, and 1956.[22] His data also reveal a positive trend in the voter turnout in Detroit from 1948 to 1956, climaxed in the 1956 election by the vote of almost eight of every ten registered Negro voters.[23] Additional confirmation of these findings comes from a study that used computer simulation.[24] It suggests that

[20]In light of this nationwide trend in the Negro turnout, it is important to caution against acceptance of either the Survey Research Center figures or the National Opinion Research Center figures at their face value. The proportions who claim to have voted or not voted are most likely exaggerated due to over-reporting. The 1956 *Statistical Abstract of the United States* reports that 62.7 per cent of the total eligible population voted in the 1952 election, while the 1963 *Abstract* reports that 63.8 per cent of the "resident" population voted in 1960. The findings presented here are exaggerated in the same direction, however, and to the same approximate degree. Specifically, the estimated over-reporting in the Survey Research Center findings is about 10 per cent and is about 8 per cent in the National Opinion Research Center data. While we are not warranted, therefore, in drawing precise numerical differences in these trends of Negro voting turnout, we are warranted in noting these trends and approximating their magnitude by comparison of the results of the Survey Research Center study with those of the National Opinion Research Center study.

[21]Because of the difficulty in obtaining registration figures for Negroes and whites separately, we have consciously ignored the issue of the proportion of registered Negro voters among those Negroes eligible to vote. There are indications, however, that registration of Negroes is quite high in some northern urban areas. In Chicago and Philadelphia, for example, the proportion of registered Negro voters for the 1948 presidential election was approximately 70 per cent. See Oscar Glantz, "The Negro Voter in Northern Industrial Cities," *Western Political Quarterly,* XIII (December, 1960), 1007.

[22]*Ibid.,* p. 1004.

[23]For an earlier report on the political participation of Detroit Negroes, see Edward H. Litchfield, "A Case Study of Negro Political Behavior in Detroit," *Public Opinion Quarterly,* V, No. 2 (June, 1941), 265–74. Even at this early date, Litchfield notes that "above all else . . . the Negro is at last becoming politically average." His participation, while once very small, has gradually approached the average" (p. 274).

[24]Simulmatics Report No. 1, "Negro Voters in Northern Cities," May, 1960, referred to in Ithiel de Sola Pool, Robert P. Abelson, and Samuel L. Popkin, *Candidates, Issues and Strategies* (Cambridge, Mass.: M.I.T. Press, 1964), pp. 94–99.

"non-voting is *not* significantly disproportionate between Negroes and comparable whites in the North, and that if there is any difference it is that Negroes vote more. It is true that lower-class people vote less than higher-class ones, so that there is some validity to the argument that the Negro voting potential is reduced by the larger proportion of Negroes in the lower income group. But the effect of this on Negro turnout is not very great since class by class there is no difference in Negro and white turnout."[25]

Table 8. *Per Cent of Voters in 1952 and 1960 Presidential Elections for Negroes and National Sample*

Voters	1952		1960–May		1960–November	
	Per Cent	N	Per Cent	N	Per Cent	N
National sample	73	1,614	72	1,505	71	1,358
Negroes	32	157	57	162	53	163

Source: 1952, Survey Research Center data, Janowitz and Marvick, *Public Opinion Quarterly* (1955-56); May, 1960, unpublished data from the National Opinion Research Center study, No. SRS-160, May, 1963; November, 1960, unpublished data from the National Opinion Research Center post-assassination study, No. SRS-350, November, 1963.

Voting data from the assassination study pertinent to subsamples of the Washington suburb and Detroit reveal the relatively high proportion of Negro turnout. Table 9, controlling for the relationship with class, presents these data. With the exception of the medium SES group in Detroit, the relationship between class and turnout is similar to that found by the Survey Research Center study. Most important, we find that 86 per cent of the Negroes reported voting in the 1960 election. Since a positive trend in the turnout from 1948 to 1956 has already been noted, it is not surprising that almost nine of every ten registered Negroes in Detroit voted in 1960.

Let us now consider regional differences in comparing Negro and white turnout. In Table 10 we compare southern and nonsouthern turnout in 1960. Again the data are taken from the two NORC studies conducted in 1963. In both surveys, we find evidence of the smaller proportion of voters in the southern section of the country. Similarity in turnout tends to be regional more than racial. The data from the May survey, for example, indicate 83 per cent of the eligible whites and 77 per cent of the eligible Negroes outside the South voted in 1960, while only 67 per cent of the eligible whites and 60 per cent of the eligible Negroes in the South voted.

Of added importance is the finding that southern Negroes were more likely to report ineligibility for the 1960 election than any other group.

[25]*Ibid.*, p. 95.

Table 9. Per Cent Voting in 1960 by Community and SES

SES	Voting			Total	
	Voted	*Did not Vote*	*Ineli-gible*	*Per Cent*	*N*
		Washington Suburb			
Low	31	58	11	100	26
Medium	65	21	14	100	68
High	75	12	13	100	99
Total	65	21	13	99	193
		Detroit			
Low	88	8	4	100	130
Medium	75	17	8	100	36
High	–	–	–	–	6
Total	86	10	4	100	172

Source: Unpublished data from the National Opinion Research Center study of mental-health-related behavior, No. 465, 1963-66.

The May data indicate that southern Negroes were twice as likely as southern whites to be ineligible to vote in 1960, 15 per cent compared to 8 per cent.[26] This information bears out other evidence on the difficulties southern Negroes encountered in registering to vote prior to the Voting Rights Act of 1965.[27]

To complete this picture of Negro voter turnout, let us consider the relationship of race, education, and turnout within each region. Table 11 presents these data for registered voters. Both within and outside the South, we find that the difference in education almost completely explains the Negro-white difference in turnout of registered voters. More education, furthermore, has an appreciably greater effect on increasing turnout in southern areas. Looking at the vote of whites and Negroes combined,

[26]Attention should be directed to the variation between the May and November figures for Negroes reporting either "not voting" or "ineligibility" to vote. While these differences are, in part, the result of sampling error, they may be due indirectly to Negro voter-registration drives in the South. Thus, the larger proportion who claim ineligibility in November would represent, in part, the recent realization of some Negroes that they did not vote in 1960 because they were prevented from registering to vote.

[27]We must caution against placing too much emphasis upon these figures since the survey data appear to inflate the proportion of registered Negro voters in the South. Donald R. Matthews and James W. Prothro, for instance, indicate that only about 28 per cent of the Negroes of voting age had registered to vote in the South for the 1960 election ("Social and Economic Factors and Negro Voter Registration in the South," *American Political Science Review,* LVII, No. 1[March, 1963], 27; see also U.S. Commission on Civil Rights, *1961 Report,* Vol. I: *Voting*).

we see that the 22 percentage points differentiate voting among low- and high-education groups in the South, compared to 9 percentage points in areas outside the South. Since the majority of southern Negroes in this sample, as in general, are less well-educated than southern whites, they are therefore less likely to vote. In short, education appears to be an important explanatory variable of the Negro-white differential in turnout of registered voters, particularly in the South.

The reader should be cautious in interpreting the differences and trends in this section. The exaggerated proportions of respondents who claim to have voted—or at least to have been eligible to vote—reflect the difficulty of obtaining accurate voting data from public-opinion surveys, even from surveys conducted immediately after presidential elections (see n. 20). These limitations notwithstanding, several observations are warranted. Of utmost importance is the evidence in the past few elections of a positive shift in the nationwide voting turnout of Negroes. This shift is particularly remarkable in contrast to the stable turnout of the nation as a whole. Although this nationwide trend probably is due largely to an increase in the turnout of southern Negroes, positive shifts are also evident in some northern urban areas, for example, Detroit. The remaining gap between the turnout of whites and Negroes appears to be chiefly the result of two factors, both of which have been primarily in evidence in the South. The first is the difficulty that Negroes have had in registering to vote, presumably due to extra-legal restrictions on their registration. The second is the generally lower educational accomplishments of Negroes. With the passage of the Voting Rights Act of 1965 and the subsequent heavy registration of Negroes in the South, the second factor represents the major handicap that Negroes must overcome in order to make their political voice more effective.

Review of the findings.—Most, if not all, of the prior research on Negro participation in associations has failed to consider the known relationship between social class and membership. When we look at the effect of SES on the membership of Negroes and whites, we find that the relationship between class and membership is much less pronounced for Negroes. Thus, we find that lower-class Negroes are more likely to belong to organizations than lower-class whites, while middle-class whites are slightly more likely to belong than middle-class Negroes. Upper-class whites, in turn, are much more likely to be "joiners" than their Negro counterparts. Further comparisons of Negroes and whites within these same SES groups show that Negroes, without exception, are more likely to participate actively in their associations. Examining membership in different kinds of organizations, we find that Negroes are more likely to belong to political and church groups than their white counterparts and equally likely to belong to civic groups. Finally, data on Negro voting in presidential elections since 1952 point to a remarkable increase in voter turnout, espe-

Table 10.   *Per Cent Voting in 1960 by Region and Race*

A. May, 1963

	Whites		Negroes	
Vote in 1960	Total	Eligible	Total	Eligible
Non-South				
Voted	77	83	69	77
Did not vote	15	17	21	23
Ineligible	8		10	
Total	100	100	100	100
N	1,013	936	52	47
South				
Voted	62	67	51	60
Did not vote	30	33	34	40
Ineligible	8		15	
Total	100	100	100	100
N	330	305	110	93

Source: Unpublished data from National Opinion Research Center study, No. SRS-160, May, 1963.

B. November, 1963

	Whites		Negroes	
Vote in 1960	Total	Eligible	Total	Eligible
Non-South				
Voted	78	83	62	68
Did not vote	15	17	29	32
Ineligible	7		9	
Total	100	100	100	100
N	873	814	63	57
South				
Voted	62	66	48	67
Did not vote	32	34	24	33
Ineligible	6		28	
Total	100	100	100	100
N	322	303	100	72

Source: Unpublished data from the National Opinion Research Center post-assassination study, November, 1963.

Table 11.   *Voting in 1960 by Region, Race, and Education (Per Cent of Registered Voters Who Voted in 1960)*

	White		Negro		White-Negro Combined	
	Per Cent	*N*	*Per Cent*	*N*	*Per Cent*	*N*
			Non-South			
Part high school or less	76	389	70	23	76	412
High-school graduate						
or more	85	545	83	24	85	549
			South			
Part high school or less	56	151	55	71	56	222
High-school graduate						
or more	77	153	82	21	78	174

Source: Unpublished data from National Opinion Research Center study, No. SRS-160, May, 1963.

cially in comparison with the stable turnout of the nation as a whole. The remaining difference between the Negro and the white turnout appears to be the result of extra-legal restrictions on Negro voter registration in the South and the generally lower educational attainment of Negroes. The enforcement of the Voting Rights Act of 1965 will undoubtedly aid in narrowing this gap between Negroes and whites.

Discussion of the Social and Political Participation of Negroes

At the outset of this paper, we presented two interpretations of the social and political participation of Negroes. The two rest on contradictory findings. One point of view maintains that Negroes are less likely than whites to participate in organizations and elections, while the other contends that Negroes are more likely to participate in organizations. The former, the "isolation" thesis, has been the more popular explanation. That it remains in vogue is evidenced by its implicit inclusion in one of the most recent analyses of "the Negro problem" in America. In *Crisis in Black and White,* Silberman writes, "Important as demonstrations have been to Negro morale, however, it would be a mistake to exaggerate their impact. They have contributed a great deal to Negro self-pride—but not enough to conquer apathy . . . mass apathy is too deeply rooted to be more than temporarily pierced by a single event, like the Birmingham demonstration, or even a series of events."[28] This kind of explanation argues that Negroes are

[28]Charles E. Silberman, *Crisis in Black and White* (New York: Random House, 1964), pp. 141–44.

"isolated" from civic affairs since they are excluded from meaningful involvement in the larger society. As a consequence, Negroes are perceived as ignorant of and indifferent to civic affairs.

In light of the data presented here, the "isolation" argument demands serious reconsideration. Although it may be true, as Silberman points out, that the majority of Negroes are apathetic, it is also correct that the majority of the white population is apathetic. The significant point is rather that in terms of over-all organizational participation—membership and activity—Negroes are not any more apathetic than whites. In fact, we found that Negroes are more likely to be active in organizations. Voting trends, moreover, indicate that Negroes are less indifferent now to civic affairs than they were ten years ago. In short, it seems that present advocates of the "isolation" thesis may be mistaking a class condition of apathy for a race condition.[29]

The opposite view of Negro participation contends that Negroes compensate for social deprivations incurred by their minority-group status through intensive participation in organizations. As Myrdal stated his case: "Membership in their own segregated associations does not help Negroes to success in the larger American society. The situation must be seen as a pathological one: Negroes are active in associations because they are not allowed to be active in much of the other organized life . . . Negroes are largely kept out, not only of politics proper, but of most purposive and creative work in the trade unions, businessmen's groups, large-scale civic improvement and charity organizations and the like."[30] The findings of this paper on Negro membership and activity in organizations confirm Myrdal's observations of two decades ago.

Myrdal's chief contribution to an understanding of the racial differences in organizational participation is that organizations fulfil different purposes for whites and Negroes. In a phrase, associations are means of *collective membership* for Negroes, whereas they are means of *collecting memberships* for whites. Since Negroes are deprived of the usual social and psychological satisfactions of everyday life, they are compelled to seek such satisfactions collectively through other means. Opportunities for association are restricted by explicit or tacit observance of segregation in public places of entertainment. The oppressive atmosphere of slum dwellings also does not offer a congenial environment for social activity. Quite naturally, then, clubs and associations become focuses for Negroes' social life. For middle- and upper-class whites, on the other hand, organi-

[29] On the remarkable degree of political "grief" that Negroes experienced after Kennedy's assassination, see: Norman Bradburn and Jacob J. Feldman, "Public Apathy and Public Grief," in B. S. Greenberg and E. B. Parker (eds.), *Communication and Crisis: Social Research on the Kennedy Assassination* (Stanford, Calif.: Stanford University Press, 1965).
[30] Myrdal *et al., op. cit.,* pp. 952–53.

zations on the whole have only a nominal significance. This significance primarily derives from the enhancement of prestige that comes with membership in the "right" kinds of organizations.

If the early experience of other ethnic groups in America can be considered a useful guide, the participation of Negroes in associations represents a significant step toward integration. In this respect, the most important consequence of activity in associations is a kind of civic education. Ideally, if not always practically, voluntary associations are models of co-operative effort; decision-making follows discussion, debate, and the reaching of a consensus among the members. Participation in associations thus offers Negroes an opportunity to acquire an understanding of the processes of co-operation and compromise that are the foundations of democratic living.[31]

In the area of pure political activity, the increase in voting turnout of Negroes may be due to a greater awareness among Negroes of the effectiveness of organized political efforts. Assuming that the voting trends together with the syndrome of activity in political and civic associations are reliable indicators, we suggest that Negroes now are a major political force in American society.

The data in this paper are diverse; therefore, the inferences drawn should be regarded as only tentative. It is important that a more comprehensive study of the social and political participation of Negroes be undertaken. Future research in this area should consider not only the types of associations to which Negroes belong but whether these are associations of the larger society or associations of the Negro community. Such information should have obvious significance in determining whether Negroes in this respect are becoming more integrated into the larger society or whether their organizational memberships contribute to a continuing segregation from it.

[31]For the ways in which voluntary associations aided Polish immigrants in adapting to America, see: Helena Znaniecki Lopata, "The Function of Voluntary Associations in an Ethnic Community, 'Polonia,' " in Ernest W. Burgess and Donald J. Bogue (eds.), *Contributions to Urban Sociology* (Chicago: University of Chicago Press, 1964).

CONVERSION

"The Making of A Black Muslim"

by John R. Howard

You were black enough to get in here. You had the courage to stay. Now be man enough to follow the honorable Elijah Muhammad. You have tried the devil's way. Now try the way of the Messenger.

> Minister William X in a West
> Coast Black Muslim Mosque

The Lost-Found Nation of Islam in the Wilderness of North America, commonly known as the Black Muslim movement, claims a small but fanatically devoted membership among the Negroes of our major cities. The way of the "Messenger" is rigorous for those who follow it. The man or woman who becomes a Muslim accepts not only an ideology but an all-encompassing code that amounts to a way of life.

A good Muslim does a full day's work on an empty stomach. When he finally has his one meal of the day in the evening, it can include no pork, nor can he have drink before or a cigarette after; strict dietary rules are standard procedure, and liquor and smoking are forbidden under any circumstances. His recreation is likely to consist of reading the Koran or participating in a demanding round of temple-centered activities, running public meetings or aggressively proselytizing on the streets by selling the Muslim newspaper, *Muhammad Speaks.*

Despite allegations of Muslim violence (adverse publicity from the slaying of Malcolm X supports the erroneous notion that Muslims preach violence), the member's life is basically ascetic. Why then in a non-ascetic, hedonistically-oriented society do people become Muslims? What is the life of a Muslim like? These are questions I asked in research among West Coast members. Specifically, I wanted to know:

•What perspective on life makes membership in such an organization attractive?

•Under what conditions does the potential recruit develop those perspectives?

•How does he happen to come to the door of the temple for his first meeting?

•The Black Muslims are a deviant organization even within the Negro community; the parents or friends of many members strongly objected to their joining. So how does the recruit handle pressures that might erode his allegiance to the organization and its beliefs?

Presenting my questions as an effort to "learn the truth" about the organization, I was able to conduct depth interviews with 19 West Coast recruits, following them through the process of their commitment to the Nation of Islam.

Two main points of appeal emerged—black nationalism and an emphasis on self-help. Some recruits were attracted primarily by the first, and some by the second. The 14 interviewees who joined the organization for its aggressive black nationalism will be called "Muslim militants." The remaining five, who were attracted more by its emphasis on hard work and rigid personal morality, may be aptly termed "Protestant Ethic Muslims."

Muslim Militants: Beating the Devil

Of the 14 Muslim militants, some came from the South, some from border states, and some from the North. All lived in California at the time of the interviews; some migrated to the state as adults, others were brought out by their families as children. They varied in age from 24 to 46, and in education from a few years of grade school to four years of college. Regardless of these substantial differences in background, there were certain broad similarities among them.

At some point, each one had experiences that led away from the institutionally-bound ties and commitments that lend stability to most people's lives. Nine had been engaged in semi-legal or criminal activities. Two had been in the military, not as a career but as a way of postponing the decision of what to do for a living. None had a stable marital history. All of them were acutely aware of being outsiders by the standards of the larger society—and all had come to focus on race bias as the factor which denied them more conventional alternatives.

Leroy X came to California in his late teens, just before World War II:

> I grew up in Kansas City, Missouri, and Missouri was a segregated state. Negroes in Kansas City were always restricted to the menial jobs. I came out here in 1940 and tried to get a job as a waiter. I was a trained waiter, but they weren't hiring any Negroes as waiters in any of the downtown hotels or restaurants. The best I could do was busboy; and they fired me from that when they found out I wasn't Filipino.

Leroy X was drafted, and after a short but stormy career was given a discharge as being psychologically unfit.

> I tried to get a job, but I couldn't so I started stealing. There was nothing

else to do—I couldn't live on air. The peckerwoods didn't seem to give a damn whether I lived or died. They wouldn't hire me and didn't seem to worry how I was going to stay alive. I started stealing.

I could get you anything you wanted—a car, drugs, women, jewelry. Crime is a business like any other. I started off stealing myself. I wound up filling orders and getting rid of stuff. I did that for fifteen years. In between I did a little time. I did time for things I never thought of doing and went free for things I really did.

In my business you had no friends, only associates, and not very close ones at that. . . . I had plenty of money. I could get anything I wanted without working for it. It wasn't enough, though.

Bernard X grew up in New York City:

As a kid . . . you always have dreams—fantasies—of yourself doing something later—being a big name singer or something that makes you outstanding. But you never draw the connection between where you are and how you're going to get there. I had to—I can't say exactly when, 13, 14, 15, 16. I saw I was nowhere and had no way of getting anywhere.

Race feeling is always with you. You always know about The Man but I don't think it is real, really real, until you have to deal with it in terms of what you are going to do with your own life. That's when you feel it. If you just disliked him before—you begin to hate him when you see him blocking you in your life. I think then a sense of inevitability hits you and you see you're not going to make it out—up—away—anywhere—and you see The Man's part in the whole thing, that's when you begin to think thoughts about him.

Frederick 2X became involved fairly early in a criminal subculture. His father obtained a "poor man's divorce" by deserting the family. His mother had children by other men. Only a tenuous sense of belonging to a family existed. He was picked up by the police for various offenses several times before reaching his teens. The police patrolling his neighborhood eventually restricted him to a two-block area. There was, of course, no legal basis for this, but he was manhandled if seen outside that area by any policeman who knew him. He graduated in his late teens from "pot" to "shooting shit" and eventually spent time in Lexington.

William 2X, formerly a shoeshine boy, related the development of his perspective this way:

You know how they always talk about us running after white women. There have always been a lot of [white] servicemen in this town—half of them would get around to asking me to get a woman for them. Some of them right out, some of them backing into it, laughing and joking and letting me know how much they were my friend, building up to asking me where they could find some woman. After a while I began to get them for them. I ran women—both black and white. . . . What I hated was they wanted me to do something for them [find women] and hated me for doing it. They figure "any nigger must know where to find it. . . . "

Things Begin to Add Up

Amos X grew up in an all-Negro town in Oklahoma and attended a Negro college. Because of this, he had almost no contact with whites during his formative years.

> One of my aunts lived in Tulsa. I went to see her once when I was in college. I walked up to the front door of the house where she worked. She really got excited and told me if I came to see her anymore to come around to the back. But that didn't mean much to me at the time. It is only in looking back on it that all these things begin to add up.

After graduating from college, Amos joined the Marines. There he began to "see how they [the whites] really felt" about him; by the end of his tour, he had concluded that "the white man is the greatest liar, the greatest cheat, the greatest hypocrite on earth." Alienated and disillusioned, he turned to professional gambling. Then, in an attempt at a more conventional way of life, he married and took a job teaching school.

> I taught English. Now I'm no expert in the slave masters' language, but I knew the way those kids talked after being in school eight and nine years was ridiculous. They said things like "mens" for "men." I drilled them and pretty soon some of them at least in class began to sound like they had been inside a school. Now the principal taught a senior class in English and his kids talked as bad as mine. When I began to straighten out his kids also he felt I was criticizing him. . . . That little black man was afraid of the [white] superintendent and all those teachers were afraid. They had a little more than other so-called Negroes and didn't give a damn about those black children they were teaching. Those were the wages of honesty. It's one thing to want to do an honest job and another thing to be able to. . . .

With the collapse of his career as a public school teacher and the break-up of his marriage, Amos went to California, where he was introduced to the Muslim movement.

> I first heard about them [the Muslims] in 1961. There was a debate here between a Muslim and a Christian minister. The Muslims said all the things about Christianity which I had been thinking but which I had never heard anyone say before. He tore the minister up.

Finding an organization that aggressively rejected the white man and the white man's religion, Amos found his own point of view crystallized. He joined without hesitation.

Norman Maghid first heard of the Muslims while he was in prison.

> I ran into one of the Brothers selling the paper about two weeks after I got out and asked him about the meetings. Whether a guy could just go and walk in. He told me about the meetings so I made it around on a Wednesday evening. I wasn't even bugged when they searched me. When they asked me about taking out my letter [joining the organization] I took one out. They seemed to know what they were talking about. I never believed

in non-violence and love my enemies, especially when my enemies don't love me.

Muhammad Soule Kabah, born into a family of debt-ridden Texas share-croppers, was recruited into the Nation of Islam after moving to California.

> I read a series of articles in the Los Angeles *Herald Dispatch,* an exchange between Minister Henry and a Christian minister. It confirmed what my grandfather had told me about my African heritage, that I had nothing to be ashamed of, that there were six thousand books on mathematics in the Library of the University of Timbucktoo while Europeans were still wearing skins. Also my father had taught me never to kow-tow to whites. My own father had fallen away. My parents didn't want me to join the Nation. They said they taught hate. That's funny isn't it? The white man can blow up a church and kill four children and the black man worries that an organization which tells you not to just take it is teaching hate.

Protestant Ethic Muslims: Up by Black Bootstraps

The Protestant Ethic Muslims all came from backgrounds with a strong tradition of Negro self-help. In two cases, the recruit's parents had been followers of Marcus Garvey; another recruit explicitly endorsed the beliefs of Booker T. Washington; and the remaining two, coming from upwardly mobile families, were firm in the belief that Negroes could achieve higher status if they were willing to work for it.

When asked what had appealed to him about the Muslims, Norman X replied:

> They thought that black people should do something for themselves. I was running this small place [a photography shop] and trying to get by. I've stuck with this place even when it was paying me barely enough to eat. Things always improve and I don't have to go to the white man for anything.

Ernestine X stressed similar reasons for joining the Muslims.

> You learned to stand up straight and do something for yourself. You learn to be a lady at all times—to keep your house clean—to teach your children good manners. There is not a girl in the M-G-T who does not know how to cook and sew. The children are very respectful; they speak only when they are spoken to. There is no such thing as letting your children talk back to you the way some people believe. The one thing they feel is the Negroes' downfall is men and sex for the women, and women and sex for the men, and they frown on sex completely unless you are married.

Despite their middle-class attitudes in many areas, Protestant Ethic Muslims denounced moderate, traditional civil rights organizations such as the NAACP, just as vigorously as the militant Muslims did. Norman X said that he had once belonged to the NAACP but had dropped out.

They spent most of their time planning the annual brotherhood dinner. Besides it was mostly whites—whites and the colored doctors and lawyers who wanted to be white. As far as most Negroes were concerned they might as well not have existed.

Lindsey X, who had owned and run his own upholstery shop for more than 30 years, viewed the conventional black bourgeoisie with equal resentment.

I never belonged to the NAACP. What they wanted never seemed real to me. I think Negroes should create jobs for themselves rather than going begging for them. That's why I never supported CORE.

In this respect Norman and Lindsey were in full accord with the more militant Amos X, who asserted:

They [the NAACP and CORE] help just one class of people. . . . Let something happen to a doctor and they are right there; but if something happens to Old Mose on the corner, you can't find them.

The interviews made it clear that most of the Protestant Ethic Muslims had joined the Nation because, at some point, they began to feel the need of organizational support for their personal systems of value. For Norman and Lindsey, it was an attempt to stop what they considered their own backsliding after coming to California. Both mentioned drinking to excess and indulging in what they regarded as a profligate way of life. Guilt feelings apparently led them to seek Muslim support in returning to more enterprising habits.

Commitment to Deviance

The Nation of Islam is a deviant organization. As such it is subject to public scorn and ridicule. Thus it faces the problem of consolidating th recruit's allegiance in an environment where substantial pressures operate to erode this allegiance. How does it deal with this problem?

The structural characteristics of the Nation tend to insulate the member from the hostility of the larger society and thus contribute to the organization's survival. To begin with, the ritual of joining the organization itself stresses commitment without questions.

At the end of the general address at a temple meeting, the minister asks those nonmembers present who are "interested in learning more about Islam" to step to the back of the temple. There they are given three blank sheets of ordinary stationery and a form letter addressed to Elijah Muhammad in Chicago;

Dear Savior Allah, Our Deliverer:
    I have attended the Teachings of Islam, two or three times, as taught by one of your ministers. I believe in it. I bear witness that there is no God but

Thee. And, that Muhammad is Thy Servant and Apostle. I desire to reclaim my Own. Please give me my Original name. My slave name is as follows:

The applicant is instructed to copy this letter verbatim on each of the three sheets of paper, giving his own name and address unabbreviated at the bottom. If he fails to copy the letter perfectly, he must repeat the whole task. No explanation is given for any of these requirements.

Formal acceptance of his letter makes the new member a Muslim, but in name only. Real commitment to the Nation of Islam comes gradually —for example, the personal commitment expressed when a chain smoker gives up cigarettes in accordance with the Muslim rules even though he knows that he could smoke unobserved. "It's not that easy to do these things," Stanley X said of the various forms of abstinence practiced by Muslims. "It takes will and discipline and time, . . . but you're a much better person after you do." Calvin X told of periodic backsliding in the beginning but added, "Once I got into the thing deep, then I stuck with it."

This commitment and the new regimen that goes with it have been credited with effecting dramatic personality changes in many members, freeing alcoholics from the bottle and drug addicts from the needle. It can be argued, however, that the organization does not change the member's fundamental orientation. To put it somewhat differently, given needs and impulses can be expressed in a variety of ways; thus, a man may give vent to his sadism by beating up strangers in an alley or by joining the police force and beating them up in the back room of the station.

"Getting into the thing deep" for a Muslim usually comes in three stages:

Participation in organizational activities—selling the Muslim newspaper, dining at the Muslim restaurant, attending and helping run Muslim meetings.

Isolation from non-Muslim social contacts—drifting away from former friends and associates because of divergent attitudes or simply because of the time consumed in Muslim activities.

Assimilation of the ideology—marking full commitment, when a Muslim has so absorbed the organization's doctrines that he automatically uses them to guide his own behavior and to interpret what happens in the world around him.

The fact that the organization can provide a full social life furthers isolation from non-Muslims. Participation is not wholly a matter of drudgery, of tramping the streets to sell the paper and studying the ideology. The organization presents programs of entertainment for its members and the public. For example, in two West Coast cities a Negro theatrical troupe called the Touring Artists put on two plays, "Jubilee Day" and "Don't You Want to Be Free." Although there was a high element of humor in both plays, the basic themes—white brutality and hypocrisy and

the necessity of developing Negro self-respect and courage—were conso-
nant with the organization's perspective. Thus the organization makes it
possible for a member to satisfy his need for diversion without going
outside to do so. At the same time, it continually reaches him with its
message through the didactic element in such entertainment.

Carl X's experiences were typical of the recruit's growing commitment
to the Nation. When asked what his friends had thought when he first
joined, he replied: "They thought I was crazy. They said, 'Man, how can
you believe all that stuff?' " He then commented that he no longer saw
much of them, and added:

> When you start going to the temple four or five times a week and selling the
> newspaper you do not have time for people who are not doing these things.
> We drifted—the friends I had—we drifted apart. . . . All the friends I have
> now are in the Nation. Another Brother and I get together regularly and
> read the Koran and other books, then ask each other questions on them like,
> "What is Allah's greatest weapon? The truth. What is the devil's greatest
> weapon? The truth. The devil keeps it hidden from men. Allah reveals it to
> man." We read and talk about the things we read and try to sharpen our
> thinking. I couldn't do that with my old friends.

Spelled out, the "stuff" that Carl X had come to believe, the official
Muslim ideology, is this:

•The so-called Negro, the American black man, is lost in ignorance. He
is unaware of his own past history and the future role which history has
destined him to play.

•Elijah Muhammad has come as the Messenger of Allah to awaken the
American black man.

•The American black man finds himself now in a lowly state, but that was
not always his condition.

•The Original Man, the first men to populate the earth, were non-white.
They enjoyed a high level of culture and reached high peaks of achievement.

•A little over 6,000 years ago a black scientist named Yakub, after considerable work, produced a mutant, a new race, the white race.

•This new race was inferior mentally, physically, and morally to the black
race. Their very whiteness, the very mark of their difference from the black
race, was an indication of their physical degeneracy and moral depravity.

•Allah, in anger at Yakub's work, ordained that the white race should rule
for a fixed amount of time and that the black man should suffer and by his
suffering gain a greater appreciation of his own spiritual worth by comparing
himself to the whites.

•The time of white dominance is drawing near its end. It is foreordained
that this race shall perish, and with its destruction the havoc, terror, and
brutality which it has spread throughout the world shall disappear.

•The major task facing the Nation of Islam is to awaken the American
black man to his destiny, to acquaint him with the course of history.

•The Nation of Islam in pursuing this task must battle against false proph-
ets, in particular those who call for integration. Integration is a plot of the
white race to forestall its own doom. The black bourgeoisie, bought off by
a few paltry favors and attempting to ingratiate themselves with the whites,
seek to spread this pernicious doctrine among so-called Negroes.

•The Nation of Islam must encourage the American black man to begin
now to assume his proper role by wresting economic control from the
whites. The American black man must gain control over his own economic
fortunes by going into business for himself and becoming economically
strong.

•The Nation of Islam must encourage the so-called Negro to give up those
habits which have been spread among them by the whites as part of the
effort to keep them weak, diseased, and demoralized. The so-called Negro
must give up such white-fostered dissolute habits as drinking, smoking, and
eating improper foods. The so-called Negro must prepare himself in mind
and body for the task of wresting control from the whites.

•The Nation of Islam must encourage the so-called Negro to seek now
his own land within the continental United States. This is due him and frees
him from the pernicious influence of the whites.

The Problem of Defection

Commitment to the Nation can diminish as well as grow. Four of the
members I interviewed later defected. Why?

These four cases can be explained in terms of a weak point in the
structure of the Nation. The organization has no effective mechanisms for
handling grievances among the rank and file. Its logic accounts for this.
Muslim doctrine assumes that there is a single, ultimate system of truth.
Elijah Muhammad and, by delegation, his ministers are in possession of
this truth. Thus only Elijah Muhammad himself can say whether a minister is doing an adequate job. The result is the implicit view that there is
nothing to be adjudicated between the hierarchy and its rank and file.

Grievances arise, however. The four defectors were, for various reasons,
all dissatisfied with Minister Gerard X. Since there were no formal mechanisms within the organization for expressing their dissatisfaction, the
only solution was to withdraw.

For most members, however, the pattern is one of steadily growing
involvement. And once the ideology is fully absorbed, there is virtually no
such thing as dispute or counterevidence. If a civil rights bill is not passed,
this proves the viciousness of whites in refusing to recognize Negro rights.
If the same bill *is* passed, it merely proves the duplicity of whites in trying
to hide their viciousness.

The ideology also provides a coherent theory of causation, provided
one is willing to accept its basic assumptions. Norman X interpreted his

victory over his wife in a court case as a sign of Allah's favor. Morris X used it to account for the day-to-day fortunes of his associates.

> Minister X had some trouble. He was sick for a long time. He almost died. I think Allah was punishing him. He didn't run the temple right. Now the Brothers make mistakes. Everyone does—but Minister X used to abuse them at the meetings. It was more a personal thing. He had a little power and it went to his head. Allah struck him down and I think he learned a little humility.

When a man reasons in this fashion, he has become a fully committed member of the Nation of Islam. His life revolves around temple-centered activities, his friends are all fellow Muslims, and he sees his own world—usually the world of an urban slum dweller—through the framework of a very powerful myth. He is still doing penance for the sins of Yakub, but the millennium is at hand. He has only to prepare.

The Nation of Islam does not in any real sense convert members. Rather it attracts Negroes who have already, through their own experiences in white America, developed a perspective congruent with that of the Muslim movement. The recruit comes to the door of the temple with the essence of his ideas already formed. The Black Muslims only give this disaffection a voice.

three

The bonds that bind men together into patterned community life are subject to stress and strain and even to deliberate acts to cut and retie them. Why are established patterns challenged? Why do old controls break down? When and why do normally critical people seem to accept the improbable message of rumors? What mobilizes otherwise meek individuals to threaten the established powers? Why does a riot develop in one city while a social movement occurs in another? Sociologists probe such questions from a concern that has come to be called "Collective Behavior."

Collective Behavior

Crowds, riots, social movements, mobs, fads, demonstrations, panics, and crazes are all part of collective behavior. These seemingly diverse activities have two general similarities. First, all tend to be relatively unstructured. That is, few formal norms or institutionalized procedures serve to guide behavior. Second, most events included under collective behavior are usually irregular or distinctive. Rather than taking place on a periodic basis they often develop suddenly and then usually cease. If such activities become permanent, they tend to develop set procedures and engage in activity on a more routine basis. Thus a protest march may evolve into a permanent organization, such as a voluntary association.

Because of the unstructured and irregular nature of collective behavior, the outcome of such phenomena is often uncertain. A crowd may suddenly become a riot; a rumor may cause a run on local banks.

Collective behavior usually constitutes a deviation or break in routine interaction because of a lack of normative guidelines to channel activity into socially accepta-ble forms. Not surprisingly, in times of stress or rapid change, certain forms of collective behavior (such as riots or panics) will more likely occur than under stable conditions. Such activity sometimes precedes the emergence of new normative patterns that will eventually gain acceptance. Therefore, through collective behav-ior pressure can be exerted and change affected.

Since Blacks have been recently undergoing a series of rapid changes in their relations with the rest of society, they have become involved in many forms of collective behavior. In fact, the entire civil rights movement is a good example of one form of collective behavior: a social movement. Blacks have had to act within the realm of collective behavior because the normal governing processes have been ineffective in ending discrimination.

The selections in this section deal with two strikingly different forms of collective behavior—a spontaneous riot, and a planned community-wide protest movement. The first article deals with the Watts riot of 1965. In the portion reprinted here Robert Conot describes the arrest of Marquette Frye, which set off the riot. Riots always have such a precipitating incident. Often the incident may seem relatively trivial. However, the initial incident serves to trigger or unleash strong emotions and frustrations that have been building up for a long period of time. This incident forcuses more general hatreds and disillusionments into a specific form of action allowing participants to express their anger. Such a precipitating incident also must be something with which most of the people involved can identify. The arrest of Frye would not have led to a riot if Blacks in Watts had not been subject to discrimination and if most of the initial rioters had not been able to identify with an apparent victim of excessive police force.

A large, angered crowd, such as the one described by Conot, can quickly build in intensity because of circular stimulation. With so many people in such close proximity, the actions of each strongly reinforce those of the others. The large number of people involved also creates a feeling of anonymity. Thus persons will do things in a large crowd that they would never even consider doing alone or in a small group.

Conot's article also shows the large role played by rumor in the beginning of a riot. Ambiguous circumstances foster rumor, so in the uncertainty surrounding the arrest of Frye and the other Blacks rumors were quick to fly. Persons in Watts believed them because they fit their pre-conceived ideas about "the Man."

L. D. Reddick's article on the Montgomery bus boycott concerns a community-wide movement in which a number of people voluntarily associated with one another to induce change. As in the Watts riot, there was a precipitating incident that set the boycott into motion. Again the arrest of Mrs. Rosa Parks was something with which Blacks could identify, and the incident brought forth the frustrated emotions of Blacks in a segregated city. The incident did not precipitate a riot, as in Watts, however, because Blacks felt that avenues of peaceful change (such as a mass boycott) were feasible. The church meetings became vital to the success of the boycott because they were the only effective means of mass communication. In this instance the movement was successful; a year after the boycott began it ended in victory as the result of a Supreme Court decision.

A CROWD BECOMES A RIOT:

WATTS *1965*

"The Stranger in the City"

by Robert Conot

On Wednesday, August 11, 1965, he [Marquette Frye] had slept late. He had slept late because he often stayed out late at night, and there wasn't any point in getting up early. When he did get up the room was already stuffy from the sun's rays ricocheting off the windows. Until a few days before it had been one of the city's really cool summers, with the temperature scarcely rising above 80. But on Monday the heat wave had descended, smothering, like a brooding hen onto an egg; and from mid-morning until late afternoon south-central Los Angeles simmered in 95-degree temperatures beneath a yellow-gray coverlet of smog. As Marquette splashed water onto his face and pulled on his slim, Italian-style pants, he decided he would accompany two of his friends, Pete and Milton, to court in Inglewood where, that afternoon, Milton was scheduled to appear for preliminary hearing on a burglary charge.

All in all, Marquette thought, things weren't too bad. Since getting out of the camp he had kept his nose clean. On July 3 he had successfully completed his two years of probation. Now, for the first time in five years, he was out from under the gun. Then, too, his stepbrother, Ronald, a year older than he, had arrived from Wyoming on Monday, and yesterday evening he had taken him around the neighborhood to introduce him to a few girls. They had had a good time partying.

Yet, one way or another, there were always problems. He hadn't had a job for months; and his girl friend, Gloria, had just told him she was pregnant.

He had his mother's gray-white 1955 Buick; and, after the hearing, he decided to go home and pick up Ronald before going over to Milton's house. It was 5 o'clock, and the breeze sucked seaward from the mountains was beginning to wipe away the pollution like grime from a dirty window. Still, the heat hadn't abated much, and it was a real pleasure when he and Ronald got over to Milton's place and were able to relax with cooling screwdrivers—vodka and orange juice.

The girls they were expecting didn't show up, so they just sat and talked. They had three or four drinks. A few minutes before 7 o'clock, when Marquette decided they'd better head home for dinner, he'd had just enough vodka to make him feel as if the world was a good place to live in after all.

He drove with verve. Slightly too fast, and not altogether in conformity with traffic regulations. As he turned north from El Segundo onto Avolon Blvd., a Negro, driving a pickup truck and waiting for the light to change, thought his behavior erratic. Coincidentally, just before the light turned green, a California Highway Patrol motorcycle officer pulled up. The truck driver, leaning from the cab, shouted to him that there seemed to be something the matter with the driver of a Buick heading north on Avalon. In response to the officer's query, he said that he "looked like he might be drunk or something."

Officer Lee Minikus gave him an informal salute in acknowledgment, gunned the cycle, and swung up Avalon Blvd. after the Buick; which was already a couple of blocks ahead.

At 65 miles an hour Minikus sped up the broad, heavily traveled street. To his right was an undeveloped area of open fields and small manufacturing plants, to his left junkyards and small businesses. Crossing 120th St. the roadway narrowed; there were stores, a café, a laundry, a beauty parlor, a neighborhood grocery featuring accounting and income-tax services. A couple of blocks farther north the neighborhood became mainly residential, consisting of recently built two-story apartment houses, interspersed here and there with old dwellings dating back to a time when the area had been used for truck farms. Lining the side streets were neat, single-family residences with well-kept lawns and plots of flowers—differing little, if at all, from other middle-class suburban neighborhoods.

As Marquette drove past 117th St., Ronald became aware of the sharp red light reflected in the rear-view mirror. He called his brother's attention to it. Marquette slowed down, then brought the car to a halt against the curb a half block north of 116th Place, stopping a few feet behind a car already parked. It just so happened that he was only a block from home—he had been planning to make a left turn onto 116th St., then left again onto Towne, which parallels Avalon.

It was just a minute or two after 7 o'clock.

At that moment, highway patrol Officer Bob Lewis, Lee Minikus's partner, was cruising on his cycle near the Harbor Freeway, six blocks to the west. Officer Wayne Wilson sat astride his cycle, watching for speeders, at an El Segundo intersection. And Officer Larry Bennett, in a CHP car, was patrolling in unincorporated county territory in the vicinity of Athens Park.

At Avalon Blvd. and 118th St., a location that Officer Minikus had just passed, Walter Gaines was working late in his barbershop. Mr. Gaines had worked long hours all of his life in order to support his closely knit family —a wife and seven children. Although he had spent most of his 40-odd years in Stockton, in the north-central part of the state, he had decided to move to Los Angeles seven years before, because Los Angeles had a barbering college, and the Stockton area, at that time, had not. Knowing that he could not afford to send his children through college, he had been determined that each of them would have a trade before he left home. So, in their early teens, while still attending high school, boys and girls alike, off he sent them to barbering school. Each of them, by the time he received his high-school diploma, also had his barbering license.

Two of his daughters were working in the shop. The younger, Joyce Ann, who would be 21 in December, had been in the shop with him until after 6 o'clock, when she had decided to go to Vergie Nash's beauty parlor, a block down on Avalon, to have her hair set.

When Marquette opened the door of the car and stepped out, he wasn't really concerned. He knew the psychology of police officers, and he was confident he would be able to handle the situation. "Mostly when an officer stops you, he'll come up to you harshly, you know. This isn't because the officer is trying to be mean to you, but because he's trying to find out what type of person you are. I mean, if you're going to be an asshole, you know he's going to treat you as such."

These were his thoughts; and he was determined that he would disarm the officer by his friendly manner.

Lee Minikus, putting down the kickstand on the cycle and taking off his gloves, saw a smiling, jaunty Marquette Frye approaching him. Marquette had on a stingy brimmed hat; pointed, Italian-style shoes; narrow, cuffless trousers; and a tailored sport shirt: they accentuated his slenderness, and made him look as if he might have stepped out of a production of *Anna Lucasta*. Minikus, on the other hand, with his boots and baggy-hipped riding trousers, his waist encircled by his gun belt, his head and face virtually hidden by the white and black crash helmet and the dark goggles covering his eyes, had the impersonality of a comic strip Batman.

Beneath this exterior he was, in actuality, a rarther good-natured man with sandy red hair, a windburned face, and a prominent nose. Like so many other officers, after a hitch in the service and a brief stint at a sedentary job, he had chosen the highway patrol as a means of escaping the eight-to-five office routine. In his middle thirties, married and with three children, he had been with the CHP almost 10 years.

"Can I see your driver's license, please?" he asked Marquette.

"Well, as it happens, you see, I was down at the New Pike in Long Beach a few days ago, and it fell out of my pocket, or some fellow could have taken it. You know how it is. I lost it, and I just haven't had time to get me a new one."

It was the truth. He had lost his driver's license. But it didn't improve the situation.

"You know you were going 50 miles an hour in a 35-mile zone?" Minikus continued.

"Aw, officer. That old car wouldn't do more than 35 if you shoved it off a cliff!" Marquette laughed.

Marquette had come right up to him. Minikus, smelling his breath, asked, "Have you been drinking?"

"Well, you see," Marquette replied, "my brother, he's been in the service, and he just came in from Wyoming. So we went over to these girls and we were sort of having a party—and I had two or three screwdrivers. But I'm not drunk, Officer, if that's what you mean."

In recent years, different jurisdictions have adopted a number of different tests in order to determine whether a person is intoxicated. The California Highway Patrol has chosen to retain the field sobriety test, a method of making the determination based on the person's physical behavior. This places a considerable burden on the officer's judgment. After checking the vehicle registration—which noted that the car belonged to Rena Frye, of 11620 Towne Ave.—and asking Marquette his name, Minikus ordered him to walk a straight line along the sidewalk, where a dirt strip divides the pavement from the curbing.

Marquette did as he was ordered. And did it rather successfully, *he* thought. "Now, would you like me to walk it backward?" he asked.

"No. Just stand there. Close your eyes. Put your finger to your nose." Minikus went on to the next test.

After Marquette's performance on that and one further test, Minikus decided that he had a 502—a drunk driver—on his hands. He went to the motorcycle, unhooked the radio mike, and called for his partner, Bob Lewis. He also asked for a transportation car to take Marquette to jail.

Returning to Marquette, Minikus began filling out a ticket. Since Marquette had no driver's license, it was necessary to ask him for all of the information—his birth date, address, the color of his eyes, the color of his hair.

"It's black, man!" Marquette replied. "I'm black all over, can't you see!" He was still jovial, doing a little jig.

"You're a real comedian, aren't you?" Minikus said good-humoredly.

While Marquette was taking his tests, people had begun to be attracted by his antics. A good many of them had been sitting on their steps or out on the lawns, and some had been congregating at the Oasis Shoeshine Stand, a hangout for Muslims, down toward Imperial Highway. A couple of dozen of them now stood around, watching the proceedings, laughing, talking among themselves, now and then making some jocose remark to Marquette or Minikus. It was a pleasant evening, a half hour before sunset.

Walking home from the store, Rosalie Sanders and her daughter Pearlie noticed the gathering. Marquette Frye had dated Pearlie, who was now married, some years before, and Rosie, as Rosalie was known, considered herself a friend of the Frye family.

"Isn't that Marquette standing there with that officer?" she asked Pearlie.

Pearlie, looking over in the indicated direction, replied that she believed it was.

Threading her way among the people, Rosie asked one of the bystanders what was going on. He answered that it looked like the boy had had a little too much to drink, and that they were going to take him to jail.

Alarmed, Rosie set out to tell Rena Frye. On the east side of Avalon Blvd., where the action was taking place, one apartment house runs lengthwise along the street, presenting its facade to the sidewalk. To the west, however, the apartment houses are aligned perpendicular to the boulevard, so that it is possible to walk between them and reach the next row of apartments facing on Towne Ave. It would take Rosie a minute, at the most, to get to the Frye apartment.

Marquette, in the meantime, although still in good humor, was becoming concerned. Minikus continued writing the ticket. Another motorcycle officer pulled up.

"Officer, you don't have to give me a ticket or take me to jail," Marquette said, talking with his hands, and using his whole body for emphasis, the way he always did when he became excited. "I live here, half a block, right around the corner. You can let my brother Ronny drive the car home, and let me walk home. I'd appreciate it, because I done came from El Segundo and Wilmington, you know, and being a half block away from home, you could, you know, let me get by with that." Having said his piece, he started to wander off.

Officer Bob Lewis had parked his cycle. "What have you got?" he inquired of Minikus.

"A deuce!" he replied, using police slang for 502.

"Who's the one under arrest?" Lewis asked, as there were now several persons within a few feet radius of the motorbike.

Minikus pointed to Marquette, who, seeing he was the subject of discussion, returned.

"Man, I'm not drunk," Marquette said. "Can't you see I'm a good fellow who wouldn't diddledybop nobody?" Still trying to make light of it, he put one hand on Minikus's cycle.

"Get your hands off that bike!" Lewis ordered.

"Now, you don't have to do me like that," Marquette replied, feeling unjustly chastened.

Although beneath their regalia it would have been difficult to tell them apart, and both had had much the same experience on the highway patrol, in personality and looks Lewis was quite different from Minikus. An extrovert, with short-cropped light hair and a full-fleshed face, Lewis laughs easily, likes his good time, and, since divorcing his wife, has had a sharp eye for the girls. After spending seven years in the southeast Los Angeles sector, he had, in 1964, been transferred to Lake Tahoe. A few months at the California-Nevada resort had convinced him that, with nightclubs and casinos all around, the cost of living was too high. So he had asked for, and received, a transfer back to Los Angeles.

Ronald, during this time, had not stirred from the front seat of the car. He was 22 years old, the youngest of four children of Wallace Frye's previous marriage to Mary Etta Riggs. Born in Arkansas, he had been raised in Superior, Wyo., where his mother had remarried after the divorce. In 1961, following graduation from high school, he had joined the air force, becoming a mechanic and reaching the rank of airman second class. Discharged in June, he had come to Los Angeles, hoping to enroll in IBM School. Slow-spoken and quite handsome, his temperament was the opposite of Marquette's mercurial one. He figured that, whatever trouble Marquette was in, it would be better to let him work out of it by himself.

"Do you want to store the vehicle?" Lewis asked Minikus. It is standard procedure to have a car put in storage when the driver is unable to operate it, since, if it is left on the street there is danger of its being stripped.

Minikus replied in the affirmative. Lewis started walking back toward his cycle to get a storage report form. As he did, the transportation car, driven by Officer Bennett, arrived. Almost simultaneously, a truck from the South East Tow Co. in Compton, three miles away, appeared.

The driver, Joseph Lee Gabel, inquired as to which vehicle was involved. Lewis indicated to him that he was to take the Buick.

As Ronald saw the tow truck stop, then back around the parked car with apparent intent to hook onto the Buick, he decided that he'd better intervene. He went back to the motorcycle, identified himself to Minikus, told him he was Marquette's brother, and asked him if he could take the car. Minikus wanted to know if he had identification, and Ronald pulled out his wallet to show him his driver's license.

That was when Rena, wearing a loose shift, her hair in disarray, came hurrying across the street. The past spring she had had a major operation, from which she was only now fully recovering.

Seeing the tow truck operator unwinding the hook, she went up to him, and, out of breath, asked him what was going on. When he replied that he was going to tow the car away, she remonstrated with him, telling him it was hers.

"Lady, I got nothing to do with it," he answered. "You'd better talk to them officers."

Catching sight of Ronald conversing with Minikus, she went back to where they were standing. Having had the foresight to bring her driver's license along, she showed it to Minikus. Since it checked with the registration of the car, he agreed, after momentary consultation with Lewis, that she could take the Buick. Walking forward, he informed Gabel that they were making out a "no hold" on the vehicle, and that he wouldn't be needed.

Observing his mother arrive on the scene, Marquette had moved around one of the trees and toward the wall of the apartment house, some 15 feet from the curb. A couple of the men were kidding him about going to jail. From his euphoric mood he was plunging into despair. After two years of watching his step and not getting into any trouble, here he was in a mess again. Nothing ever seemed to go right for him. Nothing.

The crowd continued to swell. One lane of the street was blocked. Cars were slowing down, their occupants craning their necks. Some of the drivers parked and joined the onlookers, more than 30 of whom were now gathered on the east side in the vicinity of the vehicles, with another 15 or 20 watching from across the boulevard.

One of the spectators had engaged Minikus in conversation. Lewis was replacing the storage forms in the cycle box. Bennett had alighted from the patrol car to join them. Rena was walking over toward Marquette.

"Let me have the keys to the car," she said to him. "You know better than to drive after you've been drinking."

"Momma, I'm *not* drunk and I am *not* going to jail." He pulled away from her.

The noise the people were making was increasing. As Lewis straightened up from the cycle he thought, for a moment, that Marquette had disappeared. Then he spotted him by the building, and called to Minikus, "We're going to have to get Frye out of that crowd!"

They started toward Marquette, whose unhappiness was increasing. As he spoke to his mother, his voice broke. He was almost crying. Spotting the officers, he started backing away, his feet shuffling, his arms waving.

"Come on, Marquette, you're coming with us." Minikus reached toward him.

Marquette slapped his hand away. "I'm not going to no sonofabitching jail!" he cried out. "I haven't did anything to be taken to jail."

"Go with them and make it easy on yourself," Rena said, caught between him and the officers.

All the old anger, the old frustration, welled up within Marquette. What right had they to treat him like this?

"You motherfucking white cops, you're not taking me anywhere!" he screamed, whipping his body about as if he were half boxer, half dancer.

There was a growl from the crowd, now about 100 in number. Many had just arrived, and, not having witnessed the beginning of the incident, had little knowledge of what the dispute was about. Marquette's defiance struck a responsive chord. The officers were white; they were outsiders; and, most of all, they were police. Years of reciprocal distrust, reciprocal contempt, and reciprocal insults had created a situation in which the residents assumed every officer to be in the wrong until he had proven himself right, just as the officers assumed every Negro guilty until he had proven his innocence. The people began to close in on the three highway patrolmen. What, a few minutes before, had seemed to be an entirely innocuous situation, was taking on an ugly tenor.

Lewis returned quickly to the motorcycle to broadcast a Code 1199—Officer Needs Help!—over the radio. Minikus retrieved the riot baton from Lewis's motorcycle, and Bennett got his shotgun from the patrol car. Together Minikus and Bennett advanced on the crowd, pushing the people back.

In the vicinity, when the Code 1199 call went out, were motorcycle Offiicers Wayne Wilson and Veale J. Fondville of the highway patrol. Turning on their red lights, and with their sirens screaming, they headed for Avalon and 116th Place.

Minikus and Bennett were once more within striking distance of Marquette. While Bennett used the shotgun to keep spectators at bay, Minikus tried to duck beneath Marquette's flailing arms in order to grab him from behind.

"Hit those blue-eyed bastards!" a voice yelled.

Marquette and Minikus came into contact. Marquette, grabbing for the riot baton, got one hand on it—there was a brief scuffle before Minikus was able to regain control of it.

"Go ahead, you motherfuckers! Why don't you kill me? You'll have to kill me before you take me to jail!" Marquette shouted, dancing away from Minikus. At that moment, it would have been easy enough for Marquette to escape into the crowd, but he made no effort to do so.

Nearby, Ronald, involved despite himself, concerned about Marquette being hurt, was remonstrating with Lewis.

"You'll have to stay out of the way!" Lewis tried to brush past him.

"But he's my brother!" Ronald pleaded.

Officer Wilson, as he arrived on the scene, riot baton in hand even before he had the kickstand of the motorcycle down, was confronted by an image of blurred chaos. A chunky man, about 40, with a reddish face and short-cropped hair, he went into action with no more opportunity to assess the situation than those Negro spectators who had arrived late and assumed from what they saw that there was violent conflict between Marquette and the officers.

Wilson glimpsed the crowd—grown to perhaps 150, but seeming larger and more menacing because of the noise and the narrow confines of the action. He heard them shouting. He was well aware of their hostility.

Close by he saw one officer in what appeared to be a dispute with a Negro youth. A few feet farther off, there was a fight between another Negro and an officer.

Rushing toward Ronald and Lewis, and without speaking to either, Wilson jabbed the riot baton into the pit of Ronald's stomach. As Ronald doubled over, he jabbed again. Ronald rolled to the ground.

With one adversary dispatched, it was but a half dozen steps to where Marquette was fending off Minikus. Wilson swung the baton. He caught Marquette with a glancing blow to the forehead, above the left eye. As Marquette turned instinctively to meet him, Wilson jabbed him hard in the stomach. Marquette doubled over. Instantly Minikus caught his head in a vise, and, with the fight gone out of him, had no trouble leading him to the patrol car. Throwing him across the front seat, Minikus pulled Marquette's arms behind him, and, bending over him, started to handcuff his wrists.

Rena Frye, distraught at having seen both Ronald and Marquette struck down, believed the latter to be under further attack in the police car. Rushing to his aid and trying to pull Minikus away, she, a foot shorter than the officer, sprawled awkwardly across his back. As she pulled at him she suddenly felt herself lifted up. Struggling, the back of Minikus's shirt bunched in her fist, she was torn away by Officer Fondville. Off balance, a strip of the ripped shirt in her hand, she stumbled onto the back of Officer Wilson. Both momentarily went to the ground.

Straightening up, Rena was grabbed by Fondville. Bending her over the trunk of the car, he forced her arms behind her, handcuffed her, and placed her in the rear seat.

"Put your legs inside," he ordered her.

"I wouldn't do anything for you, you white Southern bastard!" she spat at him, tears streaming down her face.

Ronald objected: "What are you arresting her for?"

Getting no answer, he became more insistent. A moment later he received his reply. Handcuffed, he too was placed inside the car.

The Negro crowd, continuing to swell, incensed by the altercation, pressed in. There were isolated shouts of: "Come on, let's get them!" "Leave the old lady alone!" "We've got no rights at all—it's just like Selma!" "Those white motherfuckers got no cause to do that!"

More highway patrol officers were arriving. With riot batons and shotguns, they kept the people back from the car.

In the front seat, Minikus had finished handcuffing Marquette. Pulling him upright on the seat, he was closing the door when Marquette, cursing, lashed out with his foot. He caught the door sharply, swinging it open, and partially springing it. As he did, one of the newly arrived officers, Taylor, kicked his feet back inside of the car, then helped Minikus cuff Marquette's legs together.

The sound of sirens was exploding from all directions as Los Angeles police sped to the scene to assist. As Sgt. V. Nicholson of the highway patrol arrived, it became evident to him that the cars converging at high speed were in danger of crashing into each other. Since the situation appeared now to be under control, he went on the radio to order the units to veer off.

Responding to the lure of the sirens, hundreds of people flocked to the area. Four blocks south of 116th Place, at Virgie Nash's beauty parlor, Joyce Ann Gaines and Joan Nash, Virgie's daughter, were unable to suppress their curiosity. Despite the fact that Joyce Ann had a headful of pink curlers and was wearing a green barber's smock to protect her white capris, they ventured into the street. As they kept asking people what was happening, and received vague, or unknowing answers in reply, they drifted farther and farther to the north, until, finally they came upon the scene shortly before 7:30 p.m.—just as all of the Fryes had been hustled into the police car.

Joyce Ann Gaines, a sociology student at Compton Junior College, is a slender, eye-catchingly attractive girl with light brown hair and a matching complexion; even the fact that she was walking around with her hair up in curlers could not hide this attractiveness. As she made her way toward the front of the crowd and asked what had happened, people were quick to tell her, "The boy in the front seat, he was already bleeding and handcuffed, and one of the cops kicked him!"

"That lady in back—they jerked her around till she was screaming with the pain!"

"With all those cops, you'd think they were fighting in Vietnam!"

"We can't even go peaceful in our own way. It's just like the South!"

Joe Gabel, under the direction of Minikus, was once more hitching the Buick onto his tow truck when Jimmy Ticey walked up to him. The Ticey brothers operate the T and T Wrecking Yard twenty blocks to the south on Avalon Blvd., and Jimmy, drawn like the others by the sirens, had arrived two or three minutes before.

"Why," he asked Gabel, "are you impounding this boy's car? I mean, being legally parked, why are you all impounding?"

"What's it to you?" An officer snapped back at him. "You want to get yourself in trouble?"

"No. No." Ticey shrugged. "It's nothing to me."

He walked off, and, caught up in the agitation of the crowd, was pushed toward the spot where Joyce Ann Gaines was standing. Among the police he noticed an officer he knew, Bill Davis. Davis, because of his size—six feet five inches, and 235 pounds—stood out clearly from the rest. The residents of the area called him "Wild Bill."

Traffic on Avalon Blvd. had come to a halt. A half block to the south, one of the well-worn red buses of the South Los Angeles Transportation

Co.—a subsidiary concern servicing the area, since the city does not feel it worthwhile to send its buses that far out—had had to stop. Behind it a number of cars and trucks were stacking up. The sun had disappeared into the haze of the Pacific Ocean, leaving only a few red reflections in a sky that was rapidly darkening. Driven by Bennett, the CHP car with the Fryes pulled away from the curb. Behind it, the tow truck, with the Buick hanging from its winch like a slaughtered animal, was escorted from the scene.

The police prepared to withdraw. There was the throaty sound of motorcycle engines being kicked into life as the officers separated themselves from the crowd and waited for the signal to be given to leave.

"Come on," Joan Nash said to Joyce Gaines. "Let's get back. I've got customers waiting for me."

Officers Vaughan and Taylor of the highway patrol were on their cycles, their backs half turned to the people. There were taunts from the crowd:

"Look at the yellow-bellies run!"

"Stay a while. We'll make it interesting for you mothers!"

The officers ignored the taunts. Then, suddenly, Vaughan felt something sting the back of his neck. Instinctively slapping his hand to the area, his fingers came off wet. Whirling around he saw, disappearing among the people, the back of a girl with pink curlers in her hair.

"Goddam! She spit on me!" he exclaimed to Sgt. Nicholson, who was sitting on a cycle a few feet away. Nicholson, and his partner, Gilbert, jumped off their bikes and plunged into the crowd after the girl.

"Let it go! It's not worth it!" another officer called out. But it was too late. The two highway patrolmen had been swallowed up by the people.

Within seconds the other officers dismounted to go to their assistance. At the point where they disappeared into the crowd a seething agitation began. Officer Pattee, fearful, broadcast a new Code 1199—Officer Needs Help!—call. The first cars that had left the scene, already a block or two away, swung back. Several new units, including some from the Sheriff's Department, raced to respond.

"Hey, pink lady!" someone called to Joyce Ann Gaines as she made her way through the crowd. They kidded her about the curlers in her hair, and she laughed. Then with startling suddenness, an arm snaked itself about the lower part of her face; she felt herself pulled backward.

"Who's that? What are you doing?" she giggled, thinking it was someone playing a joke. Dragged backward, trying to turn her head, she started to lose her balance and instinctively put out her arms to support herself.

Officer Gilbert, certain in his own mind after Vaughan's indication that the girl had spit on a fellow officer, was determined to bring her out of the crowd. Joan Nash grabbed Joyce Ann's extended arm and hung on. Pulled in opposite directions, Joyce Ann, struggling, called for help.

"She hasn't did a thing, and look at what they're doing to her!" Joan cried.

Jimmy Ticey, going to Joan Nash's aid, attempted to wrest Joyce Gaines away from Gilbert.

Other officers became involved in the melee.

"Wild Bill! Help us! Look at what they're doing to her. Don't let 'em do that to her, Wild Bill!" Jimmy Ticey shouted to Off. Davis.

Several patrolmen, not knowing to whom Ticey was calling, presumed he was exhorting others in the crowd to help Joyce Ann Gaines resist arrest. They jumped on him, pinioning his arms.

An officer, shorter than the others, broke Joan Nash's hold on her friend. He drew back his baton, threatening her.

"Go ahead, I dare you to hit me!" she screamed. "I dare you to hit me, 'cause I haven't did a thing!"

"You leave my sister alone!" Janet Nash hurled at him.

Gilbert, not for one moment releasing his hold on Joyce Ann, the elbow of his arm clamped tightly across her chin, half walked, half dragged her backward out into the street. As she struggled and kicked, the pink curlers in her hair loosened and were scattered about the pavement. Bent backward, wearing the barber's smock, she took on a pregnant appearance. Away from the crowd, out as she was in the arena of the street, hundreds of people could see her.

"Look at what they're doing to that pregnant girl!" a woman shouted.

"Oh those motherfuckers!" an anguished voice cried out.

One Negro officer, Ronald Farwell, of the Los Angeles police was among those attempting to contain the crowd. "What kind of a brother are you, when you let them do that to a girl?" he was castigated and cursed.

As Sgt. Nicholson was handcuffing Jimmy Ticey, the latter was still calling out to "Wild Bill" for help. Davis came over and told him to calm down.

"Just go quietly, and you'll be all right," he promised him.

Lee Castruita, of the LAPD, had been one of those leaving the scene when another officer had called out: "There they go again!" Returning, he found himself rushing to the assistance of Officer Gilbert. As Gilbert held Joyce Gaines, Castruita handcuffed her, then started walking her toward his patrol car. Despite the handcuffs, she was more than he could handle.

"Someone give me a hand!" Castruita called out, and Los Angeles police officer Harvey Eubank ran to help him.

Together they walked the girl to Castruita's patrol car, only to discover it immovably jammed between several others. Continuing along the line of police cars, they found one at the end that had the key in the ignition. Placing Joyce Ann in the car, the officers jumped in. Unable to turn the auto around, Castruita backed it rapidly two blocks north on Avalon Blvd., to the intersection of Imperial. Here he swung into a service station and made his turn.

"Help me! Help me! Don't let the bastards take me to jail!" Joyce Gaines called out. Her resentment flaring, she bombarded the officers with invectives.

Returning to his patrol car, LAPD Officer C. A. Willig of the 77th St. division discovered that it had been stolen.

Heading north on Avalon toward the 77th St. station, Castruita and Eubank heard on the radio that they were driving a stolen car.

"Be quiet!" Castruita snapped at Joyce Gaines. He had unhooked the radio mike, and was attempting to report that he was transporting a prisoner to the station in Willig's car. "Can't you see I'm trying to broadcast?"

"I don't have to be quiet—I don't give a good goddam if you ever broadcast!" she cried, starting a shouting match between her and the officers.

Several blocks farther on, Castruita hailed a police car heading in the opposite direction. He asked them to call the station and report he was bringing in a prisoner.

Eubank got out and exchanged places with the passenger officer in the other car. The exchange between Joyce Ann and the new officer became even more acerbic.

"Why? Why? Why," she shouted, "are you doing this to me? What have I done?" She leaned forward awkwardly in the seat, trying to get an answer out of Castruita.

The new officer pulled her back. She lashed out at him with her foot.

"If you try that once more, I'll give you a kick that'll push your teeth down your throat!" he snapped.

"I'd look right stupid trying to kick you with these handcuffs on me!" she retorted, falling silent for the remainder of the five-minute ride to the station.

Along the two-block stretch of Avalon Blvd., decades of distrust, of resentment, of antipathy, of pride ground into the dust had found a focal point in the arrest of Joyce Ann Gaines. In the manner with which the police had handled the girl the people saw, or thought they saw, the contempt of the white man for the Negro. They felt, collectively, his heel grinding in their faces. They were stricken once more by the sting of his power.

"Goddam!" a woman called out. "Goddam! They'd never treat a white woman like that!"

"What kind of men are you, anyways?" another challenged. "What kind of men are you, anyways, to let them do that to our people?"

"It's a shame! It's a pitiful, crying shame!"

"Blue-eyed white devils! We is going to get you! Oh, shit! We is going to get you!"

"Motherfuckers!" It came from all sides of the crowd. "Motherfuckers!"

The police officers, although they had long worked in a culture of antagonism, had never seen hatred of such intensity. Sgt. Richard Rankin —a sergeant of two weeks' standing—of the 77th St. police station was the senior city police officer on the scene. To him it seemed, and rightly so, that the continued presence of the officers could only incite the crowd further; that it would only lead to one incident after another, each bigger than the one before. Over the loudspeaker mounted on his patrol car he ordered his men to re-form and withdraw. Once more they began disengaging themselves from the crowd.

Gabriel Pope had made his way to the scene from the corner of Imperial and Avalon Blvd. at about 7:15. For the past 30 minutes, a two-thirds empty pop bottle in his hand, he had been wandering back and forth between 116th Place and the rose-lavender painted church at the corner of 116th St. and Avalon. Strongly built, just slightly over six feet tall, he had been born in Los Angeles in 1946, the fourth child of Sam and Tessie Pope. Sam and Tessie had both been raised in Woodville, Miss. In 1942, shortly after the beginning of the war, Sam Pope had gone to work in the Armstrong Rubber Co. plant in Natchez. Two years later he had moved his parents and his family to the West Coast, where, in the same job, the money was better. By the time Gabriel was born, however, returning veterans had begun to press Sam Pope for his job, and, under the pressure, his marriage had started showing cracks.

When Sam picked up Tessie at the hospital after she had given birth to Gabriel, they had stopped off at his parents' place to show them the child.

"What a beautiful baby!" his mother had exclaimed. "I'd like to have another beautiful baby like that myself!"

Two weeks later Tessie had returned with the baby and its accoutrements. She hadn't seen Sam for 10 days, and three children were enough for her to take care of, she said. So, since Sam's mother liked the baby so much, she might as well have it for a while.

Gabriel stayed with his paternal grandparents for the next eight years. For him, they became his parents. He saw his father every two or three months, and his mother even less frequently. Then, in 1954, his grandmother died. His grandfather, past 75, was not able to take care of himself, much less an 8-year-old boy.

Gabe, as everyone called him, returned to live with his mother. . . .

Before he was 18 he'd been stopped and questioned by the police twice, both times for curfew violation. Los Angeles has an ordinance prohibiting any person below the age of 18 from being on the street after 10 p.m. unless accompanied by a near relative. From a practical standpoint the ordinance is difficult to enforce, and on Friday and Saturday nights Hollywood Blvd is jammed with teenagers that the police ignore as long as they behave themselves. In the high crime area of southeast Los Angeles, however, anything that moves at night is liable to be stopped, and the ordinance provides a handy catch-all. . . .

It was around Easter time that, as Gabe was driving down Central Ave. with Lada [Gabriel's girlfriend] in the car, the police stopped him. They made him get out of the car and stand spreadeagled against its side as they searched him. When he protested and wanted to know what it was all about, they told him to shut up:

"We can do it here, or down at the station, buddy. Take your choice!"

After patting him down, they made Lada get out of the car also. Then they took out the seats, and threw them onto the sidewalk. After that, they did the same with the paraphernalia in the trunk. When they couldn't find any contraband, they called in on the police radio to run a make on him, and, while waiting for a reply, filled out an FI (field interrogation) slip on him. When he continued to press them as to what it was about they said that there had been a burglary in the area, and that his vehicle fitted the description of the one used by the suspects. He knew that wasn't true. He knew—in his own mind—they'd stopped him only because he had a sharp-looking car, and they wanted to harass him.

When they got the word back on the radio, they said, "It looks like you check out okay, Gabriel."

They handed him back his driver's license and drove off, leaving him standing there with the car gutted and its contents piled in a heap. "Motherfuckers!" he cried in rage after them, shaking with the fury and the helplessness of his humiliation.

Here, in August, four months later, all that old feeling welled up in him as he watched the police pull out. All the old feeling of being stomped into the ground, of having no right to his own manhood, of having to crawl before the white man. Of the white man abusing Negro women, and the Negro man standing by in cowardly indifference—the girl with the pink curlers could just as well have been Lada.

"It burn your soul, but what can you do?" said a woman next to him, and her words were like a solo to the orchestra of imprecations rising about him. Without conscious thought of his action he darted into the street and hurled the empty pop bottle in his hand toward the last of the departing black-and-white cars. Striking the rear fender of Sgt. Rankin's car, it shattered. And it was as if in that shattering the thousand people lining the street found their own release. It was as if in one violent contortion the bonds of restraint were snapped. Rocks, bottles, pieces of wood and iron—whatever missiles came to hand—were projected against the sides and windows of the bus and automobiles that, halted for the past 20 minutes by the jammed street, unwittingly started through the gauntlet. The people had not been able to overcome the power of the police. But they could, and would, vent their fury on other white people. The white people who used the police to keep them from asserting their rights.

It was 7:45 p.m. Amidst the rending sounds of tearing metal, splintering glass, cries of bewilderment and shouts of triumph, the Los Angeles uprising had begun.

PROTEST MOVEMENT

"The Bus Boycott in Montgomery"

by L.D. Reddick

Before last December, a visitor to Montgomery would have noticed Negroes standing up in the city buses, while there were empty seats right before them. Somebody could then explain that according to local practice, these unoccupied seats were reserved for "whites only." No matter how packed a bus might be with Negro passengers, they were prohibited from sitting in the first 4 seats (which hold about 10 persons). Theoretically, the last 3 back seats (holding about 10 persons) were similarly reserved for Negroes. In fact this was not so. Moreover, if white passengers were already occupying all of their reserved seats and additional white passengers boarded the bus, Negro passengers, sitting in the unreserved section immediately behind the whites, might be asked to get up and "move back" by the bus driver. At times this was done courteously; all-too-often it was an undisguised insult.

Race relations in Montgomery have traditionally been "good" in the sense that Negroes have seldom challenged their state of subordination. The structure of the society was more or less set. Opposition seemed futile. Personal difficulties might be adjusted through some prominent Negro, who would speak with an influential white person. This was the established pattern of paternalism; and it did not disturb the status quo.

But for some reason on Thursday afternoon, December 1, 1955, Mrs. Rosa Parks refused to "move back" when she was ordered to do so by the bus driver. She was *not* sitting in the section reserved for whites (as the *New York Times* mistakenly reported) but in the first seat of the unreserved section. At the time every seat in the bus was taken. So the command for her to "move back" meant that she would have to stand while a white male passenger, who had just taken the bus, would sit. And so she was arrested and for a brief moment jailed.

Mrs. Parks was ideally fitted for her role. She is attractive and quiet, a churchgoer who looks like the symbol of Mother's Day. Her trial was set for the following Monday, December 5. Out of nowhere, it seems, written and mimeographed appeals appeared in the Negro community, saying: ". . . This has to be stopped . . . if Negroes did not ride the buses they could not operate . . . every Negro stay off the buses Monday in protest of this arrest and trial . . . "

Only a fraction of Negro bus riders saw these unsigned appeals but one of the notices did fall into the hands of the local paper, which put it on the front page. Negroes laugh when they tell about this. They say that the newspaper was mostly interested in letting the white folks know what the Negroes were up to. But through this story many Negroes got the news of the Monday plan for the first time. At the Sunday church service, Negro ministers hammered home their endorsement of the projected one-day "protest"—as they consistently called the boycott.

Physically, Montgomery is ideally fitted for a bus boycott. It is just 27.9 square miles in area. Its population, 130,000, is about 40 per cent Negro. Most residents *could* walk to most places in the city.

The judge who tried Mrs. Parks, had he looked into his crystal ball, would have probably dismissed the case. Instead, he found her guilty, fining her $14. She appealed.

All day long on December 5 Negroes stayed off the buses. They did so with such enthusiasm that there was a general feeling that "we ought to continue this."

The Negro ministers had hastily scheduled a mass meeting for Monday evening. Normally, the church holds about 1500 persons. Hours before meeting time, 7:00 p.m., people began filling up the place. By 7 o'clock every seat had been taken and some 3 or 4 thousand standees over-flowed into the street. Outdoor loudspeakers were set up.

Nobody expected such a response. The Negro ministers, rising to the occasion, improvised a declaration of principles. Amid the singing of hymns and some first class oratory—led by Rev. M. L. King Jr.—the audience unanimously adopted the following declaration as read by Rev. Ralph Abernathy: Negroes were not to resume riding the buses until (1) courteous treatment by bus operators was guaranteed; (2) passengers were seated on a first come, first serve basis—Negroes seating from the back of the bus toward the front while whites seat from the front toward the back; (3) Negro bus operators were employed on predominately Negro routes.

Then without the usual money-raising salesmanship, the crowd—inside and outside of the church—filed in and placed dimes, quarters and dollars on the collection table. This was altogether spontaneous.

Since the Negro ministers were cagey about revealing who was directing the movement, that seemed to whet the appetite of the reporters. As a matter of fact, at this point every thing was *ad hoc* and tentative. The emergence of King and Abernathy was almost by chance. No leader was calling the shots. As Abernathy said later, it was never "a one-man show." The indignation and demands for action by the "common people" swept everyone along like a flood.

//

There had been a long history of abuse by the bus operators. Almost everybody could tell of some unfortunate personal experience that he himself had had or seen. Montgomery Negroes were fed up with the bus service in particular and, like Negroes throughout the South, with race relations in general. The outrage of the Emmett Till murder was alive in everybody's mind. The silence and inaction of the Federal Government, in the face of the daily abuse, beatings and killings of Negro citizens, was maddening. Negroes have no faith at all in Southern law-making and law-enforcing agencies, for these instruments of "justice" are all in the hands of "the brothers of the hoodlums who attack us."

Negroes themselves wanted to get into action. Here and elsewhere they were willing to fight it out—if the fighting was "fair." But Negroes knew on whose side the police and the lily-white militia would be when they came in to "put down disorder." And after that—there would be the local judges and juries. To remain human, the Negroes simply could not stand by and do nothing. Under the circumstances, the channel into which the Negroes of Montgomery have poured their energies and resentments is the best answer thus far to the question of what to do. Here is organized struggle and group solidarity. It is legal, nonviolent and effective.

And so the one-day boycott passed into an indefinite protest that, as of this writing, has run for fourteen weeks.

Both the press and the police expected violence. Early newspaper stories started off in this fashion: "Negro goon squads reportedly have been organized here to intimidate Negroes who ride . . . in violation of a Negro boycott . . . " This was untrue.

The police were equally sure of the image in their minds. Accordingly, they arrested a college student, saying that he had pulled a Negro woman from a bus as she was attempting to get on it. In court it came out that the two were good friends and that they were merrily crossing the street, arm in arm, near a bus. She had told the cops this before the arrest was made but the police believed that there were goons—there had to be—so they saw what they were looking for: "believing is seeing."

The first reaction of the bus company officials was one of arrogance. They pretended that the Negroes were demanding that the company violate the law. This was absurd. The law required segregation, but did not specify the manner of seating so long as it was segregated. The bus company summarily rejected the proposal of the Negroes.

The city commission sided with the bus company, condemning the boycott and declaring that "first come, first serve" would be illegal. And so almost everybody—the bus company, the city commissioners and the white public—expected Negroes to be back on the buses in a few days.

This was only the first of a series of misjudgments on the part of the city fathers. All along they demonstrated that their conception of the Negro was the stereotype of the tired field hand or the witless house servant who could be cajoled or forced to do what the white folks wanted him to do. Even now, after 14 weeks of "education," the commissioners seem not to comprehend the intelligence, resourcefulness and resolve of the people with whom they are dealing.

III

The ex-bus riders soon found themselves face to face with a practical problem: since the buses were taboo, how were the Negroes to get about the city? At first, they called upon the taxis for cheap-rate jitney service. The police stopped this by warning the taxis that by law they must charge a minimum fare of 45 cents. Next, private cars began giving "friends" a lift, along the bus routes. The charge was 15 cents for "gasoline expense." The cops stopped this, too, by insisting that drivers had to have a taxi permit and license.

In reply, the Negroes organized a voluntary motor pool. Almost overnight Montgomery saw a network of private cars spread over the city, picking up and depositing passengers, from dawn until early evening. It was a marvel of quick organization. Even the local press had to concede that the pick-up system moved with "military precision." Some transportation problems that the bus company had grappled with for twenty years were, apparently, solved overnight.

The police searched the books for laws that would dry up the motor pool. One old rule forbade more than three persons to sit on the front seat of an automobile. Lights, brakes, even the position of license tags, were checked by the police frequently. Minor regulations that are seldom invoked in this normally easy-going town were resurrected and severely enforced. Negro taxi drivers really caught it!

The Negro community of Montgomery has neither its own radio station (as does Atlanta, Ga.) nor a widely-read local newspaper. Communication is by word of mouth and through churches mainly. This is probably why frequent mass meetings have proved a necessity. The pattern was established during the first week of the boycott: mass meetings each Monday and Thursday evening. It has been adhered to ever since.

These twice-a-week get-togethers are the soul of the boycott; the Montgomery Improvement Association is the brains. The meetings are rotated from church to church. The speakers, in turn, represent the various denominations. Thus the ground is cut from under any institutional or sectarian jealousy. Rev. King and Rev. Abernathy make it plain by their words and by their sharing of the speakers' platform that they are not self-appointed "leaders" but only "spokesmen" of the movement. Incidentally, the people have "fallen in love" with King, a boyish-looking Ph.D. They look upon Abernathy, also young and an M.A., as a tower of strength. These two men symbolize the poise, the thoughtfulness and the ability of the independent ministers. They are the real and obvious leaders of this mass upsurge. The more vulnerable intellectuals stay discreetly in the background. Rufus Lewis, an ex-football coach and presently a civic-minded business man, is the cool-headed chairman of the motor pool committee.

People come hours ahead of time to get a seat at these mass meetings. A few read papers and books while waiting, but mostly the audiences sing. Hymns such as "Onward Christian Soldiers," "Abide With Me" and "Higher Ground" are moving but the really stirring songs are the lined, camp-meeting tunes, of low pitch and long meter. These seem to recapture the long history of the Negro's suffering and struggle.

IV

By 7 p.m., the time the meeting starts, virtually every inch of space is taken, including standing room. Often as many listeners are outside as inside. Many others do not come at all because they know they cannot get near the church. It is curious that meetings were never scheduled in different parts of the city at different hours on the same night or rotated to different parts of the city on different nights—in order to accommodate the crowds. This suggestion was made but the planning committee never got around to it or concluded that "the people prefer to be together," as several persons had said.

The mass meeting pattern is relatively simple: songs, prayer, latest news and plans, a "pep talk," collection. Often the pastor in whose church the meeting was held would preside or, after preliminary remarks, would turn the meeting over to some official of the Montgomery Improvement Association.

The meetings are serious but thoroughly relaxed. There are quips and jokes—a great deal of genial humor. All classes are present in the audiences but the bulk of the attendants are working class people. It is here that morale is built and sustained. Unity is expressed in words and in the little kindnesses that the people show to each other. The automobile-owning folk, who never rode the buses, and the maids and day-laborers, who depended upon the buses, have come to know each other. The inter-denominational, inter-class integration of the Negro community has called forth much comment. Moreover, the mass meetings have given many persons some place to go; something to think about; something to absorb their energies. There is high purpose these days in the Negro community.

Few whites attend these meetings although they are open to all. Aside from a Lutheran minister who has a Negro congregation, no local white preacher has publicly identified himself with the Negro cause. Many, of course, give assurances privately. A few are in "hot water" for real or suspected sympathies with the boycotters.

But the main force that keeps the people and their leaders together is the idea of the movement itself. These people know that they are fighting a big battle and that it is a vital part of a larger war. Messages and money contributions from many parts of the nation as well as from remote parts of the world have confirmed this belief.

At first, the demands of the boycotters were limited—courtesy, fair play, fair employment. These were all within the segregation laws of the city and state. At one point, the Negroes would have called off the boycott for just the "first come, first serve" arrangement. That day, of course, has long since passed.

Apparently to impress the Negro community with what it could lose, the bus company abruptly stopped all service to Negro neighborhoods. This was supposed to bring Negroes to their knees, crying for the buses. But nobody was impressed. Instead, doubtful would-be bus riders were pushed into the motor pool. The water, they found, was just "fine." On second thought, the bus company decided to re-establish the discontinued lines. So the buses were put back on the routes in the Negro areas. They continued to roll empty.

For about a month negotiations were on and off. Neither side would yield. The boycott held its own. This meant that 75 per cent of the bus riding public was "out," and it cut some $3,000 from each day's revenue. Moreover, fewer whites—probably out of sympathy with the boycott— seem to be riding.

To counteract this economic squeeze, the mayor called on the white public to support the buses. The so-called White Citizens Council solicited contributions for the poor suffering bus company. No figures were ever given out but the general impression is that very few persons were willing to subsidize the National City Lines, an economic giant that is spread out over the cities and towns of the Middle West and South and has its main office in Chicago. A forced subsidy was made possible by raising the bus fare from 10 to 15 cents. At which point, additional whites stayed off the buses.

V

To break the impasse, the city commission pulled a fast one. On Sunday, January 22, the Negro community was astounded to read in the morning paper that a settlement had been reached. The article said: "The above aggreement is concurred in by all three members of the City Commission, as well as by representatives of the bus company and the group representing the Negroes of Montgomery." The terms of the "agreement" were: (1) courtesy to all; (2) white reserve section at the front of the bus, Negro reserve section at rear of bus; (3) special, all-Negro buses during the rush hours. "First come, first serve" would obtain for the unreserved, middle section. The city commission stated that it had nothing to do with the question of employment. The declaration of courtesy carried no machinery for assuring its practice. In short, this latest "agreement" was merely a re-statement of the *status quo ante bellum.* Nevertheless, it sounded like a settlement and many persons who read the story felt that the boycott was over. Some whites were jubilant. Some Negroes were ill. Why had the "leaders" given in?, they asked.

A careful reading of the article raises the question whether it was just poor reporting or something much worse. For example, the names of the "prominent ministers" were not given. Other omissions were equally strange. If this was a release from the city commission, would any newspaper naively print such an important front-page story without first checking with the known Negro representatives, who had been negotiating with the bus company and city commission for weeks? Obviously, this announcement was a calculated maneuver to get the ex-bus riders back on the buses Sunday morning. Perhaps once the spell of not riding was broken, the boycott would dissolve.

The Negroes foiled this maneuver by a combination of luck and quick action. The story had been sent out Saturday evening by the Associated Press. As it came over the wires into the office of the *Minneapolis Tribune,* the reporter Carl T. Rowan, who had been down to Montgomery to cover the boycott, did what any good reporter would do: he called Rev. M. L. King Jr. to verify the story.

King was amazed. He knew absolutely nothing about any settlement. Rowan then contacted one of the Montgomery commissioners who confirmed the story but refused to give the names of the Negro ministers involved. Under prodding, the commissioner did reveal the denominations of the ministers. Rowan then called King again. This clue was enough. King and his colleagues by a process of checking soon identified the "three prominent Negro ministers." It turned out that they were neither prominent nor members of the negotiating committee.

It was now late Saturday night. Like minute men, the ministers of the Montgomery Improvement Association went themselves or sent messages to all of the night clubs and taverns in the Negro community, informing the Saturday night revellers of the attempted hoax. Rev. King himself humorously stated that he got a chance to see the insides of many a night spot! Result: word got around so well that the next day the buses rolled empty as usual. At the Sunday morning services, the ministers excoriated

the "fake settlement" and repeated that the "protest" was
commissioners lost face. The Negroes were brought closer .

By the next day, the "three prominent Negro ministers" ι
repudiated the commission's press announcement. One of the ι
before an open meeting that he had been "tricked" into the con ͜͜ on
the basis of a telephone invitation, asking that he join in a discussion of
group insurance for the city. This man said that neither he nor the other
two Negroes present agreed to any settlement, declaring that they were
unauthorized to speak for the ex-bus riders.

Few persons thought that these three Negro ministers would dare challenge the veracity of the city fathers; but they did. This, everybody was
sure, would make front page news. But the local press reduced the sensa-
tional disclosure to a bare statement of denial that was buried near the
end of a long story. When the local dailies did not print his statement, one
of the three ministers purchased space for a three-inch ad saying: "The
rumor that is out that I agreed with the commissioners on the proposal
that they issued is an untrue statement." These words have never been
contradicted.

Things now took a turn for the worse. The mayor and the other commissioners embarked upon a "get tough" policy. With a show of anger the
mayor denounced the boycott, declared that the white people did not care
if another Negro ever rode the buses again, and called upon white employers to stop taking their Negro employees to and from work. He said
that white businessmen informed him that they were discharging Negro
workers who were participating in the boycott. All three commissioners
let it be known that they had joined the White Citizens Council. Even the
timid member of the trio mustered up enough bravado to go on television
and join the "get tough with Negroes" act. All this, of course, was the
traditional, Confederate, flag-waving appeal to white supremacy.

It was to be a field day. The police would "cut the legs off" the boycott
by a campaign of arrests for real and imaginary traffic infractions. Negro
drivers, who appeared to be in the motor pool, would be questioned about
their employment, the balance due on the purchase of their automobiles
and the firms with which they had their insurance.

VI

For a moment the protest movement seemed to be wavering. Again,
Negroes saw that the very instruments of law and order were being used
against them. Surely, a man had the right to give someone a ride in his
own automobile. Persons who had not received a traffic ticket in years
were booked. Some ex-bus riders, while waiting to be picked up, were told
that there was a law against hitchhiking; others were accused of "loud
talking," walking on lawns and "congregating in white neighborhoods."

The daily press printed next to nothing about the wholesale arrests and harassment.

Under such heavy blows the voluntary pick-up system began to weaken. Some drivers were already tired; others disliked "tangling with the law"; still others feared that they could not stand much more provocation without striking back.

The high point of the "get tough" operation was the arrest of Rev. King himself. But if this move was intended to frighten King, it fell flat. He calmly submitted to arrest and jailing. At first, he was not to be let out on bond. The news spread through the Negro community like wildfire. Negroes began rushing down to the jail in such numbers that King was released without having even to sign his own bond.

Meanwhile, a group of Negro business and professional men asked the city for permission to operate a jitney service. This was turned down on the grounds that sufficient transportation was already available. The mayor said, let them ride the buses now rolling empty through the streets. A strange stand for one who didn't care if another Negro ever rode a bus again!

But the city did care. It stood to lose part of the $20,000 in taxes it received from the bus company each year. Downtown merchants cared, too, for some of their businesses were off by as much as a third since the boycott had begun. Most of all, the bus company cared—each day it cared more and more. It let it be known that it would agree to any seating arrangement that the city commissioners would approve.

The worst was yet to come. The inflammatory appeals seemed to give the signal to the violent enemies. A stick of dynamite was thrown on the porch of Rev. King's home. The job was amateurish; the damage slight; the intent vicious. Within minutes hundreds of Negroes flocked to King's home; also the police. It was at this moment that non-violent resistance almost faded. Many Negroes wanted to launch a counter-offensive. Rev. King, standing on the front porch of his "bombed" home, pleaded with the angry Negroes: "We are not harmed. Do not get your weapons. Let us not answer hate with hate, violence with violence. But we will continue to stay off the buses." Probably this saved the city from a race riot.

There had been other incidents. Some Negro and white high school students had clashed; one or more cars of white youths had made commando raids on the nearby Negro college, dashing through the campus with lights out, throwing out bags of water, eggs, rocks and a tiny flaming cross. One evening the commandos were ambushed and bombarded with bricks. Another commando car was captured by special police. Another clumsy bomb-thrower hit the fence of E. D. Nixon, the president of the local NAACP chapter.

This flurry of violence had no noticeable effect on the boycott. The leaders were careful but nobody seemed to be at all afraid. On the other hand, it helped convince the patient hopefuls that an all-out fight was the only kind that made any sense.

For two months the Negroes had clung to the hope of a settlement on the basis of their limited demands. But the failure of negotiations and the crude brutality of the "get tough" policy convinced the most conservative ex-bus riders that an attack had to be made upon bus segregation itself. Accordingly, on February 1 a suit was filed in the local federal courts, asking for the end of bus jim crow on the grounds that it is contrary to the 14th Amendment of the Constitution of the United States. Furthermore, the court was asked to stop the city commissioners from violating the civil rights of Negro motorists and pedestrians.

This was a sobering jolt for the city commissioners. The "get tough" policy evaporated overnight. The city fathers, who had been making speeches at the drop of the hat, lapsed into their usual quietude.

VII

Meanwhile, a fresh effort was made to re-open negotiations. This time a white business men's club intervened. Many of them had stores that had been hurt. It is estimated that the boycott has cost Montgomery $1,-000,000. The business men's club met several times, separately, with the city commission and a committee from the Montgomery Improvement Association. Chicago Negroes had thrown a picket line around the offices of the parent bus company, so it was more willing than ever to come to terms. The city commissioners, however, remained adamant. They seem to feel that they can not afford to yield. So the best that the business men could offer was little more than the old "fake" settlement that had been palmed off on the "three prominent Negro ministers."

Some of the drivers in the motor pool were becoming exhausted. Twelve or thirteen weeks of free, voluntary service, four or five hours per day, is fatiguing. Most of these drivers have jobs and other obligations. Several of the leaders felt that maybe the boycott might as well be called off since in the end the courts would settle the issue. Understandably, people were becoming battle-weary. For over three months, life had been like a military operation for the Negro Improvement Association.

So the leaders, though reluctantly, submitted the proposals of the business men to the rank and file at one of the mass meetings. The answer was an almost total rejection. Out of approximately four thousand persons present, *only two* voted in favor of calling off the boycott. The morale of the masses, once again, revived the morale of the leaders.

To date the latest move to break the boycott has been the indictment of the leaders of the Improvement Association. This was based on an old anti-labor law of doubtful constitutionality. And again nobody was frightened. Nobody tried to hide. Many inquired of the sheriff's office: "Is my name on that Grand Jury list?" If it was, the caller let it be known that he would come down immediately. Confident, orderly, loyal to each other, the Negroes again manifested their collective will and *esprit de corps.*

Social Processes

four

What forces operate to keep Black Americans at the bottom of America's stratification system? Are the dominant middle-class norms the best standards for Blacks to follow or should they forge their own? Should race be a criterion for social position in the United States today?

Stratification

Stratification is basically the study of social inequality. In all complex societies, families or groups can be ranked in terms of prestige, power, and privileges. Thus some persons rank very high in power while others rank very low. Very often such differences become translated into an entire life-style for a large group of people within a certain society, and such a group is usually called a class. Thus sociologists speak of an American upper class and attempt to describe the living patterns of families that belong to it. Economic opportunities become very important in such a discussion, since persons following similar economic pursuits will tend to exhibit similar life-styles.

Stratification has strong implications for human behavior. The opportunities open to an individual, the rewards he receives, and the amount of power available to him are all dependent upon his position in the stratification system of his society.

In looking at societies throughout the world we find a great complexity of stratification systems. In some societies the position of an individual is relatively fixed at birth; his place in the system is ascribed to him, and he has little opportunity for mobility. In other societies positions depend upon achievement. In these the individual has choice; various positions and the means of preparing to fill them are relatively open. Many societies, such as the United States, exhibit a combination of the two types. When race is used as a criterion for stratification, a particularly rigid system results.

To be born Black in America puts strong limitations on the opportunities open to the individual. It is not surprising, therefore, that most Blacks are members of the lower class. Yet life-styles differ significantly within the Black community. Some members exhibit what might be termed "middle-class" modes of behavior. Such persons are, for example, very concerned with respectability and getting ahead.

They emphasize the importance of education and expect their children to attend college. It is thus possible to depict a separate stratification system within the Black community. This frame of reference would especially apply to the South where a caste system restricts interaction between Blacks and other members of society.

In the first part of this article, St. Clair Drake discusses the differences between the stratification systems of the North and the South. Researchers have tended to see the South as an example of a remarkably rigid stratification system in which the barriers between Blacks and the rest of society are strongly enforced by those in power. Liberal Whites, attempting to break the barrier, find themselves faced with economic and social ostracism by the rest of society. In the North the stratification system is composed of a single set of classes with various ethnic groups starting at the bottom and slowly moving upward.

Drake then examines the life-styles that emerge within the ghetto. Although the majority of Black Americans are labeled lower-class, a significant portion follow middle-class and even upper-class patterns. Note, however, that such status does not mean acceptance within the larger society. Whether lower or upper class, Blacks must largely manage their own social affairs.

C. Eric Lincoln examines the ideals of many Blacks. Being raised in America, they come to desire owning their own homes and having two cars as much as do their White counterparts. But, as Lincoln points out, the avenues for success traditionally followed by other Americans are often closed to them. Even when such Black families accumulate the necessary wealth to leave the ghetto they often cannot. Thus they must emulate middle-class standards under much more difficult economic and social conditions. Blacks who do leave the ghetto may live like their White neighbors, but still not be completely accepted. Such Black families then experience difficult identity problems.

CASTE AND CLASS—
STYLES OF LIFE

"The Social and Economic Status
of the Negro in the United States
by St. Clair Drake

Caste, Class, and "Victimization"

During the 1930's, W. Lloyd Warner and Allison Davis developed and popularized a conceptual scheme for analyzing race relations in the Southern region of the United States which viewed Negro-white relations as organized by a color-caste system that shaped economic and political relations as well as family and kinship structures, and which was reinforced by the legal system. Within each of the two castes (superordinate white and subordinate Negro), social classes existed, status being based upon possession of money, education, and family background as reflected in distinctive styles of behavior. "Exploitation" in the Marxist sense was present within this caste-class system, but also much more; for an entire socio-cultural system, not just the economic order, functioned to distribute power and prestige unevenly between whites and Negroes and to punish any individuals who questioned the system by word or behavior.[1]

Students of the situation in the North rarely conceptualized race relations in terms of caste, but tended rather to view specific communities as areas in which *ethnic* groups were involved in continuous competition and conflict, resulting in a hierarchy persisting through time, with now one, and again another, ethnic group at the bottom as previous newcomers moved "up." Each ethnic group developed a social class structure within

---

[1]The first systematic formulation of a caste-class hypothesis to explain American race relations appeared in an article by W. Lloyd Warner and Allison Davis, "A Comparative Study of American Caste," one of several contributions to a volume edited by Edgar Thompson, *Race Relations and the Race Problem* (Raleigh, N. C., 1939). The field research upon which much of the article was based was published later as Allison Davis, Burleigh Gardner, and Mary Gardner, *Deep South* (Chicago, 1941). For a Marxist criticism of the caste-class interpretation of American race relations see Oliver Cromwell Cox, *Caste, Class and Race* (New York, 1948).

it, but as individuals acquired better jobs, more education, and some sophistication, they and their families often detached themselves from immigrant colonies (usually located in slum areas) and sometimes from all
ethnic institutions as well. They tended to become part of the middle
class. The Negroes who migrated North in large numbers during World
War I were the latest arrivals in this fluid and highly competitive situation,
but their high visibility became a crucial factor limiting their upward
mobility. Upwardly mobile Negroes could not "disappear" into the middle
class of the larger society as did European ethnics.[2]

Thus, on the eve of World War II, students of race relations in the
United States generally described the status of Negroes as one in which
they played subordinate roles in a caste system in the South and an
ethnic-class system in the North. The actions of persons toward those of
another race were explained not in terms of some vaguely defined emotions connected with "prejudice," but rather in terms of the behavior they
felt was expected of them by others in various positions within the social
structure, and as attempts to protect and maximize whatever power and
prestige accrued to them at their locus in the system. John Dollard, a
psychologist, in his *Caste and Class in a Southern Town,* added an additional dimension. He analyzes the situation in terms of the "gains" and
"losses"—sexual, psychological, economic, and political—which both
Negroes and whites sustained at different levels in the Southern caste-
class system.[3]

The caste-class analysis still provides a useful frame of reference for
studying the behavior of individuals and groups located at various positions in the social structure. It can also serve as a starting point for
viewing the *processes* of race relations in terms of their consequences. Of
the racial and ethnic groups in America only Negroes have been subjected
to caste-deprivations; and the ethnic-class system has operated to their
disadvantage as compared with European immigrants. In other words,
Negroes in America have been subject to "victimization" in the sense that
a system of social relations operates in such a way as to deprive them of
a chance to share in the more desirable material and non-material products of a society which is dependent, in part, upon their labor and
loyalty. They are "victimized," also, because they do not have the same
degree of access which others have to the attributes needed for rising in

---

[2]Analysis of inter-ethnic mobility in terms of conflict, accommodation, and assimilation
characterized the work of "The Chicago School" of Sociology during the 1920's and early
1930's. For more sophisticated analysis, note W. L. Warner and Leo Strole, *The Social
Systems of American Ethnic Groups* (New Haven, Conn., 1946), in which studies of comparative mobility rates of various ethnic groups are made. Nathan Glazer and Patrick D.
Moynihan, in *Beyond The Melting Pot* (Cambridge, Mass., 1963), have recently suggested
that ethnic solidarities are much more enduring than earlier sociologists had expected them
to be.

[3]John Dollard, in association with Allison Davis, has added other dimensions to his
analysis in *Children of Bondage* (Washington; D. C., 1940).

the general class system—money, education, "contacts," and "know-how."

The concept of "victimization" implies, too, that some people are used as means to other people's ends—without their consent—and that the social system is so structured that it can be deliberately manipulated to the disadvantage of some groups by the clever, the vicious, and the cynical, as well as by the powerful. The callous and indifferent unconsciously and unintentionally reinforce the system by their inaction or inertia. The "victims," their autonomy curtailed and their self-esteem weakened by the operation of the caste-class system, are confronted with "identity problems." Their social condition is essentially one of "powerlessness."

Individual "victims" may or may not accept the rationalizations given for the denial to them of power and prestige. They may or may not be aware of and concerned about their position in the system, but, when they do become concerned, victimization takes on important social psychological dimensions. Individuals then suffer feelings of "relative deprivation" which give rise to reactions ranging from despair, apathy, and withdrawal to convert and overt aggression. An effective analysis of the position of the Negro in these terms (although the word "victimization" is never used) may be found in Thomas F. Pettigrew's *A Profile of the Negro American* (1964).

Concepts developed by Max Weber are useful for assessing the degree of victimization existing within the American caste-class system.[4] Individuals and groups can be compared by examining what he refers to as "life chances," that is, the extent to which people have access to economic and political power. *Direct victimization* might be defined as the operation of sanctions which deny access to power, which limit the franchise, sustain job discrimination, permit unequal pay for similar work, or provide inferior training or no training at all. *Indirect victimization* is revealed in the consequences which flow from a social structure which decreases *"life chances,"* such as high morbidity and mortality rates, low longevity rates, a high incidence of psychopathology, or the persistence of personality traits and attitudes which impose disadvantages in competition or excite derogatory and invidious comparisons with other groups. Max Weber also compared individuals and groups in terms of differences in *"life styles,"* those ways of behaving which vary in the amount of esteem, honor, and prestige attached to them. Differences in "life chances" may make it impossible to acquire the money or education (or may limit the contacts) necessary for adopting and maintaining prestigious life styles. The key to understanding many aspects of race relations may be found in the fact that, in American society, the protection of their familiar and cherished life styles is a dominating concern of the white

---

[4]For a discussion of these concepts see Hans Gerth and C. Wright Mills, *From Max Weber: Essays in Sociology* (New York, 1946), chapter on "Caste, Class and Party."

middle classes, who, because many Negroes have life styles differing from their own, have tried to segregate them into all-Negro neighborhoods, voluntary associations, and churches.[5] (Marxist sociologists tend to over-emphasize protection of economic interests as a dynamic factor in American race relations, important though it is.) . . .

Folkways and Classways Within the Black Ghetto

Black Ghettos in America are, on the whole, "run down" in appearance and overcrowded, and their inhabitants bear the physical and psychological scars of those whose "life chances" are not equal to those of other Americans. Like the European immigrants before them, they inherited the worst housing in the city. Within the past decade, the white "flight to the suburbs" has released relatively new and well-kept property on the margins of some of the old Black Belts. Here, "gilded ghettos" have grown up, indistinguishable from any other middle-class neighborhoods except by the color of the residents' skin.[6] The power mower in the yard, the steak grill on the rear lawn, a well stocked library and equally well stocked bar in the rumpus room—these mark the homes of well-to-do Negroes living in the more desirable portions of the Black Belt. Many of them would flee to suburbia, too, if housing were available to Negroes there.

But the character of the Black Ghetto is not set by the newer "gilded," not-yet run down portions of it, but by the older sections where unemployment rates are high and the masses of people work with their hands —where the median level of education is just above graduation from grade school and many of the people are likely to be recent migrants from rural areas.[7]

The "ghettoization" of the Negro has resulted in the emergence of a ghetto subculture with a distinctive ethos, most pronounced, perhaps, in Harlem, but recognizable in all Negro neighborhoods. For the average Negro who walks the streets of any American Black Ghetto, the smell of barbecued ribs, fried shrimps, and chicken emanating from numerous restaurants gives olfactory reinforcement to a feeling of "at-homeness." The beat of "gut music" spilling into the street from ubiquitous tavern juke boxes and the sound of tambourines and rich harmony behind the crude

[5]The distinguished psychotherapist, Bruno Bettelheim, of the Orthogenic School of the University of Chicago, in a provocative and perceptive article in *The Nation,* October 19, 1963 ("Class, Color and Prejudice"), contends that protection of social class values is a more important variable than race prejudice in structuring relations between Negroes and whites in the North of the U.S.A.

[6]Professor Everett C. Hughes makes some original and highly pertinent remarks about new Negro middle-class communities in his introduction to the 1962 edition of Drake and Cayton's *Black Metropolis.*

[7]Thomas F. Pettigrew, *A Profile of the Negro American* (Princeton, N. J., 1964) pp. 180–181.

folk art on the windows of store-front churches give auditory confirmation to the universal belief that "We Negroes have 'soul.' " The bedlam of an occasional brawl, the shouted obscenities of street corner "foul mouths," and the whine of police sirens break the monotony of waiting for the number that never "falls," the horses that neither win, place, nor show, and the "good job" that never materializes. The insouciant swagger of teen-age drop-outs (the "cats") masks the hurt of their aimless existence and contrasts sharply with the ragged clothing and dejected demeanor of "skid-row" types who have long since stopped trying to keep up appearances and who escape it all by becoming "winoes." The spontaneous vigor of the children who crowd streets and playgrounds (with Cassius Clay, Ernie Banks, the Harlem Globe Trotters, and black stars of stage, screen, and television as their role models) and the cheerful rushing about of adults, free from the occupational pressures of the "white world" in which they work, create an atmosphere of warmth and superficial intimacy which obscures the unpleasant facts of life in the overcrowded rooms behind the doors, the lack of adequate maintenance standards, and the too prevalent vermin and rats.

This is a world whose urban "folkways" the upwardly mobile Negro middle class deplores as a "drag" on "The Race," which the upper classes wince at as an embarassment, and which race leaders point to as proof that Negroes have been victimized. But for the masses of the ghetto dwellers this is a warm and familiar milieu, preferable to the sanitary coldness of middle-class neighborhoods and a counterpart of the communities of the foreign-born, each of which has its own distinctive subcultural flavor. The arguments in the barbershop, the gossip in the beauty parlors, the "jiving" of bar girls and waitresses, the click of poolroom balls, the stomping of feet in the dance halls, the shouting in the churches are all *theirs*—and the white men who run the pawnshops, supermarts, drug stores, and grocery stores, the policemen on horseback, the teachers in blackboard jungles—all these are aliens, conceptualized collectively as "The Man," intruders on the Black Man's "turf." When an occasional riot breaks out, "The Man" and his property become targets of aggression upon which pent-up frustrations are vented. When someone during the Harlem riots of 1964 begged the street crowds to go home, the cry came back, "Baby, we *are* home!"

But the inhabitants of the Black Ghetto are not a homogeneous mass. Although, in Marxian terms, nearly all of them are "proletarians," with nothing to sell but their labor, variations in "life style" differentiate them into social classes based more upon differences in education and basic values (crystallized, in part, around occupational differences) than in meaningful differences in income. The American caste-class system has served, over the years, to concentrate the Negro population in the low-income sector of the economy. In 1961, six out of every ten Negro families had an income of less than $4000.00 per year. This situation among whites was just the reverse: six out of every ten white families had *over* $4000.00 a year at their disposal. (In the South, eight out of ten Negro families were below the $4000.00 level.) This is the income gap. Discrimination in employment creates a job ceiling, most Negroes being in blue-collar jobs.

With 60 per cent of America's Negro families earning less than $4000.00 a year, social strata emerge between the upper and lower boundaries of "no earned income" and $4000.00. Some families live a "middle-class style of life," placing heavy emphasis upon decorous public behavior and general respectability, insisting that their children "get an education" and "make something out of themselves." They prize family stability, and an unwed mother is something much more serious than "just a girl who had an accident"; pre-marital and extra-marital sexual relations, if indulged in at all, must be discreet. Social life is organized around churches and a welter of voluntary associations of all types, and, for women, "the cult of clothes" is so important that fashion shows are a popular fund raising activity even in churches. For both men and women, owning a home and going into business are highly desired goals, the former often being a realistic one, the latter a mere fantasy.

Within the same income range, and not always at the lower margin of it, other families live a "lower-class life-style" being part of the "organized" lower class, while at the lowest income levels an "unorganized" lower class exists whose members tend always to become *dis*organized—functioning in an anomic situation where gambling, excessive drinking, the use of narcotics, and sexual promiscuity are prevalent forms of behavior, and violent interpersonal relations reflect an ethos of suspicion and resentment which suffuses this deviant subculture. It is within this milieu that criminal and semi-criminal activities burgeon.

The "organized" lower class is oriented primarily around churches whose preachers, often semi-literate, exhort them to "be in the 'world' but not of it." Conventional middle-class morality and Pauline Puritanism are preached, although a general attitude of "the spirit is willing but the flesh is weak" prevails except among a minority fully committed to the Pentecostal sects. They boast, "We *live* the life"—a way of life that has been portrayed with great insight by James Baldwin in *Go Tell it on the Mountain* and *The Fire Next Time.*

Young people with talent find wide scope for expressing it in choirs, quartets, and sextets which travel from church to church (often bearing colorful names like The Four Heavenly Trumpets or the Six Singing Stars of Zion) and sometimes traveling from city to city. Such groups channel their aggressions in widely advertised "Battles of Song" and develop their talent in church pageants such as "Heaven Bound" or "Queen Esther" and fund-raising events where winners are crowned King and Queen.

These activities provide fun as well as a testing ground for talent. Some lucky young church people eventually find their fortune in the secular world as did singers Sam Cooke and Nat King Cole, while others remain in the church world as nationally known gospel singers or famous evangelists.

Adults as well as young people find satisfaction and prestige in serving as ushers and deacons, "mothers," and decaconesses, Sunday-school teachers and choir leaders. National conventions of Negro denominations and national societies of ushers and gospel singers not only develop a continent-wide nexus of associations within the organized lower class, but also throw the more ambitious and capable individuals into meaningful contact with middle-class church members who operate as role models for the less talented persons who seek to move upward. That prestige and sometimes money come so easily in these circles may be a factor militating against a pattern of delaying gratifications and seeking mobility into professional and semi-professional pursuits through higher education.

Lower-class families and institutions are constantly on the move, for in recent years the Negro lower class has suffered from projects to redevelop the inner city. By historic accident, the decision to check the expansion of physical deterioration in metropolitan areas came at a time when Negroes were the main inhabitants of substandard housing. (If urban redevelopment had been necessary sixty years ago immigrants, not Negroes, would have suffered.) In protest against large-scale demolition of areas where they live, Negroes have coined a slogan, "Slum clearance is Negro clearance." They resent the price in terms of the inconvenience thrust upon them in order to redevelop American cities,[8] and the evidence shows that, in some cities, there is no net gain in improved housing after relocation.

At the opposite pole from the Negro lower class in both life styles and life chances is the small Negro upper class whose solid core is a group in the professions, along with well-to-do businessmen who have had some higher education, but including, also, a scattering of individuals who have had college training but do not have a job commensurate with their education. These men and their spouses and children form a cohesive upper-class stratum in most Negro communities. Within this group are individuals who maintain some type of contact—though seldom any social relations—with members of the local white power élite; but whether or not they participate in occupational associations with their white peers depends upon the region of the country in which they live. (It is from this group that Negro "Exhibit A's" are recruited when white liberals are

[8]The issue of the extent to which Negroes have been victimized by urban redevelopment is discussed briefly by Robert C. Weaver in *The Urban Complex: Human Values in Urban Life* (New York, 1964). See also Martin Anderson, *The Federal Bulldozer: A Critical Analysis of Urban Renewal: 1949–1962* (Cambridge, Mass., 1964).

carrying on campaigns to "increase interracial understanding.") They must always think of themselves as symbols of racial advancement as well as individuals, and they often provide the basic leadership at local levels for organizations such as the N.A.A.C.P. and the Urban League. They must lend sympathetic support to the more militant civil rights organizations, too, by financial contributions, if not action.[9]

The life styles of the Negro upper class are similar to those of the white upper *middle* class, but it is only in rare instances that Negroes have been incorporated into the clique and associational life of this group or have intermarried into it. (Their participation in activities of the white upper class occurs more often than with those whites who have similar life styles because of Negro upper-class participation as members of various civic boards and interracial associations to which wealthy white people contribute.) Living "well" with highly developed skills, having enough money to travel, Negroes at this social level do not experience victimization in the same fashion as do the members of the lower class. Their victimization flows primarily from the fact that the social system keeps them "half in and half out," preventing the free and easy contact with their occupational peers which they need; and it often keeps them from making the kind of significant intellectual and social contributions to the national welfare that they might make if they were white. (They are also forced to experience various types of nervous strain and dissipation of energy over petty annoyances and deprivations which only the sensitive and the cultivated feel. Most barbershops, for instance, are not yet desegrated, and taxi drivers, even in the North, sometimes refuse Negro passengers.)

The Negro upper class has created a social world of its own in which a universe of discourse and uniformity of behavior and outlook are maintained by the interaction on national and local levels of members of Negro Greek-letter fraternities and sororities, college and alumni associations, professional associations, and civic and social clubs. It is probable that if all caste barriers were dropped, a large proportion of the Negro upper class would welcome complete social integration, and that these all-Negro institutions would be left in the hands of the Negro middle class, as the most capable and sophisticated Negroes moved into the orbit of the general society. Their sense of pride and dignity does not even allow them to imagine such a fate, and they pursue their social activities and play their roles as "race leaders" with little feeling of inferiority or deprivation, but always with a tragic sense of the irony of it all.

The Negro middle class covers a very wide income range, and whatever cohesion it has comes from the network of churches and social clubs to which many of its members devote a great deal of time and money. What sociologists call the Negro middle class is merely a collection of people

[9]St. Clair Drake and Horace R. Cayton, *Black Metropolis* (New York, 1962) Chap. 23, "Advancing the Race."

who have similar life styles and aspirations, whose basic goals are "living well," being "respectable," and not being crude. Middle-class Negroes, by and large, are not concerned about mobility into the Negro upper class or integration with whites. They want their "rights" and "good jobs," as well as enough money to get those goods and services which make life comfortable. They want to expand continuously their level of consumption. But they also desire "decent" schools for their children, and here the degree of victimization experienced by Negroes is most clear and the ambivalence toward policies of change most sharp. Ghetto schools are, on the whole, inferior. In fact, some of the most convincing evidence that residential segregation perpetuates inequality can be found by comparing data on school districts in Northern urban areas where *de facto* school segregation exists. (Table 1 presents such data for Chicago in 1962.)

Table 1. Comparison of White, Integrated, and Negro Schools in Chicago: 1962

Indices of Comparison	Type of School		
	White	Integrated	Negro
Total appropriation per pupil	$342.00	$320.00	$269.00
Annual teachers' salary per pupil	256.00	231.00	220.00
Per cent uncertified teachers	12.00	23.00	49.00
Number of pupils per classroom	30.95	34.95	46.80
Library resource books per pupil	5.00	3.50	2.50
Expenditures per pupil other than teachers' salaries	86.00	90.00	49.00

Adapted from a table in the U.S. Commission on Civil Rights report, *Public Schools, Negro and White* (Washington, D.C., 1962), pp. 241-248.

Awareness of the poor quality of education grew as the protest movement against *de facto* school segregation in the North gathered momentum. But while the fight was going on, doubt about the desirability of forcing the issue was always present within some sections of the broad Negro middle class. Those in opposition asked, "Are we not saying that our teachers can't teach our own children as well as whites can, or that our children can't learn unless they're around whites? Aren't we insulting ourselves?" Those who want to stress Negro history and achievement and to use the schools to build race pride also express doubts about the value of mixed schools. In fact, the desirability of race consciousness and racial solidarity seems to be taken for granted in this stratum, and sometimes there is an expression of contempt for the behavior of whites of their own and lower income levels. In the present period one even occasionally hears a remark such as "Who'd want to be integrated with *those* awful white people?"

Marxist critics would dismiss the whole configuration of Negro folkways and classways as a subculture which reinforces "false consciousness," which prevents Negroes from facing the full extent of their victimization, which keeps them from ever focusing upon what they could be because they are so busy enjoying what they are—or rationalizing their subordination and exclusion. Gunnar Myrdal, in *An American Dilemma,* goes so far as to refer to the Negro community as a "pathological" growth within American society.[10] Some novelists and poets, on the other hand, romanticize it, and some Black Nationalists glorify it. A sober analysis of the civil rights movement would suggest, however, that the striking fact about all levels of the Negro community is the absence of "false consciousness," and the presence of a keen awareness of the extent of their victimization, as well as knowledge of the forces which maintain it. Not lack of knowledge but a sense of powerlessness is the key to the Negro reaction to the caste-class system.

Few Negroes believe that Black Ghettos will disappear within the next two decades despite much talk about "open occupancy" and "freedom of residence." There is an increasing tendency among Negroes to discuss what the quality of life could be within Negro communities as they grow larger and larger. At one extreme this interest slides over into Black Nationalist reactions such as the statement by a Chicago Negro leader who said, "Let all of the white people flee to the suburbs. We'll show them that the Black Man can run the second largest city in America better than the white man. Let them go. If any of them want to come back and integrate with *us* we'll accept them."

It is probable that the Black Belts of America will increase in size rather than decrease during the next decade, for no city seems likely to commit itself to "open occupancy" (although a committee in New York has been discussing a ten-year-plan for dismantling Harlem).[11] And even if a race-free market were to appear Negroes would remain segregated unless drastic changes took place in the job ceiling and income gap. Controlled integration will probably continue, with a few upper- and upper-middle-class Negroes trickling into the suburbs and into carefully regulated mixed neighborhoods and mixed buildings within the city limits.[12] The basic

[10]See section on "The Negro Community as a Pathological Form of an American Community," Chap. 43 of Gunnar Myrdal, *An American Dilemma* (New York, 1944), p. 927.

[11]A report appeared on the front page of *The New York Times,* April 5, 1965, stating that a commission was at work trying to elaborate plans for "integrating" Harlem by 1975. Columbia University was said to be co-operating in the research aspects of the project.

[12]A successful experiment in "controlled integration" has been described by Julia Abrahamson in *A Neighborhood Finds Itself*·(New York, 1959).

problem of the next decade will be how to change Black Ghettos into relatively stable and attractive "colored communities." Here the social implications of low incomes become decisive.

THE MIDDLE CLASS
"The Negro's Middle-Class Dream"
by C. Eric Lincoln

A famous professor at a large university used to begin one of his lectures in social psychology with a description of the characteristics of a typical American family. After he had described the family's income, address, religion, the kind of car they drove, organizations to which they belonged, and the occupation of the father, he would then demand to know what social class the family belonged to. But before the students could answer, the professor would add as an apparent afterthought: "Oh yes, I forgot to mention that this is a *Negro* family!" Inevitably the students were stymied. What had begun as a simple problem became insolubly complex by the addition of the word "Negro."

Where do Negroes fit into the prevailing American class structure? Most sociologists say they don't. Negroes have a *parallel* social structure, somewhat—but not entirely—analogous to that of whites. This social parallelism, or two-caste society, is created by the color barrier which, with the rarest exceptions, prevents lateral movement from class to class between Negroes and whites. As a prominent Negro matron said in Detroit, "We Negroes and whites visit each other at times, and frequently we belong to the same civic organizations and attend the same functions, but the lines are there, and no one has to say where they are."

The Negro class structure had its roots in the institution of American slavery, which, in ignoring the African's cultural presumptions, leveled all classes and force-fused highly disparate individuals and groups into one conglomerate mass—"the Negro slave," or simply "the Negro," a word which, in America, became synonymous with "slave" or the "descendent of slaves." Prince and servant, Eboe and Mandingo, Moslem and spirit-worshiper were all the same to the slavemaster, who saw them only as commodities to be bought and sold, or as a labor supply for his vast plantations.

Whatever the basis of past distinctions, the Negro social structure in America had to evolve out of conditions connected with plantation life, and within a context which recognized the absolute superiority of the white slave owner (although not necessarily that of the small, nonslaveholding white farmers, who were looked upon by house servants and slave owners alike as "poor white trash").

The Negro's "society," then, had four more or less distinct social classes. In ascending order, they were: (1) field hands (who had least contact with the socializing influences of the white environment); (2) mechanics and artisans (bricklayers, carpenters, ironworkers, bakers, etc., who were frequently hired out by the month or the year to merchants or builders in the cities); (3) valets, butlers, maids, cooks, and other household servants (whose frequent personal contact with whites made them the most "acculturated" class), and (4) free Negroes (who had bought their freedom or had become free by manumission—often because of faithfulness or some heroic exploit).

As slaves, the house-servant class had by far the highest proportion of mulattoes. While this did not by any means exempt them from the normal vigors incident to being slaves, including sale, the light-skinned mistresses of the slavemasters were often granted petty privileges and their children were more frequently given their freedom than those of any other class.

At the end of the slave period the mulattoes sought to establish themselves as a distinct occupational and social class within the Negro subculture. For the most part they continued as servants and retainers to their erstwhile masters—as dressmakers, barbers, coachmen, and the like. For more than a generation they clung tenaciously to a certain degree of status derived from catering exclusively to the "quality" folk (as they had done in slavery) under the then current slogan of (serving) "mighty few white folks and no niggers a-tall!"

By the turn of the century, however, as the economy of the South began to revive, the mulatto "retainers" were progressively displaced by European immigrants and poor whites who were suddenly willing to do "Negro work." From that date neither occupation nor color has been a reliable index of social standing among Negroes.

Today a light skin is not an automatic key to social status. In this day of the Negro's increasing race pride and his subtle impulse to nationalism, a light skin *can* be a handicap, especially if it is associated with "recent" miscegenation. Mass education and the indiscriminate rise to power and money of significant numbers of Negroes irrespective of their grandparents' station in the slave society have all but destroyed the effectiveness of the Negro's private color bar. Leadership in civil rights as well as in the professions has long since passed from the mulatto class. As a matter of fact, the number of mulattoes in the general Negro population seems to be declining steadily and there is no evidence that legal integration will soon replace clandestine miscegenation in restoring the ratio of light color.

There is no unanimity of opinion as to what proportion of today's Negroes fall into the traditional "lower," "middle," and "upper" classes of the Negro social structure. Prof. Tillman Cothran, head of the graduate department of sociology at Atlanta University, estimates that "not more than 25 per cent of the Negro population can be called middle class by any reasonable standards. And not more than 5 per cent can be called upper class."

Other sociologists have argued that if one applies the full spectrum of criteria by which the white social structure is measured—ranging from income to education, affiliation, residence, etc.—the Negro middle class is reduced to 4 per cent or 5 per cent of the Negro population, and the Negro upper class vanishes altogether.

Such an estimate is, I think, too drastic. If the theory of parallel social structure is valid (and there seems to be no other way to measure "class" in an essentially segregated society), certainly it can be shown that Negroes and whites of similar education and income exhibit many of the same desires, restraints, conformities, and general patterns of behavior.

America's self-image is that of an essentially equalitarian society best represented by the middle class. Most Americans concede that there are a few snobs and millionaires at the top, and a few poor people in Appalachia, or somewhere, at the bottom, but America is middle-class, and most Americans identify themselves as belonging to the middle class.

Implicit in this identification is a belief in "democracy" and "fair play," and also the expectation of "the good life"—a home, a car, a regular vacation, an education for the children, regular promotions, and maybe even extras like a boat or a summer place. Despite the pessimism of the sociologists, more and more Negroes share this dream, and to an increasing degree they are making it come true for themselves and their children.

The Negro middle class is made up primarily of Negro professionals, with schoolteachers probably constituting the largest single bloc. Teachers along with doctors, lawyers, college professors, small businessmen, ministers, and postal workers have traditionally made up the bulk of the Negro middle class.

However, the recent availability of new kinds of jobs not previously held by Negroes has begun to modify the character of this group. Technicians, politicians, clerical and sales personnel, social workers, labor-union officials, minor government bureaucrats, and an increasing managerial class in such agencies as federal housing and local units of national corporations have helped to broaden the occupational range of the Negro middle class.

Under the Kennedy-Johnson Administration a few Negroes have been appointed to the upper echelons of government officialdom, and within the past two or three years a few Negroes have reached executive status in white corporations. A recent dinner in New York honored seven Negroes who were vice-presidents or held managerial positions in major firms. In Washington, Dr. James Nabrit, President of Howard University, and Dr. Frank Jones have been elected to the board of directors of a major bank. And in that city several Negroes have been elected to the Board of Trade.

It is difficult to set a salary range for a given social class because social status does not depend on money alone. Some upper-class whites are impoverished, but their families have once held fortunes and they have traditions of culture and attainment. Since the American Negro's family traditions seldom antedate the Civil War, Negro society puts an undue emphasis on money and material acquisitions. It is often said by Negro critics themselves that "anybody with a dollar, no matter where he stole it, can belong to Negro society."

Most Negroes, like most other Americans, earn their living legitimately, of course, but because of job discrimination and lack of skills, the total income of the typical middle-class Negro family will be substantially lower than that of a typical white family of the middle class. An arbitrary figure of $7,500 a year as the average income of a middle-class family would severely limit the number of Negroes who could be called middle-class.

Some Negro families do exceed a $7,500 income, but the vast majority of those who do are families in which both husband and wife work full time. Very frequently among home-buying Negroes, the head of the family works at two jobs, and occasionally at three. Such supplementary work or "moonlighting"—often driving a taxi, waiting on tables, tending bar, or bell-hopping—is known as "a hustle," a term quite familiar to the Negro middle class.

In many of the large cities of the North such as New York or Boston where undeveloped land is nonexistent, the middle-class Negro, who has the means and the desire to live elsewhere, is locked in the black ghetto. Only with difficulty can he find a house or apartment outside the ghetto in a white community. As a consequence, many Negroes despair of ever leaving the slums, no matter what their education or income.

Money that would normally go for a new house is spent in the hopeless task of refurbishing antiquated apartments, or in conspicuous consumption which somehow helps them to forget the horror of living in the nation's Harlems. (In the South the housing problem is not nearly so acute. Space for building can be had in most Southern cities, although it is likely to be in a segregated community.)

The style of living of the Negro middle class does not differ radically from that of its white counterpart. Bridge is a favorite pastime among both men and women. Those who have the leisure belong to innumerable social clubs. An increasing number of Negro men play golf and participate in water sports where facilities are available. In the South fishing and hunting are favorite pastimes, but only if one has the full regalia of dress and all the latest equipment shown in the sports magazines.

To a far greater degree than whites, Negroes maintain affiliation in the graduate chapters of their college fraternities and sororities, and these organizations are important indexes of social stratification. Women of a given sorority tend to marry men of its fraternal opposite number. Together the eight major Negro sororities and fraternities constitute the nucleus of any imaginary "blue book" of Negro society.

The children of the Negro middle class are taught to aspire to middle-class standards. They take lessons in piano and creative dancing on Saturday mornings and attend carefully planned parties on Saturday night. A few are sent East to private schools.

Sometimes the interpretation of middle-class values takes an unusual twist. A Negro matron in a Memphis department store, for example, refused to corral her two children who were busily chasing through the store and littering the aisles with merchandise. She explained: "The white kids do it and the salesclerks think its cute. I don't want my children inhibited by feeling that they can't do anything other kids can do."

In Washington, among those aspiring to the middle class, or those who are recently "in," status is measured by the quantity and the cost of whiskey served one's guests. The most conspicuous feature in such a home will be the bar appointments, and it is considered equally insulting for a guest to refuse a drink as it is for the host to offer his guests "cheap whiskey." One Washingtonian gained prominence in his set by consistently being first to serve rare and expensive imports before they were well known in the Negro community. He learned what was "in" by frequenting an exclusive liquor store patronized by high government officials.

It used to be said that the difference between a Negro making $50 a week and driving a Cadillac and a white man making $100 a week and driving a Chevrolet was that the Negro, having nowhere to live, needed the bigger car to sleep in! On Atlanta's West Side, where the Cadillac (or Lincoln) frequently comes with a split-level ranch house, it is popular to have the main (or "status") car match the house in color and appointments.

A second car for the Negro professional family is not unusual. Unlike most white middle-class families having two cars, the Negro's second car is likely to be as big and expensive as his first. An expensive automobile to drive to work is often as much a matter of personal prestige for the working Negro woman as for her husband. Hence, it is common to see large numbers of Pontiacs, Oldsmobiles, and Mercurys parked near the schools where Negro women are employed as teachers.

A cottage at Oak Bluffs, on Martha's Vineyard, or in Maine or Upper Michigan can be claimed by a few. A very small number of Negroes go to Europe and to the Caribbean or Mexico on vacation. A sort of pilgrimage of Africa has high status value for those seeking to "understand their pre-Western heritage."

Some Negroes are in the middle class because there is nowhere else for them to go. These few might be considered "upper class," but there is a certain incongruity in talking about a Negro "upper class" so long as the color barrier operates to bar Negroes who are otherwise qualified from full participation in American social life. "There may not be an upper class," says Clarence Coleman, southeastern director of the National Urban League, "but there is a 'power elite' which abstracts itself from the rank and file of the middle class and participates to an important extent in the decision-making of the white power structure where Negroes are concerned."

Certainly this power elite does exist. But where it was not created by the white establishment, its power derives from white recognition and respect. Militant civil rights leaders have discovered this again and again when the white establishment has refused to negotiate with the Negro community except through "recognized channels."

The Negro middle class, like any middle class, is preoccupied with making secure its hard-won social position. This is a characteristic of middle-class aspirations.

Because of this preoccupation the Negro middle class has been criticized for not being more deeply and realistically involved in the struggle for civil rights. The criticism is well placed, for given more manpower, more money, and more dedication, it is obvious that more walls could be breached. But this is not the whole story, and the lack of total involvement may not be an accurate index of middle-class feelings and intentions.

Much of the criticism has come from within the ranks of the middle class itself. The Urban League's Clarence Coleman sees the middle class as the buffer between the militants, whose aspirations are frequently unrealistic in terms of present possibilities, and the power elite which seems concerned to protect itself and its privileged positions from too rapid social change.

James A. Tillman, Jr., executive director of the Greater Minneapolis Fair Housing Program and a frequent writer on problems of social change, describes the Negro middle class as "that class of Negroes who have bought the inane, invalid, and self-defeating notion that the black man can be integrated into a hostile white society without conflict."

Tillman denounces the power elite as "the fixers and go-betweens who cover up rather than expose the violent nature of racism. They are," he declares, "the most dangerous clique in America."

Tillman's sentiments are echoed by Cecil Moore, militant civil rights attorney and head of the Philadelphia NAACP. Moore, who himself came from an accomplished West Virginia family, insists that "the Negro middle class, and all those who consider themselves above the middle class, 'subsist on the blood of the brother down under,' the brother they are supposed to be leading. Who do these Negroes think they're kidding?" he asks, and then answers his own question. "They're kidding nobody but the white folks who are willing to pay 'philanthropy' to keep from having to come to grips with the central problem, which is 'full and complete citizenship for all Americans, *right now!*' "

Despite all such criticism, however, the Negro middle class has borne the brunt of the civil rights protest. Critics of the so-called "Black Bourgeoisie" have not always given them credit for the maturity and social responsibility upon which the Negro's fight for first-class citizenship has finally depended. The civil rights fight, at least insofar as it visualizes an integrated society, is a middle-class fight. The NAACP, CORE, the Urban League, and the followers of Dr. Martin Luther King are all middle-class. (Indeed, the lower-class Negro has yet to be stirred by the promise of integration. He is more concerned with such immediate needs as jobs and housing than with abstract values like integration. He looks neither to Martin Luther King nor to Roy Wilkins; in fact, the leader of the black masses has yet to appear.)

In Atlanta and other Southern cities during the massive sit-ins of 1962–63, housewives baked pies, made sandwiches, and provided transportation for the students. Negro businessmen donated food, gasoline, and other supplies. Then doctors, nurses, professors, and businessmen walked the picket lines. Similar middle-class support has assisted the activities of CORE in New York, Cleveland, and other cities in the North. Voter registration is essentially a middle-class project.

Middle-class leadership and support of the civil rights movement has not been without ambivalence. Desegregated schools frequently mean that Negro teachers will lose their jobs. Negro businessmen often lose their most competent clerical help to recently desegregated industries. Negro restaurants, drugstores, real estate firms, and the like may be adversely affected by desegregation. Some Negro churches have lost members to white churches. In a fully integrated society the Negro middle class would lose its identity. Indeed, it would cease to exist.

Some Negroes recognize all this, of course, and fight against it. Nor can it be said that the majority of the middle class is active in the rights struggle. What can be said is that the struggle is for the most part led, financed, and supported by the Negro middle class and, of course, its white allies.

Certainly Negro leadership has become a "profession," and in some cases a lucrative one. Yet most Negroes trying to help improve things are in search of neither fame nor fortune and may be themselves disadvantaged by the race issue. A. Maceo Walker and Jesse Turner of Memphis, for example, both executive officers of a sensitive banking business that has important white as well as Negro depositors, come to mind. These men and others like them have little to gain for themselves personally, yet they have given leadership to the civil rights movement in their city for years. Other cases could be cited across the country.

In Washington, I talked with the distinguished Negro attorney, Belford Lawson, and his wife, Marjorie McKenzie, who, as associate judge of the Juvenile Court there, is no less distinguished. The Lawsons were undisturbed about the "black backlash" against the Negro middle class, although they felt that the middle class was just beginning to realize its responsibilities to the Negro masses. Nor did they recognize a middle-class backlash against the lower class (which has been roundly criticized by some Negroes for rioting in the streets and undoing the patient and painful accomplishments of middle-class leaders).

"We must press on to the next phase," Lawson said. "And it would be foolish to wait until all of us have reached the place a few of us have reached today. Negroes, like other people, move at different rates of speed. Our circumstances vary. Now we have a handful of civil rights and no money. Our next front is economic. We want to buy stocks in banks and corporations and sit on their boards. Every time a Negro reaches an executive position in a major corporation, he is in a better position to help that Negro in the streets without a job."

Mr. Lawson believes that it is time to move on into the American mainstream. "Breaking into the white man's economy" he believes to be essential to any further progress on the part of Negroes. "In Washington," he says, "where many social and cultural affairs are integrated, many doors would open if the Negro would only push on them."

Negroes are pushing—for status and respectability and economic security. They are less concerned with integration for integration's sake than they are with being comfortable—middle-class—and unhindered in enjoying all that America has to offer. The riots in the city streets are not the work of sinister Communist agents, except where such agents move in to exploit an already festering social situation. Nor are they the work of hopheads and hoodlums bent on the destruction of the fruits of years of patient interracial effort.

They are the social expressions of pent-up anxiety and frustration which derive from the hopelessness of the conditions under which those people live. *They* cannot appropriate the "middle-class image," the American norm for democratic living.

I sat recently in a comfortable middle-class home in northwest Washington talking with Jerry Coward and his wife, both schoolteachers in the District of Columbia school system. "You know, when we moved into this neighborhood five years ago," Jerry said, "the whites all threatened to move out. A few stayed. And since that time two brand-new white families have moved in, right down the block. Professional people, too. When white people start moving into, instead of away from, a Negro neighborhood, I guess we've got it made."

I guess they have.

five

What causes people to deviate from norms? Or, put another way, what causes people to conform? Does society ever actually cause deviance by labeling certain behavior as deviant, or is a deviant always defined solely by the act itself? What relationship does opportunity have to deviance? Black Americans are now questioning the idea that all behavior which does not conform to White middle-class standards must necessarily be considered deviant.

Deviance

Deviance involves a failure to conform to the norms of society. Where the society is simple and homogeneous, such as a hunting-and-gathering band, deviance is relatively easy to depict. Such societies contain a high degree of value consensus; most norms apply to all members. Deviant behavior in such a setting is quickly noted and controlled. In complex, industrial societies, however, universal norms are few. Because such societies are composed of many different groups, each having somewhat separate norms, deviance is more difficult to determine. What would be conformity for a farm family would be deviancy for an urban, wealthy family. What is one man's conformity is another man's deviance.

Because complex societies often contain such diverse groups, it is important in a discussion of deviance to determine just what norms will be used for reference. The most pervasive norms in American society seem to revolve around norms common to the middle class, such as thrift, personal honesty, cleanliness, and goal deferment. By such standards a member of a delinquent gang is, of course, a deviant. However, a gang member is not a deviant by the standards of his own gang. He conforms to the norms of his gang just as a middle-class businessman conforms to the norms of his company when he is at work.

Persons in the lower class are likely to exhibit more deviance than other members of society for a number of reasons. Families with limited resources usually have more difficulty following the traditional routes of success, yet they often desire the same goals as other members of the society, and are therefore, more likely to seek new and different ways of achieving these goals. Such ways may often be viewed by other members of society as undesirable.

Within a complex society special interest groups that have power will support political candidates and the passage of laws that benefit their own interests. It is not surprising, therefore, that in the United States most income tax deductions favor business interests. Members of the lower class often find themselves in violation of laws simply because they have such a limited influence on law makers. Prosperous persons also have more understanding of the law and are therefore less likely to violate it through ignorance.

The higher rate of crimes among the lower class is also partly due to the procedures used by law enforcement agencies to detect deviance. The police are highly sensitive to those kinds of crimes that are commonly committed by members of the lower class and therefore tend to more heavily patrol lower-class neighborhoods. Some forms of deviance more common to the middle and upper classes often go undetected. Examples would include tax evasion and embezzlement. It is also the case that some activities are seen as being deviant when committed by members of the lower class but are evaluated differently when performed by others. Many forms of juvenile delinquency fit this pattern.

Deviance would normally be expected to call forth negative sanctions to ensure conformity. Yet some deviance may be tolerated. New members of a group, for example, are usually given a certain period of time to adapt to the norms of the group. Some forms of deviance may even be rewarded: Combat medals are given to soldiers who exhibit extreme bravery on the battle field. Saints, geniuses, adventurers, and heroes usually exhibit socially approved forms of deviance.

Blacks in America have distinct norms and values, although there are strong differences between social classes. While Blacks in the middle class tend to follow norms that are similar to those followed by the rest of middle-class society, some of the norms and values of lower-class Blacks are considered deviant by middle-class standards. However, within the Black community, such Blacks are not seen as deviants.

Alphonso Pinkney's article covers a wide range of deviance although the stress is upon criminal activities. Note particularly the relation between social class and type of crime committed. Black Americans tend to be involved in relatively fewer crimes of embezzlement and forgery than their white counterparts because they do not have access to positions that permit the commission of such crimes. One cannot dip into the till at the bank unless he works there first. The lower economic position of Blacks also means that they are more likely to be convicted when charged with an offense and likely to spend more time in jail.

Harold Finestone examines the deviant role of the heroin addict. With few models of success in the ghetto, young Blacks often see the "Cat" as a figure of admiration. His ability to "hustle" and "play it cool" cause him to stand out from the drudgery of ghetto existence. In a very real sense his role is an adaption to oppressive conditions in the ghetto and provides him with certain satisfactions that he is unable to obtain in any other way. The language of the "Cat" illustrates a feature found in many deviant roles. The use of slang terms serves to bind members of a deviant group together and set them off from the rest of society.

THE STATISTICS

"Social Deviance"

by Alphonso Pinkney

"I can conceive of no Negro native to this country who has not, by the age of puberty, been irreparably scarred by the conditions of his life. . . . The wonder is not that so many are ruined but that so many survive."[1] This statement by James Baldwin capsules the role of environmental factors in producing in black Americans deviations from the professed norms of the larger society. Black people are forced to live under harsh conditions in the United States; yet high standards of civic responsibility are expected of them.

No discussion of social deviance among black Americans can ignore the role of racism in American life. Individuals, social agencies, and social institutions responsible for the enforcement of social norms in American society operate within a long-established framework which precludes equality of treatment for black citizens. In no case is this situation more pronounced than in the relationship between the police and the black community. Policemen, like citizens in general, operate with a set of assumptions about black people which predisposes them to differential treatment.[2] In this regard policemen do not differ significantly from other public officials in the United States. Therefore such circumstances must enter into any disucssion of the extent and causes of social deviance among black people in the United States.

In this chapter attention is focused on three areas in which behavior is reported to exceed the "tolerance limit of the community."[3] Crime and delinquency, mental illness, and drug addiction have been selected because of the availability of research findings in these areas and because other areas (e.g., family disorganization) are discussed elsewhere.

---

[1]James Baldwin, *Notes of a Native Son* (Boston: Beacon Press, 1957), p. 71.

[2]See, for example, Aaron V. Cicourel, *The Social Organization of Juvenile Justice* (New York: Wiley, 1968); Jerome H. Skolnick, *Justice Without Trial: Law Enforcement in Democratic Society* (New York: Wiley, 1966).

[3]See Marshall B. Clinard, *Sociology of Deviant Behavior* (New York: Holt, 1963), pp. 22–31.

Crime and Delinquency

Statistics on crime and delinquency in the United States are notoriously inaccurate. In addition to differences among various administrative agencies in compiling statistics on criminal and delinquent behavior, special problems arise in connection with black people.[4] The position occupied by black people in a racist society means that they are more likely than whites to be arrested, indicted, and convicted. Furthermore, black people are less likely than white persons to receive probation, parole, suspended sentence, pardon, or commutation of the death sentence.[5] In short, black people are discriminated against in the administration of justice, just as they are in virtually every aspect of American life. The relative proportion of crimes recorded for black people, therefore, must be questioned.

For a variety of reasons, official statistics on Negro criminality are exaggerated.[6] Many acts that are considered crimes among black persons are not so considered when they are committed by white persons. In several political subdivisions laws relating to such practices as segregation and vagrancy are especially designed for black people. Black men have been arrested and convicted for such acts as "looking at a white woman" and refusing to comply with the racial etiquette of the South. Black people are frequently blamed and falsely convicted for crimes which have actually been committed by white persons.

Black people are especially vulnerable to misuse of power by the police. Police sometimes arrest Negroes on the slightest suspicion and obtain "confessions" through the excessive use of force. Similarly, Negroes are often arrested in police raids as a means of earning fees. Once arrested, Negroes face a series of acts of discrimination in the courts, on the part of juries, judges, and prosecutors. Anti-Negro prejudice on the part of court officials frequently results in Negroes' being convicted for crimes which they have not committed. One of the most clear-cut cases of discriminatory behavior is the disproportionately high percentage of black people executed under capital punishment. For example, between 1930 and 1963, 54 percent of the 3,833 persons executed in the United States were black.[7]

Because they are poor and frequently unable to pay fines, convicted Negroes are less likely than convicted white persons to escape prison

[4]See, for example, Ronald H. Beattie, "Problems of Criminal Statistics in the United States," *The Journal of Criminal Law, Criminology and Police Science,* Vol. 46 (July–August 1955), 178–86.
[5]See Donald Cressy, "Crime," *Contemporary Social Problems,* eds. Robert K. Merton and Robert A. Nisbet (New York: Harcourt, Brace, 1966), pp. 151–53; Guy B. Johnson, "The Negro and Crime," *The Annals of the American Academy of Political and Social Science,* Vol. 271 (September 1941), 93–104; Gunnar Myrdal, *An American Dilemma* (New York: Harper, 1944), pp. 966–79.
[6]This discussion relies heavily on Johnson, *op. cit.,* pp. 95–103.
[7]*The Negro Handbook* (Chicago: Johnson Publishing Co., 1966), p. 111.

sentences. On their arrival at prison, Negroes again encounter a series of acts of discrimination. Prison officials share the same anti-Negro prejudice that pervades the larger society. Black prisoners are frequently required to perform the most difficult work tasks. They are less likely to be pardoned because they cannot usually exert the political pressure necessary for such acts. Similarly, they are discriminated against in the use of parole as a method of release and rehabilitation.

Despite the many shortcomings in collecting crime statistics and in the administration of justice for black people, official reports usually form the basis for estimating the extent of criminal behavior in the United States. These statistics report that the crime rate for black people exceeds that for whites in all categories. The proportionate number of arrests is greater, as is the rate of commitments to state and federal prisons.

Crime

Official crime statistics in the United States have been reported yearly since 1930 by the Federal Bureau of Investigation (FBI) of the Department of Justice. These data are based on the number of arrests reported by police departments throughout the United States. In 1965 reports were received from law enforcement agencies having jurisdiction over 92 percent of the population. Reports are made in accordance with a handbook supplied to local law enforcement officials by the FBI. This handbook outlines the procedures for scoring and classifying crimes. Thus the annual report of the FBI is the most comprehensive index of arrests available.

According to the 1965 report, Negroes, comprising 10.8 percent of the population, accounted for 28.4 percent of the arrests for criminal acts (see Table 1). The proportion of arrests varied by offenses charged. Nearly three-fourths (73.2 percent) of all persons arrested for gambling were Negroes, compared with only 14.2 percent of the persons arrested for embezzlement. In all categories of offenses, however, the rate of arrests for black people was higher than that for white persons. Assuming that the arrests reported by the FBI represent a reasonably reliable indicator of conventional crimes committed in the United States, arrests for specific offenses in which Negroes significantly exceed their proportion in the total population may provide some clues to an explanation of differential rates of criminality among black and white persons.

Inspection of the table reveals little about the crimes for which black people are arrested other than the general observation that they were vastly overrepresented in the total arrests when compared with their numbers in the population. However, a few patterns emerge. (1) The rate of arrests for those crimes which are defined as "serious" (the first seven in the table) was greater than for "minor" crimes. For example, black people accounted for at least one-half of the arrests for murder and nonnegligent

Table 1. Total Arrests and Negro Arrests, United States, 1965

Offense Charged	Total	Negro	Percent Negro
All Arrests	4,743,123	1,347,994	28.4
1. Criminal homicide			
(a) murder and nonnegligent manslaughter	6,509	3,704	56.9
(b) manslaughter by negligence	2,457	541	22.0
2. Forcible rape	9,328	4,665	50.0
3. Robbery	39,854	22,546	56.6
4. Aggravated assault	70,285	36,558	52.0
5. Burglary (breaking and entering)	181,429	59,673	32.9
6. Larceny (theft)	364,072	109,792	30.2
7. Auto theft	93,108	26,372	28.3
8. Other assaults	193,475	73,284	37.9
9. Arson	5,516	1,127	20.4
10. Forgery and counterfeiting	27,477	5,440	19.8
11. Fraud	49,537	8,252	16.6
12. Embezzlement	6,781	966	14.2
13. Stolen property (buying, receiving, or possessing)	15,869	5,463	34.4
14. Vandalism	82,798	16,074	19.4
15. Weapons: carrying, possessing, etc.	49,731	26,226	52.7
16. Prostitution and commercialized vice	30,635	17,598	57.4
17. Sex offenses (except forcible rape and prostitution)	53,422	13,759	25.7
18. Narcotic drug laws	31,294	12,069	38.6
19. Gambling	86,627	64,135	73.2
20. Offenses against family and children	59,958	19,699	32.9
21. Driving under the influence of alcohol	231,899	38,966	16.8
22. Liquor laws	167,815	31,929	19.0
23. Drunkenness	1,516,548	354,158	23.4
24. Disorderly conduct	503,849	179,506	35.6
25. Vagrancy	115,305	28,161	24.4
26. All other offenses (except traffic)	511,121	135,946	26.6
27. Suspicion	76,183	21,721	28.8
28. Curfew and loitering violations	71,138	14,521	20.4
29. Runaways	88,103	15,142	17.2

Source: Compiled from Federal Bureau of Investigation, Uniform Crime Reports—1965, Table 25, p. 117.

manslaughter, forcible rape, robbery, and aggravated assault. (2) The arrest rate for black people was lowest for crimes which are directly related to socioeconomic status. These crimes, which include forgery and counterfeiting, fraud, and embezzlement, generally involve the use and misappropriation of money and defrauding. They usually involve larger financial transactions than Negroes are capable of engaging in *and* positions in the social structure of business which are usually denied black people. (3) The arrest rate for black people was especially high for the illegal possession of weapons (52.7 percent of total), prostitution and commercialized vice

(57.4 percent of total), and gambling (73.2 percent ot total). The latter two crimes are clearly related to the precarious economic position which black people occupy, whereas the possession of weapons is no doubt a function of the frustrations which result from this depressed state.

The arrest rate for black people may be compared with the rate of court commitments involving felony prisoners and with the characteristics of prisoners in state prisons. In 1960 black people accounted for 35 percent of all court commitments for felony prisoners and 38.7 percent of all prisoners confined in state prisons.[8] There is a sizable discrepancy between the arrest rate of black people (30 percent of the total in 1960), the rate of court commitments, and the proportion of prisoners in state prisons. This discrepancy between arrests and commitments represents, among other things, discrimination on the part of court personnel, the inability of black people to pay cash fines in lieu of prison sentences, and the lack of access to bail and efficient legal counsel. The discrepancy between the rate of commitment and the state prison census no doubt reflects discrimination against black people insofar as pardon and parole are concerned.

Despite the shortcomings enumerated above, it is likely that black people commit a disproportionately high percentage of crimes in the United States.[9] Numerous reasons for this phenomenon may be advanced. (1) In the United States black people occupy a separate and subordinate economic and social position which leads to frustration. Their frustrations are usually displaced in acts of aggression against fellow Negroes, thus leading to a high proportion of intraracial criminal acts. (2) As Myrdal has demonstrated, the caste system under which black people live operates in such a way as to prevent them from indentifying with the society and the law. The very legal system itself is manipulated to discriminate against black people.[10] (3) Black persons, far more than white persons, are forced to live in deteriorated sections of cities. These areas are characterized by widespread social disorganization and organization in terms of criminal values, as well as poverty, poor housing, restrictions on settlement, and limited outlets for recreation and employment. "Out of these and similar conditions arise elements conducive to greater criminality, as well as other forms of pathology, among the Negro population."[11] (4) The high

---

[8]U.S. Department of Justice, Federal Bureau of Prisons, *National Prisoner Statistics* (Washington, D.C.: Federal Bureau of Prisons, 1960), pp. 40, 57.

[9]See, for example, J. T. Blue, "The Relationship of Juvenile Delinquency, Race, and Economic Status," *Journal of Negro Education,* Vol. 17 (Fall 1948), 469–77; Earl R. Moses, "Differentials in Crime Rates Between Negroes and Whites Based on Comparisons of Four Socio-Economically Equated Areas," *American Sociological Review,* Vol. 12 (August 1947), 411–20.

[10]Myrdal, *op. cit.,* pp. 975–76.

[11]Moses, *op. cit.,* p. 420; See also Albert K. Cohen, *Delinquent Boys* (Glencoe, Ill.: Free Press, 1955); and W. B. Miller, "Lower Class Culture as a Generating Milieu of Gang Delinquency," *Journal of Social Issues,* Vol. 14 (1958), 5–19.

crime rate among black people is partially a function of their reaction to having their means to success blocked by discriminatory behavior. "Crime may thus be utilized as a means of escape, ego enhancement, expression of aggression, or upward mobility."[12] Black people have internalized the cultural goals of the larger society, but the socially acceptable means for achieving these goals are unavailable to them. (5) Black people are over-represented in the lower class, and recorded crime tends to be concentrated in this class.[13] "White-collar crime," the middle- and upper-class speciality, is far less likely to be recorded as such.[14] Lower-class people, both black and white, live in a society in which they are surrounded by affluence, yet they must live in poverty. The association between economics and recorded crime is a pronounced one.

Juvenile delinquency

It is impossible to estimate the amount of juvenile crime committed in the United States for the same reasons that statistics on crime in general are unreliable indicators of criminal behavior.[15] Age, rather than offense, is the defining characteristic of juvenile delinquents, and the age at which an offender is defined as a juvenile varies from state to state. Usually, however, juveniles are defined as persons under the age of 18. As with adults, black youths are far more likely to be arrested for criminal acts than white youths. In 1965, for example, the FBI reported that Negroes accounted for 23 percent of all arrests of persons under 18 years of age.[16] Other investigations corroborate these findings.[17] The same factors operating to inflate the Negro crime rate in general must be considered in any discussion of juvenile delinquency among Negroes. Black youths encounter the same types of discrimination as do black adults. Studies report that black youths accused of criminal acts are more likely to be institutionalized than white youths and that they are likely to be committed younger, for less serious offenses, and with fewer court appearances.[18]

[12]Thomas F. Pettigrew, *A Profile of the Negro American* (Princeton, N.J.: Van Nostrand, 1964), p. 156.

[13]Albert J. Reiss, Jr., and Albert L. Rhodes, "The Distribution of Juvenile Delinquency in the Social Structure," *American Sociological Review,* Vol. 26 (October 1961), 720–32; Calvin F. Schmid, "Urban Crime Areas: Part I," *American Sociological Review,* Vol. 25 (August 1960), 527–42; Calvin F. Schmid, "Urban Crime Areas: Part II," *American Sociological Review,* Vol. 25 (October 1960), 655–78.

[14]E. H. Sutherland, *White Collar Crime* (New York: The Dryden Press, 1949).

[15]See Albert K. Cohen and James F. Short, "Juvenile Delinquency," in Merton and Nisbet (eds), *op. cit.,* pp. 90–91.

[16]Federal Bureau of Investigation, *Uniform Crime Reports—1965* (Washington, D.C.: Government Printing Office, 1966), p. 118.

[17]Joseph H. Douglass, "The Extent and Characteristics of Juvenile Delinquency Among Negroes in the United States," *Journal of Negro Education,* Vol. 28 (Summer 1959), 214–29.

[18]Sidney Axelrod, "Negro and White Male Institutionalized Delinquents," *American Journal of Sociology,* Vol. 57 (May 1952), 569–74; Mary H. Diggs, "Some Problems and Needs of Negro Children as Revealed by Comparative Delinquency and Crime Statistics," *Journal*

Even when allowances are made for discrimination against black youths and for inaccuracies in reporting, rates of juvenile delinquency among Negroes are reported to be especially high compared to white youths in large urban centers. For example, between 1951 and 1962 the rate for central Harlem was reported to be at least twice as high as the rate for New York City as a whole.[19] Data on delinquency from predominantly Negro sections of several other cities—St. Louis, Missouri; Boston, Massachusetts; Minneapolis, Minnesota; Cleveland, Ohio; and Syracuse, New York—indicate that the rates in these sections vary anywhere from twice to four times the rates for the cities as a whole.[20] It is reported that in 1960, almost one-third (31 percent) of the juvenile delinquents in the Lexington, Kentucky, Standard Metropolitan Statistical Area were Negroes, although nonwhites comprised only 15 percent of the population from ages 5 to 19.[21] The likelihood, then, is that Negro (and other minority) youths commit a disproportionately high percentage of acts of juvenile crime in the United States.

In addition to factors contributing to the high crime rate among black people in general (as enumerated above), black youths in the United States are distinguishable from youths in the dominant society in ways which are likely to contribute to nonconforming behavior. Even when compared with black adults, black youths are especially vulnerable to arrest. For example, in one city where two-thirds of the police interviewed openly admitted anti-Negro prejudice, a policeman was asked why he had apprehended a Negro youth. He replied that he "looked suspicious," which he explained by saying, "He was a Negro wearing dark glasses at midnight."[22] The appearance of black youths frequently corresponds to the policeman's perception of the confirmed delinquent.

The family in which the black youth lives serves to contribute to non-conforming behavior as defined by the dominant middle-class society. The black family, with its lower-class status, is more likely than the white family to be characterized by disorganization.[23] The family is frequently incomplete, often lacking the father. The incidence of juvenile delinquency among children from broken homes is greater than among children who come from homes where both parents are present. In such families the mother is frequently required to work outside the home, and

of Negro Education, Vol. 19 (1950), 290–97; Irving Piliavin and Scott Briar, "Police Encounters with Juveniles," *American Journal of Sociology,* Vol. 60 (September 1964), 206–14.

[19] *Youth in the Ghetto* (New York: Harlem Youth Opportunities Unlimited, 1964). p. 138.

[20] Kenneth Clark, *Dark Ghetto* (New York: Harper & Row, 1965), pp. 86–87.

[21] James K. Ball, Alan Ross, and Alice Simpson, "Incidence and Estimated Prevalence of Recorded Delinquency in a Metropolitan Area," *American Sociological Review,* Vol. 29 (February 1964), 90–93.

[22] Piliavin and Briar, *op. cit.,* p. 212.

[23] Ruth S. Cavan, "Negro Family Disorganization and Juvenile Delinquency," *Journal of Negro Education,* Vol. 28 (Summer 1959), 230–39.

the child lacks parental supervision or guidance. Interpersonal relations between parents and children in lower-class families are frequently characterized by indifference, hostility, fear, and the absence of sympathy and kindness. These elements are reported to be associated with delinquency in youth.[24]

Within the black community the youths frequently see aggressive behavior as a means of obtaining and maintaining status.[25] Having been rejected, as well as subjected to constant threats, by the larger society and by middle-class Negroes, these youths resort to aggressive behavior. "Deviant conduct, therefore, might be approached as a nonconforming means of survival in a segregated, presumably hostile society."[26] Techniques are thereby developed for dealing with the emotional frustrations which black youths encounter.

Finally, acts of deviance on the part of black youths are much more likely to come to the attention of official agencies than are those of white youths.[27] Deviant acts on the part of white youths are more likely to be handled by private social agencies, whereas for black youths they are handled by legal authorities.

Mental Illness

Statistics on the incidence of mental illness among black people are both insufficient and contradictory. Since black people are separated from the larger society by a caste barrier which relegates them to a precarious existence, the assumption is frequently made that they are more likely to be scarred by their existence than are white Americans. This theory holds that for black people the U.S. social environment is one of oppression and that this situtation adversely affects their mental health. Numerous social pressures to which Negroes, more than white Americans, are exposed leave their impact on their personalities. Such circumstances, it is assumed, contribute to differentially high rates of mental illness among black people.

Mental illness is usually divided into two types, psychoses and psychoneuroses. Psychoses are more easily diagnosed and are therefore more often studied. However, studies show conflicting findings. For a period of some three decades one researcher had studied the incidence of mental illness among black persons, compared with white persons, in New York State. The statistics for New York State are reasonably complete for

[24]See Sheldon Glueck and Eleanor Glueck, *Unraveling Juvenile Delinquency* (Cambridge, Mass.: Harvard, 1950).

[25]Kenneth Clark, "Color, Class, Personality and Juvenile Delinquency." *Journal of Negro Education,* Vol. 28 (Summer 1959), 240–51.

[26]Mozell Hill, "The Metropolis and Juvenile Delinquency Among Negroes," *Journal of Negro Education,* Vol. 28 (Summer 1959), 278.

[27]Douglass, *op. cit.,* p. 215.

patients hospitalized for psychoses because they are collected by a central agency from both public and private hospitals. Malzberg reports that in 1930 and 1931, the rate of first admissions of Negroes to mental hospitals or mental wards in other hospitals was 150.6 per 100,000 population, compared with 87.7 whites per 100,000 population, or a ratio of 1.7 to 1.[28] By 1939 both black and white rates had increased, but the Negro rate of increase is reported to have been greater—48 percent, compared with a 14 percent increase among whites.[29] He reports that between 1948 and 1951, Negroes continued to have significantly higher rates of hospitalization for psychoses than whites.[30] Moreover, in 1960 and 1961, Negroes constituted only 8.4 percent of the population of New York State but accounted for 13.8 percent of the admissions to mental hospitals.[31] Although the differential between blacks and whites had diminished, blacks were still overrepresented in first admissions to mental hospitals in New York State.

The data from New York State show a persistent excess of psychoses among Negroes. Findings from other states frequently differ, however.[32] It is reported that in Pennsylvania from 1943 to 1947 the incidence of mental illness was higher for blacks than for whites. In South Carolina the numbers of Negroes in state mental hospitals in 1948 were proportionate to their numbers in the population. A comparable finding is reported for Mississippi from 1945 to 1947. Data from Louisiana report that the incidence of mental illness among whites was greater than among Negroes in 1941. A study in Illinois reports no greater incidence of psychoses among blacks than among whites in 1948.[33] A study of the Cincinnati, Ohio, General Hospital revealed that the proportion of Negro admissions to the psychiatric wards was not significantly higher than the ratio of Negroes in the population of that city.[34]

A recent, impressively comprehensive study in Baltimore, Maryland, reports that Negroes do not have higher rates of psychoses than do whites.[35] Data reported in this study are based on sample surveys and on

[28]Benjamin Malzberg, *Statistical Data for the Study of Mental Disease Among Negroes in New York State, 1939–1941* (Albany, N.Y.: State Department of Mental Hygiene, 1955), p. 1.

[29]*Ibid.,* p. 9.

[30]Benjamin Malzberg, *The Mental Health of the Negro* (Albany, N.Y.: Research Foundation for Mental Hygiene, 1962).

[31]Benjamin Malzberg, *New Data on Mental Disease Among Negroes in New York State, 1960–1961* (Albany, N.Y.: Research Foundation for Mental Hygiene, 1965).

[32]Data for Pennsylvania, South Carolina, and Louisiana are reported in Ernest Y. Williams and Claude P. Carmichael, "The Incidence of Mental Disease in the Negro," *Journal of Negro Education,* Vol. 18 (Summer 1949), 276–82

[33]Helen V. McLean, "The Emotional Health of Negroes," *Journal of Negro Education,* Vol. 18 (Summer 1949), 283–90.

[34]A. B. Sclare, "Cultural Determinants in the Neurotic Negro," *British Journal of Medical Psychology,* Vol. 26 (1953), 279–88.

[35]Benjamin Pasamanick, "Some Misconceptions Concerning Differences in Racial Preva-

public and private institutional rates. In state hospitals nonwhite rates were higher, but in private hospitals and Veterans Administration hospitals rates were higher among whites. And, among the noninstitutional population the white rate of psychosis was more than 10 times as great as the black rate. The overall rate from all sources in Baltimore was 9.46 per 1,000 whites, compared with 7.04 per 1,000 Negroes. Finally, a widely publicized study reported that in Virginia the rates of black mentally ill patients have always been higher than those for whites and that in recent years there has been a significant increase in the Negro rate.[36]

The findings from these diverse studies are so contradictory as to make generalizations hazardous. Nevertheless, the assumption that black people suffer disproportionately high rates of the most serious forms of mental illness persists.[37] Furthermore, two recent studies report an inverse correlation between social class and the incidence of psychoses.[38] Since Negroes are overrepresented among the poor, it might be expected that psychoses would be more prevalent among them. On the other hand, it is generally reported that white Americans, more than Negroes, are likely to suffer from psychoneuroses, the milder form of mental illness. Pasamanick reports that in Baltimore the rate of psychoneuroses among whites was more than twice as great as among blacks. The rate among whites was reported to be 62 per 1,000 population, compared with 28 per 1,000 among Negroes.[39] Williams and Carmichael report that the incidence of psychoneuroses among black people in state hospitals is much lower than among whites. In New York State it is reported that the rate of psychoneuroses among whites was three times as great as among Negroes from 1949 to 1951.[40] Both Hollingshead and Redlich, and Srole, *et al.,* report a direct correlation between social class and the prevalence of psychoneuroses. Again, since black people are underrepresented among the middle class, it might be expected that the incidence of psychoneuroses among them would be lower than among white Americans. Although the data on psychoneuroses are less complete, they are also less contradictory than data on psychoses.

Psychoses are usually considered to be of two types, organic and functional. Studies reporting the differential incidence of mental illness among blacks and whites report that blacks are more likely to suffer from such

lence of Mental Disease," *American Journal of Orthopsychiatry,* Vol. 33 (January 1963), 72–86; Benjamin Pasamanick, "A Survey of Mental Disease in the Urban Population," *American Journal of Psychiatry,* Vol. 119 (October 1962), 299–305.

[36]David C. Wilson and Edna M. Lantz, "Culture Change and Negro State Hospital Admissions," *American Journal of Psychiatry,* Vol. 114 (July 1957), 25–32.

[37]Cf. Thomas F. Pettigrew, *op. cit.,* p. 75.

[38]See August B. Hollingshead and Frederick C. Redlich, *Social Class and Mental Illness* (New York: Wiley, 1958); Leo Srole *et al., Mental Health in the Metropolis: The Midtown Manhattan Study* (New York: McGraw-Hill, 1962).

[39]Pasamanick, *op. cit.,* p. 83.

[40]Malzberg, *New Data on Mental Disease . . . ,* pp. 58–59.

organic psychoses as general paresis and alcoholic psychoses and from such functional psychoses as dementia praecox (schizophrenia); whites are more likely to suffer from manic depressive (functional) psychoses.[41] Pettigrew, after a review of studies of mental illness among Negroes, concluded: "Particular psychoses contribute disproportionately to the greater Negro rates. Schizophrenia, the bizarre condition of social withdrawal and personality disorganization, is especially frequent among Negro first admissions."[42] Therefore it is reported that the incidence of mental illness among black people is greater for both organic and functional psychoses.

Pasamanick reports that in Baltimore nonwhites have higher rates of mental deficiency than do whites. He reports that between 1952 and 1955 the rate was 21.3 per 1,000 Negro population, compared with 13.2 per 1,000 white population. He attributes this difference to environmental (rather than hereditary) factors, such as lack of motivation and less stimulation among poor people.

Conflicting data on the differential incidence of mental illness among blacks and whites usually result from incompleteness and from difficulties in diagnosing mental illness. As one writer has concluded, " . . . inadequate appreciation of the sociological dimensions in the differential racial environments may lead the researcher or clinician to overlook variations in the development of the personality with consequent difficulties in assessing etiological factors, accurate diagnosis, or therapeutic proceedings."[43] Nevertheless, differentially high rates, when reported, are usually explained in terms of social factors. For example, the Malzberg studies explain the differential in New York State as a function of migration, which results in a more precarious standard of living. Furthermore, statistics are more often reported for public than private institutions. Because black people are overrepresented in the lower class, they are forced to seek treatment in public institutions, whereas white Americans seek care in private institutions or through noninstitutional arrangements. Black people are often denied treatment in private hospitals and clinics. Williams and Carmichael reported in 1949 that "No private institution in the United States at the present time will accept the Negro as a mental patient, and the number of whites treated in these institutions is difficult to evaluate. . . . "[44]

Data from Southern states which generally show that black people are proportionately represented in mental hospitals no doubt reflect a tend-

---

[41]Malzberg, *Statistical Data for the Study of Mental Disease . . .* , pp. 4–6; Malzberg, *New Data on Mental Disease . . .* , pp. 51–59; Benjamin Malzberg, "Mental Disease Among Native and Foreign Born Negroes in New York State," *Journal of Negro Education,* Vol. 25 (Spring 1956), 175–81; Wilson and Lantz, *op. cit.,* p. 32.

[42]Pettigrew, *op. cit.,* p. 75

[43]R. A. Schermerhorn, "Psychiatric Disorders Among Negroes: A Sociological Note," *American Journal of Psychiatry,* Vol. 112 (May 1956), 882.

[44]Williams and Carmichael, *op. cit.,* pp. 281–82.

ency to hospitalize only the most severe cases of mental illness among black people. This tendency may result in underenumeration. On the other hand, the overrepresentation of black people in some studies may reflect faulty diagnoses. Clinical studies on mental illness among black people which frequently report extreme paranoia may actually describe an accurate perception of the hostile environment in which they are forced to live. As Kardiner and Ovesey have written, "Such anxieties mean one thing in the white and another in the Negro. In the white they mean paranoid tendencies; but not in the Negro. For the latter, to see hostility in the environment is a normal perception."[45] Or, as Schermerhorn has written, " . . . mistakes in diagnosis could result from uncritical use of case history materials in a Negro patient, if given the same weight that they were given for a white patient. For example, the irregular school attendance or job history of a Negro patient may be less a sign of neurotic instability than of economic deprivation and the consequent ability to do nothing but odd jobs."[46]

The harshness of the environment in which black people are forced to live may contribute to their being reported as overrepresented among Americans suffering from functional psychoses. Studies indicate that the culture in which one lives plays an important role in the incidence of psychoses and that the incidence varies from culture to culture.[47] The effect of American culture on the personalities of black people has been summarized by Kardiner and Ovesey: Cultural factors " . . . force the Negro to live within the confines of a caste system which not only interferes seriously with all varieties of social mobility through class lines, but, simultaneously, tends to stifle effective protest by the threat of hostile retaliation by the majority of whites. Such oppression cannot but leave a permanent impact on the Negro's personality."[48] That living in a state of oppression in the United States has contributed to a disproportionately high incidence of mental illness among black people is usually assumed, but empirical data, where they exist, are so contradictory as to preclude firm generalizations.

Drug Addiction

Data on the extent of drug addiction in the United States are extremely crude because the use of narcotics for nonmedical purposes is generally

[45]Abram Kardiner and Lionel Ovesey, *The Mark of Oppression* (New York: World, 1962), p. 343.

[46]Schermerhorn, *op. cit.,* pp. 881–82.

[47]See Joseph W. Eaton and Robert J. Weil, *Culture and Mental Disorders* (New York: Free Press, 1955).

[48]Kardiner and Ovesey, *op. cit.,* p. 11. For a review of cultural factors in mental illness in one Negro community see Seymour Parker and Robert J. Kleiner, *Mental Illness in the Urban Negro Community* (New York: Free Press, 1966).

prohibited by federal, state, and municipal laws. Nonmedical users and dispensers of narcotics must exercise secrecy in these activities, and addicts usually become known only when they are arrested or when they seek treatment. Therefore, published statistics probably represent a small fraction of the narcotics addicts in the United States.

There are several types of addicting drugs commonly used in the United States. They may be classified in two broad types, stimulants and depressants.[49] The stimulants include cocaine, benzedrine, and mescaline. The depressants, which induce sleep and lessen nervous tension, include morphine and all its derivatives (e.g., heroin, diladuid, and codeine), synthetic analgesics (e.g., methadone and demerol), and the hypnotics and sedatives (e.g., bromides and the barbiturates). Although habitual marijuana use is considered a form of drug addiction by lawmakers and narcotics control personnel, it is not considered by medical practitioners to be a form of drug addiction because it does not entail physiological dependence.

Recent statistics show that among drug addicts heroin (a depressant) is used by a vast majority.[50] An earlier study of 1,036 patients in a federal hospital for narcotic addicts reported that morphine was preferred by the patients and that it was the first used and the last used by a majority of them. This drug was followed in expressed preference and usage by heroin.[51] The typical addict is likely to take heroin, morphine, or a similar drug intravenously. In recent years such practices as glue sniffing, gasoline addiction, and the use of hallucinogenic drugs (LSD-25, psilocybin, and mescaline) have reportedly increased, especially among younger Americans.

The Federal Bureau of Narcotics was created in 1930 to implement laws governing the use and sale of narcotics and to supervise the production and importation of these drugs. One of its primary functions is the apprehension of violators of an elaborate network of narcotics control laws. According to the Federal Bureau of Narcotics, which compiles statistics on drug addiction from state police reports, there were approximately 60,000 drug addicts in the United States in 1965. This figure is obviously a gross underenumeration, as one study estimated that there were 90,000 addicts in New York City alone.[52] Estimates of the number of narcotic addicts in New York vary widely. The Federal Bureau of Narcotics estimates the number at 35,000, the New York State Narcotic Addiction Control Commission estimates the number at 60,000, and the New York City Narcotics Coordinator estimates the number at 100,000.[53]

[49] Facts About Narcotics Addiction (New York: Department of Health, n.d.).

[50] Bureau of Narcotics, Annual Report on Narcotic Addiction in the United States (Washington, D.C.: Treasury Department, 1966), Table I.

[51] Michael J. Pescor, "A Statistical Analysis of the Clinical Records of Hospitalized Drug Addicts," Public Health Reports, Supplement 143 (1938), Appendix, p. 24.

[52] Report of Study of Drug Addiction Among Teenagers (New York: Mayor's Committee on Drug Addiction, 1951).

It is invariably reported that black people are overrepresented among drug addicts in the United States. The Federal Bureau of Narcotics reports that in 1965 more than one-half (51.6 percent) of all narcotics addicts in the United States were Negroes.[54] Similarly, the New York City Health Department reports that 47.8 percent of all newly reported habitual users of narcotic drugs in 1964 were Negroes.[55] It is generally believed that from 40 to 60 percent of all addicts in the United States live in New York, and in central Harlem the rate is reported to be approximately seven times as high as that in New York City as a whole.[56]

Although data on drug addiction are inadequate, all available evidence indicates that black people are disproportionately represented among reported narcotic addicts. (It must be remembered, however, that the liklihood is that reported addicts represent a small proportion of those addicted to the use of narcotics.) A vast majority of known narcotic addicts use depressant drugs, such as heroin and morphine, which serve as a means of escape from the precarious existence which black people in the United States lead. Clausen describes their effects: "Their depressant actions include relief of pain, muscular relaxation, drowsiness or lethargy, and (before extreme tolerance has been developed) euphoria, a sense of well-being and contentment."[57] Similarly, other economically deprived groups, such as Puerto Ricans and Mexican Americans, are overrepresented among reported narcotic addicts. In 1965 Puerto Ricans accounted for 13.1 percent of all narcotic addicts reported by the Federal Bureau of Narcotics; Mexican Americans accounted for 5.6 percent.[58]

Drug addiction in the United States is an urban phenomenon. More than one-half (51.6 percent) of the addicts reported by the Federal Bureau of Narcotics live in New York, primarily in New York City. One-fourth live in California and Illinois, mainly in Los Angeles and Chicago. The remaining one-fourth live in other large cities, such as Detroit, Philadelphia, Washington, D.C., Baltimore, and Newark. Each of these cities contains large proportions of deprived Negroes. Drug addiction is most prevalent in urban areas because of the lack of institutional (family, religious) controls, the accessibility of supply, greater anonymity (decreasing the likelihood of detection), and the presence of social norms favorable to such behavior.

Drug addiction is most acute among young males. Approximately 82

[53] *The New York Times,* March 27, 1967, p. 26, col. 8. For a comprehensive report of narcotic drug use in the United States, see the series in *The New York Times,* January 8–12, 1968.

[54] Bureau of Narcotics, *Annual Report. . . .*

[55] *Narcotics Register Project, Report Number 1* (New York: Department of Health, 1966), Table 4.

[56] *Youth in the Ghetto,* pp. 144–45.

[57] John A. Clausen, "Drug Addiction," in Merton and Nisbet (eds.), *op. cit.,* p. 197.

[58] Federal Bureau of Narcotics, *Annual Report. . . .*

percent of all reported addicts were male, and almost half (46.5 percent) of them were between the ages of 21 and 30. Fifty percent were over 30 years of age, and nearly 38 percent were between 31 and 40. Of addicts under 21 years of age, black youths were vastly overrepresented, but the proportion is significantly lower than among the older addicts. Negroes constituted only one-fourth of the addicts under 21 years of age, and Puerto Ricans constituted another one-fifth. These figures indicate that within the category with the highest rates of unemployment, young adult black and Puerto Rican males, the rate of drug addiction is highest. Furthermore, the high rate of drug addiction among adolescents no doubt reflects the increasing use of drugs among middle-class white youth.

Drug addiction is most prevalent in those sections of metropolitan centers that are most often inhabited by members of ethnic minorities. Certain social characteristics prevail throughout these areas.[59] These areas have high rates of crime, prostitution, and illegitimacy. Family disorganization is widespread, and the areas are densely populated. Living quarters tend to be deteriorated, and families frequently live in cramped quarters, often with several people sharing a single bedroom. Mothers frequently work outside the home, and fathers experience difficulties providing support for the family. Children rely heavily on peer groups for support, which often results in gangs and other youth groups within which social pressures force experimentation with narcotics.

According to one researcher, a distinctive subculture of drug addicts exists.[60] Within this subculture the young drug addict displays a highly developed sense of taste in clothes, speaks with a distinctive vocabulary, thrives on the exploitation of women, and, in genera, maintains a superior attitude accompanied by a disdain for work and the conventional daily routine. He is frequently able to live without working, and his main purpose in life is to experience the "kick," and unconventional experience which serves to distinguish him from those he defines as "squares." The ultimate "kick" is the use of heroin because of the extreme proscription on its use in conventional middle-class society.

The habitual use of narcotics is expensive. The New York City Health Department estimates that addicts require $75 a day for drugs. Because of the precarious economic existence of most reported addicts, such a sum of money is far beyond their means. Therefore it is said that they resort to other criminal acts to maintain their "habit." There is some evidence of a correlation between narcotics usage and crime; however, addicts are not prone to crimes of violence. Rather, their criminal behavior is likely

---

[59]See Clausen, *op. cit.,* pp. 210–12; Isidor Chein, "Narcotics Use Among Juveniles," in *Narcotic Addiction,* eds. John A. O'Donnell and John C. Ball (New York: Harper & Row, 1966), pp. 123–41.

[60]See Harold Finestone, "Cats, Kicks, and Color," *Social Problems,* Vol. 18 (July 1957), 3–13.

to involve some type of theft. For example, "According to 1951 Chicago data, arrests for nonviolent property offenses are proportionately higher among addicts, whereas arrests of addicts for violent offenses against the person, such as rape and aggravated assault, are only a fraction of the proportion among the population at large."[61] Addicts are most likely to be convicted of larceny and robbery.

Recent reports by the Federal Bureau of Narcotics show a decline in the number of narcotic addicts among black people. At the same time an increase in narcotic addicts is reported among whites. In the decade from 1956 to 1966 the proportion of Negro addicts is reported to have declined from 57.8 percent of the total to 40.2 percent.[62] Several explanations for this decline have been advanced: increasing racial pride, brought about the civil rights movement; increased education on the effects of drug addiction; and increased observations by Negroes of the harmful effects of narcotics on relatives and friends.

The evidence indicates that black people are overrepresented among drug addicts in the United States. Despite the shortcomings of the data, they are persuasive. The daily experiences of black people, in many regards, are traumatic. They face indignities which most white persons are spared. The use of narcotizing drugs represents one means of escaping from a harsh environment.

Data on crime and delinquency, mental illness, and drug addiction among black Americans are inadequate and, in some cases, contradictory. However, it is frequently reported that black people contribute disproportionately high rates to each of these social problems in the United States. Because of discrimination in the administration of justice, the reported differentially high crime and delinquency rates among black people must be questioned. It is virtually impossible for black Americans to secure impartial treatment at any step in the judicial process. It is possible that black people commit proportionately more conventional crimes than white Americans, but economic and social factors are responsible. The racist nature of American society frequently forces them to resort to nonconforming behavior as a means of surviving the daily hazards to which they are subjected.

The inadequacy of statistics on mental illness renders the making of firm generalizations impossible. Furthermore, subcultural differences between black Americans and mental heath personnel call the validity of such diagnoses into question. As a form of social deviance the extent of drug addiction as reported in official sources is questionable. The likelihood is, however, that the precarious existence which black people lead gives rise to disproportionately high rates of drug addiction.

When black people deviate disproportionately from the norms of so-

[61]Clinard, *op. cit.,* p. 312.
[62]*The New York Times,* March 6, 1967, p. ·1, col. 4.

ciety, such behavior must be explained as resulting from the social environment. These phenomena (crime and delinquency, mental illness, and drug addiction) are referred to as "social problems" because they are products of the society in which they are found. For black citizens American society is one which has, through the years, made it difficult for them to conform to standards of behavior which the society sets for all citizens.

DEVIANT ROLE: DRUG ADDICT

"Cats, Kicks, and Color"

by Harold Finestone

Growing recognition that the most recent manifestation of the use of opiates in this country has been predominantly a young peoples' problem has resulted in some speculation as to the nature of this generation of drug users. Is it possible to form an accurate conception as to what "manner of man" is represented by the current species of young drug addict? Intensive interviews between 1951 and 1953 with over fifty male colored users of heroin in their late teens and early twenties selected from several of the areas of highest incidence of drug use in Chicago served to elicit from them the expression of many common attitudes, values, schemes of behavior, and general social orientation. Moreover, since there was every reason to believe that such similarities had preceded their introduction to heroin, it appeared that it was by virtue of such shared features that they had been unusually receptive to the spread of opiate use. Methodologically, their common patterns of behavior suggested the heuristic value of the construction of a social type. The task of this paper is to depict this social type, and to present a hypothetical formulation to account for the form it has taken.

No special justification appears to be necessary for concentrating in this paper on the social type of the young colored drug user. One of the distinctive properties of the distribution of drug use as a social problem, at least in Chicago, is its high degree of both spatial and racial concentration. In fact, it is a problem which in this city can be pinpointed with great accuracy as having its incidence preponderantly among the young male colored persons in a comparatively few local community areas. The following delineation of the generic characteristics of young colored drug users constitutes in many respects an ideal type. No single drug addict exemplified all of the traits to be depicted but all of them revealed several of them to a marked degree.

The young drug user was a creature of contrasts. Playing the role of the fugitive and pariah as he was inevitably forced to do, he turned up for interviews in a uniformly ragged and dirty condition. And yet he talked with an air of superiority derived from his identification with an elite group, the society of "cats." He came in wearing a non-functional tie clip attached to his sport shirt and an expensive hat as the only indications that he was concerned with his appearance and yet displayed in his conversation a highly developed sense of taste in men's clothing and a high valuation upon dressing well. He came from what were externally the drabbest, most overcrowded, and physically deteriorated sections of the city and yet discussed his pattern of living as though it were a consciously cultivated work of art.

Despite the location of his social world in the "asphalt jungle" of the "Blackbelt" he strictly eschewed the use of force and violence as a technique for achieving his ends or for the settling of problematic situations. He achieved his goals by indirection, relying, rather, on persuasion and on a repertoire of manipulative techniques. To deal with a variety of challenging situations, such as those arising out of his contacts with the police, with his past or potential victims, and with jilted "chicks," etc., he used his wits and his conversational ability. To be able to confront such contingencies with adequacy and without resort to violence was to be "cool." His idea was to get what he wanted through persuasion and ingratiation; to use the other fellow by deliberately outwitting him. Indeed, he regarded himself as immeasurably superior to the "gorilla," a person who resorted to force.

The image of himself as "operator" was projected onto the whole world about him and led to a complete scepticism as to other persons' motives. He could relate to people by outsmarting them, or through open-handed and often ruinous generosity, but his world seemed to preclude any relationship which was not part of the "scheme" or did not lend itself to an "angle." The most difficult puzzle for him to solve was the "Square," the honest man. On the one hand the "square" was the hard-working plodder who lived by routine and who took honesty and the other virtues at their face value. As such he constituted the prize victim for the cat. On the other hand the cat harbored the sneaking suspicion that some squares were smarter than he, because they could enjoy all the forbidden pleasures which were his stock in trade and maintain a reputation for respectability in the bargain.

The cat had a large, colorful, and discriminating vocabulary which dealt with all phases of his experience with drugs. In addition, he never seemed to content himself with the conventional world for even the most commonplace objects. Thus he used "pad" for house, "pecks" for food, "flicks" for movies, "stick hall" for pool hall, "dig the scene" for observe, "box" for record player, "bread" for money, etc. In each instance the word he used was more concrete or earthier than the conventional word and such as to reveal an attitude of subtle ridicule towards the dignity and conventionality inherent in the common usage.

His soft convincing manner of speaking, the shocking earthiness and fancifulness of his vocabulary, together with the formidable gifts of charm and ingratiation which he deployed, all contributed to the dominant impression which the young drug user made as a person. Such traits would seem to have fitted naturally into a role which some cats had already played or aspired to play, that of the pimp. To be supported in idleness and luxury through the labors of one or more attractive "chicks" who shoplifted or engaged in prostitution or both and dutifully handed over the proceeds was one of his favorite fantasies. In contrast with the milieu of the white underworld, the pimp was not an object of opprobrium but of prestige.

The theme of the exploitation of the woman goes close to the heart of the cat's orientation to life, that is, his attitude towards work. Part of the cat's sense of superiority stems from his aristocratic disdain for work, and for the subordination of self to superiors and to the repetitive daily routine entailed by work, which he regards as intolerable. The "square" is a person who toils for regular wages and who takes orders from his superiors without complaint.

In contrast with the "square," the cat gets by without working. Instead he keeps himself in "bread" by a set of ingenious variations on "begging, borrowing, or stealing." Each cat has his "hustle,"[1] and a "hustle" is any non-violent means of "making some bread" which does not require work. One of the legendary heroes of the cat is the man who is such a skillful con-man that he can sell "State Street" to his victim. Concretely, the cat is a petty thief, pickpocket, or pool shark, or is engaged in a variety of other illegal activities of the "conning" variety. A very few cats are actually living off the proceeds of their women "on the hustle."

The main purpose of life for the cat is to experience the "kick." Just as every cat takes pride in his "hustle," so every cat cultivates his "kick," A "kick" is any act tabooed by "squares" that heightens and intensifies the present moment of experience and differentiates it as much as possible from the humdrum routine of daily life. Sex in any of its conventional expressions is not a "kick" since this would not serve to distinguish the cat from the "square," but orgies of sex behavior and a dabbling in the various perversions and byways of sex pass muster as "kicks." Some "cats" are on a alcohol "kick," others on a marihuana "kick" and others on a heroin "kick." There is some interchangeability among these various "kicks" but the tendency is to select your "kick" and stay with it. Many of these young drug users, however, had progressed from the alcohol to

[1]Finestone, Harold, "Narcotics and Criminality," *Law and Contemporary Problems,* 22 (Winter, 1957), 60–85.

the marihuana to the heroin "kick." Each "kick" has its own lore of appreciation and connoisseurship into which only its devotees are initiated.

In addition to his "kick" the cat sets great store on the enjoyment of music and on proper dress. To enjoy one's "kick" without a background of popular music is inconceivable. The cat's world of music has a distinctive galaxy of stars, and the brightest luminaries in his firmament are performers such as "Yardbird" (the late Charlie Parker) and disc jockeys such as Al Benson. Almost every cat is a frustrated musician who hopes some day to get his "horn" out of pawn, take lessons, and earn fame and fortune in the field of "progressive music."

The cat places a great deal of emphasis upon clothing and exercises his sartorial talents upon a skeletal base of suit, sport shirt, and hat. The suit itself must be conservative in color. Gaiety is introduced through the selection of the sport shirt and the various accessories, all so chosen and harmonized as to reveal an exquisite sense of taste. When the cat was not talking about getting his clothes out of pawn, he talked about getting them out of the cleaners. With nonchalant pride one drug user insisted that the most expensive sport shirts and hats in the city of Chicago were sold in a certain haberdashery on the South Side. The ideal cat would always appear in public impeccably dressed and be able to sport a complete change of outfit several times a day.

The cat seeks through a harmonious combination of charm, ingratiating speech, dress, music, the proper dedication to his "kick," and unrestrained generosity to make of his day to day life itself a gracious work of art. Everything is to be pleasant and everything he does and values is to contribute to a cultivated aesthetic approach to living. The "cool cat" exemplifies all of these elements in proper balance. He demonstrates his ability to "play it cool" in his unruffled manner of dealing with outsiders such as the police, and in the self-assurance with which he confronts emergencies in the society of "cats." Moreover, the "cat" feels himself to be any man's equal. He is convinced that he can go anywhere and mingle easily with anyone. For example, he rejects the type of music designated "the blues" because for him it symbolizes attitudes of submission and resignation which are repugnant and alien to his customary frame of mind.

It can be seen now why heroin use should make such a powerful appeal to the cat. It was the ultimate "kick." No substance was more profoundly tabooed by conventional middle-class society. Rugular heroin use provides a sense of maximal social differentiation from the "square." The cat was at last engaged, he felt, in an activity completely beyond the comprehension of the "square." No other "kick" offered such an instantaneous intensification of the immediate moment of experience and set it apart from everyday experience in such spectacular fashion. Any words used by the cat to apply to the "kick," the experience of "being high," he applied to heroin in the superlative. It was the "greatest kick of them all."

In the formulation now to be presented the cat as a social type is viewed as a manifestation of a process of social change in which a new type of self-conception has been emerging among the adolescents of the lower socio-economic levels of the colored population in large urban centers. It is a self-conception rooted in the types of accommodation to a subordinate status achieved historically by the colored race in this country, a self-conception which has become increasingly articulated as it responded to and selected various themes from the many available to it in the milieu of the modern metropolis. Blumer's classification of social movements into general, specific, or expressive, appears to provide a useful framework for the analysis of the social type of the cat.[2]

In terms of these categories the cat as a social type is the personal counterpart of an expressive social movement. The context for such a movement must include the broader community, which, by its policies of social segregation and discrimination, has withheld from individuals of the colored population the opportunity to achieve or to identify with status positions in the larger society. The social type of the cat is an expression of one possible type of adaptation to such blocking and frustration, in which a segment of the population turns in upon itself and attempts to develop within itself criteria for the achievement of social status and the rudiments of a satisfactory social life. Within his own isolated social world the cat attempts to give form and purpose to dispositions derived from the dominant social order.

What are these dispositions and in what sense may they be said to be derived from the dominant social order? Among the various interrelated facets of the life of the cat two themes are central, those of the "hustle" and the "kick." It is to be noted that they are in direct antithesis to two of the central values of the dominant culture, the "hustle" versus the paramount importance of the occupation for the male in our society, and the "kick" versus the importance of regulating conduct in terms of its future consequences. Thus, there appears to be a relationship of conflict between the central themes of the social type of the cat and those of the dominant social order. As a form of expressive behavior, however, the social type of the cat represents an indirect rather than a direct attack against central conventional values.

It is interesting to speculate on the reasons why a type such as the cat should emerge rather than a social movement with the objective of changing the social order. The forces coercing the selective process among colored male adolescents in the direction of expressive social movements are probably to be traced to the long tradition of accommodation to a

[2]Blumer, Herbert, "Social Movements," in Robert E. Park, ed., *An Outline of the Principles of Sociology* (New York: Barnes & Noble, 1939), pp. 255–78.

subordinate status on the part of the Negro as well as to the social climate since the Second World War, which does not seem to have been favorable to the formation of specific social movements.

The themes of the "hustle" and "kick" in the social orientation of the cat are facts which appear to be overdetermined. For example, to grasp the meaning of the "hustle" to the cat one must understand it as a rejection of the obligation of the adult male to work. When asked for the reasons underlying his rejection of work the cat did not refer to the uncongenial and relatively unskilled and low paid jobs which, in large part, were the sole types of employment available to him. He emphasized rather that the routine of a job and the demand that he should apply himself continuously to his work task were the features that made work intolerable for him. The self-constraint required by work was construed as an unwarranted damper upon his love of spontaneity. The other undesirable element from his point of view was the authoritarian setting of most types of work with which he was familiar.

There are undoubtedly many reasons for the cat's rejection of work but the reasons he actually verbalized are particularly significant when interpreted as devices for sustaining his self-conception. The cat's feeling of superiority would be openly challenged were he to confront certain of the social realities of his situation, such as the discrimination exercised against colored persons looking for work and the fact that only the lowest status jobs are available to him. He avoided any mention of these factors which would have forced him to confront his true position in society and thus posed a threat to his carefully cherished sense of superiority.

In emphasizing as he does the importance of the "kick" the cat is attacking the value our society places upon planning for the future and the responsibility of the individual for such planning. Planning always requires some subordination and disciplining of present behavior in the interest of future rewards. The individual plans to go to college, plans for his career, plans for his family and children, etc. Such an orientation on the part of the individual is merely the personal and subjective counterpart of a stable social order and of stable social institutions, which not only permit but sanction an orderly progression of expectations with reference to others and to one's self. Where such stable institutions are absent or in the inchoate stages of development, there is little social sanction for such planning in the experience of the individual. Whatever studies are available strongly suggest that such are the conditions which tend to prevail in the lower socio-economic levels of the Negro urban community.[3] Stable family and community organization is lacking in those areas of the city where drug use is concentrated. A social milieu which does not encourage the subordination and disciplining of present conduct in the interests of

---

[3]Drake, St. Clair, and Horace R. Cayton, "Lower Class: Sex and Family," *Black Metropolis* (New York: Harcourt, Brace & Co., 1945), pp. 564–99.

future rewards tends by default to enhance the present. The "kick" appears to be a logical culmination of this emphasis.

Accepting the emergence of the self-conception of the cat as evidence of a developing expressive social movement, we may phrase the central theoretical problem as follows: What are the distinctive and generic features of the cat's social orientation? Taking a cue from the work of Huizinga as developed in *Homo Ludens,*[4] we propose that the generic characteristics of the social type of the cat are those of play. In what follows, Huizinga's conception of play as a distinctive type of human activity will be presented and then applied as a tool of analysis for rendering intelligible the various facets of the social orientation of the cat. It is believed that the concept of play indicates accurately the type of expressive social movement which receives its embodiment in the cat.

According to Huizinga the concept of play is a primary element of human experience and as such is not susceptible to exact definition.

"The *fun* of playing resists all analysis, all logical interpretation . . . Nevertheless it is precisely this fun-element that characterizes the essence of play."[5] The common image of the young colored drug addict pictures him as a pitiful figure, a trapped unfortunate. There is a certain amount of truth in this image but it does not correspond to the conception which the young colored addict has of himself or to the impression that he tries to communicate to others. If it were entirely true it would be difficult to square with the fact that substantial numbers of young colored persons continue to become drug users. The cat experiences and manifests a certain zest in his mode of life which is far from self-pity. This fun element seemed to come particularly to the fore as the cat recounted his search for "kicks," the adventure of his life on the streets, and the intensity of his contest against the whole world to maintain his supply of drugs. Early in the cycle of heroin use itself there was invariably a "honeymoon" stage when the cat abandoned himself most completely to the experience of the drug. For some cats this "honeymoon" stage, in terms of their ecstatic preoccupation with the drug, was perpetual. For others it passed, but the exigencies of an insatiable habit never seemed to destroy completely the cat's sense of excitement in his way of life.

While Huizinga declines to define play, he does enumerate three characteristics which he considers to be proper to play. Each one of them when applied to the cat serves to indicate a generic feature of his social orientation.

(a) "First and foremost . . . all play is a voluntary activity."[6] "Here we have the first main characteristic of play: that it is free, is in fact free-

---

[4]Huizinga, Johan, *Homo Ludens, A Study of the Play Element in Culture* (Boston: Beacon Press, 1955).
[5]*Ibid.,* p. 3.
[6]*Ibid.,* p. 7.

dom."[7] The concept of an expressive social movement assumes a social situation where existing social arrangements are frustrating and are no longer accepted as legitimate and yet where collective activity directed towards the modification of these limitations is not possible. The cat is "free" in the sense that he is a pre-eminent candidate for new forms of social organization and novel social practices. He is attempting to escape from certain features of the historical traditions of the Negro which he regards as humiliating. As an adolescent or young adult he is not only fully assimilated into such social institutions as the family, school, church, or industry which may be available to him. Moreover, the social institutions which the Negroes brought with them when they migrated to the city have not as yet achieved stability or an adequate functioning relationship to the urban environment. As a Negro, and particularly as a Negro of low socio-economic status, he is excluded from many socializing experiences which adolescents in more advantaged sectors of the society take for granted. He lives in communities where the capacity of the population for effective collective action is extremely limited, and consequently there are few effective controls on his conduct besides that exercised by his peer group itself. He is fascinated by the varied "scenes" which the big city spreads out before him. Granted this setting, the cat adopts an adventurous attitude to life and is free to give his allegiance to new forms of activity.

> (b) . . . A second characteristic is closely connected with this (that is, the first characteristic of freedom), namely, that play is not "ordinary" or "real" life. It is rather a stepping out of "real" life into a temporary sphere of activity with a disposition all of its own. Every child knows perfectly well that he is "only pretending," or that it was "only for fun." . . . This "only pretending" quality of play betrays a consciousness of the inferiority of play compared with "seriousness," a feeling that seems to be something as primary as play itself. Nevertheless . . . the consciousness of play being "only a pretend" does not by any means prevent it from proceeding with the utmost seriousness, with an absorption, a devotion that passes into rapture and, temporarily at least, completely abolishes that troublesome "only" feeling.[8]

It is implicit in the notion of an expressive social movement that, since direct collective action to modify the sources of dissatisfaction and restlessness is not possible, all such movements should appear under one guise, as forms of "escape." Persons viewing the problem of addiction from the perspective of the established social structure have been prone to make this interpretation. It is a gross oversimplification, however, as considered from the perspective of the young drug addict himself. The emergence of the self-conception of the cat is an attempt to deal with the

[7] *Ibid.,* p. 8.
[8] *Ibid.*

problems of status and identity in a situation where participation in the life of the broader community is denied, but where the colored adolescent is becoming increasingly sensitive to the values, the goals, and the notions of success which obtain in the dominant social order.

> The caste pressures thus make it exceedingly difficult for an American Negro to preserve a true perspective of himself and his own group in relation to the larger white society. The increasing abstract knowledge of the world outside—of its opportunities, its rewards, its different norms of competition and cooperation—which results from the proceeding acculturation at the same time as there is increasing group isolation, only increases the tensions.[9]

Such conditions of group isolation would appear to be fairly uniform throughout the Negro group. Although this isolation may be experienced differently at different social levels of the Negro community, certain features of the adaptations arrived at in response to this problem will tend to reveal similarities. Since the struggle for status takes place on a stage where there is acute sensitivity to the values and status criteria of the dominant white group, but where access to the means through which such values may be achieved is prohibited, the status struggle turning in on itself will assume a variety of distorted forms. Exclusion from the "serious" concerns of the broader community will result in such adaptations manifesting a strong element of "play."

Frazier in *Black Bourgeoisie* discusses the social adaptation of the Negro middle class as "The World of Make-Believe."[10]

> The emphasis upon "social" life or "society" is one of the main props of the world of make-believe into which the black bourgeoisie has sought an escape from its inferiority and frustrations in American society. This world of make-believe, to be sure, is a reflection of the values of American society, but it lacks the economic basis that would give it roots in the world of reality.[11]

In the Negro lower classes the effects of frustrations deriving from subordination to the whites may not be experienced as personally or as directly as it is by the Negro middle class, but the massive effects of residential segregation and the lack of stable social institutions and community organization are such as to reinforce strong feelings of group isolation even at the lowest levels of the society.

It is here suggested that the function performed by the emergence of the social type of the cat among Negro lower class adolescents is analogous to that performed by "The World of Make-Believe" in the Negro middle class. The development of a social type such as that of the cat is only possible in a situation where there is isolation from the broader

[9]Myrdal, Gunnar, *An American Dilemma* (New York: Harper & Brothers, 1944), p. 760.
[10]Frazier, E. Franklin, *Black Bourgeoisie* (Glencoe, Illinois: Free Press, 1957).
[11]*Ibid.*, p. 237.

community but great sensitivity to its goals, where the peer group pressures are extremely powerful, where institutional structures are weak, where models of success in the illegitimate world have strong appeals, where specific social movements are not possible, and where novel forms of behavior have great prestige. To give significance to his experience, the young male addict has developed the conception of a heroic figure, the "ideal cat," a person who is completely adequate to all situations, who controls his "kick" rather than letting it control him, who has a lucrative "hustle," who has no illusions as to what makes the world "tick," who is any man's equal, who basks in the admiration of his brother cats and associated "chicks," who hob-nobs with "celebs" of the musical world, and who in time himself may become a celebrity.

The cat throws himself into his way of life with a great deal of intensity but he cannot escape completely from the perspective, the judgments, and the sanctions of the dominant social order. He has to make place in his scheme of life for police, lockups, jails, and penitentiaries, to say nothing of the agonies of withdrawal distress. He is forced eventually to confront the fact that his role as a cat with its associated attitudes is largely a pose, a form of fantasy with little basis in fact. With the realization that he is addicted he comes only too well to know that he is a "junky," and he is fully aware of the conventional attitudes towards addicts as well as of the counterrationalizations provided by his peer group. It is possible that the cat's vacillation with regard to seeking a cure for his addiction is due to a conflict of perspectives, whether to view his habit from the cat's or the dominant social order's point of view.

> (c) Play is distinct from "ordinary" life both as to locality and duration. This is the third main characteristic of play: its secludedness, its limitedness. It is "played out" within certain limits of time and place. It contains its own course and meaning.[12]

It is this limited, esoteric character of heroin use which gives to the cat the feeling of belonging to an elite. It is the restricted extent of the distribution of drug use, the scheming and intrigue associated with underground "connections" through which drugs are obtained, the secret lore of the appreciation of the drug's effects, which give the cat the exhilaration of participating in a conspiracy. Contrary to popular conception most drug users were not anxious to proselyte new users. Of course spreading the habit would have the function of increasing the possible sources of supply. But an equally strong disposition was to keep the knowledge of drug use secret, to impress and dazzle the audience with one's knowledge of being "in the know." When proselyting did occur, as in jails or lockups, it was proselyting on the part of a devotee who condescended to share with the uninitiated a highly prized practice and set of attitudes.

[12]Huizinga, p. 9.

As he elaborates his analysis of play Huizinga brings to the fore additional aspects of the concept which also have their apt counterpart in the way of life of the cat. For instance, as was discussed earlier, the cat's appreciation of "progressive music" is an essential part of his social orientation. About this topic Huizinga remarks, "Music, as we have hinted before, is the highest and purest expression of the *facultas ludendi.*"[13] The cat's attitude towards music has a sacred, almost mystical quality. "Progressive music" opens doors to a type of highly valued experience which for him can be had in no other way. It is more important to him than eating and is second only to the "kick." He may have to give up his hope of dressing according to his standards but he never gives up music.

Huizinga also observes, "Many and close are the links that connect play with beauty."[14] He refers to the "profoundly aesthetic quality of play."[15] The aesthetic emphasis which seems so central to the style of living of the cat is a subtle elusive accent permeating his whole outlook but coming to clearest expression in a constellation of interests, the "kick," clothing, and music. And it certainly reaches a level of awareness in their language. Language is utilized by the cat with a conscious relish, with many variations and individual turns of phrase indicating the value placed upon creative expression in this medium.

It is to be noted that much of the description of the cat's attributes did not deal exclusively with elements unique to him. Many of the features mentioned are prevalent among adolescents in all reaches of the status scale. Dress, music, language, and the search for pleasure are all familiar themes of the adolescent world. For instance, in his description of the adolescent "youth culture" Talcott Parsons would appear to be presenting the generic traits of a "play-form" with particular reference to its expression in the middle class.

> It is at the point of emergence into adolescence that there first begins to develop a set of patterns and behavior phenomena which involve a highly complex combination of age grading and sex role elements. These may be referred to together as the phenomena of the "youth culture." . . .
>
> Perhaps the best single point of reference for characterizing the youth culture lies in its contrast with the dominant pattern of the adult male role. By contrast with the emphasis on responsibility in this role, the orientation of the youth culture is more or less specifically irresponsible. One of its dominant roles is "having a good time." . . . It is very definitely a rounded humanistic pattern rather than one of competence in the performance of specified functions.[16]

Such significant similarities between this description and the themes of

[13]p. 187.

[14]p. 7.

[15]p. 2.

[16]Parsons, Talcott,"Age and Sex in the Social Structure," *Essays in Sociological Theory Pure and Applied* (Glencoe, Illinois: Free Press, 1949), pp. 220–21.

the social type of the cat only tend to reinforce the notion that the recent spread of heroin use was a problem of adolescence. The cat is an adolescent sharing many of the interests of his age-mates everywhere but confronted by a special set of problems of color, tradition, and identity.

The social orientation of the cat, with its emphasis on non-violence, was quite in contrast to the orientation of the smaller group of young white drug users who were interviewed in the course of this study. The latter's type of adjustment placed a heavy stress upon violence. Their crimes tended to represent direct attacks against persons and property. The general disposition they manifested was one of "nerve" and brashness rather than one of "playing it cool." They did not cultivate the amenities of language, music, or dress to nearly the same extent as the cat. Their social orientation was expressed as a direct rather than an indirect attack on the dominant values of our society. This indicates that the "youth culture" despite its generic features may vary significantly in different social settings.

In his paper, "Some Jewish Types of Personality," Louis Wirth made the following suggestive comments about the relationship between the social type and its setting.

> A detailed analysis of the crucial personality types in any given area or cultural group shows that they depend upon a set of habits and attitudes in the group for their existence and are the direct expressions of the values of the group. As the life of the group changes there appears a host of new social types, mainly outgrowths and transfromations of previous patterns which have become fixed through experience.[17]

What are some of the sources of the various elements going to make up the social type of the cat which may be sought in his traditions? The following suggestions are offered as little more than speculation at the present time. The emphasis upon nonviolence on the part of the cat, upon manipulative techniques rather than overt attack, is a stress upon the indirect rather than the direct way towards one's goal. May not the cat in this emphasis be betraying his debt to the "Uncle Tom" type of adjustment, despite his wish to dissociate himself from earlier patterns of accommodation to the dominant white society? May not the "kick" itself be a cultural lineal descendant of the ecstatic moment of religious possession so dear to revivalist and store-front religion? Similarly, may not the emphasis upon the exploitation of the woman have its origin in the traditionally greater economic stability of the colored woman?

W.I. Thomas in one of his references to the problems raised by the city environment stated, "Evidently the chief problem is the young American

[17] Wirth, Louis, "Some Jewish Types of Personality," in Ernest W. Burgess, ed., *The Urban Community* (Chicago: University of Chicago Press, 1926), p. 112.

person."[18] In discussing the type of inquiry that would be desirable in this area he states that it should

> . . . lead to a more critical discrimination between that type of disorganiza-
> tion in the youth which is a real but frustrated tendency to organize on a
> higher plane, or one more correspondent with the moving environment, and
> that type of disorganization which is simply the abandonment of standards.
> It is also along this line . . . that we shall gain light on the relation of
> fantastic phantasying to realistic phantasying. . . . [19]

Posed in this way the problem becomes one of evaluating the social type of the cat in relation to the processes of social change. This social type is difficult to judge according to the criterion suggested by Thomas. Since many of the cat's interests are merely an extreme form of the adolescent "youth culture," in part the problem becomes one of determining how functional the period of adolescence is as preparation for subsequent adult status. However, the central phases of the social orientation of the cat, the "hustle" and the "kick," do represent a kind of disorganization which indicates the abandonment of conventional standards. The young ad-dicted cat is "going nowhere." With advancing age he cannot shed his addiction the way he can many of the other trappings of adolescence. He faces only the bleak prospect, as time goes on, of increasing demoraliza-tion. Although the plight of the young colored addict is intimately tied to the conditions and fate of his racial group, his social orientation seems to represent a dead-end type of adjustment. Just as Handlin in *The Uprooted* suggests that the first generation of immigrant peoples to our society tends to be a sacrificed generation,[20] it may be that the unique problems of Negro migrants to our metropolitan areas will lead to a few or several sacrificed generations in the course of the tortuous process of urbaniza-tion.

The discussion of the social type of the cat leads inevitably to the issue of social control. Any attempt to intervene or modify the social processes producing the "cat" as a social type must have the objective of reducing his group isolation. For instance, because of such isolation and because of the cat's sensitivity to the gestures of his peers, the most significant role models of a given generation of cats tend to be the cats of the preceding age group. Where, in a period of rapid change, the schemes of behavior of the role models no longer correspond to the possibilities in the actual situation, it is possible for attitudes to be transmitted to a younger genera-tion which evidence a kind of "cultural lag." Thus the condition of the labor market in Chicago is such as to suggest the existence of plentiful

[18]Thomas, William I., "The Problem of Personality in the Urban Environment," in Ernest W. Burgess, ed., *The Urban Community* (Chicago: University of Chicago Press, 1926), p. 46.
[19]*Ibid.*, p. 47.
[20]Hardlin, Oscar, *The Uprooted* (New York: Grosset and Dunlap, 1951), p. 243.

employment opportunities for the Negro in a variety of fields. But because such openings are not mediated to him through role models it is possible that the cat is unable to take advantage of these opportunities or of the facilities available for training for such positions.

The social type of the cat is a product of social change. The type of social orientation which it has elaborated indicates an all too acute awareness of the values of the broader social order. In an open class society where upward mobility is positively sanctioned, an awareness and sensitivity to the dominant values is the first stage in their eventual assimilation. Insofar as the social type of the cat represents a reaction to a feeling of exclusion from access to the means towards the goals of our society, all measures such as improved educational opportunities which put these means within his grasp will hasten the extinction of this social type. Just as the "hoodlum" and "gangster" types tend to disappear as the various more recently arrived white ethnic groups tend to move up in the status scale of the community,[21] so it can confidently be expected that the cat as a social type will tend to disappear as such opportunities become more prevalent among the colored population.

[21]Bell, Daniel, "Crime as an American Way of Life," *Antioch Review,* 13 (June, 1953), 131–54.

six

Change is constantly occurring, yet much change is resisted. Why are some changes accepted while others rejected? Why does change sometimes occur smoothly and at other times precipitate violence? Can Black Power be effective in producing needed change or is Coalition Politics the best method? Can White Americans learn to accept Black Americans as individuals and vice versa?

Social Change

All societies change, yet all change tends to be initially resisted. Persons are often reluctant to adapt to new patterns. It takes a certain impetus or force to induce societal change. When change does occur the new product or idea tends to be interpreted in light of the existing culture, so that there is often consistency between the old patterns and the new. Certain changes may also be far-reaching and affect all aspects of a given society. The automobile, for example, has wrought changes in nearly every area of American life.

In analyzing change we must first consider the social setting within which the change takes place. If the setting contains established avenues for the expression of grievances and sufficient procedures for bringing about orderly change, we would expect social change to follow such routes. Disruptive forms of change would be much more likely in a setting with few such processes.

Within a given setting change is more likely to occur if diverse groups of people are present or if mobility is high, conditions which are especially apparent in urban areas. Exposure to such diversity increases the likelihood of change.

When a group organizes to promote change, such as in a social movement, their relative power within the community may determine how successful they are likely to be. Also important would be their ability to organize, the communication facilities open to them, the community resources they have at their disposal, and the relative power of groups likely to oppose such a change. Blacks have often faced strong power blocs in their attempts to combat discrimination.

Since change is much more likely to be accepted if it is compatible with the existing norms and values of the society, advocates will attempt to demonstrate the compatibility of the proposed change. For example, civil rights advocates have stressed the compatibility of equality for Blacks with the general values of liberty and freedom found in the American ethos. Likewise, opponents usually attempt to *demonstrate the incompatibility of the proposed change by linking it with some-thing to which negative values are already held. Thus opponents of civil rights activity have labeled proponents Communists or "outside agitators."*

In the past two decades there have been increasing efforts by Blacks to organize and oppose discrimination. Many factors have contributed toward this increasing tempo of change within the Black community: the migration of Blacks into urban areas, the rising aspiration level of Blacks, increased mass media coverage of civil rights activity, and the concern of the federal government with America's image abroad. Unfortunately, legitimate avenues for the expression of grievances are often denied to Blacks, necessitating the use of more radical forms of expression and protest.

The article by Charles Moskos on integration in the armed forces examines the relative effectiveness of directed change within a large organization. We see how rapidly integration can be brought about when those that hold the power in an organization become committed to it. Admittedly, the military is conducive to such change because of its rigid authority structure. However, it is important to note that integration has been successful only in the more formal aspects of the military. At informal levels segregation continues. Thus off-base recreational activities and informal peer group interaction are still conducted largely on a segregated basis. The military may be an indication of what to expect in the immediate future for race relations in the United States.

Moskos also examines the effects of integration upon attitudinal change. Such alterations in attitudes seem to follow, rather than precede, actual behavioral changes. Many civil rights advocates have tried rather unsuccessfully to change the negative attitudes that persons have toward integration, hoping that behavioral changes would follow. Changing actual behavior first might be more effective.

Black Power could be an important force for change. The two articles reprinted here present opposing views on this subject. David Danzig argues that the old civil rights coalition of Blacks and Liberal Whites is dying. He sees its place being taken by "the Negro Movement," in which Blacks will attempt to remold their communities on their own. Danzig examines the disillusionment of Blacks with their supposedly liberal allies and the view that only through Black Power can any meaningful change occur. Such persons argue that other ethnic groups used economic and political power to gain equality, so that we should not be surprised if Blacks now do the same. Bayard Rustin sees Blacks as too few in number and too weak in power to achieve success without forming some kind of coalition with other underprivileged groups. He foresees the possibility of a liberal-labor-civil rights coalition that would work to modify the Democratic Party. Since Rustin feels that politicans with only Black support have not done and will not do a very effective job in representing the Black community, he feels that it is only through some sort of coalition that Blacks can achieve success.

DELIBERATE CHANGE

"Racial Relations in the Armed Forces"

by Charles C. Moskos, Jr.

On July 28, 1948, President Truman issued an executive order abolishing racial segregation in the armed forces of the United States. By the middle 1950's this policy was an accomplished fact. The lessons of the racial integration of the military are many. Within a remarkably short period the makeup of a major American institution underwent a far-reaching transformation.[1] Because of the favorable contrast in the military performance of integrated black servicemen with that of all-Negro units, the integration of the armed forces is a demonstration of how changes in social organization can bring about a marked and rapid improvement in individual and

[1]Materials covering racial matters in the military are quite extensive. A primary source are those United States government reports dealing with racial relations in the armed forces: President's Committee on Equality of Treatment and Opportunity in the Armed Forces ("Fahy Committee"), *Freedom to Serve: Equality of Treatment and Opportunity in the Armed Forces,* Washington: Government Printing Office, 1950; U.S. Commission on Civil Rights, "The Negro in the Armed Forces," *Civil Rights '63,* Washington: Government Printing Office, 1963, pp. 169–224; President's Committee on Equal Opportunity in the Armed Forces ("Gesell Committee"), "Initial Report: Equality of Treatment and Opportunity for Negro Personnel Stationed within the United States," mimeographed, June, 1963, and "Final Report: Military Personnel Stationed Overseas and Membership and Participation in the National Guard," mimeographed, November, 1964. An invaluable source of information pertaining to racial composition rates within the armed forces are the statistical breakdowns periodically issued by the office of Civil Rights and Industrial Relations ("CR&IR") in the Department of Defense.

Another source of data is found in Operations Research Office ("ORO"), *Project Clear: The Utilization of Negro Manpower in the Army,* Chevy Chase, Md.: Operations Research Office, Johns Hopkins University, April, 1955. The ORO surveys queried several thousand servicemen during the Korean Conflict on a variety of items relating to attitudes toward racial integration in the Army. The findings of Project Clear, classified until 1965, are now available for professional scrutiny. Some comparable data were obtained from the section dealing with Negro soldiers in Samuel A. Stouffer et al., *The American Soldier: Adjustment during Army Life,* Vol. I, Princeton, N.J.: Princeton University Press, 1949, pp. 486–599.

Much of the information for the findings presented in this chapter are based on my participant observations while on active duty in the Army (1956–58), and subsequent field trips as a researcher to various overseas military installations: Germany and Korea in 1965, the Dominican Republic in 1966, and Viet Nam in 1965 and 1967. Additionally, sixty-seven formal interviews with black soldiers in Germany were conducted in 1965. These interviews were with soldiers who made up almost all of the total black enlisted personnel in two Army companies.

group achievement. The desegregated military, moreover, offers itself as a graphic example of the abilities of both whites and blacks to adjust to egalitarian racial practises with relatively little strain. Further, an examination of the racial situation in the contemporary armed services can serve as a partial guideline as to what one might expect in a racially integrated America. At the same time, the desegregation of the military can also be used to trace some of the mutual permeations between the internal organization of the military and the racial and social cleavages found in the larger setting of American society. For it is also the case that the military establishment—as in other areas of American life—will be increasingly subject to the new challenges of black separatism as well as the persistencies of white racism.

Desegrating the Military [2]

Blacks have taken part in all of this country's wars. An estimated 5,000 blacks, mostly in integrated units, fought on the American side in the War of Independence. (But over twenty thousand black slaves—on the promise of manumission—joined the British as soldiers, supply handlers, and scouts.) Several thousand blacks saw service in the War of 1812. During the Civil War 180,000 blacks were recruited into the Union Army and served in segregated regiments. Following the Civil War four Negro regiments were established and were active in the Indian wars on the Western frontier and later fought with distinction in Cuba during the Spanish-American War. In the early twentieth century, however, owing to a gen-

[2] This background of the black serviceman's role in the American military is derived, in addition to the sources cited above, from Seymour J. Schoenfeld, *The Negro in the Armed Forces,* Washington: Associated Publishers, 1945; Herbert Aptheker, *Essays in the History of the American Negro,* New York: International Publishers, 1945; Arnold M. Rose, "Army Policies toward Negro Soldiers," *Annals of the American Academy of Political and Social Science,* Vol. CCXLIV (March, 1946), pp. 90–94; Paul C. Davis, "The Negro in the Armed Services," *Virginia Quarterly,* Vol. XXIV (Autumn, 1948), pp. 499–520; David G. Mandelbaum, *Soldiers Groups and Negro Groups,* Berkeley: University of California Press, 1952; Lee Nichols, *Breakthrough on the Color Front,* New York: Random House, 1954; Eli Ginzburg, "The Negro Soldier," in his *The Negro Potential,* New York: Columbia University Press, 1956, pp. 61–91; Benjamin Quarles, *The Negro in the Making of America,* New York: Collier Books, 1964, *passim;* Ulysses Lee, *The Employment of Negro Troops,* Special Studies on the United States Army in World War II by the Office of the Chief of Military History, Washington: Government Printing Office, 1966; and Richard J. Stillman, II, *Integration of the Negro in the U.S. Armed Forces,* New York: Praeger, 1968.

Blacks have not been the only racial or ethnic group to occupy a unique position in the American military. Indians served in separate battalions in the Civil War and were used as scouts in the frontier wars. Filipinos have long been a major source of recruitment for stewards in the Navy. The much decorated 442nd ("Go For Broke") Infantry Regiment of World War II was composed entirely of Japanese-Americans. Also in World War II, a separate battalion of Norwegian-Americans was drawn up for intended service in Scandanavia. The participation of Puerto Ricans in the American military deserves special attention. A recent case of large-scale use of non-American soldiers are the Korean fillers or "Katusas" (from Korean Augmentation to the U.S. Army) who make up roughly one-sixth of the troop strength of the Eighth Army.

eral rise in American racial tensions and specific outbreaks of violence between black troops and whites, official opinion began to turn against the use of black soldiers. Evaluation of black soldiers was further lowered by events in World War I. The combat performance of the all-Negro 92nd Infantry Division, one of its regiments having fled in the German offensive at Meuse Argonne, came under heavy criticism. Yet it was also observed that black units operating under French command, in a more racially tolerant situation, performed well.

In the interval between the two World Wars, the Army not only remained segregated but also adopted a policy of a Negro quota that was to keep the number of blacks in the Army proportionate to the total population. Never in the pre-World War II period, however, did the number of blacks approach this quota. On the eve of Pearl Harbor, blacks constituted 5.9 percent of the Army; and there were only five black officers, three of whom were chaplains. During World War II blacks entered the Army in larger numbers, but at no time did they exceed 10 percent of total personnel. Black soldiers remained in segregated units, and approximately three-quarters served in the quartermaster, engineer, and transportation corps. To make matters worse from the viewpoint of "the right to fight," a slogan loudly echoed by Negro organizations in the United States, even black combat units were frequently used for heavy duty labor. This was highlighted when the 2nd Cavalry was broken up into service units owing to command apprehension over the combat qualities, even though untested, of this all-Negro division. The record of those black units that did see combat in World War II was mixed. The performance of the 92nd Infantry Division again came under heavy criticism, this time for alleged unreliability in the Italian campaign.

An important exception to the general pattern of utilization of black troops in World War II occurred in the winter months of 1944–45 in the Ardennes battle. Desperate shortages of combat personnel resulted in the Army asking for black volunteers. The plan was to have platoons (approximately 40 men) of blacks serve in companies (approximately 200 men) previously all-white. Some 2,500 blacks volunteered for this assignment. Both in terms of black combat performance and white soldier's reactions, the Ardennes experiment was an unqualified success. This incident would later be used to support arguments for integration.

After World War II, pressure from Negro and liberal groups coupled with an acknowledgement that black soldiers were being poorly utilized led the Army to reexamine its racial policies. A report by an Army board in 1945, while holding racial integration to be a desirable goal and while making recommendations to improve black opportunity in the Army, concluded that practical considerations required a maintenance of segregation and the quota system. In light of World War II experiences, the report further recommended that black personnel be exclusively assigned to support rather than combat units. Another Army board report came out in 1950 with essentially the same conclusions.[3] Both reports placed heavy stress on the supervisory and disciplinary problems resulting from the disproportionate number of blacks, as established by Army entrance examinations, found in the lower mental and aptitude levels. In 1950, for example, 60 percent of the black personnel fell into the Army's lowest categories compared with 29 percent of the white soldiers. From the standpoint of the performance requirements of the military, such facts could not be lightly dismissed.

After the Truman desegregation order of 1948, however, the die was cast. The President followed his edict by setting up a committee, chaired by Charles Fahy, to pursue the implementation of equal treatment and opportunity for armed forces personnel. Under the impetus of the Fahy committee, the Army abolished the quota system in 1950, and was beginning to integrate some training camps when the conflict in Korea broke out. The Korean Conflict was the coup de grâce for segregation in the Army. Manpower requirements in the field for combat soldiers resulted in many instances of *ad hoc* integration. As was true in the Ardennes experience, black soldiers in previously all-white units performed well in combat. As integration in Korea became more standard, observers consistently noted that the fighting abilities of blacks differed little from those of whites.[4] This contrasted with the blemished record of the all-Negro 24th Infantry Regiment.[5] Its performance in the Korean Conflict was judged to be so poor that its divisional commander recommended the unit be dissolved as quickly as possible. Concurrent with events in Korea, integration was introduced in the United States. By 1956, three years after the end of the Korean Conflict, the remnants of Army Jim Crow disappeared at home and in overseas installations. At the time of the Truman order, blacks constituted 8.8 percent of Army personnel. In 1967 the figure was 11.2 percent.

In each of the other services, the history of desegregation varied from the Army pattern. The Army Air Corps, like its parent body, generally assigned blacks to segregated support units. (However, a unique military venture taken during the war was the formation of three all-Negro, including officers, air combat units.) At the end of World War II the proportion of blacks in the Army Air Corps was only 4 percent, less than half what it was in the Army. Upon its establishment as an independent service in

---

[3]The 1945 and 1950 Army board reports are commonly referred to by the names of the officers who headed these boards: respectively, Lieutenant General Alvan C. Gillem, Jr., and Lieutenant General S.J. Chamberlin.

[4]These evaluations are summarized in ORO, *op. cit.,* pp. 16–19, 47–105, and 582–83.

[5]The notoriety of the 24th Infantry Regiment was aggravated by a song—"The Bug-Out Buggie"—attributed to it: "When them Chinese mortars begin to thud/ The old Deuce-Four begin to bug/ When they started falling 'round the CP [command post] tent/ Everybody wonder where the high brass went/ They were buggin' out/ Just movin' on."

1947, the Air Force began to take steps toward integration even before the Truman order. By the time of the Fahy committee report in 1950, the Air Force was already largely integrated. Since integration there has been a substantial increase in the proportion of blacks serving in the Air Force, from less than 5 percent in 1949 to 9.1 percent in 1967.

Although large numbers of blacks had served in the Navy during the Civil War and for some period afterward, restrictive policies were introduced in the early 1900's, and by the end of World War I only about 1 percent of Navy personnel were blacks. In 1920 the Navy adopted a policy of total racial exclusion and barred all black enlistments. This policy was slightly changed in 1932 when blacks, along with Filipinos, were again allowed to join the Navy but only as stewards in the messman's branch. Further modifications were made in Navy policy in 1942 when some openings in general service were created. Black sailors in these positions, however, were limited to segregated harbor and shore assignments. In 1944, in the first effort toward desegregation in any of the armed services, a small number of black sailors in general service were integrated on ocean-going vessels. After the end of World War II the Navy, again ahead of the other services, began to take major steps toward elimination of racial barriers. Even in the integrated Navy of today, however, black sailors are still overproportionately concentrated in the messman's branch. Also, despite the early steps toward integration taken by the Navy, the proportion of black sailors has remained fairly constant over the past two decades, averaging between 4 and 5 percent of total personnel.

The Marine Corps has gone from a policy of exclusion to segregation to integration. Before World War II there were no black Marines, In 1942 blacks were accepted into the Marine Corps but assigned to segregated units where they were heavy-duty laborers, ammunition handlers, and anti-aircraft gunners. After the war small-scale integration of black Marines into white units was begun. In 1949 and 1950 Marine Corps training units were integrated, and by 1954 the color line was largely erased throughout the Corps. Since integration began, the proportion of blacks has increased markedly. In 1949 less then 2 percent of all Marines were black compared with 9.6 percent in 1967.

Although the various military services are all similar in being formally integrated today, they differ in their proportion of blacks. As shown in Table 1, black membership in the total armed forces in 1967 was 9.0 percent, lower than the 11–12 percent constituting the black proportion in the total population. It is certain, however, that among those *eligible,* a higher proportion of blacks than whites enter the armed forces. That is, a much larger number of blacks do not meet the entrance standards required by the military services. For the years 1960 through 1966, about 55 percent of blacks did not pass the preinduction mental examinations given to selective service registrants, almost four times the about 15 percent of whites who failed these same tests.[6] Because of the relatively low number of blacks obtaining student or occupational deferments, however, it is the Army drawing upon the draft that is the only military service where the percentage of blacks approximates the national proportion. Thus, despite the higher number of blacks who fail to meet induction standards, Army statistics for 1960–1967 show blacks constituted about 15 percent of those drafted.

Even if one takes into account the Army's reliance on the selective service for much of its personnel, the figures in Table 1 also show important differences in the number of blacks in those services meeting their manpower requirements solely through voluntary enlistments; in 1967, for example, the 4.3 percent black in the Navy is lower than 9.6 percent for the Marine Corps or the 9.1 percent for the Air Force. Moreover, the Army, besides its drawing upon the draft, also has the highest black initial enlistment rate of any of the services. For the 1961–1966 period, the Army drew 10.9 percent of its volunteer incoming personnel from blacks as compared with 9.8 percent for the Air Force, 7.2 percent for the Marine Corps, and 4.2 percent for the Navy.

Table 1. *Blacks in the Armed Forces as a Percentage of Total Personnel by Selected Years*

Year	Total Armed Forces	Army	Navy	Air Force	Marine Corps
1945	7.3	9.8	5.0	4.0*	3.6
1949	5.9	8.6	4.0	4.5	1.9
1954	7.9	11.3	3.2	7.5	5.9
1962	8.2	11.3	4.7	7.8	7.0
1965	9.5	12.8	5.2	9.2	8.3
1967	9.0	11.2	4.3	9.1	9.6

Source: Defense Department statistics.
*1945 Air Force figures refer to Army Air Corps.

There are also diverse patterns between the individual services as to the rank or grade distribution of blacks. Looking at Table 2, we find the ratio of black to white officers in 1967 was roughly 1 to 30 in the Army, 1 to 60 in the Air Force, 1 to 150 in the Marine Corps, and 1 to 300 in the Navy. Among enlisted men across all four services, blacks are underrepresented in the very top enlisted ranks (but least so in the Army). We also find a disproportionate concentration of blacks in the lower NCO levels in each of the armed forces. This is especially so in the Army where one out of every five staff sergeants is a black. An assessment of these data

[6]Bernard D. Karpinos, *Supplement to Health of the Army,* Washington: Office of the Surgeon General, Department of the Army, 1967, pp. 14–15.

reveals that the Army, followed by the Air Force, has not only the largest proportion of blacks in its total personnel, but also the most equitable distribution of blacks throughout its ranks. Although the Navy was the first service to integrate and the Army the last, in a kind of tortoise and hare fashion, it is the Army that has become the most representative service for blacks.

Table 2. Blacks as a Percentage of Total Personnel in Each Grade for Each Service (December 31, 1967)

Grade*	Army	Navy	Air Force	Marine Corps
Officers:				
0–7 and up (generals)	–	–	.2	–
0–6 (colonel)	.5	–	.8	–
0–5 (lt. colonel)	2.7	.1	.6	.1
0–4 (major)	5.6	.3	1.7	.3
0–3 (captain)	4.2	.5	2.1	.5
0–2 (1st lt.)	3.1	.4	2.7	1.4
0–1 (2nd lt.)	2.7	.3	1.9	.6
Total Officers	3.4	.3	1.8	.7
Enlisted Men:				
E–9 (sgt. major)	4.9	1.5	1.8	1.3
E–8 (master sgt.)	9.5	2.3	3.1	2.9
E–7 (sgt. 1st class)	13.9	3.9	4.5	5.9
E–6 (staff sgt.)	19.9	6.2	7.7	11.7
E–5 (sergeant)	13.7	6.4	13.4	10.8
E–4 (specialist 4)	10.6	4.4	12.5	8.6
E–3 (pvt. 1st class)	10.8	3.8	9.2	9.9
E–2 (private)	11.1	4.5	10.8	12.8
E–1 (recruit)	11.4	5.7	12.4	12.1
Total Enlisted Men	12.1	4.7	10.4	10.3

Source: Defense Department statistics.
*Army titles given in parentheses have equivalent pay grades in other services.

Changing Military Requirements and Black Participation

A pervasive trend within the military establishment singled out by students of this institution is the long-term trend toward greater technical complexity and narrowing of civilian-military occupational skills. An indicator, albeit a crude one, of this trend is the decreasing proportion of men assigned to combat arms. Given in Table 3, along with concomitant white-black distributions, are figures comparing the percentage of Army enlisted personnel in combat arms (e.g. infantry, armor, artillery) for the years of 1945, 1962, and 1967. We find that the proportion of men in combat arms—that is, traditional military specialties—drops from 44.5 percent in 1945 to 26.0 percent in 1962 and to 23.5 percent in 1967. Also, the percentages of white personnel in traditional military specialties closely approximate the total proportional decrease in the combat arms over the twenty-two year period.

Table 3. White and Black Army Personnel in Combat Arms, Selected Years

Category	1945*	1962	1967
Blacks as percentage of total personnel	10.5	12.2	12.1
Percentage of total personnel in combat arms	44.5	26.0	23.5
Percentage of total white personnel in combat arms	48.2	24.9	22.8
Percentage of total black personnel in combat arms	12.1	33.4	28.6

Source: Defense Department statistics.
*Excludes Army Air Corps.

For black soldiers, however, a different picture emerges. While the percentage of black enlisted men in the Army increased only slightly, the likelihood of a black serving in a combat arm is well over two times greater in the 1960's than it was at the end of World War II. Further, when impressionistic observations are made within the combat arms, the black proportion is noticeably higher in line rather than staff assignments, and in infantry rather than other combat arms. In many airborne and Marine line companies, the number of blacks approaches half the unit strength. Put in another way, the direction of assignment of black soldiers in the desegregated military is testimony to the continuing consequences of differential racial opportunity originating in the larger society. That is, even though integration of the military has led to great improvement in the performance of black servicemen, the social and particularly educational deprivations suffered by the black in American society can be mitigated but not eliminated by the racial egalitarian policies of the armed forces.[7]

Yet it is also true that the probabilities of a black being assigned to a combat arm are noticeably greater even when certain control variables are introduced. The data given in Table 4 is derived from complete Department of Defense manpower statistics for the year ending December 31, 1965. To sharpen the analysis, the grade and cohort that is modal for permanently assigned enlisted men in the Army and Marine Corps is used: servicemen who occupy the pay grade E-4 (corporal or specialist fourth class) with less than four years of military service. These manpower

[7]World War II evidence shows much of the incidence of pyschoneurotic breakdown among Negro soldiers, compared to Caucasians, was associated with psychological handicaps originating before entrance into military service. Arnold M. Rose, "Psychoneurotic Breakdown among Negro Soldiers," *Phylon,* Vol. XVII (1956), pp. 61–73.

statistics concerning proportional assignment in combat arms, in additional to racial breakdowns, also allow for categorization based on the Armed Forces Qualification Test (AFQT), a prime indicator of civilian socio-educational background.

Table 4. *Army and Marine Corps Enlisted Personnel (Pay Grade E-4) in Combat Arms by AFQT Level and Race (December 31, 1965)*

	Percent in Combat Arms	
Category	Army	Marine Corps
AFQT Level I	9.5 (5,835)	16.3 (1,459)
White	9.4 (5,719)	16.1 (1,426)
Black	15.5 (116)	24.2 (33)
AFQT Level II	13.7 (30,743)	29.9 (8,786)
White	13.5 (29,648)	29.4 (8,438)
Black	20.1 (1,095)	40.2 (348)
AFQT Level III	22.3 (51,156)	45.5 (8,729)
White	21.3 (44,079)	45.1 (7,687)
Black	28.5 (7,077)	54.0 (1,042)
AFQT Level IV and V	30.7 (14,232)	55.3 (2,027)
White	26.2 (8,362)	52.9 (1,616)
Black	37.1 (5,870)	64.5 (411)
Total Grade E-4*	20.1 (102,056)	38.1 (21,001)
White	18.3 (87,898)	36.7 (19,167)
Black	31.3 (14,158)	53.2 (1,834)

Source: Defense Department statistics. Number of cases on which percentages based given in parentheses.
*Pay grade E-4 with under four years of military service.

Table 4 reveals that combat arms assignment is markedly higher for blacks compared to whites even within each of the AFQT levels. It is also the case, however, that regardless of race, the lower the AFQT level, the greater the likelihood of combat assignment. These Department of Defense statistics also show that when AFQT level and race are looked at in unison, there are pronounced effects on assignment probabilities. Thus, blacks in the lowest AFQT levels (IV and V) are about four times more likely to be assigned to combat arms than are whites in AFQT level I: 37.1 percent to 9.4 percent in the Army; and 64.5 percent to 16.1 percent in the Marine Corps. These findings, however, need not be interpreted as a reflection on the "status" of the black in the integrated military. Actually there is evidence that higher prestige—but not envy—is generally accorded combat personnel by those in non-combat activities within the military.[8] And taken within the historical context of the "right to fight"

[8]Stouffer *et al., op. cit.,* Vol. II, pp. 242–89; Raymond W. Mack, "The Prestige System of an Air Base," *American Sociological Review,* Vol. XIX (June, 1954), pp. 281–87; Morris Janowitz, *The Professional Soldier,* Glencoe, Ill.: Free Press, 1960, pp. 31–36.

voiced by Negro organizations with reference to the segregated military of World War II, the black soldier's current overrepresentation in the combat arms might be construed as a kind of ironic step forward.[9]

As is to be expected, the overconcentration of blacks in combat units is all too obviously shown in the casualty reports from Viet Nam. As documented in Table 5, during the 1961–1966 period, blacks constituted 10.6 percent of military personnel in Southeast Asia while accounting for 16.0 percent of those killed in action. This reflects the high casualities suffered by the Army and Marine Corps—about 95 percent of all American losses in Viet Nam—compared to the Navy and Air Force. In 1967 and the first six months of 1968, however, the proportion of black combat deaths dropped to between 13 and 14 percent. Yet even in these later figures, black combat deaths were still about 3 percentage points above the proportion of blacks stationed in Southeast Asia, and about 5 percentage points above the total black proportion in the American military.

Table 5. *Blacks as Percentage of Men Assigned to Southeast Asia* and Killed in Action for Each Service (1961-June, 1968)*

Time Period	Army	Navy	Air Force	Marine Corps	Total Armed Forces
			Blacks in Southeast Asia		
1961–1966	12.6	5.4	10.3	8.0	10.6
1967	11.1	4.7	10.5	8.2	9.8
Jan.–June 1968	11.7	4.8	10.5	10.1	10.5
			Killed in Action		
1961–1966	20.0	.5	1.5	11.0	16.0
1967	13.5	2.9	5.2	12.8	12.7
Jan.–June 1968	13.3	2.6	1.5	14.1	13.0
1961–June 1968	15.1	2.2	2.7	12.8	13.7

Source: Defense Department statistics.
*Vietnam, Thailand, and off-shore ships.

Despite the greater likelihood for blacks to be assigned to combat arms and resultant high casualty rates in wartime, the fact remains that the

[9]There are, as should be expected, differences among black soldiers as to their desire to see combat. From data not shown here, 1965 interviews with black soldiers stationed in Germany revealed reluctance to go to Viet Nam was greatest among those with high-school or better education, and Northern home residence. This is in direct contrast with the findings reported in *The American Soldier*. In the segregated Army of World War II, Northern and more highly educated Negro soldiers were most likely to want to get into combat, an outcome of the onus of inferiority felt to accompany service in support units. Stouffer *et al. op. cit.,* Vol. I, pp. 523–24.

military at the enlisted ranks has become a major avenue of career mobility for many black men.[10] This state of affairs reflects not only the "pull" of the appeals offered by a racially integrated institution, but also the "push" generated by the plight of the black in the American economy. Indeed, there is rather conclusive evidence that the gap between black and white job opportunities in the civilian economy has not significantly altered over the past quarter-century. An insight into the causes underlying volunteer initial enlistments can be gained by looking at reasons given for entering the armed forces. Based on responses elicited in the 1964 NORC survey, the motivations of volunteers were grouped into four categories: (1) *personal,* e.g. get away from home, travel excitement; (2) *patriotic,* e.g. serve one's country; (3) *draft motivated,* e.g. increase options in choice of service and time of entry; and (4) *self-advancement,* e.g. learn a trade, receive an education, military as a career. As shown in Table 6, reasons for service entry among volunteers are reported by race holding educational level constant. There are only slight differences between whites and blacks with regard to personal or patriotic motivations for service entry. The variation between the races is found almost entirely in their differing mentions of draft motivated *versus* self-advancement reasons. Within each educational level, black volunteers mention self-advancement almost twice as often as whites. Conversely, whites are markedly more likely to state they entered the service to avoid the draft. In other words, the draft serves as a major inducement for whites to volunteer, while the belief that self-advancement will be furthered in the military is much more typical of black enlistees.

Moreover, once within the military the black serviceman is much more likely than his white counterpart to have "found a home." As noted earlier, in all four services there is an overrepresen'ation of black NCO's, especially at the junior levels. The disproporti nate concentration of blacks at these grades implies a higher than aver e reenlistment rate as such ranks are not normally attained until after a second enlistment. This assumption is supported by the data presented in Table 7. We find for the years 1964–1967 that the service-wide black reenlistment rate is approximately twice that of white servicemen. (Data from the 1964 NORC survey also show that 50.0 percent of blacks who were making a career of military life were initially draftees, as contrasted with 21.3 percent of the white career soldiers who similarly first entered the service through the draft.) Indeed, except for 1967, about half of all first-term black servicemen chose to remain in the armed forces for at least a second term. Even in 1967 when there is a sharp (but cross-racial) drop in reenlistments, the

---

[10]The emphasis on academic education for officer careers effectively limits most black opportunities to the enlisted levels. On this point, see Kurt Lang, "Technology and Career Management in the Military Establishment," in Morris Janowitz, ed., *The New Military,* New York: Russell Sage Foundation, 1964, pp. 39–81.

Table 6. Service Entry Reasons of Enlisted Volunteers, by Education and Race (Percentage Distribution)

Category	Personal	Patriotic	Draft-Motivated	Self Advancement	Total (N)
Less than high school					
White	33.2	13.5	27.5	25.8	100.0 (6,913)
Black	26.7	17.8	12.5	43.0	100.0 (911)
High school graduate					
White	27.8	10.9	39.5	21.8	100.0 (20,757)
Black	28.8	7.1	25.5	38.6	100.0 (2,440)
Some college					
White	27.5	10.7	47.2	14.6	100.0 (7,947)
Black	30.8	7.7	34.0	27.5	100.0 (701)
Total white	28.8	11.4	39.1	20.7	100.0 (35,617)
Total black	28.7	9.6	24.5	37.2	100.0 (4,052)

Source: 1964 NORC survey.

black reenlistment rate remains at twice that of whites.[11] The greater likelihood of blacks to select a service career suggests that the military establishment is undergoing a significant change in its NCO core. At the minimum, it is very probable that as the present cohort of black junior NCOs attains seniority there will be much greater black representation in the very top NCO grades. The expansion of the armed forces arising from the war in Viet Nam and the resulting "opening up of rank" has undoubtedly accelerated this development.

That black servicemen have a more favorable view of military life than whites is indicated not only in their higher reenlistment rates, but also more directly in the 1964 NORC survey data reported in Table 8. Whether broken down by branch of service, educational level, pay grade, or military occupational specialty, black servicemen compared to whites consistently have a less negative view of life in the military. In fact, inspection of Table 8 will show there is no category or subgroup in which whites are more favorably disposed toward military service than their black counterparts. It should be reiterated, however, that the relatively benign terms in which black men regard military life speak not only of the racial desegregation of the armed forces, but, more profoundly, of the existing state of affairs for blacks in American society at large.

[11]Some have attributed the sharp drop in the 1967 reenlistment rate to servicemen seeking to avoid a second tour of duty in Viet Nam. Although this factor undoubtedly explains some of the decline, the 1967 reenlistment data is suspect on other grounds. A substantial change in the mix of "first-term enlistees" and "inductees" (i.e. the greater number of draftees making up first-term servicemen) has made comparison of reenlistments for 1967 to earlier years questionable. Personal communication, Jack Moskowitz, Deputy Assistant Secretary, Department of Defense.

Table 7. First-Term Reenlistment Rates in the Armed Services, by Race, 1964-1967

Race	Army	Navy	Air Force	Marine Corps
1964:				
White	18.5%	20.9%	26.3%	12.9%
Black	49.3	39.9	48.8	25.1
1965:				
White	13.7	24.2	19.1	18.9
Black	49.3	44.8	39.2	38.9
1966				
White	20.0	17.6	16.0	10.5
Black	66.5	24.7	30.1	19.5
1967:				
White	12.8	16.7	17.3	9.7
Black	31.7	22.5	26.9	15.9

Source: Defense Department Statistics.

Attitudes of Soldiers

So far the discussion has sought to document the degree of penetration and the kind of distribution characterizing black servicemen in the integrated military establishment. We now turn to certain survey and interview data dealing more directly with the question of soldiers' attitudes toward military desegregation. Commenting on the difficulties of social analysis, the authors of *The American Soldier* wrote that few problems are "more formidable than that of obtaining dependable records of attitudes toward racial separation in the Army."[12] Without underestimating the continuing difficulty of this problem, an opportunity exists to compare attitudes toward racial integration held by American soldiers in two different periods. This is done by contrasting responses to equivalent items given in World War II as reported in *The American Soldier* with those reported in Project Clear, a study sponsored by the Defense Department during the Korean Conflict. The Project Clear surveys, conducted by the Operations Research Office ("ORO") of Johns Hopkins University, queried several thousand servicemen in both Korea and the United States on a variety of items relating to attitudes toward racial integration in the Army.[13]

[12]Stouffer *et al., op. cit.,* p. 566.

[13]What methodological bias exists is that the Korean Conflict question was a stronger description of racial integration than the item used in World War II. Compare, "What is your feeling about serving in a platoon containing both whites and colored soldiers, all

Table 8. Enlisted Personnel Not *Liking Military Life by Race and Selected Groupings (Percent Distribution)*

Category	White	Black
Services:		
Army	51.4 (15,007)	35.2 (2,641)
Navy	44.2 (11,158)	29.6 (699)
Air Force	36.1 (12,593)	27.0 (1,414)
Marine Corps	46.5 (3,262)	35.3 (300)
Total military by education:		
Less than high school	42.8 (8,431)	28.5 (1,084)
High school graduate	43.2 (24,027)	31.3 (2,985)
Some college	49.3 (9,562)	38.9 (985)
Army enlisted men by military occupation:		
Combat	49.5 (3,192)	36.1 (777)
Technical	52.9 (3,390)	35.6 (556)
Administrative	54.1 (2,976)	35.5 (352)
Service	52.5 (4,221)	33.0 (690)
Army enlisted men by pay grade		
E–1 – E–2	54.2 (2,992)	39.9 (571)
E–3 – E–4	69.6 (7,183)	48.9 (1,197)
E–5 – E–6	25.5 (3,826)	14.7 (797)
E–7 – E–9	12.9 (1,016)	4.9 (81)

Source: 1964 NORC survey. Number of cases on which percentages based given in parentheses.

In both *The American Soldier* and Project Clear (the surveys under consideration were conducted in 1943 and 1951, respectively) large samples of Army personnel in segregated military settings were categorized as to whether they were favorable, indifferent, or opposed to racial integration in Army units. We find, as presented in Table 9, massive shifts in soldiers' attitudes over the eight-year period, shifts showing a much more positive disposition toward racial integration among both whites and blacks in the later year. A look at the distribution of attitudes held by white soldiers reveals opposition to integration goes from 84 percent in

working and training together, sleeping in the same barracks and eating in the same mess hall?" with "Do you think white and Negro soldiers should be in separate outfits or should they be together in the same outfits?". Respectively, ORO, *op. cit.,* p. 453, and Stouffer *et al., op. cit.,* p. 568.

1943 to less than half in 1951. That such a change could occur in less than a decade counters viewpoints that see basic social attitudes in large populations being prone to glacial-like changes.

Table 9. Attitudes of White and Black Soldiers Toward Racial Integration in the Segregated Army, 1943 and 1951

Attitude Toward Integration	White Soldiers		Black Soldiers	
	1943	*1951*	*1943*	*1951*
Favorable	12%	25%	37%	90%
Indifferent	4	31	27	6
Oppose	84	44	36	4
Total	100%	100%	100%	100%
(N)	(4,800)	(1,983)	(3,000)	(1,384)

Source: 1943 data from Stouffer et al., *The American Soldier*, Vol. I, 1949, p. 568; 1951 data from ORO, *Project Clear*, 1955, pp. 322, 433.

Yet, an even more remarkable change is found among the black soldiers. Where in 1945, favorable, indifferent, or opposing attitudes were roughly equally distributed among the black soldiers, by 1951 opposition or indifference to racial integration had become negligible. Such a finding is strongly indicative of a reformation in black public opinion from traditional acquiescence to Jim Crow to the ground swell that laid the basis for the subsequent civil rights movement. It may be argued, of course, that recent developments—separatist tendencies within the black community in the late 1960's—have eclipsed the 1951 findings. Nevertheless, the data is still convincing that on the eve of integration, black soldiers overwhelmingly rejected a segregated armed forces.

Moreover, while the data on black responses toward integration given in Table 9 were elicited during the segregated military of 1943 and 1951, we also have evidence on how black soldiers react to military integration in a more contemporary setting. As reported in Table 10, the Army is thought to be much more racially egalitarian than civilian life. Only 16 percent of sixty-seven black soldiers interviewed in 1965 said civilian life was more racially equal or no different than the Army. By region, as might be expected, we find Southern blacks more likely than Northern blacks to take a favorable view of racial relations in the Army when these are compared to civilian life. The data in Table 10 support the proposition that, despite existing deviations from military policy at the level of informal discrimination, the military establishment stands in sharp and favorable contrast to the racial relations prevalent in the larger American society.

One of the most celebrated findings of *The American Soldier* was the

Table 10.   Attitudes of Black Soldiers in 1965 Comparing Racial Equality in Military and Civilian Life, Total and by Home Region

Where More Racial Equality	Total	Home Region	
		North	South
Military life	84%	75%	93%
Civilian life	3	6	0
No difference	13	19	7
Total	100%	100%	100%
(N)	(67)	(36)	(31)

discovery that the more contact white soldiers had with black troops, the more favorable was their reaction toward racial integration.[14] This conclusion is consistently supported in the surveys conducted by Project Clear. Again and again, comparisons of white soldiers in integrated units with those in segregated units show the former to be more supportive of desegregation. Illustrative of this pattern are the data shown in Table 11. Among combat infantrymen in Korea, 51 percent in all-white units prefer segregation compared to 31 percent in integrated units. For enlisted personnel stationed in the United States, strong objection to integration characterizes 44 percent serving in segregated units while less than one-fifth of the men in integrated units feel the same way. Seventy-nine percent of officers on segregated posts rate blacks worse than white soldiers as compared with 28 percent holding similar beliefs on integrated posts.

Official Policy and Actual Practice

For the man newly entering the armed forces, it is hard to conceive that the military was one of America's most segregated institutions some two decades ago. For today color barriers at the formal level are absent throughout the military establishment. Equal treatment regardless of race is official policy in such non-duty facilities as swimming pools, chapels, barbershops, post exchanges, movie theaters, snack bars, and dependents' housing as well as in the more strictly military endeavors involved in the assignment, promotion, and living conditions of members of the armed services.[15] Moreover, white personnel are often commanded by black superiors, a situation rarely obtaining in civilian life. In brief, military life

[14]*Ibid.,* p. 594.

[15]The comprehensive scope of military integration is found in the official guidelines set forth under "Equal Opportunity and Treatment of Military Personnel," in *Army Regulation 66-21, Air Force Regulation 35-78,* and *Secretary of the Navy Instruction 5350.6.*

Table 11. Racial Attitudes of White Soldiers in Segregated and Integrated
Military Settings, 1951 (Percent Distribution)

Racial Attitudes	All-White Units	Integrated Units
Combat infantrymen in Korea saying segregated outfits better	51% (195)	31% (1,024)
Enlisted personnel in the U.S. strongly objecting to racial integration	44% (1,983)	17% (1,683)
Officers rating Negroes worse than white soldiers	79% (233)	28% (385)

Source: ORO, *Project Clear*, 1955, pp. 141, 322, 333, 356. Number of cases on which percentages based given in parentheses.

is characterized by an interracial equalitarianism of a quantity and of a kind that is seldom found in the other major institutions of American society.

Some measure of the extent and thoroughness of military desegregation is found in comparing the 1950 President's committee ("Fahy committee") report dealing with racial integration and the 1963 and 1964 reports of a second President's committee ("Gesell committee"). Where the earlier report dealt entirely with internal military organization, the later reports address themselves primarily to off-base discrimination.[16] Thus in order to implement its policy of equal opportunity, the military began to exert pressure on local communities where segregated residential patterns affected military personnel. Since 1963 commanders of military installations have been under instructions to persuade apartment and trailer court owners to end segregation voluntarily. These informal efforts had little or no success. In 1967 an important precedent was set when segregated housing was declared off limits to all military personnel in the area adjacent to Andrews Air Force Base, Maryland. In 1968 the Defense Department announced a nationwide policy forbidding any serviceman to rent lodgings where racial discrimination was practised. Whatever one's value priorities—concern over military influence on civilian society *versus* integrated housing—the ramifications of this policy are significant and deserve careful examination.

In their performance of military duties, whites and blacks work together with little open display of racial animosity. This is not to say racial tension is negligible in the military. Incidents between the races do occur, but

[16]Cf. the Fahy committee report (1950) with the Gesell committee reports (1963 and 1964).

such confrontations are almost always off-duty, if not off-base. (Excepting, importantly, military stockades where racial strife is compounded by the problems of incarceration.) Additionally it must be stressed that conflict situations stemming from non-racial causes characterize most sources of friction in the military establishment, for example, enlisted men *versus* officers, lower-ranking enlisted men *versus* non-commissioned officers, soldiers of middle-class background *versus* those of the working class, draftees *versus* volunteers, line units *versus* staff units, rear echelon *versus* front echelon, newly arrived units *versus* earlier stationed units, etc.

Yet the fact remains that the general pattern of day-to-day relationships *off the job* is usually one of mutual racial exclusivism. As one black soldier put it, "A man can be my best buddy in the Army, but he won't ask me to go to town with him." Closest friendships normally develop within races between individuals of similar educational and social background. Beyond one's hard core of friends there exists a level of friendly acquaintances. Here the pattern seems to be one of educational similarities overriding racial differences. On the whole, racial integration at informal levels works best on-duty vis-à-vis off-duty, on-base vis-à-vis off-base, basic training and maneuvers vis-à-vis garrison, sea vis-à-vis shore duty, and—most especially—combat vis-à-vis non-combat. In other words, the behavior of servicemen resembles the racial (and class) separatism of the larger American society, the more they are removed from the military environment.

For nearly all white soldiers the military is a first experience with close and equal contact with a large group of blacks. There has developed what has become practically a military custom: the look over the shoulder, upon the telling of a racial joke, to see if there are any blacks in hearing distance. Some racial animosity is reflected in accusations that black soldiers use the defense of racial discrimination to avoid disciplinary punishment. Many white soldiers claim they like Negroes as individuals but "can't stand them in bunches." In a few extreme cases, white married personnel may even live off the military base and pay higher rents rather than live in integrated military housing. On the whole, however, the segregationist-inclined white soldier regards racial integration as something to be accepted pragmatically, if reluctantly, as are so many situations in military life.

The most overt source of racial unrest in the military community centers in dancing situations. A commentary on American mores is a finding reported in Project Clear: three-quarters of a large sample of white soldiers said they would not mind Negro couples on the same dance floor, but approximately the same number disapproved of Negro soldiers dancing with white girls.[17] In many non-commissioned officer (NCO) clubs,

[17]ORO, *op. cit.,* p. 388.

the likelihood of interracial dancing partners is a constant producer of tension. In fact, the only major exception to integration within the military community is on a number of large posts where there are two or more NCO clubs. In such situations one of the clubs usually becomes tacitly designated as the black club.

Although there is general support for racial integration by black soldiers, tensions are also evident among black military personnel. Black officers are sometimes seen as being too strict or "chicken" when it comes to enforcing military discipline on black enlisted men. As one black soldier said, "I'm proud when I see a Negro officer, but not in my company." Similarly, black noncoms are alleged to pick on blacks when it comes time to assign men unpleasant duties. There is also the tendency among some of the lower-ranking black enlisted men, especially draftees, to view black NCOs as "Uncle Toms" or "handkerchief heads." This view may be expected to become somewhat more prevalent in the wake of the growing militancy among black youths in civilian society. In the same vein, self-imposed informal segregation on the part of many blacks will become more overt. Nevertheless, the fact remains—and will indefinitely be so—that the military is a sought after career choice for many black men.

One black writer, who served in the segregated Army and later had two sons in the integrated military, has proposed that what was thought by soldiers in all-Negro units to be racial discrimination was often nothing more than routine harassment of lower-ranking enlisted personnel.[18] In fact, the analogy between enlisted men vis-à-vis officers in the military and blacks vis-à-vis whites in the larger society has often been noted.[19] It has been less frequently observed, however, that enlisted men's behavior is often similar to many of the stereotypes associated with Negroes, for example, laziness, boisterousness, emphasis on sexual prowess, consciously acting stupid, obsequiousness in front of superiors combined with ridicule of absent superiors, etc. Placement of white adult males in a subordinate position within a rigidly stratified system, that is, appears to produce behavior not all that different from the so-called personality traits commonly held to be an outcome of cultural or psychological patterns unique to Negro life. Indeed, it might be argued that relatively little adjustment on the part of the command structure was required when the infusion of blacks into the enlisted ranks occured as the military establishment was desegregated. It is suggested, in other words, one factor contributing to the generally smooth racial integration of the military was due to the standard treatment—"like Negroes"—accorded to all lower-ranking enlisted personnel.

[18]James Anderson, "Father and Sons: An Evaluation of Military Racial Relations in Two Generations," term paper, University of Michigan, December, 1965.
[19]Stouffer and his accociates, for example, report enlisted men as compared to officers, as Negro soldiers to white soldiers, were more prone to have "low spirits," to be less desirous of entering combat, and to be more dissatisfied than perceived by others. Stouffer *et al., op. cit,* Vol. II, p. 345, and Vol. I, pp. 392–94, 506, 521, and 538.

The Black Soldier Overseas

Some special remarks are needed concerning black servicemen overseas. Suffice it to say for prefatory purposes, the American soldier, be he either white or black, is usually in a place where he does not understand the language, is received with mixed feelings by the local population, spends the greater part of his time in a transplanted American environment, sometimes plays the role of tourist, is relatively affluent in relation to the local economy, takes advantage and is at the mercy of a comprador class, and in comparison with his counterpart at home is more heavily involved in military duties.

In general, the pattern of racial relations observed in the United States —integration in the military setting and racial exclusivism off-duty—prevails in overseas assignments as well. This norm is reflected in one of the most characteristic features of American military life overseas, a bifurcation of the vice structure into groups that pander almost exclusively (or assert they do) to only one of the races. A frequent claim of local bar owners is that they discourage racially mixed trade because of the demands of their G.I. clientele. And, indeed, many of the establishments catering to American personnel that ring most military installations are segregated in practice. To a similar degree this is true of shore towns where Navy personnel take liberty. Violation of these implicit taboos can lead to physical threat if not violence.

The pattern of off-duty separatism is most pronounced in Japan and Germany, and somewhat less so in Korea (though the Sam Gak Chi area in Seoul has long been a gathering point for black servicemen). Combat conditions in Viet Nam make the issue of off-duty racial relations academic for those troops in the field. In the cities, however, racial separatism off-duty is readily apparent. It is said that the riverfront district in Saigon, Kanh Hoi, frequented by black American soldiers was formerly patronized by Senegalese troops during the French occupation. In off-duty areas on Okinawa racial separatism is complicated by interservice rivalries and a fourfold ecological pattern shows up: white-Army, black-Army, white-Marines, and black-Marines. A major exception to the norm of off-duty racial separatism occurred in the Dominican Republic. There all troops were restricted and leaving the military compound necessitated soldiers collaborating if they were not to be detected; such ventures were often as not interracial.

In Germany one impact of that country's economic boom has been to depress the relative position of the American soldier vis-à-vis the German working man. In the Germany of ten or fifteen years ago (or the Korea and Viet Nam of today) all American military personnel were affluent by local standards with all that implied. This was (and is in Korea and Viet Nam) an especially novel experience for the black soldier. The status drop

of American soldiers in Germany has particularly affected the black serviceman who has the additional handicap of being black in a country
where there are no black women. The old "good duty" days for black
soldiers in Germany have come to an end as he finds his previous access
to other than prostitutes severely reduced. The German economic boom
has affected black soldiers in another way. In recent years there has been
some friction between foreign laborers (mostly from Mediterranean countries) and black soldiers. Both groups of men apparently are competing for
the same girls. At the same time, the foreign workers have little contact
with white American soldiers who move in a different segment of the vice
structure.

Nonetheless, overseas duty for the black serviceman, in Germany as
well as in the Far East, gives him an opportunity, even if peripheral, to
witness societies where racial discrimination is less practiced than it is in
his home country. Although the level of black acceptance in societies
other than America is usually exaggerated, the black soldier is hard put
not to make invidious comparisons with the American scene.[20] In interviews conducted in 1965 with black servicemen in Germany, 64 percent
said there was more racial equality in Germany than America, 30 percent
saw little difference between the two countries, and only 6 percent believed blacks were treated better in the United States.

Observers of overseas American personnel have told the writer that
black soldiers are more likely than whites to learn local languages (though
for both groups of servicemen this is a very small number). Evidence for
this supposition is given in Table 12. Three German-national barbers, who
were permanently hired to cut the hair of all the men in one battalion,
were asked by the writer to evaluate the German language proficiency of
the individual personnel in that battalion.[21] When these evaluations were
correlated with race, it was found that black soldiers were five times more
likely to know "conversational" German, and three times more likely to
know "some" German than were white soldiers.[22] Actually, the likelihood
of black soldiers compared to whites in learning the language of the

---

[20]A social-distance study conducted among Korean college students found the following
placement, from near to far: Chinese, Europeans and white Americans, Filipinos, Indians
(from India), and black Americans. Personal communication, Man Gap Lee, Seoul National
University.

The less than favorable reception of black soldiers—compared to whites—in overseas
locales is also illustrated in the Japanese film *The Saga of Postwar Cruelty* (1968), a portrayal
of the American occupation from 1945 to 1952. Made by one of Japan's leading directors
—Tetsuji Takechi—the film loses no time in making its point. Even before the titles are
completed, a Japanese girl is seized, raped, and killed by a drunken black soldier.

[21]These barbers were focal points of much of the battalion's gossip and between themselves saw every man in the battalion on the average of at least twice a month.

[22]These same data, in tables not shown here, reveal that there is an *inverse* correlation
between formal education (as ascertained from battalion personnel records) and likelihood
of learning German: This reflects the greater probability of black soldiers, compared to
whites, to learn German while averaging fewer years of formal education.

country in which they are stationed may be even greater than indicated in Table 12. Several of the German-speaking white soldiers were of German ethnic background and acquired some knowledge of the language in their home environments back in the United States.

Table 12. Command of German Language of White and Black Soldiers in a German-Based U.S. Army Battalion, 1965 (Percent Distribution)

Command of German*	White Soldiers	Black Soldiers
Conversational	1.4	7.4
Some	3.0	7.4
Little or none	95.6	85.2
Total	100.0	100.0
(N)	(629)	(98)

*Based on evaluations of German-national battalion barbers.

It is more than coincidence that a widely seen German television commerical in 1965—in which white and black American soldiers were portrayed—only the black soldiers spoke German. Similarly, a study of American troops in Japan reported: "In general, Negro soldiers learned to speak Japanese more quickly and expertly than did the white soldiers (whose efforts in this direction were very halting.)"[23] The strong weight of evidence, then, is that black servicemen overseas, perhaps because of the more favorable racial climate, are more willing to take advantage of informal participation and interaction with local populations.

Race at Home and War Abroad

It is important to remember that the desegregation of the armed forces antedated both the beginnings of the civil rights movement in the late 1950's and the black power movement a decade later. In the light of subsequent developments in the domestic racial picture, it is likely that severe disciplinary problems—if not outright organized mutiny—would have occurred had military integration not come about when it did. The timing of desegregation in the military, that is, defused an ingredient—all-black units—which would have been explosive in this nation's current racial strife. One has only to be reminded of the embroilments between black units and whites that were an ever present problem in the segregated military. On the other hand, the armed forces were remarkably free of racial turmoil from the middle 1950's through the middle 1960's.

Nevertheless, it is also the case that the military establishment—at least

[23]William Caudill, "American Soldiers in a Japanese Community," unpublished manuscript, p. 34.

into the foreseeable future—will no longer be immune from the racial and
class conflcts occurring in the larger American society. Incidents with
racial overtones have become more frequent in recent years. Two of the
most dramatic occurred in the summer of 1968. Over 250 black prisoners
took part in a race riot in the Long Binh stockade outside Saigon. The
stockade was not brought under complete military control for close to a
month. At about the same time in the United States, forty-three black
soldiers at Fort Hood, Texas, refused to leave as part of the force assigned
to guard the Democratic Convention. The soliders feared they might be
used to combat Chicago blacks. That black soldiers may find they owe
higher fealty to the black community than to the U.S. Army is a possibility that haunts commanders. The likelihood of such an eventuality, however, will be serious only if the Army is regularly summoned into action
in black ghettos. Sensitive to the civil rights issue and spectre of black
power in the military, the armed forces have been surprisingly mild (up
to this writing) in their handling of black servicemen involved in racial
incidents. Neither the Long Binh rioters nor the "Fort Hood 43" received
anything approaching maximum sentences, many cases being dismissed
outright. Such a policy of lenient treatment coupled with internal racially
egalitarian practises will most likely be sufficient—barring repeated military interventions in black ghettos—to preclude any widespread black
disaffection within the armed forces.

The nature of black participation in the military organization has also
become inextricable with broader criticisms of American's politico-mili-
tary policies. Though originally focusing on the war in Viet Nam, radical
attacks have come to include a questioning of the very legitimacy of
military service.[24] Much attention has been given to the relationship between elements of the black militant movement with the movement
against the war in Viet Nam. Yet the black movement as a whole has
remained largely removed from those white radical groups vociferously
attacking the military services. Indeed, the anti-war movement has aggravated not only the already existing cleavages between black moderate
and black militant leaders but has also revealed differences between black
demands and the goals of white radicals. The pertinent question appears
to be not so much what are the implications of the black movement for
the military establishment, but what are the effects of the Viet Nam war
on internal developments within the black movement itself. Although it
would be premature to offer a definite statement on any future interpene-

[24]Even in the Civil War there were black spokesmen who opposed black participation in
the Union Army. Frederick Douglass attacked them as follows. "They tell you this is the
'white man's' war; that you will be no 'better off after than before the war'; that the getting
of you into the army is to 'sacrifice you on the first opportunity.' Believe them not; cowards
themselves, they do not wish to have their cowardice shamed by your brave example. Leave
them to their timidity, or to whatever motive may hold them back." Quoted in Ronald Segal,
The Race War, Bantam, 1967, pp. 198–99.

trations between the black movement and anti-military groups, a major turning away of blacks *per se* from military commitment is viewed as highly doubtful. Most likely, and somewhat paradoxically, we will witness more vocal anti-military sentiment within certain black militant groups at the same time that the armed forces increasingly become a leading avenue of career opportunity for many black men.

Nevertheless, there has usually been and is today a presumption on the part of America's military opponents that Negroes should be less committed soldiers than whites. Whether for tactical or ideological reasons, the black serviceman has been frequently defined as a special target for propaganda by forces opposing America in military conflicts. In World War II the Japanese directed radio appeals specifically to Negro servicemen in the Pacific theater. The Chinese in the Korean Conflict used racial arguments on Negro prisoners of war. Yet a careful study of American POW behavior in Korea made no mention of differences in black and white behavior except to note that the resegregation of black POWs by the Chinese had a boomerang effect on Communist indoctrination methods.[25]

The recent military interventions of the United States on the international scene raises again the question of the motivation and performance of black soldiers in combat. A spokesman for the National Liberation Front of South Viet Nam asserted as early as 1965 that "liberation forces have a special attitude toward American soldiers who happen to be Negroes." In the same vein, upon release of three American POWs (two of them black) in early 1968, the clandestine Viet Cong radio announced it was a gesture of "solidarity and support for American Negroes." My observations as well as those of others found no differences in white or black combat performance in Viet Nam. In the Dominican Republic, where the proportion of blacks in line units ran as high as 40 percent, a pamphlet was distributed to black soldiers exhorting them to "turn your guns on your white oppressors and join your Dominican brothers."[26] Again, my personal observations buttressed by comment from Dominicans revealed no significant differences between white and black military performance.[27]

My appraisal is that among officers and NCO's there was no discernible difference between the races concerning military commitment in either

[25]Albert D. Biderman, *March to Calumny,* New York: Macmillan, 1964, p. 60.

[26]A copy of the entire pamphlet is reproduced in the Dominican news magazine *Ahora* (no. 108, September 18, 1965). Although many whites were unaware of the pamphlet's existence, virtually every black soldier I talked to in Santo Domingo said he had seen the pamphlet. The effectiveness of the pamphlet on black soldiers was minimal, among other reasons, because it asserted black equality existed in the Dominican Republic, a statement belied by brief observation of the Dominican scene.

[27]Similarly in an interview with a black reporter, the commandant of "constitutionalist rebel" forces in Santo Domingo stated that to his dismay Negro American soldiers fought no differently than whites. Laurence Harvey, "Report from the Dominican Republic," *Realist,* June, 1965, p. 18.

the Dominican Republic or Viet Nam. Among black soldiers in the lower enlisted ranks, however, there was a somewhat greater disenchantment compared to white as to the mertis of America's recent military ventures. Such unease, however, has little effect on military performance, most especially in the actual combat situation. Close living, strict discipline and common danger all serve to preclude racial conflict between whites and blacks in field units. The evidence strongly suggests that the racial integration of the armed forces, coming about when it did, effectively precluded any potential success on the part of America's military opponents to differentiate black from white soldiers.

It is also probable, however, that military experience will contribute to an activist posture on the part of black servicemen returning to civilian life. The black ex-serviceman, that is, will be less willing to accommodate himself to second-class citizenship after participating in the racially egalitarian military system. Further, especially in situations where blacks are intimidated by physical threat or force, techniques of violence and organizational skills acquired in military service will be a new factor in the black movement. Robert F. Williams, the first leading advocate of armed self-defense for blacks explicitly states that his Marine Corps experience led to his beliefs.[28] (Williams, whose exact whereabouts are unknown, is listed as the honorary head of the ultra-militant Revolutionary Action Movement—RAM.) It also seems more than coincidence that the ten founders of the Deacons for Defense and Justice a paramilitary group organized in 1964 to counter Ku Klux Klan terrorism, were all veterans of Korea or World War II.[29] Moreover, black veterans returning from Viet Nam are alleged to be prominent in the membership of newly formed para-military groups in urban ghettos (e.g. the Black Panthers in the San Francisco Bay area, the Zulu 1200's in St. Louis, the Invaders in Memphis, the US organization in Los Angeles). Yet, the future role of the Viet Nam veteran in the black movement is hard to assess. Undoubtedly, most black veterans—like most people—will eschew politico-revolutionary activity and seek to improve their lives along individual lines. But we can also expect—as was the case after previous American wars—that black veterans will play a leading role in their race's struggle for dignity and equality.

Although the military was until recent times one of America's most segregated institutions, it has leaped into the forefront of racial equality in the past decades. What features of the military establishment can account for this about-face? There is a combination of mutually supporting factors that operate in the generally successful racial integration of the armed forces. For one thing, the military—an institution revolving around techniques of violence—is to an important degree discontinuous from

[28]Robert F. Williams, *Negroes with Guns,* New York: Marzani and Munsell, 1962.
[29]*The Militant,* November 22, 1965, p. 1.

other areas of social life. And this apartness served to allow, once the course had been decided, a rapid and complete racial integration. The path of desegregation was further made easier by characteristics peculiar or at least more pronounced in the military compared to other institutions. With its hierarchical power structure, predicated on stable and patterned relationships, decisions need take relatively little account of the personal desires of service personnel. Additionally, because roles and activities are more defined and specific in the military than in most other social arenas, conflicts that might have ensued within a more diffuse and ambiguous setting were largely absent. Likewise, desegregation was facilitated by the pervasiveness in the military of a bureaucratic ethos, with its concomitant formality and high social distance, that mitigated tensions arising from individual or personal feelings.

At the same time it must also be remembered that the military establishment has means of coercion not readily available in most civilian pursuits. Violations of norms are both more visible and subject to quicker sanctions. The military is premised, moreover, on the accountability of its members for effective performance. Owing to the aptly termed "chain of command," failures in policy implementation can be pinpointed. This in turn means that satisfactory carrying out of stated policy advances one's own position. In other words, it is to each individual's personal interest, if he anticipates receiving the rewards of a military career, to insure that decisions going through him are executed with minimum difficulty. Or put in another way, whatever the internal policy decided upon, racial integration being a paramount but only one example, the military establishment is uniquely suited to realize its implementation.

What implications does the military integration experience have for civilian society? Although it is certainly true that the means by which racial desegregation was accomplished in the military establishment are not easily transferable to the civilian community, the end result of integration in the contemporary armed forces can suggest some qualities of what —if it came about—an integrated American society would be *within the context of the prevailing structural and value system.* Equality of treatment would be the rule in formal and task-specific relationships. Racial animosity would diminish but not disappear. We would expect primary group ties and informal association to remain largely within one's own racial group. But even at primary group levels, the integrated society would exhibit a much higher interracial intimacy than exists in the nonintegrated society. We would also expect a sharp improvement in black mobility and performance in the occupational sphere even taking into consideration on-going social and educational handicaps arising from existing inequities. Yet, because of these inequities, blacks would still be overconcentrated in less skilled and less rewarded positions.

Such a description of the racially integrated society is, of course, what one finds in today's military establishment. Moreover, despite inequities suffered by blacks both in being more likely to be drafted and once in the service being more likely to assignment in combat units, blacks, nevertheless, are still much more favorably disposed toward military life than whites. It is a commentary on our nation that many black youths by seeking to enter and remain in the armed forces are saying that it is even worth the risk of being killed in order to have a chance to learn a trade, to make it in a small way, to get away from a dead-end existence, and to become part of the only institution in this society which seems really to be integrated.

BLACK POWER AND
"THE MOVEMENT": TWO VIEWS

"In Defense of 'Black Power'"

by David Danzig

When the Mississippi marchers trekked across the state chanting "Black Power," they were addressing themselves to other Negroes, mostly sharecroppers, tenant farmers, and small-town residents who crowded the line of march as it passed their way. The slogan no doubt meant different things to the many demonstrators who shouted it in preference to last year's "Freedom Now," just as it did to the commentators in the North who were subsequently disturbed by it. But in the context of the Mississippi march, the new slogan was clearly an appeal to Negroes to build political strength around the vote.

This effort to encourage Negroes to see themselves as a power bloc, and to act as one, is entirely in keeping with American minority politics, and yet an attempt is apparently being made by both the advocates and the opponents of "black power" to present it as something of a departure. Indeed, the slogan of the Mississippi march, followed by the belligerent tone of the CORE convention in Baltimore last June, called forth a response from liberals, both white and black, which seemed to suggest that Stokely Carmichael and Floyd McKissick had just invented bloc politics and were converting this startling invention into a movement to take over America. To Martin Luther King, "black power" meant the substitution of "one tyranny for another." To Vice President Humphrey, Roy Wilkins, and the New York *Times,* it meant black nationalism and "racism in reverse." To others it meant nothing less than that the Negroes were out to achieve "black supremacy." Everyone, of course, agreed on the right of Negroes to use the ballot to improve their lot, but conditions were often implicitly set on how they should behave collectively. Rarely, in the course of all the excitement over "black power," did anyone seek to deal with the realities underlying the current thrust of Negro social action.

Of these realities, the primary one is the steady build-up of group feeling among Negroes during the past twenty years. That such feeling would express itself as color consciousness was to be expected, but "buy black," "vote black," and "hire black" hardly indicate that Negroes have embraced a mystique of color. On the contrary, what such slogans betoken is a new political realism based on the perception that group solidarity is the only road to Negro salvation.

In general, most Negro organizations—from the moderate NAACP, Urban League, and Southern Christian Leadership Conference to the militant CORE and SNCC, to say nothing of the aggressive nationalists and the anti-white Black Muslims—share this perception. Thus, while the NAACP has not excluded whites from positions of leadership in the organization, as SNCC has done, Jack Greenberg, the white head of the NAACP Defense Fund, was aked not to attend the very NAACP conference at which Roy Wilkins denounced "black power": a less obvious and more typical concession to the rising feeling among Negroes that important posts in the civil-rights field should be filled by their own people. And while only SNCC of the major organizations withdrew from the recent White House Conference "To Fulfill These Rights," the remaining Negro groups united to keep the conference centered exclusively on Negro interests, showing little inclination to put the problems of other minorities like the Puerto Ricans and the Mexicans on the agenda. The national leaderships of NAACP, CORE, SNCC, and the SCLC still include some whites, but they are so few as to suggest a reverse "tokenism." The local branches of these organizations, which are rather more representative of majority sentiment than the national headquarters and less concerned with questions of public image, are by now primarily, if not entirely, Negro.

The call for group solidarity embodied in "black power"—like the many signs that Negroes are now determined to run their own organizations—is so far from anything which could legitimately be called racism that one is at first puzzled to account for all the excitement the new slogan has generated. Much of it, of course, can be put down to public relations and position-taking, but there does seem to be an undercurrent of real anxiety in the air as well. The white man's persistent fears of the black man—fears which stem from the not unreasonable idea that an oppressed minority may decide at any moment to retaliate against the majority—have spread from the South to the North, updated by Watts, mounting city crime and violence, Negro impatience with the ineffectiveness of poverty and civil-rights programs, and the swelling chorus among Negroes of anti-white rhetoric. "Black power," with its separatist connotations, gives shape to these fears. The extent of the anxiety is suggested by the contrast between the universal white condemnation of the new slogan and the tolerant editorials that greeted the Watts riots a year ago. Are violent outbreaks such as Watts less frightening than the vision of a powerfully organized Negro bloc? If so, it may be because in the final analysis Watts stands for a kind of group delinquency that always ends in political impotence, while the term "black power" suggests an organized, disciplined group.

At any rate, if the liberals have been unable to put their fingers on the cause of their growing dissatisfaction with the civil-rights movement in the last few years, the Mississippi militants have given them a helping hand. When Roy Wilkins said that "black power" means "black death," he was warning the Negroes against provoking an explosion of repressive white counterpower. Whether or not there is any substance to this warning, the picture of bitter conflict among contending blocs, each acting out of its own self-interest, is deeply disturbing to liberals: is *this* what they have been striving for in the name of the free and open society? And if the civil-rights movement is losing its idealism and becoming a movement "merely" to advance Negro interests, does it deserve liberal support?

As it happens, however, "black power" in various forms has been around for some time, and the issue which the slogan has raised is but the latest and—here is the main novelty—the most explicit in a long series of conflicts between the white liberal and the Negro. It all began with the adoption by the civil-rights movement of militant direct-action tactics like mass demonstrations, sit-ins, and boycotts—a phase which reflected and coincided with the growing involvement of Negroes themselves in the movement. Such tactics seemed suited to conditions in the South, but they made many liberals uncomfortable when they were exported to the North, particularly as the cry of "Freedom Now" that usually accompanied them was so perplexing to liberal ears. What specific injustice were the militants seeking to redress? What relevance did "Freedom Now" have to New York, Chicago, and Seattle? (As though to provide the general confusion with a symbol in the form of a caricature, there was the protestor who manacled himself to a railing outside Mayor Wagner's office and shouted "Freedom Now!" as he tried to prevent a baffled policeman from unchaining him.) Some white liberal groups—the unions and the churches, for example—had their own traditions of militancy, and could understand what the Negroes were doing, but *black* militancy was in general a new experience for the white man. In time, the issue of aggressive tactics more and more distinguished white from black within the civil-rights coalition and militant declarations became part of the rhetoric of Negro leadership.

The Negroes' demand for special consideration was another source of tension. While the liberal coalition thought it was correcting an injustice by repairing the New Deal's failure to take in the Negro, the Negro himself found that the problem of unemployment had grown so serious that it could no longer be dealt with by the normal processes of non-discrimination. But the new Negro demand for compensatory hiring and preferential treatment that was formulated to meet this situation turned out to be totally unacceptable to the liberals, for it conflicted with the traditional liberal ideal of equal opportunity and equal treatment of people according to their individual merits. Accordingly, these demands were condemned as "reverse discrimination" and rejected as public policy; nevertheless, an unofficial policy of deliberately seeking Negro applicants in a ratio relative to their numerical proportion in the community has been adopted wherever Negroes have been strong enough to apply group pressure. Recently, to take only one example of many, Secretary of Labor Wirtz announced that the government, in a complete reversal of its earlier practice, was requiring information as to race on all job applications. Thus, Negro group pressure for jobs has countermanded one of the early achievements of the liberal coalition in eliminating all reference to race and religion from the formal hiring procedure—an achievement which was once counted a great victory for the forces of "nondiscrimination."

Disillusion with the liberal ideal of color blindness and the adoption of a strategy of color consciousness is characteristic of the Negro militants and is, indeed, at the heart of what "black power" is all about. But Negroes as such have been organizing on a color conscious basis to seek their common interests in many areas without the blessing of the slogan of "black power." Thus far, the signs are still undramatic—they include the formation of the Negro American Labor Council to look after Negro interests in the unions, and of associations like the Guardian Society to look after Negro interests in the New York Police Department, as well as the fact that Negro congressmen have been meeting as a bloc in the Democratic party—but the tendency is unmistakable: in the civil-rights movement, in the poverty program, and on both the local and national political scenes, the idea of unity based on color is taking a stronger and stronger hold among Negroes.

It is this growing Negro group solidarity—verbal as well as organizational, emotional as well as political—which, even more than the current lack of clarity over goals and the dissension over methods, accounts for the crisis within the civil-rights coalition that has come into sharp visibility since the cry of "black power" began to be heard in the land. The crisis has manifested itself most clearly in a growing crop of defectors, both Negro and white, from the movement. The white defectors include: (1) former civil-rights activists, some of many years' standing, who have had the ground cut out from under them by the Negro takeover of the field; (2) liberals like Lillian Smith who are willing to make excuses for the violence of Watts but not for anti-white slogans; (3) long-time Jewish supporters of civil rights, who are disturbed at sporadic outbursts of illiberalism and anti-Semitism in the movement; and (4) those whites who for some time have been losing interest as what they deem to be the proper goals of the movement are progressively attained through court decisions and legislation.

The Negro defectors are numerically small: they mostly include young militants who, having few roots in the past, take the achievements of the movement for granted. They tend to see the civil-rights program as the political patronage doled out to the upper-class Negroes mortgaged to the Johnson administration—an "opening to the Left" that balances Johnson's over-extended Right; and equality of opportunity they see as inapplicable to the ghetto Negro, in whom they are primarily interested. No one as yet knows to what extent the young militants derive their mandate from the real feelings of the masses of Negroes—unless it is Adam Clayton Powell, to whom they are a "new breed of cats" taking the place of the "fading aristocratic colonials of the civil-rights movement."

Aside from such political sniping, there is little inclination on the part of civil-rights leaders to take public stock of these ailments of the movement. At the last NAACP convention, the very significant rejection by the Mississippi Marchers of Roy Wilkins's request that the demonstration be used to marshal support for the 1966 civil-rights bill was merely mentioned in passing, and Vice President Humphrey's reference, in his speech at the convention, to Negroes and whites "marching with a common spirit" honored history more than it described the present. Humphrey's only allusion to the declining support of the movement was in the remark: "The time has come to broaden the base of the civil-rights movement . . . to reach out into the community and enlist vital new sources of energy and strength." Where one might look for these additional sources of energy and strength to compensate for the drying up of the old sources, the Vice President did not say. What he and others seem unwilling to face are the clear indications that the particular phase of the struggle for Negro rights in which many of the old civil-rights supporters were involved may have come to an end—that the civil-rights movement, which originated with whites and at its height became a nationwide coalition of whites and blacks, now faces the prospect of becoming an all-black movement.

For the truth is that there are great differences between the civil-rights movement and the "Negro Revolution,"* and these differences, papered over for so long by certain historical exigencies, are now surfacing into full view. The civil-rights movement was and is essentially concerned with the structure of law and social justice: its goals were equality before the law and equality of individual opportunity. As a movement, it was begun by people whose aim was not to aid the Negro as such but to bring American

*This distinction was aptly drawn by James Meredith in "Big Changes are Coming," in the *Saturday Evening Post,* August 13, 1966.

society into closer conformity with constitutional principle. For the greatest part of its history, civil rights was the white liberals' cause. Liberals expounded the moral basis for human rights in religion and politics, developed the theory of human equality in the physical and social sciences, led the intellectual offensive against racism, and took the intiative in founding the civil-rights organizations. Not long ago, retiring President Arthur Spingarn told his NAACP audience that when he picketed for Negro rights in Memphis, Tennessee, in 1914, "not one Negro would join me." What was true of the NAACP, with respect to the role of whites, was also true of most of the earlier philanthropic and educational institutions established to benefit Negroes, and it applied even more to the Urban League established some years later. From the time of the abolitionist movement to World War II, civil rights remained the cause of a small reformist group whose influence was more a matter of persuasive than of political power. What changed civil rights almost overnight from a peripheral moral issue to our major domestic movement was the emergence of the Negroes themselves as a nationwide bloc.

Perhaps the first clear indication of this shift came in 1941 with the March on Washington Movement, organized by A. Philip Randolph and later joined by Walter White and other Negro leaders. The single goal of the new movement was to muster Negro political power to force a reluctant President Roosevelt to establish a national FEPC. In threatening a protest demonstration unless its demands were met, the March on Washington Movement served notice that notwithstanding the snowballing patriotic war effort, the Negro had begun to regard his own needs as a priority. This threat of direct mass action by Negroes produced Executive Order 8802 of June 1941, the first major concession on the national level to the Negro bloc. It was soon to be followed by many more.

To be sure, the Negro bloc did not act alone. An alliance was forged with the forces of labor, humanism, religious radicalism, and political liberalism to fiight for civil rights and to realize standards of social justice and civic morality that had previously been enshrined only in the rhetoric of American democracy. As time went on, the new movement caught the imagination of a significant part of the nation, filling the idealistic void left by the de-radicalization of labor and the waning of the New Deal. To the politically starved youth of the late 50's and early 60's, it offered excitement, a chance to break with the past, and a practical outlet for social idealism; to fairminded adults, it promised a long overdue correction of chronic injustice; and from the indifferent, the opportunists, and the hostile, it commanded political respect.

During the life of the coalition, four major civil-rights laws were passed, several executive orders eliminating segregation under federal jurisdiction were issued, and a number of epochal legal decisions such as *Brown vs. Board of Education of Topeka* were handed down; more than thirty-one states and a hundred cities legislated public responsibility for civil rights, some more effectively than others; and administrative agencies with varying degrees of powers were established on the national, state, and local levels to enforce compliance with the new laws. Many corporations, voluntary organizations, and institutions of all kinds hastened to make sure that at least their public images accorded with the new policy; many others set up and financed departments of civil rights to foster integration among their own constituencies and in the community at large. New civil-rights bodies came into being: the Southern Regional Council, the Southern Christian Leadership Conference, the Congress of Racial Equality, and SNCC were all products of the coalition, as were a number of coordinating agencies (the Leadership Conference on Civil Rights, the Civil Liberties Clearing House, and the National Conference on Religion and Race) which took in hundreds of large national organizations. In all, the combined annual budgets of the public and voluntary agencies working to strengthen civil rights has been estimated at many millions of dollars, and their professional staffs number more than two-thousand.

So far as actual achievement is concerned, the coalition can point to some radical changes in the formal structure of American society: (1) the reconstruction of the legal basis of civil rights, (2) the fixing of federal responsibility to intervene where possible to enforce civil rights; (3) the establishment of equality before the law as the public policy of the nation. With these accomplishments—which will, no doubt, be strengthened by further legislation as the federal government makes good on its commitment to the civil-rights agencies—the climax of the coalition program seems to have been reached. For virtually everything that was envisaged by the liberal as legal "civil rights" has either already been done, or been accepted (at least in principle) by the federal government as its responsibility, and while much remains to be done, it does not command the wholehearted support of the coalition. That this fact has not yet been widely recognized has not prevented it from making itself felt in action. It was, after all, only three years ago that an estimated three-hundred thousand persons converged on Washington in response to the call from religious, labor, and civil-rights agencies. This massive demonstration of white and black contrasts sharply with the recent, almost all-Negro Mississippi March, a fraction of its size. And in the short period between the two marches, coalition bodies like the Conference on Religion and Race and the Leadership Conference on Civil Rights have atrophied or all but vanished from the scene along with their once prominent white civil-rights leaders. We have, indeed, reached a point where even the well-informed could hardly name a nationally-known civil-rights leader who is white—unless it happened to be Lyndon Johnson or Hubert Humphrey.

What all this adds up to is that the civil-rights coalition is being phased out, and that its place is being taken by a new force in American life, *the*

Negro movement. The difference between the two can be summed up in the contrast between the coalition's belief that what is good for democracy is good for the Negro, and the Negro movement's belief that what is good for the Negro, is good for democracy. The goal of the liberals has been to change the formal social order—not their personal human relations or those of their children—and they support civil rights as a necessary part of a moral democratic order. The Negro movement, on the other hand, is a self-interest movement which is for civil rights because it serves Negro welfare. Not that Negroes are not also liberals; but Negroes when acting collectively as a group are, like all other groups, motivated predominantly by self-interest. Thus motivated, Negroes might, for example, mount a campaign to elect a Negro as mayor of Newark (where there is a Negro majority), and while such a campaign might be a good thing, it would by no stretch of the imagination fall within the domain of civil-rights—or even the moral equivalent thereof.

Though one cannot speak of the Negro movement as though it were monolithic and had clearly defined priorities and goals, one might perhaps describe its broad aspirations as directed toward "the good life." The "good life" not only includes an end to second-class citizenship but it also envisages an equitable share of the abundance of the "great society." But if the Negro movement can be said to be centered on material welfare, it has a redemptive side as well: it seeks a rediscovery of pride and confidence and it couples communal self-assertion with individual self-respect.

"Black power," the first slogan to emphasize this idea of communal self-assertion, originally jolted white ears in the South, but it is essentially a Northern product, having as it does a particularly pointed meaning on the home ground of the liberal coalition. In the cities, where expectations have been escalated by reassuring civil-rights bills while little else has been forthcoming, "black power" is an attack upon the civil-rights agencies whose solution to the race problem presupposes the disappearance of the ghetto but prescribes for this herculean task nothing more than "equality of opportunity" and the one-by-one absorption of "deserving" Negroes into white society.

It should hardly be necessary to detail the dismal deprivations that continue to dog the lives of most Negroes. To the great majority, and their number continues to increase, the ghetto sets the boundaries of their world and conditions the most intimate and essential acts of their daily existence. Those who live close to its vital center find their lives quite unaffected by the social reforms of the last two decades. They are daily witnesses to the capacity of the ghetto to replenish itself at its core more rapidly than it can be skimmed off at the periphery by the escape of those few Negroes who fight their way to its outer edge. The rest have come to look upon "equal opportunity" as the password of those who wish to flee "black destiny" through integration with whites. "Black power" is the slogan for those Negroes who know that their destiny as individuals will be ruled by the fate of their group as a whole.

The outlook behind "black power" accepts the ghetto as its starting point; in this view, the ghetto, built by two centuries of organized inequality, stands as a monumental social institution that will not "wither away" through mere cessation of the policies that created it. Thus, the "black-power" outlook calls for an attack on the Negro liberals of the civil-rights agencies who, like their white counterparts, offer only a philosophy of integration with whites and a program of "opportunity" which can have relevance only for the few. It is to be expected that the Negro "rights" agencies should return this attack, but to accuse those who wish to organize the ghetto of being racist is to betray a dismal ignorance of the way American society actually works.

In setting off on the road to political power through group loyalty, the Negro is naturally being criticized by those who deplore pluralism, but the same charge was leveled in an earlier period against the Irish, the Italians, the Poles, and others—to, it might be added, no avail. Then as now, the critics, ignoring the role of group power in our social structure, blandly assumed that the so-called majority Americans were a mass of disinterested individuals acting only for the welfare of the entire community. The truth, of course, is that American society is organized along religio-ethnic lines, not only in politics (where the influence of "blocs" is commonly recognized) but in many other areas as well—social, professional, and to some extent economic.

To the American Negro, who throughout his history has confronted white society as a homogeneous, monolithic "power structure," the pluralism of the Northern cities is a fairly recent experience. His first concrete encounters with the reality of American ethnic groups must have contained a great shock for the Negro—the shock of discovering that what stood in the way of integration was not laws or the policies of institutions, but people, many of whom had been his allies in the grand coalition which passed the national laws that were supposed to lead him to a new place in the world. The Negro discovered, moreover, that those who dominated the neighborhoods in which he had sought to send his children to school were not simply whites: in Gary, Indiana, they were Poles; in Cleveland, they were Italians; in Jackson Heights and White Plains, they were Jews; and in Boston and Philadelphia, they were Irish. Nor were these the only encounters the Negro had with the various ethnic establishments. Negroes moving into the Lower East Side of New York found their way blocked into the Italian- and Jewish-controlled political clubs; and in the powerful building-trades unions, the Irish leadership was not about to dilute its strength with new and untrusted members. It is not that these ethnic groups are more prejudiced than others; it is simply that—in contrast to the case in the upper middle class and among the very wealthy—their color prejudice coincides with ethnic solidarity and self-interest.

The lesson for the Negro in all this was clear: to make his way in a pluralistic society, he too needed organized strength. But judging from the horror with which his announcement of this discovery has been greeted, white America has yet to learn what its own successful experience with minorities demonstrates: that minority solidarity is in great part a defensive stance toward a hostile society, not a conspiracy to take over the country. Indeed, it is probably only through collective action that aggrieved minorities can behave responsibly toward themselves and society in general. It is not the *organized* Negroes who represent a threat to white society, but rather the disorganized, the disenfranchised, and the hopeless—who, it should be emphasized, are still very much with us even though the program of the civil-rights coalition has made such progress.

It is, to be sure, a long step from the recognition of the need for power to the building and strengthening of indigenous social and political institutions within the ghetto from which power can be drawn. The Negro as yet has few such institutions. Unlike most of the other religioethnic minorities, he lacks a network of unifying social traditions, and this is why he must depend on political action through color consciousness as his main instrument of solidarity. That solidarity entails a certain degree of "separatism" goes without saying, but the separatism of a strengthened and enriched Negro community need be no more absolute than that, say, of the Jewish community. There is no reason, after all, why the Negro should not be able to live, as most Americans do, in two worlds at once—one of them largely integrated and the other primarily separated.

In short, to the extent that "black power" expresses a determination to build a Negro community which would be something more than a euphemism for the ghetto, it is a valid and necessary cry; to the extent that it expresses a despair of the one-by-one absorption of "deserving" Negroes into the general society and puts its faith instead in collective action aimed at dealing with a collective fate, it is an intelligent response to the realities of American life.

On the other side, however, "black power" is not by itself an adequate substitute for the coalition which provided the now obsolescent civil-rights movement with its constituency, if only because the Negroes as a minority will continue to need allies. A Negro movement based primarily on self-interest is a necessity, but a Negro movement based *exclusively* on self-interest is doomed to failure. The dilemma is real and cannot be escaped by blaming the Negro militants for alienating white supporters by their anti-white rhetoric: even if every Negro in America daily professed his great love for the whites, the coalition would still be breaking up for having fulfilled so much of the civil-rights program which brought it together, and for having no program on which it can agree to deal with the economic plight of the Negro masses.

The answer may lie in a new coalition program, organized around the cities as that of the old coalition was organized around the federal government. In claiming—as other self-interest groups have done in the past and with a like measure of truth—that what is good for the Negro is good for America, the new Negro movement will be asked, as others have been asked, to make the claim stick. This it could do if, while building itself up as a political bloc, it also threw its weight behind an alliance of all the urban blocs whose purpose would be to press for a genuine assault on the problems of the American city. The American liberal has needed the Negro as victim to activate his idealism on the national level in the past. Paradoxically enough, he now needs the Negro as a seeker for power to activate his idealism on the local scene—that newest frontier of social injustice and unrest.

" 'Black Power' and Coalition Politics"

by Bayard Rustin

There are two Americas—black and white—and nothing has more clearly revealed the divisions between them than the debate currently raging around the slogan of "black power." Despite—or perhaps because of—the fact that this slogan lacks any clear definition, it has succeeded in galvanizing emotions on all sides, with many whites seeing it as the expression of a new racism and many Negroes taking it as a warning to white people that Negroes will no longer tolerate brutality and violence. But even within the Negro community itself, "black power" has touched off a major debate—the most bitter the community has experienced since the days of Booker T. Washington and W. E. B. Du Bois, and one which threatens to ravage the entire civil-rights movement. Indeed, a serious split has already developed between advocates of "black power" like Floyd McKissick of CORE and Stokely Carmichael of SNCC on the one hand, and Dr. Martin Luther King of SCLC, Roy Wilkins of the NAACP, and Whitney Young of the Urban League on the other.

There is no question, then, that great passions are involved in the debate over the idea of "black power"; nor, as we shall see, is there any question that these passions have their roots in the psychological and political frustrations of the Negro community. Nevertheless, I would contend that "black power" not only lacks any real value for the civil-rights movement, but that its propagation is positively harmful. It diverts the movement from a meaningful debate over strategy and tactics, it isolates · the Negro community, and it encourages the growth of anti-Negro forces.

In its simplest and most innocent guise, "black power" merely means the effort to elect Negroes to office in proportion to Negro strength within the population. There is, of course, nothing wrong with such an objective in itself, and nothing inherently radical in the idea of pursuing it. But in Stokely Carmichael's extravagant rhetoric about "taking over" in districts of the South where Negroes are in the majority, it is important to recognize that Southern Negroes are only in a position to win a maximum of two congressional seats and control of eighty local counties.[1] (Carmichael, incidentally, is in the paradoxical position of screaming at liberals—wanting only to "get whitey off my back"—and simultaneously needing their support: after all, he can talk about Negroes taking over Lowndes County only because there is a fairly liberal federal government to protect him should Governor Wallace decide to eliminate this pocket of black power.) Now there might be a certain value in having two Negro congressmen from the South, but obviously they could do nothing by themselves to reconstruct the face of America. Eighty sheriffs, eighty tax assessors, and eighty school-board members might ease the tension for a while in their communities, but they alone could not create jobs and build low-cost housing; they alone could not supply quality integrated education.

The relevant question, moreover, is not whether a politician is black or white, but what forces he represents. Manhattan has had a succession of Negro borough presidents, and yet the schools are increasingly segregated. Adam Clayton Powell and William Dawson have both been in Congress for many years; the former is responsible for a rider on school intergration that never gets passed, and the latter is responsible for keeping the Negroes of Chicago tied to a mayor who had to see riots and death before he would put eight-dollar sprinklers on water hydrants in the summer. I am not for one minute arguing that Powell, Dawson, and Mrs. Motley should be impeached. What I am saying is that if a politician is elected because he is black and is deemed to be entitled to a "slice of the pie," he will behave in one way; if he is elected by a constituency pressing for social reform, he will, whether he is white or black, behave in another way.

Southern Negroes, despite exhortations from SNCC to organize themselves into a Black Panther party, are going to stay in the Democratic party—to them it is the party of progress, the New Deal, the New Frontier, and the Great Society—and they are right to stay. For SNCC's Black Panther perspective is simultaneously utopian and reactionary—the former for the by now obvious reason that one-tenth of the population cannot accomplish much by itself, the latter because such a party would

---

[1] See "The Negroes Enter Southern Politics" by Pat Watters, *Dissent,* July-August 1966.

remove Negroes from the main area of political struggle in this country (particularly in the one-party South, where the decisive battles are fought out in Democratic primaries), and would give priority to the issue of race precisely at a time when the fundamental questions facing the Negro and American society alike are economic and social. It is no accident that the two main proponents of "black power," Carmichael and McKissick, should now be co-sponsoring a conference with Adam Clayton Powell and Elijah Muhammad, and that the leaders of New York CORE should recently have supported the machine candidate for Surrogate—because he was the choice of a Negro boss—rather than the candidate of the reform movement. By contrast, Martin Luther King is working in Chicago with the Industrial Union Department of the AFL-CIO and with religious groups in a coalition which, if successful, will mean the end or at least the weakening of the Daley-Dawson machine.

The winning of the right of Negroes to vote in the South insures the eventual transformation of the Democratic party, now controlled primarily by Northern machine politicians and Southern Dixiecrats. The Negro vote will eliminate the Dixiecrats from the party and from Congress, which means that the crucial question facing us today is who will replace them in the South. Unless civil-rights leaders (in such towns as Jackson, Mississippi; Birmingham, Alabama; and even to a certain extent Atlanta) can organize grass-roots clubs whose members will have a genuine political voice, the Dixiecrats might well be succeeded by black moderates and black Southern-style machine politicians, who would do little to push for needed legislation in Congress and little to improve local conditions in the South. While I myself would prefer Negro machines to a situation in which Negroes have no power at all, it seems to me that there is a better alternative today—a liberal-labor-civil rights coalition which would work to make the Democratic party truly responsive to the aspirations of the poor, and which would develop support for programs (specifically those outlined in A. Philip Randolph's $100 billion Freedom Budget) aimed at the reconstruction of American society in the interests of greater social justice. The advocates of "black power" have no such programs in mind; what they are in fact arguing for (perhaps unconsciously) is the creation of a *new black establishment.*

Nor, it might be added, are they leading the Negro people along the same road which they imagine immigrant groups traveled so successfully in the past. Proponents of "black power"—accepting a historical myth perpetrated by moderates—like to say that the Irish and the Jews and the Italians, by sticking together and demanding their share, finally won enough power to overcome their initial disabilities. But the truth is that it was through alliances with other groups (in political machines or as part of the trade-union movement) that the Irish and the Jews and the Italians acquired the power to win their rightful place in American society. They did not "pull themselves up by their own bootstraps"—no group in American society has ever done so; and they most certainly did not make isolation their primary tactic.

In some quarters, "black power" connotes not an effort to increase the number of Negroes in elective office but rather a repudiation of nonviolence in favor of Negro "self-defense." Actually this is a false issue, since no one has ever argued that Negroes should not defend themselves as individuals from attack.[2] Non-violence has been advocated as a *tactic* for organized demonstrations in a society where Negroes are a minority and where the majority controls the police. Proponents of non-violence do not, for example, deny that James Meredith has the right to carry a gun for protection when he visits his mother in Mississippi; what they question is the wisdom of his carrying a gun while participating in a demonstration.

There is, as well, a tactical side to the new emphasis on "self-defense" and the suggestion that non-violence be abandoned. The reasoning here is that turning the other cheek is not the way to win respect, and that only if the Negro succeeds in frightening the white man will the white man begin taking him seriously. The trouble with this reasoning is that it fails to recognize that fear is more likely to bring hostility to the surface than respect; and far from prodding the "white power structure" into action, the new militant leadership, by raising the slogan of black power and lowering the banner of non-violence, has obscured the moral issue facing this nation, and permitted the President and Vice President to lecture us about "racism in reverse" instead of proposing more meaningful programs for dealing with the problems of unemployment, housing, and education.

"Black power" is, of course, a somewhat nationalistic slogan and its sudden rise to popularity among Negroes signifies a concomitant rise in nationalist sentiment (Malcolm X's autobiography is quoted nowadays in Grenada, Mississippi as well as in Harlem). We have seen such nationalistic turns and withdrawals back into the ghetto before, and when we look at the conditions which brought them about, we find that they have much in common with the conditions of Negro life at the present moment: conditions which lead to despair over the goal of integration and to the belief that the ghetto will last forever.

It may, in the light of the many juridical and legislative victories which have been achieved in the past few years, seem strange that despair should be so widespread among Negroes today. But anyone to whom it seems strange should reflect on the fact that despite these victories *Negroes today are in worse economic shape, live in worse slums, and attend more highly segregated schools than in 1954*. Thus—to recite the appalling, and

---

[2]As far back as 1934, A. Philip Randolph, Walter White, then executive secretary of the NAACP, Lester Granger, then executive director of the Urban League, and I joined a committee to try to save the life of Odell Waller. Waller, a sharecropper, had murdered his white boss in self-defense.

appallingly familiar, statistical litany once again—more Negroes are unemployed today than in 1954; the gap between the wages of the Negro worker and the white worker is wider; while the unemployment rate among white youths is decreasing, the rate among Negro youths has increased to *32 per cent* (and among Negro girls the rise is even more startling). Even the one gain which has been registered, a decrease in the unemployment rate among Negro adults, is deceptive, for it represents men who have been called back to work after a period of being laid off. In any event, unemployment among Negro men is still twice that of whites, and no new jobs have been created.

So too with housing, which is deteriorating in the North (and yet the housing provisions of the 1966 civil-rights bill are weaker than the anti-discrimination laws in several states which contain the worst ghettos even with these laws on their books). And so too with schools: according to figures issued recently by the Department of Health, Education and Welfare, 65 per cent of first-grade Negro students in this country attend schools that are from 90 to 100 per cent black. (If in 1954, when the Supreme Court handed down the desegregation decision, you had been the Negro parent of a first-grade child, the chances are that this past June you would have attended that child's graduation from a segregated high school.)

To put all this in the simplest and most concrete terms: the day-to-day lot of the ghetto Negro has not been improved by the various judicial and legislative measures of the past decade.

Negroes are thus in a situation similar to that of the turn of the century, when Booker T. Washington advised them to "cast down their buckets" (that is to say, accommodate to segregation and disenfranchisement) and when even his leading opponent, W. E. B. Du Bois, was forced to advocate the development of a group economy in place of the direct-action boycotts, general strikes, and protest techniques which had been used in the 1880's, before the enactment of the Jim Crow laws. For all their differences, both Washington and Du Bois then found it impossible to believe that Negroes could ever be integrated into American society, and each in his own way therefore counseled withdrawal into the ghetto, self-help and economic self-determination.

World War I aroused new hope in Negroes that the rights removed at the turn of the century would be restored. More than 360,000 Negroes entered military service and went overseas; many left the South seeking the good life in the North and hoping to share in the temporary prosperity created by the war. But all these hopes were quickly smashed at the end of the fighting. In the first year following the war, more than seventy Negroes were lynched, and during the last six months of that year, there were some twenty-four riots throughout America. White mobs took over whole cities, flogging, burning, shooting, and torturing at will, and when

Negroes tried to defend themselves, the violence only increased. Along with this, Negroes were excluded from unions and pushed out of jobs they had won during the war, including federal jobs.

In the course of this period of dashed hope and spreading segregation—the same period, incidentally, when a reorganized Ku Klux Klan was achieving a membership which was to reach into the millions—the largest mass movement ever to take root among working-class Negroes, Marcus Garvey's "Back to Africa" movement, was born. "Buy Black" became a slogan in the ghettos; faith in integration was virtually snuffed out in the Negro community until the 1930's when the CIO reawakened the old dream of a Negro-labor alliance by announcing a policy of non-discrimination and when the New Deal admitted Negroes into relief programs, WPA jobs, and public housing. No sooner did jobs begin to open up and Negroes begin to be welcomed into mainstream organizations than "Buy Black" campaigns gave way to "Don't Buy Where You Can't Work" movements. A. Philip Randolph was able to organize a massive March on Washington demanding a wartime FEPC; CORE was born and with it the non-violent sit-in technique; the NAACP succeeded in putting an end to the white primaries in 1944. Altogether, World War II was a period of hope for Negroes, and the economic progress they made through wartime industry continued steadily until about 1948 and remained stable for a time. Meanwhile, the non-violent movement of the 1950's and 60's achieved the desegregation of public accommodations and established the right to vote.

Yet at the end of this long fight, the Southern Negro is too poor to use those integrated facilities and too intimidated and disorganized to use the vote to maximum advantage, while the economic position of the Northern Negro deteriorates rapidly.

The promise of meaningful work and decent wages once held out by the anti-poverty programs has not been fulfilled. Because there has been a lack of the necessary funds, the program has in many cases been reduced to wrangling for positions on boards or for lucrative staff jobs. Negro professionals working for the program have earned handsome salaries—ranging from $14- to $25,000—while young boys have been asked to plant trees at $1.25 an hour. Nor have the Job Corps camps made a significant dent in unemployment among Negro youths; indeed, the main beneficiaries of this program seem to be the private companies who are contracted to set up the camps.

Then there is the war in Vietnam, which poses many ironies for the Negro community. On the one hand, Negroes are bitterly aware of the fact that more and more money is being spent on the war, while the anti-poverty program is being cut; on the other hand, Negro youths are enlisting in great numbers, as though to say that it is worth the risk of being killed to learn a trade, to leave a dead-end situation, and to join the only institution in this society which seems really to be integrated.

The youths who rioted in Watts, Cleveland, Omaha, Chicago, and Portland are the members of a truly hopeless and lost generation. They can see the alien world of affluence unfold before them on the TV screen. But they have already failed in their inferior segregated schools. Their grandfathers were sharecroppers, their grandmothers were domestics, and their mothers are domestics too. Many have never met their fathers. Mistreated by the local storekeeper, suspected by the policeman on the beat, disliked by their teachers, they cannot stand more failures and would rather retreat into the world of heroin than risk looking for a job downtown or having their friends see them push a rack in the garment district. Floyd McKissick and Stokely Carmichael may accuse Roy Wilkins of being out of touch with the Negro ghetto, but nothing more clearly demonstrates their own alienation from ghetto youth than their repeated exhortations to these young men to oppose the Vietnam war when so many of them tragically see it as their only way out. Yet there is no need to labor the significance of the fact that the rice fields of Vietnam and the Green Berets have more to offer a Negro boy than the streets of Mississippi or the towns of Alabama or 125th Street in New York.

The Vietnam war is also partly responsible for the growing disillusion with non-violence among Negroes. The ghetto Negro does not in general ask whether the United States is right or wrong to be in Southeast Asia. He does, however, wonder why he is exhorted to non-violence when the United States has been waging a fantastically brutal war, and it puzzles him to be told that he must turn the other cheek in our own South while we must fight for freedom in South Vietnam.

Thus, as in roughly similar circumstances in the past—circumstances, I repeat, which in the aggregate foster the belief that the ghetto is destined to last forever—Negroes are once again turning to nationalistic slogans, with "black power" affording the same emotional release as "Back to Africa" and "Buy Black" did in earlier periods of frustration and hopelessness. This is not only the case with the ordinary Negro in the ghetto; it is also the case with leaders like McKissick and Carmichael, neither of whom began as a nationalist or was at first cynical about the possibilities of integration.[3] It took countless beatings and 24 jailings—that, and the absence of strong and continual support from the liberal community—to persuade Carmichael that his earlier faith in coalition politics was mistaken, that nothing was to be gained from working with whites, and that an alliance with the black nationalists was desirable. In the areas of the South where SNCC has been working so nobly, implementation of the Civil Rights Acts of 1964 and 1965 has been slow and ineffective. Negroes in many rural areas cannot walk into the courthouse and register to vote. Despite the voting-rights bill, they must file complaints and the Justice

[3]On Carmichael's background, see "Two for SNCC" by Robert Penn Warren in the April 1965 COMMENTARY—ED.

Department must be called to send federal registrars. Nor do children attend integrated schools as a matter of course. There, too, complaints must be filed and the Department of Health, Education and Welfare must be notified. Neither department has been doing an effective job of enforcing the bills. The feeling of isolation increases among SNCC workers as each legislative victory turns out to be only a token victory—significant on the national level, but not affecting the day-to-day lives of Negroes. Carmichael and his colleagues are wrong in refusing to support the 1966 bill, but one can understand why they feel as they do.

It is, in short, the growing conviction that the Negroes cannot win—a conviction with much grounding in experience—which accounts for the new popularity of "black power." So far as the ghetto Negro is concerned, this conviction expresses itself in hostility first toward the people closest to him who have held out the most promise and failed to deliver (Martin Luther King, Roy Wilkins, etc.), then toward those who have proclaimed themselves his friends (the liberals and the labor movement), and finally toward the only oppressors he can see (the local storekeeper and the policeman on the corner). On the leadership level, the conviction that the Negroes cannot win takes other forms, principally the adoption of what I have called a "no-win" policy. Why bother with programs when their enactment results only in "sham"? Why concern ourselves with the image of the movement when nothing significant has been gained for all the sacrifices made by SNCC and CORE? Why compromise with reluctant white allies when nothing of consequence can be achieved anyway? Why indeed have anything to do with whites at all?

On this last point, it is extremely important for white liberals to understand—as, one gathers from their references to "racism in reverse," the President and the Vice President of the United States do not—that there is all the difference in the world between saying, "If you don't want me, I don't want you" (which is what some proponents of "black power" have in effect been saying) and the statement, "Whatever you do, I don't want you" (which is what racism declares). It is, in other words, both absurd and immoral to equate the despairing response of the victim with the contemptuous assertion of the oppressor. It would, moreover, be tragic if white liberals allowed verbal hostility on the part of Negroes to drive them out of the movement or to curtail their support for civil rights. The issue was injustice before "black power" became popular, and the issue is still injustice.

In any event, even if "black power" had not emerged as a slogan, problems would have arisen in the relation between whites and Negroes in the civil-rights movment. In the North, it was inevitable that Negroes would eventually wish to run their own movement and would rebel against the presence of whites in positions of leadership as yet another sign of white supremacy. In the South, the well-intentioned white volunteer had the cards stacked against him from the beginning. Not only could he leave the struggle any time he chose to do so, but a higher value was set on his safety by the press and the government—apparent in the differing degrees of excitement generated by the imprisonment or murder of whites and Negroes. The white person's importance to the movement in the South was thus an ironic outgrowth of racism and was therefore bound to create resentment.

But again: however understandable all this may be as a response to objective conditions and to the seeming irrelevance of so many hard-won victories to the day-to-day life of the mass of Negroes, the fact remains that the quasi-nationalist sentiments and "no-win" policy lying behind the slogan of "black power" do no service to the Negro. Some nationalist emotion is, of course, inevitable, and "black power" must be seen as part of the psychological rejection of white supremacy, part of the rebellion against the stereotypes which have been ascribed to Negroes for three hundred years. Nevertheless, pride, confidence, and a new identity cannot be won by glorifying blackness or attacking whites; they can only come from meaningful action, from good jobs, and from real victories such as were achieved on the streets of Montgomery, Birmingham, and Selma. When SNCC and CORE went into the South, they awakened the country, but now they emerge isolated and demoralized, shouting a slogan that may afford a momentary satisfaction but that is calculated to destroy them and their movement. Already their frustrated call is being answered with counterdemands for law and order and with opposition to police review boards. Already they have diverted the entire civil-rights movement from the hard task of developing strategies to realign the major parties of this country, and embroiled it in a debate that can only lead more and more to politics by frustration.

On the other side, however—the more important side, let it be said—it is the business of those who reject the negative aspects of "black power" not to preach but to act. Some weeks ago President Johnson, speaking at Fort Campbell, Kentucky, asserted that riots impeded reform, created fear, and antagonized the Negro's traditional friends. Mr. Johnson, according to the New York *Times,* expressed sympathy for the plight of the poor, the jobless, and the ill-housed. The government, he noted, has been working to relieve their circumstances, but "all this takes time."

One cannot argue with the President's position that riots are destructive or that they frighten away allies. Nor can one find fault with his sympathy for the plight of the poor; surely the poor need sympathy. But one can question whether the government has been working seriously enough to eliminate the conditions which lead to frustration-politics and riots. The President's very words, "all this takes time," will be understood by the poor for precisely what they are—an excuse instead of a real program, a cover-up for the failure to establish real priorities, and an indication that the administration has no real commitment to create new jobs, better housing, and integrated schools.

For the truth is that it need only take ten years to eliminate poverty—ten years and the $100 billion Freedom Budget recently proposed by A. Philip Randolph. In his introduction to the budget (which was drawn up in consultation with the nation's leading economists, and which will be published later this month), Mr. Randolph points out: "The programs urged in the Freedom Budget attack all of the major causes of poverty—unemployment and underemployment, substandard pay, inadequate social insurance and welfare payments to those who cannot or should not be employed; bad housing; deficiencies in health services, education, and training; and fiscal and monetary policies which tend to redistribute income regressively rather than progressively. The Freedom Budget leaves no room for discrimination in any form because its programs are addressed to all who need more opportunity and improved income and living standards, not to just some of them."

The legislative precedent Mr. Randolph has in mind is the 1945 Full Employment bill. This bill—conceived in its original form by Roosevelt to prevent a postwar depression—would have made it public policy for the government to step in if the private economy could not provide enough employment. As passed finally by Congress in 1946, with many of its teeth removed, the bill had the result of preventing the Negro worker, who had finally reached a pay level about 55 per cent that of the white wage, from making any further progress in closing that discriminatory gap; and instead, he was pushed back by the chronically high unemployment rates of the 50's. Had the original bill been passed, the public sector of our economy would have been able to insure fair and full employment. Today, with the spiralling thrust of automation, it is even more imperative that we have a legally binding commitment to this goal.

Let me interject a word here to those who say that Negroes are asking for another handout and are refusing to help themselves. From the end of the 19th century up to the last generation, the United States absorbed and provided economic opportunity for tens of millions of immigrants. These people were usually uneducated and a good many could not speak English. They had nothing but their hard work to offer and they labored long hours, often in miserable sweatshops and unsafe mines. Yet in a burgeoning economy with a need for unskilled labor, they were able to find jobs, and as industrialization proceeded, they were gradually able to move up the ladder to greater skills. Negroes who have been driven off the farm into a city life for which they are not prepared and who have entered an economy in which there is less and less need for unskilled labor, cannot be compared with these immigrants of old. The tenements which were jammed by newcomers were way-stations of hope; the ghettos of today have become dead-ends of despair. Yet just as the older generation of immigrants—in its most decisive act of self-help—organized the trade-union movement and then in alliance with many middle-class elements went on to improve its own lot and the condition of American society generally, so the Negro of today is struggling to go beyond the gains of the past and, in alliance with liberals and labor, to guarantee full and fair employment to all Americans.

Mr. Randolph's Freedom Budget not only rests on the Employment Act of 1946, but on a precedent set by Harry Truman when he believed freedom was threatened in Europe. In 1947, the Marshall Plan was put into effect and 3 per cent of the gross national product was spent in foreign aid. If we were to allocate a similar proportion of our GNP to destroy the economic and social consequences of racism and poverty at home today, it might mean spending more than 20 billion dollars a year, although I think it quite possible that we can fulfill these goals with a much smaller sum. It would be intolerable, however, if our plan for domestic social reform were less audacious and less far-reaching than our international programs of a generation ago.

We must see, therefore, in the current debate over "black power," a fantastic challenge to American society to live up to its proclaimed principles in the area of race by transforming itself so that all men may live equally and under justice. We must see to it that in rejecting "black power," we do not also reject the principle of Negro equality. Those people who would use the current debate and/or the riots to abandon the civil-rights movement leave us no choice but to question their original motivation.

If anything, the next period will be more serious and difficult than the preceding ones. It is much easier to establish the Negro's right to sit at a Woolworth's counter than to fight for an integrated community. It takes very little imagination to understand that the Negro should have the right to vote, but it demands much creativity, patience, and political stamina to plan, dvelop, and implement programs and priorities. It is one thing to organize sentiment behind laws that do not disturb consensus politics, and quite another to win battles for the redistribution of wealth. Many people who marched in Selma are not prepared to support a bill for a $2.00 minimum wage, to say nothing of supporting a redefinition of work or a guaranteed annual income.

It is here that we who advocate coalitions and integration and who object to the "black power" concept have a massive job to do. We must see to it that the liberal-labor-civil rights coalition is maintained and, indeed, strengthened so that it can fight effectively for a Freedom Budget. We are responsible for the growth of the "black power" concept because we have not used our own power to insure the full implementation of the bills whose passage we were strong enough to win, and we have not mounted the necessary campaign for winning a decent minimum wage and extended benefits. "Black power" is a slogan directed primarily against liberals by those who once counted liberals among their closest friends. It is up to the liberal movement to prove that coalition and integration are better alternatives.

seven

How does migration affect behavior? What happens to Black Americans when they move into urban areas? Are Black residential patterns following the same steps taken by previous ethnic groups which moved toward eventual assimilation? As the urban movement of Blacks continues, Black Americans could well end up being the most urbanized group in America. The problems of the cities and the problems of Blacks are inevitably linked.

Population Dynamics

As a consequence of industrialization the world's population has grown rapidly. Technological change in the areas of food production and distribution, sanitation, and disease control first brought about a rapid lowering of the death rate. There followed a decline in the birth rate as smaller families became the norm. Large families are valuable in a rural environment, since the children can aid in the growing of food. In urban areas children seldom have any economic function. Among the poor, large numbers of children cause a definite hardship. In Western Europe and in the United States the trend has been toward having fewer children, although the continually declining death rate has still meant a steadily increasing population.

Many factors concerning a given population can affect behavior. A dense population with limited resources, such as in India, is likely to have a very low standard of living. A growing population will mean increasing demand for goods and services, whereas a declining population will cause a decreasing market. If a population is thinly spread out, urbanization and industrialization are likely to be limited.

Variations in the composition and distribution of a population will have social consequences. The United States, for example, is witnessing an increase in the proportion of older people in the general population. This has meant an increasing demand by the aged for such goods and services as increased social security benefits, better medical care, recreational equipment designed for their use, and a function other than retirement to perform. The "baby boom" following World War II placed enormous pressures upon the schools and colleges and resulted in the creation of a vast market for teen-age products.

A changing sex ratio will affect the possibilities for marriage within a society. The loss by European nations of so many young men in World War II meant that many women could not marry. It also meant that there were openings for women in the job market, so many of them choose a career. In the United States the norm is for women to marry men several years older than themselves. When the population grows suddenly, as it did after World War II, a frequent outcome is that there are fewer men in the appropriate age groupings. In such a situation, women would either have to remain single or marry men their own age.

Within a society certain communities may contain select populations. Washington, D. C., has a high proportion of young female clerical personnel; St. Petersburg, Florida, has a high proportion of older persons; and San Diego, California, has a high proportion of young, military personnel. Such communities tend to reflect the interests and consequences of such special groupings.

Over a period of time populations may change through migration. Such movements of people may occur between nations or within a society. Migrants tend to be younger persons, particularly if the area to which they are moving is on a frontier. Migrants are also more likely to be male, causing a sex imbalance both in the place from which they came and in the place to which they are migrating. Within the United States there have been increasing numbers of persons moving into the urban areas, causing rapid growth around the nation's major cities. These movements have left many rural areas nearly devoid of young, married couples. The future for America seems to be one of increasing urbanism, although the present trend is for movement into the suburban areas of a city, rather than into the city itself.

C. Horace Hamilton describes the great urban migration by Black Americans within the last 50 years. While it is true that Blacks have tended to move out of the South, it is also true that they have increasingly moved into the urban areas of the country, even within the South. In fact, Blacks are now more urban than Whites, and the trend seems likely to continue. The urban movement by Blacks has had a profound effect upon their attitudes and actions. Migrants move expecting better conditions. When Blacks have not found them in the cities, their proximity to one another has aided the formation of social and protest movements to demand equality.

The article by Karl and Almd' Taeuber on residential segregation in Chicago calls into question the thesis that Blacks will follow the distribution patterns set by previous ethnic groups which moved toward eventual assimilation. Black Americans are the most segregated ethnic group in Chicago and there is no indication of any change.

MIGRATION

"The Negro Leaves the South"

by C. Horace Hamilton

The migration of Negro population from rural to urban communities, from southern states[1] to the metropolitan centers of the nation, has been and will continue for many years to be a major cause of human misery, social maladjustment, and interracial misunderstanding. A major thesis of this paper is that population increase and migration have been and will continue to be important contributing causal factors in race conflict and in the kind, magnitude, and rate of the adjustments needed to be made.

As recent as 1910, just before the first World War, about 9 out of every 10 Negroes lived in the southern part of the United States and 8 out of every 10 southern Negroes lived in rural areas. Over three-fourths of Negro farmers were farm tenants and more than half of the tenants were sharecroppers. Many others were wage workers on farms and in the small towns and cities of the South. Before 1910 both white and Negro farmers of the South were poor, had low standards of living, little formal education, and few institutional services. Health conditions were also bad. Malaria, intestinal parasites, dysentery, pellagra, contagious diseases, typhoid, scarlet fever, tuberculosis, and other diseases were common. Death rates, especially infant mortality rates, were high in comparison with the rest of the nation. These conditions were generally accepted because they had been a part of rural life for generations and few people believed they could be improved.

A hundred years is actually a short period in the history of the human race. During this time, however, the American Negro has made the transition from slavery to what we now call, euphemistically, "Modern industrial civilization." During this 100 years the Negro has not only had to

Paper read at the 1963 Annual Meeting of the American Association for the Advancement of Science at Cleveland, Ohio, December 27, 1963.

[1]Except as otherwise noted the South of this paper includes the 17 state U.S. Census South, including not only 11 southeastern states from Louisiana to Florida to Virginia to Kentucky but also Texas, Oklahoma, Maryland, West Virginia, Delaware, and the District of Columbia.

Data on Negro population are presented when available and appropriate; but in some cases it will be necessary to use the nonwhite classification.

make the transition from farm sharecropping and primitive living conditions to working and living in the city, but he has found his progress impeded by social and psychological barriers over which he had little control. Social relations and statuses firmly imbedded in the folkways and traditions of a society have been difficult to change and have changed very slowly. The Negro's place in southern society was also reinforced by both state and federal legislation. The first national civil rights law, providing for equal treatment in all public accommodations, was declared to be unconstitutional in 1875. In terms of sociological time, and considering the difficulties involved, it is surprising that the Negro has been able to move so rapidly, even in many southern communities, toward his goals of equality and first-class citizenship.

I. Population Growth

The rapid growth of the Negro population in recent years has been due not only to some increase in the birth rate following the last war but more significantly to the great decrease in the Negro mortality rate.

From 1790 to 1930 (with the exception of one decade) the Negro population of the nation grew at a slower rate than did the white population. Since 1930, the Negro population has grown more rapidly than the white. In the early history of the nation (1790–1830) Negroes comprised about one-fifth of the total population; but by 1930 the percentage of Negroes had dropped to only 9.7 and since has increased to 10.5. Unless relative white-Negro fertility rates change, the percentage of Negroes will continue to increase slowly, reaching about 11.8 by 1980. It will likely be many decades, if ever, before the percentage of Negroes in the nation again reaches 18 or 19 percent.

Since 1860 the Negro population of the nation has increased over fourfold, rising from 4,442,000 to 18,860,000 in 1960. Today (late 1963) the Negro population of the nation is just about, if not over, 20,000,000. Between 1950 and 1960, the Negro population increased by 25 percent, or a total of 3.8 million. The increase in the preceding decade was only 2,176,000, or 17 percent of the 1940 figure, 12,866,000. A reasonable projection, based on assumed constant mortality and fertility rates, would result in a 1970 Negro population of about 23,339,000; and in 1980, 29,532,000. Thus, between 1960 and 1980, over ten and one-half million Negroes will be added to the nation's population. Although Negroes make up only one-ninth of the nation's total population, they will likely contribute about one-sixth of the total population increase of the United States between 1960 and 1980. Of course, during the next few years, as and if Negroes become more prosperous and better educated, the rate of natural increase may slow down. Be that as it may, the changing distribution of the Negro population is equally as significant as the growth rate.

II. Regional Differences in Negro Population Growth

The Negro population of the South is growing very slowly (about 10 percent a decade). The Negro population of nonsouthern regions increased 56 percent during the past decade and 62.5 per cent in the preceding decade. Northward migration underlies this very large differential in growth. During the next two decades the decennial rate of population increase in the North will likely drop to about 45 percent, because of the rapidly increasing size of the population base in relation to the number of mirgrants from southern states. Even so, the total number of Negroes likely to be added to nonsouthern areas will be relatively very large indeed. Whereas 2,720,000 Negroes were added to nonsouthern areas in the 1950 decade, about 3,365,000 will be added in the 1960's, and 4,943,000 may be added during the 1970's; this would result in a 1980 Negro population in nonsouthern communities of 15,845,000, or about 54 percent of the Nation's projected total of 29,532,000.

The South's percentage of the nation's Negro population, which was over 90 percent before 1900 and had dropped to only 77 percent by 1940, reached 60 percent in 1960. The South's share of Negro population will likely drop to 54 percent by 1970 and to only 46 percent in 1980. As I shall show presently, the South's share of Negro population may drop ultimately to about 28 percent. In spite of this decline in its share of the Negro population, the absolute size of the South's Negro population continues to increase. By 1980, its Negro population is expected to reach about 13,700,000.

Although the South's Negro population will likely continue to grow, the proportion of the South's total population which is Negro will decline. One hundred years ago, over 36 percent of the South's population were Negroes, by 1930 only one-fourth were Negroes, and in 1960 only 20.6 percent. By 1980, only 18.8 percent of the South's population will likely be Negroes.

In other major regions, the proportion of Negro population will continue to rise sharply—reaching 9.0 percent of all nonsouthern people by 1980, as compared with 4.7 percent in 1950 and 6.1 percent in 1960. Ratewise, the West's Negro population is growing most rapidly; with increases of 234 percent in the 1950's and 88 percent in the 1960's.

III. Rural Negro Population and Southern Agriculture

In the meantime, the rural Negro population will decline in numbers and remain almost wholly southern. In 1960, 93 percent of the rural Negro population lived in the South. On the contrary, about 95 percent of the Negro population outside the South was urban. At the same time, the percentage of southern Negroes who live in urban centers is rising rapidly.

In 1960, for the first time in our history, the American Negro became more urban than the American white, when 73.2 percent of the Negroes were found to be living in cities, as compared with only 69.5 for the whites. Even in the South Negroes were found to be as urban as the whites. In several southern states this condition has existed for a hundred years.

The decline in rural Negro population is largely (but not entirely) due to a very great decline in the opportunity for Negroes in agriculture. As in the nation, southern farms have become highly mechanized and consequently fewer agricultural tenants, sharecroppers, and laborers are needed. Furthermore, cotton has decreased in importance as a farm enterprise and cotton culture has shifted westward. Only in tobacco farming, and a few other intensive types of farming requiring a lot of manual labor, are many Negro laborers and tenants in demand. Truck farming is expanding in some parts of the South, but its labor requirements are highly seasonal. For this reason, truck farmers depend to a great extent on migratory farm labor.

. . . In 1920, there were just under a million Negro farmers in the South, and the number remained about 800,000 until 1935 when crop-control programs were introduced and the rate of mechanization began to increase. During World War II the number of Negro farmers fluctuated between 600,000 and 700,000 and after the war, under the impact of still greater mechanization, the number of Negro farmers skidded downward very rapidly, reaching a low of only 265,000 in 1959. All tenure classes declined—owners, part-owners, tenants, and sharecroppers. However, a hard core of Negro farm owners, about 127,000, remained, along with 73,000 sharecroppers and 65,000 other tenants.

In spite of the ambitious home- and farm-ownership programs of the United States Farmers Home Administration (formerly the Farm Security Administration), the number of southern Negro farm owners never exceeded 218,000. Generally, land was not sold to Negroes and, of course, where it was for sale, few sharecroppers and tenants could afford to buy it. Also, many Negro farm owners have very small farms which are used primarily for residential and subsistence purposes. These limitations have operated to "push" Negroes out of the country and ultimately out of the South.

In addition to agricultural changes and the difficulties of buying land, southern Negro farm families (as well as most white farmers) have traditionally produced a large surplus crop of babies—many more than are needed to replace farmers who die or who move away. Consequently, migration, short of living in abject poverty if not actually starving, is the only recourse for this surplus youth population.

In the long run, which has already run out for the southern Negro farmer, birth control offers one solution to the surplus production of babies. But birth control has never been taught systematically to Negro sharecroppers. Employers and landlords have always thought that a high Negro birth rate was a good thing because it provided a large supply of cheap labor. Now northern and western communities, beset with the problem of large Negro families, are getting interested in birth-control programs as a means of reducing the cost of welfare, health, and other services.

IV. Southern Migration History

Migration from the South is actually not a recent phenomenon. It started in the early history of this country when slaves went North to escape their southern masters. The importation of slaves to America was prohibited in 1808, but nevertheless many were brought in and sold clandestinely. But by the early 1800's, the natural increase in the slave population was the prime factor in the increase of the Negro population in the South. The production of cotton, rice, and indigo in the South on colonial type plantations favored the use of Negro slave labor and large numbers of children.

A growing number of free Negroes undoubtedly contributed to the early migratory movement out of the South, but heavy migration did not take place until after 1890, . . . the net migration out of the South was less than 10,000 per year. After 1890, possibly because of heavy natural increase, a leveling-off of agricultural expansion, and possibly also due to urbanization in the North, Negro migration increased substantially to over 30,000 per year. There also began to be a redistribution, by migration, of Negroes within the South. This was due, in part, to the beginnings of southern urban growth and urbanization.

Another spurt in migration from the South got underway in the decade just preceding the first World War—about 56,000 net leaving in an average year. Migration of white people out of the South also picked up rapidly in this decade.

It was in the decade of the 1920's, a period of urban expansion and industrialization following the first World War, that both white and Negro migration out of the South reached a very high level—just under 100,000 (net) Negroes leaving in an average year and a slightly smaller number of white people.

The invasion of southern cotton fields by the boll weevil is also thought to be an important factor in pushing Negroes out of the deep South to the middle and upper South and ultimately out of the South altogether.

In the decade of the 1930's, lightning struck in the form of a nationwide and worldwide economic depression. There was plenty of surplus rural Negro population in the South, but there was very little economic opportunity in the North and West. As a result, net migration of both white and

Negro people from the South dropped about 50 percent under the previous decade.

In terms of net migration from the South by decades, the peak movement was reached in the 1940's, the decade of World War II and the early postwar period. The total net movement out of the South during this decade amounted to 2,135,000, of which over three-fourths were Negroes. Except before 1910, this was the first decade in which the Negro movement out of the South greatly exceeded the out-migration of whites. Also, in this decade, migration of both whites and Negroes from a few southern states decreased to zero and actually went over on the plus side for both whites and Negroes. . . .

In the decade of the 1950's, migration of Negroes from the South continued at a fast pace only slightly below the rate of the previous decade. The net out-migration of southern whites slowed down in most southern states, and there was a net migration of white people to six states—Delaware, Maryland, Virginia, Florida, Louisiana, and Texas. It was in this decade that Florida gained not only 1,516,000 white people by migration but also 101,000 Negroes. Delaware, Maryland, and the District of Columbia also gained Negro population by migration.

During the 1950's states that lost the most Negro population by migration, relatively, were Arkansas, West Virginia, Mississippi, South Carolina, Alabama, Georgia, and North Carolina. These states lost from one-fifth to over one-third of their 1950 Negro populations.

V. Age and Sex of Migrants

. . . Among Negro men and women, the heaviest rates of out-migration occurred in the 1940 cohort 15–19 years of age (25–29 in 1950—average age 20–24 during the decade). Rates for Negro men and women were also high in the adjoining age classes.

Among the older age classes of both whites and Negroes, the South either gained or had low losses of population by migration.

This heavy migration of youth will cause the number of young Negro workers in nonsouthern areas to double within a ten-year period; as a result also many other social, educational, and civic problems will be intensified, perhaps beyond the present expectations of most political and civic leaders.

VI. State of Birth Data

With all its limitations,[2] U.S. Census data on the state of birth show some important aspects of migration from the South to the North and West. . . .

[2]See Everett Lee *et al., Population Distribution and Economic Growth, United States, 1870–1950,* Vol. I: *Methodological Considerations and Reference Tables* (Philadelphia:

These data may be summarized briefly as follows:

1. The great volume of Negro migration from the South to the non-South during the last two census decades is shown by the fact that the number of nonwhites born in the South (mostly Negroes) but living in the North and West increased from 1,549,000 in 1940 to 3,248,736 in 1960, or 110 percent. Even so, only 43 percent of the nonwhite population living outside the South in 1960 was born in the South, but in 1950 the comparable percentage was 50. The drop from 50 to 43 percent is due to the heavy migration of Negroes from the South before 1950 and to their natural increase.

2. The most rapidly increasing population component, shown by the state of birth data, is the nonwhite population living outside the South and born outside the South. Between 1940 and 1960 this component increased by 156 percent, that is, from 1,667,000 to 4,266,727. This fact shows that the nonsouthern regions are now developing, by natural increase, their own homegrown Negro populations who have no direct cultural contact with the South; but, obviously, the influence of their southern cultural heritage, transmitted by friends and relatives, will be in evidence for many years. In 1960 the median age of this nonsouthern native nonwhite contingent was about 12 years.

3. The net migration of Negroes born in the non-South to the South is extremely small, numbering only 156,000 in 1960. This suggests that migration of northern and western Negroes to the South is a one-way street. But such is not the case with Negroes who were born in the South and who left the South and returned between date of birth and the 1960 Census. From the analysis of data showing state of birth and states of residence in 1955 *and* 1960, it is seen that about 100,000 native southern Negroes moved from the South between birth and 1955, but returned to the South before 1960. Unfortunately, we cannot be very precise here because of the high percentage of Negroes whose 1955 place of residence was unknown.

4. There is a very large interchange of migrants between states within the South. Actually, the State of birth data show that 17,696,000 natives (white and nonwhite) of the southern states have moved to other states but that 7,752,000 of these moved to other southern states. Among the 4,717,000 nonwhites who have left their state of birth, 1,460,000 had migrated to other southern states and 3,257,000 had migrated from the South.

American Philosophical Society, 1957). For a discussion of the nature and uses of these data, see pp. 57–64.

VII. Place of Residence in 1955

The census data on place of residence in 1955 offer an opportunity to study migration over a definite short period of time and to observe the volume of migration to and from the South. One shortcoming of these data, however, is that the 1955 place of residence of a large proportion of movers is unreported. However, we have assumed that most of these were truly migrants, that is, that they had moved across county lines. On this assumption, we have distributed this number of unreported nonwhite movers to the various major regions in direct proportion to the known migrants by their region of residence in 1955. . . .

The South (17 states) lost by migration a nonwhite population of 370,-000 during the five-year period 1955–60, being the difference between an out-movement of 516,000 and an in-movement of 146,000. Considering the much larger net loss by migration over the entire decade cited earlier in this paper, a net out-migration of only 370,000 southern Negroes seems to be unusually small. However, the earlier data include migration of children under 10 years of age in 1960, but the latter data do not include children under 5 in 1960. Another difference between these two sources of data is that the 10-year data include net migration among the population abroad, whereas the 5-year data include only the movement within the United States. Allowing for these and some other differences in the two types of data, we conclude that the migration of nonwhites from the South must have slowed down substantially during the latter half of the 1950–60 decade.

The above-mentioned data on regions of birth in 1955 and 1960 provide a basis for predicting the future distribution by region of the nonwhite population of the nation. On the assumptions that the rates of migration from one region to another will remain constant for several decades, it can be shown that the distribution of population by regions will finally reach an equilibrium state beyond which there will be no further changes in the proportional distribution by regions. Although the assumption of static migration patterns is manifestly unrealistic, we can make projections which show the consequences of current migration rates. These projections are analogous to the prediction of a future stable age distribution under assumptions of constant specific natality and mortality rates.

Our analysis of the place of residence data leads to the prediction that the distribution of the nonwhite population of the nation (50 states) will be as follows:

Northeast   21
North Central   25
South   28
West   26

The West will include a sizable number of nonwhites other than Negroes.

VIII. Concentration of Negro Migrants in Metropolitan Central Cities

Evidence that most migrants from the South have settled in the central cities of metropolitan areas is shown in a number of ways based on the 1960 *United States Census of Population: Report on Standard Metropolitan Statistical Areas.* A few of the important significant summary statements based on census data are:

1. In 1960, 64.5 percent of the nation's total Negro population lived in Standard Metropolitan Statistical Areas and 79.7 percent of the nation's Negro metropolitan population lived in the central cities of the metropolitan areas.

2. Between 1940 and 1960 the Negro metropolitan population of the nation more than doubled—increasing from 5,840,000 to 12,194,000.

3. About 85 percent of the 1950–60 increase in the nation's Negro metropolitan population occurred in the central cities.

4. The Negro metropolitan population of the non-South, both in and outside of central cities, is increasing more rapidly than in the South.

5. The central cities of the metropolitan South have a higher percent of Negroes than similar areas in the non-South; but, the South's percent is about constant at 25 percent, whereas the non-South percentage is rising rapidly, being 13.7 in 1960 as compared with the South's 25.8.

6. The percent of population Negro in the South's metropolitan ring is decreasing; but the corresponding percent in the non-South is low and stable being only 2.7 percent in 1960 as compared with the South's 11.5. Under pressure of population increase the percent population Negro in the nonsouthern metropolitan rings will likely increase in the future.

IX. Educational Selectivity of Migration

The rate of migration regardless of direction (to or from the South) is positively correlated with level of education; but the South is losing more of the better educated Negroes than it is gaining—relative to the poorly educated. In other words, the rate of net out-migration of Negroes, especially young Negroes, is positively correlated with years of school completed. Several older studies[3] show this but more recently some valuable confirmation of the relationship between education and

[3]For example, see C. Horace Hamilton, "Educational Selectivity of Net Migration from the South," *Social Forces,* XXXVIII (October, 1959), 33–42 and Elmer H. Johnson, "Methodological Note on Measuring Selection in Differential Migration," *Social Forces,* XXXIII (March, 1955), 289–92.

migration is found in the 1960 Census report on Life Time and Recent Migration.[4]

Although a complete analysis of these data is not yet available, some preliminary study of the data pertaining to the migration of young Negroes from the South Atlantic Division during the period 1955–60 confirms the results of previous studies. . . .

Although the South loses its best educated Negroes, the general educational level of Negro migrants is below that of white people living in the same communities. . . . The white population of metropolitan areas in all regions is better educated than the nonwhite. However, the color differential in school years completed is much greater in the South than in the North and West. Were it not for educational selectivity in migration, the educational level of nonsouthern Negroes would be lower than it is.

X. Major Occupational Changes

The migration of Negroes from the South is associated with certain major changes in the occupational structure. That is to say, social mobility and geographical mobility are closely associated. A change in kind of job may or may not always involve a change in community of residence. In the case of the southern Negro, however, the decline in agricultural employment made it almost inevitable that large numbers of Negroes would change occupations and places of residence more or less simultaneously.
. . .

A quick review of the data leads to the following broad generalizations:
1. The migration of Negroes out of southern agriculture and out of the South to a very great extent represents a shift from one low socioeconomic status to another. The Negro workers who have moved into the urban centers of the nonsouthern states, if employed, are employed in such occupational classes as (in order of gross numbers) operatives, service workers, private-household workers, and other types of unskilled and semi-skilled workers.

For example, it may be noted that between 1940 and 1950 in the nonsouthern states the number of Negro men employed as operatives and kindred workers increased by about 329,000 or 286 percent. Similar employment among Negro women increased 162,000 or 365 percent. In terms of percentage distribution, Negro men and women have, relative to other occupations, moved heavily into the operative and kindred classes of occupations. Similar statements can be made with reference to service workers and other laborers.

During the 20-year period, 1940–60, in the non-South there was an increase of 14.5 million jobs and Negroes filled 13.8 percent of these. On

[4] *United States Census of Population: Life Time and Recent Migration,* PC (2) 2D, Table S.

the other hand, in the same regions there was an increase of 5.3 million low-status jobs and Negroes filled 25 percent of these. Low-status jobs include operatives, service workers, other laborers, and the like.

Similarly, in this region and time period, there was an increase of 2,-500,000 in craftsmen and kindred workers (a middle-status class) and Negroes filled only 7.5 percent of these new positions. In the same period, there was an increase of 8,347,000 in high status white collar positions and Negroes filled 6.2 percent of them.

In the South, in the same 20-year period, Negroes got 23 percent of the increase in low-status jobs, 8 percent of the middle-status jobs, and 6 percent of the high-status jobs. On the other hand, in the South, 35 percent of the decrease of 2,692,000 agricultural workers was among the nonwhite. The number of nonwhite agricultural workers in the South declined 952,000.

During the same period, in the non-South there was a decrease of 4,141,000 agricultural workers and about one-fifth of these occurred among the nonwhite.

2. Although the great majority of Negro migrants from the South have moved into the low-status jobs of the metropolitan centers of the North and West, there has been a noteworthy percentage of increase of Negro workers in middle- and upper-status occupations. There has also been a substantial improvement in the percentage distribution of Negroes in certain occupations. . . .

The increases in the employment of Negroes in the high-status white collar occupations were relatively very great—in both South and non-South. In the South, although the total number of Negro workers declined by 160,000, the number employed in professional, technical, and kindred occupations actually increased from 91,000 to 170,000. This means that the proportion of southern Negroes employed in the high-status white collar occupations increased substantially, but from a very low level in 1940. In the case of Negro males, the proportions increased from 1.5 to 2.9, as compared with 4.5 and 7.5 for Negro females. The fact that school-teaching is included in the professional classification accounts for the relatively high standing of Negro females in the South.

In the case of southern whites, the proportion of men in the high-status white collar occupations increased from 5.0 percent to 10.0 percent—or from 406,000 to 1,024,000—as compared with 15.6 and 14.0 percent in the case of white females—the numbers rising from 325,000 to 668,000.

In the nonsouthern states, between 1940 and 1960, the number of Negroes employed in the high-status white collar occupations (professional, technical, and kindred) increased from 35,000 to 165,000; as compared with an increase of whites from 2,496,000 to 5,170,000. Although the total number of employed Negro workers in the nonsouthern states increased by 96 percent, the number in the high-status white collar occupations increased by 371 percent. As a result, the proportion of Negro males in these occupations went up from 3.1 to 4.8, and that of Negro females from 3.7 to 7.2. During the same period the corresponding figures for white males rose from 6.3 to 11.3 and that of white females fell from 14.0 to 13.7.

Although these data show that the status of Negro workers is still substantially below that of the white, they show also that Negroes are definitely, but slowly, rising in the social structure.

In the middle-class white collar occupations (clerical and kindred), Negroes have also increased substantially—relative to the white percentage increases and to the increase of all Negroes employed. In the nonsouthern states the number of Negro clerical and kindred workers increased from 51,000 in 1940 to 345,000 in 1960—a little less than sevenfold. Even in the southern states the number of Negro clerical workers increased from 40,000 to 150,000. . . .

With regard to clerical work, Negroes still lag far behind whites, but in the nonsouthern states Negroes, especially females, are moving in quite rapidly.

Following the same line of analysis as used above, it may also be shown that Negroes have moved rapidly into the skilled jobs classed as craftsmen and kindred. Since this is largely a man's area, the data presented below apply only to males. The number of nonwhite male craftsmen increased 110 percent in the South and 303 percent in the non-South as compared with 101 percent and 58 percent, respectively, in the case of white males. . . .

If the above analysis seems to be over-optimistic, a similar analysis of a group of low-status occupations will appear to be somewhat less than encouraging, particularly in the South. In this class of occupations we include private-household workers, service workers, farm laborers, and other (miscellaneous, including unknown) workers. . . .

Nonsouthern nonwhites have made much more progress in moving out of the low-status jobs than have southern nonwhites. By the same token, it appears that nonwhite males of the non-South have moved out of low-status jobs more rapidly than have either nonsouthern white males or southern nonwhite males.

On the other hand, nonsouthern nonwhite females have been more successful than any other sex-color-regional group in moving out of the low-status jobs. Even so, more than one-half remain in low-status jobs. It is interesting to note in passing that relatively more nonsouthern whites —male and female—remain in low-status jobs than do southern whites. Possibly this situation is related to the fact that, in the South, Negroes occupy a larger percent of the low-status jobs than in the non-South.

XI. Summary

1. Migration of Negroes from the South has been going on for over a hundred years but picked up tempo about 1910, increased rapidly in the 1920's, slowed down some during the depression years, and then surged ahead rapidly during and after World War II.

2. Causal factors in this migration have been the high rate of natural increase in the South, mechanization of southern agriculture, shift of cotton production to the Southwest and West, governmental programs limiting agricultural production, and the rapid economic development in nonsouthern states.

3. Out-migration of Negroes has been heaviest from Arkansas, Mississippi, West Virginia, Alabama, North Carolina, and South Carolina.

4. The highest rates of migration are found among young people from 18 to 25 years of age. There has been a tendency for elderly people to migrate back to the South—but more so among whites than among Negroes.

5. Migration of Negroes from the South has been selective of the best educated; but, even so, the educational level of Negro migrants has been below that of the nonsouthern communities to which they have gone.

6. There is now a large and rapidly increasing indigenous Negro population in the nonsouthern states. This indigenous population is now much larger than the nonsouthern Negro population which has migrated from the South.

7. There is a very small amount of Negro migration back to the South; but there is a substantial interstate migration of Negroes within the South.

8. Ultimately, if present migration trends continue, from 75 to 85 percent of the Negro population of the nation will live outside the South.

9. Negro migrants from the South have gone almost entirely to the large metropolitan areas of the North and West. The largest percentage has settled in the central cities of these metropolitan areas.

10. The mass of Negro migrants from the South has moved into the low-status, low-wage occupations of the North and West. In terms of numbers, the greatest absolute increases by occupation have occurred in such unskilled and semi-skilled occupations as operatives, services, and miscellaneous unskilled labor. However, there are some large percentage increases in employment of Negroes in the middle and upper white collar occupational classes, as well as a significant increase in the number of Negro skilled craftsmen and kindred workers.

11. The educational level of Negroes in nonsouthern metropolitan centers is still quite low—over fifty percent have never attended high school. On the other hand, the southern white metropolitan population has a higher level of education than does the white metropolitan population of the North, but less than that of the West.

12. In spite of the heavy out-migration of Negroes, the South's Negro population is still increasing about 10 percent a decade.

13. If present rates of mortality, fertility, and migration should continue, the total Negro population will reach 23.3 million by 1970 and 29.5 million by 1980. The Negro population of the nonsouthern states should reach 10.9 million by 1970 and 15.8 million by 1980. By 1980 only 46 percent of the nation's Negro population will live in the South (17 states).

XII. Conclusion

It is not the function of this paper either to discuss the implications of the migration of Negroes from the South or to make any recommendations regarding public policies or programs.

The purpose of this paper has been to review and analyze the most recent available demographic facts of the movement of Negroes out of the South. An accurate assessment of the bare facts regarding numbers and characteristics of these migrants is indispensable to the accurate evaluation of the magnitude of the forces underlying one of the greatest problems of the day.

If the facts of this movement have any direct message in themselves, it is simply that the seriousness of the problem and the rate of movement, and of the increase of the nonsouthern metropolitan Negro population, are so great as to stagger one's imagination. Except for the world-wide population explosion itself, the movement of Negroes from the southern part of the United States has without a doubt been the greatest and most significant sociological event of our country's recent history. Its repercussions will be felt for a long time and the social problems (education, housing, health, interracial adjustment) will be most difficult to solve. The great danger is that the adjustments needed will be much too little and too late.

Perhaps one of the most obvious demographic and hence socially significant consequences of the migration of Negroes from the South to large cities is that the flood of Negro migrants cannot and will not be contained within the old corporate city limits of the metropolitan central cities. As has already occurred in many instances, Negroes are moving into heretofore all-white suburbs. This trend will no doubt continue with increased acceleration under the impact of natural increase and continued heavy migration. The addition of 8.3 million Negroes to the nonsouthern metropolitan communities during the 1960–80 period will place a great strain on the community leadership and on governments—local, state, and national.

The only general conclusion which we can draw at this time is that time tables of interracial adjustment must be speeded up. There is much to be done and everything that is done will, in the final analysis, depend on changes in basic attitudes about race and on the kinds of adjustments which are reasonable and just. Channels of communication between white and Negro leaders must be kept open and expanded. Perhaps many individuals, white and Negro, do not as yet understand and agree with many of the social measures and adjustments being advocated by our leaders. But we are living in a time of uncertainty and adventure in many other respects. Perhaps for years to come we will have to learn to live adventuresomely and courageously in human relationships, as we are learning to do in the realms of international relations and interplanetary space. Whatever the dangers of racial adjustment are—be they real or imaginary—Americans of all races must learn to take them in their stride as a part of the price for living in this great age. Perhaps the imaginary dangers will turn out to be much worse than the real ones!

RESIDENTIAL SEGREGATION

"The Negro as an Immigrant Group: Recent Trends in Racial and Ethnic Segregation in Chicago"[1]

by Karl E. Taeuber and Alma F. Taeuber

During the last half of the nineteenth century and the early decades of the twentieth, millions of immigrants from Europe entered the United States. Many of these immigrants settled initially in ethnic colonies in large northern cities and found jobs as unskilled laborers in burgeoning mass-production industries. With the onset of World War I in Europe, and with the passage of restrictive legislation in the United States in the early 1920's, the period of massive overseas migration came to an end. At the same time, however, there developed a large-scale migration of Negroes from the South to the same large northern industrial cities. Like the immigrants from abroad, the Negro migrants to northern cities filled the lowest occupational niches and rapidly developed highly segregated patterns of residence within the central cities.

[1]Paper No. 15 in the series, "Comparative Urban Research," was issued from the Population Research and Training Center, University of Chicago, under a grant from the Ford Foundation. A preliminary version of this paper was read at the 1962 annual meetings of the American Statistical Association. We appreciate the reactions of Stanley Lieberson, Judah Matras, and Margaret G. Reid to that version.

In view of many obvious similarities between the Negro migrants and the various immigrant groups preceding them, it has been suggested that northern urban Negroes are but the latest of the immigrant groups, undergoing much the same processes of adaptation to city life and of assimilation into the general social structure as the European groups preceding them.[2] The persistence of Negroes as a residentially segregated and underprivileged group at the lowest levels of socioeconomic status, however, is frequently interpreted in terms of distinctive aspects of the Negro experience, particularly their historical position in American society.[3]

The question of whether or not a northern urban Negro population can fruitfully be viewed as an immigrant population, comparable to European immigrant populations of earlier decades with respect to the nature and speed of assimilation, will be explored on the basis of data permitting analysis of recent trends in racial and ethnic segregation in Chicago.

The processes by which various immigrant groups have been absorbed into American society are complex and have been studied from a variety of viewpoints. Unfortunately there is no sociological consensus on a definition of assimilation and there is nothing approaching a definitive study of the processes of assimilation for any one immigrant group. It is beyond the scope of our task here to attempt to provide such a definition. We feel that a distinctively sociological approach to the topic must view assimilation as a process of dispersion of members of the group throughout the social structure. Cultural and psychological processes, we feel, should not be incorporated into a sociological definition, although their relationship to institutional dispersion should, of course, be retained as one focus of research on assimilation.

For our purposes, it will suffice to have a working definition of the process of assimilation considerably less sophisticated than that required for a general sociological theory. Accepting the view that both immigrant groups and Negro migrants originally settled in segregated patterns in central areas of cities and ranked very low in terms of socioeconomic measures, assimilation then consisted in large part of a process of social and economic advancement on the part of the original members of the group and their descendants, along with a decreasing residential concentration in ethnic colonies. Our concern with diminishing residential segregation as a necessary concomitant of the assimilation process derives from Myrdal's discussion of the "mechanical" importance of residential segregation in facilitating other forms of segre-

<hr>

[2]Philip M. Hauser, "On the Impact of Urbanism on Social Organization, Human Nature and the Political Order," *Confluence,* VII (Spring, 1958), 65. Elsewhere Hauser has expressed a more cautious view, emphasizing the lack of definitive knowledge; see his *Population Perspectives* (New Brunswick, N.J.: Rutgers University Press, 1960), p. 129.

[3]D. J. Bogue, "Chicago's Growing Population Problem," *Commerce,* LIX (July, 1962), 31.

gation and discrimination, and Hawley's discussion of the impact of spatial patterns on race relations.[4] Our concern with socioeconomic advance reflects the initially low status of the groups with which we are concerned, whereas a more general treatment would need to reckon with the unusually high status of some immigrant stocks, as well as with other aspects of social status and institutional dispersion than those for which we have data.

The data in Table 1 illustrate for selected immigrant groups the patterns of socioeconomic advance and residential dispersion from highly segregated ethnic colonies. For each of the larger ethnic groups, data for 1950 show the average standing on three measures of socioeconomic status, standardized for age, of the first generation (the foreign-born white, FBW) and the second generation (native white of foreign or mixed parentage, NWFMP). The nationality groups are split into "old," "new," and "newer" groups in an extension of the traditional system. On the average, comparing within the first or within the second generation, the "old" immigrant groups are the best off on these measures, the "new" groups are intermediate, and the "newer" groups are the worst off. It cannot be determined from these data to what extent the old immigrants are better off by virtue of their longer average length of residence in the United States, or to what extent they may have been better off at their time of immigration than the newer immigrants were at the time of their move.

Comparisons between the first and second generations might appear to be a more direct means for assessing the extent of socioeconomic advance, particularly since the emphasis in the literature on assimilation is on intergenerational processes rather than simply on processes of upward mobility through time in the status of the original immigrants. Comparisons of corresponding status measures for the first and second generations in Table 1 reveal, in general, the expected pattern of intergenerational advance. Data such as these, however, do not refer directly to a specific set of immigrant parents and their native-born children and must be interpreted with great caution.[5] For instance, it would be unwarranted on the basis of these data to assume that descendants of German immigrants are not as well off as their parents in terms of education. It is more credible that recent immigrants from Germany, under our immigration laws, include a large proportion of persons of high socioeconomic status.

Measures of the changing residential patterns of the immigrant groups are given in columns 7–9 of Table 1. The measure, an index of residential

---

[4]Gunnar Myrdal, *An American Dilemma* (New York: Harper & Bros., 1944), I, 618; Amos H. Hawley, "Dispersion versus Segregation: Apropos of a Solution of Race Problems," *Papers of the Michigan Academy of Science, Arts, and Letters,* XXX (1944), 667–74.

[5]For an enumeration of some of the difficulties see C. A. Price and J. Zubrzycki, "The Use of Inter-marriage Statistics as an Index of Assimilation," *Population Studies,* XVI (July, 1962), 58–69.

Table 1. Selected Characteristics (Age-Standardized) of Foreign-born and Native Ethnic Population in 1950, and Indexes of Residential Segregation of Selected Groups of Foreign Stock from Native Whites of Native Parentage, 1930 and 1960, Chicago*

Country of Origin	Per Cent High-School Graduates (Males Age 25 and Over)		Per Cent with Income above $3,000 (Persons with Income)		Per Cent with White-Collar Jobs (Employed Males)		Index of Residential Segregation (Compared with NWNP)		
	FBW	NWFMP	FBW	NWFMP	FBW	NWFMP	1930	1960	Change
"Old" immigrant groups:									
England and Wales	45	50	53	58	49	51	11	18	+ 7
Ireland	24	47	47	56	22	47	23	31	+ 8
Norway	31	47	54	57	24	51	44	37	- 7
Sweden	25	48	59	60	23	51	26	30	+ 4
Germany	37	34	53	55	34	42	22	19	- 3
"New" immigrant groups:									
Austria	29	40	54	57	33	44	30	16	-14
Czechoslovakia	25	33	44	54	22	36	59	37	-22
Italy	15	27	47	53	24	37	52	32	-20
Poland	18	25	42	49	25	30	63	38	-25
U.S.S.R.	35	60	60	69	59	74	51	44	- 7
"Newer" immigrant groups:									
Mexico	14	16	38	29	8	13	71	54	-17
Puerto Rico**	13	29	16	37	22	36	**	67	**

*Data for 1930 and 1950 refer to foreign white stock (foreign-born plus native of foreign or mixed parentage); data for 1960 refer to total foreign stock. Abbreviations used are FBW for foreign-born white, NWFMP for native white of foreign or mixed parentage, and NWMP for native white of native parentage. The three socioeconomic characteristics refer to the Standard Metropolitan Area population, while the segregation indexes are based on community areas within the city. Age-standardization was by the direct method, using age groups 25-44 and over, with the Standard Metropolitan Area age composition as a standard.

**Socioeconomic characteristics for Puerto Rican population refer to total United States; Puerto Rican population by community areas for Chicago available for 1960 only.

Source: Characteristics from U.S. Bureau of the Census, U.S. Census of Population: 1950, Vol. IV, Special Reports, Pt. 3, chap. A. "Nativity and Parentage," and chap. D. "Puerto Ricans in Continental United States." Distributions of population by community areas for 1930 and 1960 from data on file at Chicago Community Inventory, University of Chicago.

segregation between the total foreign stock (FBW + NWFMP) of each nationality and the total native whites of native parentage (NWNP), assumes a value of 100 for maximum residential segregation and a value of 0 if the residential distributions are identical.[6] The indexes were computed from the distribution of each group among the seventy-five community areas of the city of Chicago for 1930 (the last previous census year that included information on the total foreign stock) and 1960. The degree of residential segregation from the native population is highest for the "newer" immigrants and lowest for the "old" immigrants. Between 1930 and 1960, most of the ethnic groups became less segregated from the native population. Only for England, Ireland, and Sweden did the indexes fail to decline, and these were already at relatively low levels.[7]

This general approach to the measurement or assimilation of immigrant groups has been pursued for a number of cities and longer time periods by Lieberson. He found a remarkably persistent and consistent association through time between residential desegregation of an ethnic group and increasing socioeconomic similarity to native whites, and cross-sectionally between the position of each group as compared to others on measures of residential segregation and its relative levels on status measures.[8]

The index of residential segregation between Negroes and NWNP for 1930 was 84, and for 1960, 82. These values are higher than any of those for specific immigrant stocks. Furthermore, each of the immigrant stocks was highly segregated from Negroes in 1930 and 1960. There is relatively little intermixture of Negro residences with those of any group of whites. Even the "newer" immigrant groups, the Puerto Ricans and Mexicans, are not joining or replacing Negroes in established Negro areas but are moving into separate ethnic colonies of their own at the periphery of Negro areas. Negroes clearly occupy a distinctive position as the most residentially segregated of the principal migrant groups. The separation of Negroes from all groups of whites is sharper than any of the patterns of residential segregation between ethnic groups or between socioeconomic groups within the white population.[9] Apparently this pattern has developed during the last few decades. Lieberson has demonstrated that, although prior to the great Negro migrations of World War I there were

---

[6]The index of residential segregation is an index of dissimilarity between the residential distributions of each group. For further discussion, see Otis Dudley Duncan and Beverly Duncan, "A Methodological Analysis of Segregation Indexes," *American Sociological Review*, XX (April, 1955), 210–17.

[7]For a more detailed discussion of these patterns, using data for 1930 and 1950, see Otis Dudley Duncan and Stanley Lieberson, "Ethnic Segregation and Assimilation," *American Journal of Sociology*, LXIV (January, 1959), 364–74.

[8]Stanley Lieberson, *Ethnic Patterns in American Cities* (New York: Free Press of Glencoe, 1963).

[9]For a discussion of class residential segregation in Chicago see Otis Dudley Duncan and Beverly Duncan, "Residential Distribution and Occupational Stratification," *American Journal of Sociology*, LX (March, 1955), 493–503.

instances of immigrant stocks being more segregated from native whites than were Negroes, since 1920 there has been a general tendency for Negro residential segregation to be highest.[10]

Table 2. Selected Socioeconomic Characteristics (Unstandardized) of Whites and Nonwhites, Chicago, 1940, 1950, and 1960

Characteristic	Nonwhite	White
Residential segregation index, whites vs. Negroes:*		
1930		85
1940		85
1950		79
1960		83
Per cent high school graduates, ages 25+:		
1940	16	25
1950	25	37
1960	29	37
Per cent white collar, male:		
1940	17	40
1950	17	41
1960	21	40
Per cent home-owners:		
1940	7	26
1950	12	33
1960	16	39
Per cent multiple-person households with 1.01 or more persons per room:		
1940	41	17
1950	46	14
1960	34	10

*These values differ slightly from those cited in the text for Negroes as compared to native whites of native parentage.

Source: Data for 1940 from the 1940 Census Tract Bulletin for Chicago; for 1950 from Philip M. Hauser and Evelyn M. Kitagawa (eds.), *Local Community Fact Book for Chicago, 1950* (Chicago: Chicago Community Inventory, 1953); and for 1960 from the 1960 Census Tract Bulletin for Chicago.

Data pertaining specifically to the comparison between whites and non-whites (97 per cent of Chicago's non-whites are Negroes) on measures of socioeconomic status and of residential segregation are presented in Table 2. For each of four measures reflecting socioeconomic status, there was improvement in the status of the non-white population between 1940 and 1960. (For whites, improving status would be more clearly evident if the data referred to the entire metropolitan area rather than just the city of Chicago.) The indexes of residential segregation between whites and

[10]Lieberson, *op. cit.,* pp. 120–32.

Negroes, in the top panel of the table, show minor fluctuations around an extremely high level and give no indication of the decline anticipated on the basis of the socioeconomic advancement of the Negro population. That this is not an atypical finding is indicated by reference to other data showing a long term historical trend toward increasing residential segregation between whites and non-whites. Increasing racial residential segregation was evident in most large cities of the United States between 1940 and 1950, while during the 1950's, southern cities continued to increase in segregation and northern cities generally registered modest declines.[11]

In broad perspective, the historical trend toward improving socioeconomic status of immigrant groups has gone hand in hand with decreasing residential segregation. In contrast, Negro residential segregation from whites has increased steadily over past decades until it has reached universally high levels in cities throughout the United States, despite advances in the socioeconomic status of Negroes.

We have been unable to locate any data permitting a comparison between Negroes long resident in Chicago, or born and raised in the North, and Negroes with lesser periods of residence in the city. Thus we are not able to make even the crude intergenerational comparisons for Negroes that are possible for immigrant groups. The only analysis of this type possible with census data is a comparison between recent migrants and the rest of the population, and the only published data are residential distributions, with no socioeconomic characteristics. For 1960, with the seventy-five community areas of Chicago as units, the index of residential segregation between non-whites resident in the metropolitan area five years or more and native whites of native parents is 80.5. Comparing non-whites with less than five years' residence in the metropolitan area and NWNP, the index was 81.0. Comparing the recent in-migrants with the non-whites who were resident in the metropolitan area five years or more, the index was 13. Thus the recent non-white in-migrants are distributed differently from the rest of the non-white population, but each group is highly segregated from the native whites. Unfortunately, these results cannot be readily interpreted in terms of the general assimilation and dispersion processes under consideration. Possibly there are trends toward socioeconomic advancement and residential dispersion on the part of "second generation" Negroes in Chicago that are confounded in the data for the total Negro population.

Decreasing residential concentration of immigrant groups occurred despite the efforts of many nationality organizations to maintain the ethnic colonies.[12] Few Negro organizations have been as explicitly segregationist.

[11]Karl E. Taenber, "Negro Residential Segregation, 1940–1960: Changing Trends in the Large Cities of the United States" (paper read at the Annual Meetings of the American Sociological Association, 1962).
[12]David A. Wallace, "Residential Concentration of Negroes in Chicago" (unpublished Ph.D. dissertation, Harvard University, 1953).

In some immigrant groups, many members were dispersing from the ethnic colonies even while large scale immigration of that group was still under way. For every immigrant group, diminishing residential segregation has been evident since the cessation of large-scale immigration. For Negroes, however, residential segregation has increased since the first period of large-scale immigration to northern cities, and this increase in residential segregation continued during the late 1920's and 1930's when the volume of migration was at a low level. These observations tend to discredit the argument that a major barrier to residential dispersion of the Negro population of Chicago is its continuing rapid increase. However, the size of the Negro population and the magnitude of its annual increase are larger than for any single ethnic group in the past, and comparisons with smaller groups are not completely convincing. That rapid increase of Negro population does not necessarily lead to increasing residential segregation was domonstrated directly in the intercity comparative study previously cited. There was no definite relationship between increase in Negro population and increase in the value of the segregation index. Indeed, during the 1950–60 decade, there appeared to be a slight relationship in the opposite direction.[13]

More significant in accounting for the divergent trends in residential segregation may be the different urban contexts in which the immigrant and Negro populations found themselves. Comparing the residential locations of Italian-born and Polish-born in Chicago in 1899 and in 1920, Wallace observed:

> it can be seen that the areas of greatest dispersion, low proportion, and presumably of "second" settlement for many immigrants were those which were not settled at all in 1899.
>
> The implication of this fact is that so-called "assimilation" process was not reflected by the geographic dispersion of the immigrant populations into "cosmopolitan American areas." The dispersal was more directly related to an increase in housing alternatives as the city grew at the periphery.[14]

By the time the Negro concentrations were forming near the central areas of Chicago, the city was built up and the urbanized area extended well beyond the present boundaries. Residential alternatives at a price Negroes could afford and located sufficiently close in to permit inexpensive commuting were no longer available.

It has been suggested that considerable time is required for Negroes to make the transition from a "primitive folk culture" to "urbanism as a way of life."[15] Several types of data indicate that large and increasing proportions of the Negro urban population are city-born and raised. For instance, there is a rapidly decreasing color differential in the percentage of

[13]Taeuber, *op. cit.*
[14]Wallace, *op. cit.,* p. 205.
[15]Philip M. Hauser, "The Challenge of Metropolitan Growth," *Urban Land,* XVII (December, 1958), 5.

the Chicago population born in the state of Illinois. In 1960, 44 per cent of the native-born, non-white residents of Chicago were born in Illinois, as contrasted to 66 per cent of the white population.[16] National estimates for 1958 showed that of all males aged 45-64 living in metropolitan places of 500,000 or more population, 65 per cent of the non-whites, as compared to 77 per cent of the whites, had lived in this size city for twenty years or longer.[17] Estimates of the components of growth of the non-white population of Chicago indicate that between 1950 and 1960 natural increase was as important as net in-migration, and that natural increase will in the future account for rapidly increasing proportions of the growth of the non-white population.[18]

Unfortunately there is inadequate knowledge of the specific length of time under specified conditions for the required cultural transformation to occur. Wallace's observations indicate a significant degree of dispersal over time among first-generation immigrants. Such processes are more often conceived as primarily intergenerational. That many of the "first generation" Negro migrants to northern cities have lived there for twenty years or more and that in the younger adult ages there are sizable numbers of "second generation" urban Negroes suggest that there has been ample time for any necessary adjustment to urban living, at least for large proportions of the Negro population. It is also clear that if northern Negroes remain inadequately educated for urban living and fail to participate fully in the urban economy, the "primitive folk culture" of the South can less and less be assigned responsibility, and northern cities will be suffering from the neglect of their own human resources.

The "visibility" of Negroes due to skin color and other features which make the large majority of second-, third-, and later-generation descendants readily identifiable as Negroes is often cited as a basic factor in accounting for the distinctive position of Negroes in our society. It is exceedingly difficult to assess the significance of visibility. There is no other group that is strictly comparable to Negroes regarding every factor except visibility. It is not completely irrelevant, however, to note that non-white skin color, by itself, is not an insurmountable handicap in our society. The socioeconomic status of the Japanese population of Chicago in 1950 substantially exceeded that of the Negro population; and their residential segregation from whites, although high, was considerably lower than that between Negroes and

[16]Data from U.S. Bureau of the Census, *U.S. Census of Population, 1960: General Social and Economic Characteristics, Illinios.* Final Report PC(1)-15C, Tables 72 and 77.

[17]Karl E. Taeuber, "Duration-of-Residence Analysis of Internal Migration in the United States," *Milbank Memorial Fund Quarterly,* XXXIX (January, 1961), Table 3.

[18]D. J. Bogue and D. P. Dandekar, *Population Trends and Prospects for the Chicago Northwestern Indiana Consolidated Metropolitan Area: 1960 to 1990* (Chicago: Population Research and Training Center, University of Chicago, 1962).

whites.[19] Unfortunately there are no trend data available on the characteristics of the Japanese in Chicago. A more appropriate Japanese population for comparison, however, is the much larger one in the San Francisco area. A recent study there affirmed that "ethnic colonies of Japanese are gone or rapidly going" and documented their rapid socioeconomic advance.[20]

In the traditional immigrant pattern, the more recent immigrants displaced the older groups at the bottom socioeconomic levels. How do the Negroes compare with the other "newer" immigrant groups, the Mexicans and the Puerto Ricans? The limited data now available suggest that the Negroes may soon be left alone at the bottom of the social and economic scale. We have already noted (from data in Table 1) that the "newer" groups were, in 1950, of very low status compared to the other immigrant groups, and that their residential segregation from the native whites of native percentage was the highest of all the immigrant groups. For 1960, data on distribution within Chicago of persons born in Puerto Rico are available separately from data on those persons born in the United States of Puerto Rican parentage. Thus it is possible to compute indexes of residential segregation for first- and second-generation Puerto Ricans. For Chicago in 1960, these index values were 68.4 for the first generation and 64.9 for the second generation, indicating that residential dispersion has already begun for the Puerto Ricans. This difference actually understates the amount of dispersion, since the second generation consists in large proportion of children still living with their first-generation parents.

Selected socioeconomic measures for the Puerto Rican and the nonwhite populations of Chicago in 1960 are shown in Table 3. On every measure, the Puerto Rican population is less well off—it is less educated, has lower income, is more crowded, is less likely to own homes, is less well housed, and lives in older buildings. Yet the index of residential segregation (computed with respect to NWNP) for Puerto Ricans is 67 as compared with 82 for Negroes.

Up to now we have been making comparisons between Negroes and immigrant groups, demonstrating that residential dispersion has not accompanied socioeconomic advance by Negroes in the way that it did for immigrant groups. Economic status and expenditure for housing, however, are clearly correlated, and there is also a correlation between economic status and residential segregation. By virtue of variations in the type, age, and quality of housing, and in the patterns of residential choice

---

[19]Although the maximum value of the residential segregation index is less than 100 for ethnic groups of small size, this is not sufficient to vitiate the Negro-Japanese comparison.

[20]Harry H. L. Kitano, "Housing of Japanese -Americans in the San Francisco Bay Area," in Nathan Glazer and Davis McEntire (eds.), *Studies in Housing and Minority Groups* (Berkeley: University of California Press, 1960), p. 184.

by persons of varying socioeconomic status, the subareas of a city are differentiated in terms of the average status of their residents. Since Negroes are of much lower average status than whites, they would be expected to be disproportionately represented in low-status residential areas. In fact, an extreme position regarding the relationships between patterns of socioeconomic residential segregation and racial residential segregation would attribute all of the latter to the former. Such a position is sometimes offered as a counterargument to charges of racial discrimination against the real estate business. To the extent that this position is correct, it might be expected that future economic advances on the part of the Negro population should be translated into decreased residential segregation.

The task of partialing out a component of racial segregation due to economic factors involves some difficult methodological problems, and no method is entirely satisfactory.[21] Our approach utilizes indirect standardization of available census data. Let us delineate the status of a residential area in terms of, say, the income distribution of its residents. Specifically, consider for each community area of Chicago the number of families with incomes below $1,000, from $1,000–1,999, from $2,000–2,999, and so forth. For the city as a whole in 1960, 44 per cent of all families with an income below $1,000 were non-white, as were 44 per cent of families with incomes from $1,000–1,999, and 40 per cent of families with incomes from $2,000–2,999. For each community area, we can apply these city-wide percentages to the observed income distribution to obtain the number of non-white families expected if income alone determined the residential locations of whites and non-whites.

By the method of indirect standardization just outlined, we obtain an expected number of non-white and white families for each of the seventy-five community areas. We can then compute an index of residential segregation between expected numbers of non-white and white families. This index can be regarded as the amount of racial residential segregation attributable to patterns of residential differentiation of income groups. For 1950, the index of residential segregation between the numbers of whites and non-whites expected on the basis of income was 11, as compared with the actual segregation index of 79. As a rough measure, then, we can attribute 11/79, or 14 per cent, of the observed racial residential segregation in Chicago in 1950 to income differentials between whites and non-whites. For 1960, the corresponding values are 10 for the expected index, 83 for the observed index, and 12 per cent for the racial segregation attributable to income differentials.

In a recent study of the relationships between housing consumption and

[21]A general discussion of this problem can be found in the section on explanation of areal variation in Otis Dudley Duncan, Ray P. Cuzzort, and Beverly Duncan, *Statistical Geography* (Glencoe, Ill.: Free Press, 1961).

Table 3. Selected Socioeconomic Characteristics (Unstandardized) of Puerto
Ricans and Non-Whites, Chicago, 1960

Characteristic	Non-White	Puerto Rican
Residential segregation vs. whites	83	67
Per cent high school gradu- ates, total	29	11
Median family income	$4,742	$4,161
Per cent families earning <$3,000	28	27
Per cent families earning >$10,000	9	4
Per cent home-owners	16	6
Per cent substandard dwell- ings	26	33
Per cent 1.01 or more per- sons per room	34	52
Per cent housing units built since 1940	12	6
Median gross rent	$88	$79
Median number of rooms	3.9	3.7
Median number of persons	3.0	4.0

Source: Data are from the 1960 Census Tract Bulletin for Chicago.

income, Reid has demonstrated many pitfalls in the uncritical use of income distributions in the analysis of housing patterns.[22] We have therefore repeated the above analyses, using distributions by major occupational groups and distributions by educational attainment. For 1960, the index of residential segregation computed from the numbers of whites and non-whites expected on the basis of patterns of occupational differentiation is 9, and that expected on the basis of patterns of educational differentiation is 3. The results using income distributions are thus supported by the results from other measures of socioeconomic status, and the conclusion seems clear that patterns of socioeconomic differentiation of residential areas can account for only a small proportion of observed racial residential segregation.

Reid demonstrated that differences between whites and non-whites in observed patterns of housing consumption are largely attributable to income differentials between whites and non-whites. Our analysis suggests that residential segregation cannot be attributed to these differentials. Apparently the economic structure of the housing market for whites is similar to that for non-whites, even though non-whites are excluded from a large share of the housing supply for which their economic circumstances would allow them to compete.

[22]Margaret G. Reid, *Housing and Income* (Chicago: University of Chicago Press, 1962).

The judicious conclusion from our review of a variety of pieces of data is that we simply do not yet know enough about immigrant assimilation processes and any corresponding processes among Negro migrants to northern cities to be able to compare the two. We believe that this very lack of knowledge makes questionable any attempt to reason from presumed patterns of assimilation among immigrants in the past to current racial problems in northern cities. Furthermore, such evidence as we could compile indicates that it is more likely to be misleading than instructive to make such comparisons.

Our definition of assimilation as involving socioeconomic advancement and residential dispersion is simple, and greater differences between groups would appear were a more complex definition adopted. Restriction of portions of the analysis to the city of Chicago had little effect on the measures for non-whites, but probably led to an understatement of the degree of assimilation of the immigrant stocks insofar as higher-status members of these groups have moved to the suburbs. The segregation indexes probably overstate somewhat the residential isolation of small groups, such as particular immigrant stocks, as compared with large groups such as total native whites of native parents. Taking account of any of these limitations in our data would tend to increase the differences between Negroes and immigrant groups. Even so, our data showed that second-generation persons from several countries are of higher socioeconomic status than the total native whites of native parentage. Relatively few Negroes in Chicago have white-collar jobs or incomes above the median level for whites, and yet there are large numbers of adult Negroes who were born in the city. Basic differences between the Negroes and the immigrant groups seems to us implicit in the failure of residential desegregation to occur for Negroes while it has continued for the immigrant groups.

In view of the fundamental impact of residental segregation on extra-legal segregation of schools, hospitals, parks, stores, and numerous other facilities, the failure of residential dispersion to occur strikes us as an especially serious social problem. Socioeconomic advance and residential dispersion occurred simultaneously for the various immigrant groups. It is apparent that the continued residential segregation of the Negro population is an impediment to the continued "assimilation" of Negroes into full and equal participation in the economy and the society at large.

Social Institutions

A child's first conception of society occurs within the family. There his basic beliefs and values are usually shaped. Just how important is the family for socialization? Do other groups enter into the process? What happens if a child receives one set of norms from his family, another from his school, and still another from his peer group?

Family and Socialization

Because of the numerous functions that it performs, the family is one of the basic units of social organization. The family is the primary means by which sexual behavior in a society is regulated and offspring are produced. The structure of the family provides a definite network of kinship relationships and obligations for its members. Within the family young children receive the intimate and affectionate contact that is necessary for normal emotional development. And by being born into a particular family a child automatically receives a number of social statuses, such as social class and race. Such statuses may determine to a large extent the availability of future opportunities.

At birth a child is essentially a biological organism possessing little more than certain drives and needs, such as hunger. But because the human child has a great capacity for learning and the ability to use language he can easily be taught to communicate and to learn the culture of his society. This learning process begins in the family and is called socialization.

Socialization is often a direct process such as when a mother teaches her child certain manners. It may also be less deliberate. For example, much of what a child learns comes from his observations of the behavior of his parents and others. Though an individual learns much during his early youth, socialization continues throughout his life. In complex societies schools and other organizations and groups may later play an active part in this process.

Socialization transmits culture to individuals thereby providing them with the knowledge and skills necessary to participate in society. Performed effectively on all members of a society, this process can be seen as an integrative and cohesive force. Socialization also contributes to the personal development of an individual. Through learning experiences and contact with others a person develops an assessment of himself or a self identity. At the same time he begins to form the

distinct modes of behavior and way of thinking that will make up what is called
his personality.

Socialization patterns and family practices differ from society to society. The
Black family in America illustrates the additional fact that such patterns and
practices may also differ within societies. For example, because some elements of
Black culture are different from those of the general society and because of the
distinct social conditions in the ghetto, Black children often have different socialization experiences. These experiences generally do not equip Blacks for active
participation in American society, nor do they often even prepare them for the
meager opportunities available to them.

In the Black community family styles vary, especially between the social classes.
However social scientists have tended to direct most of their attention to the lower
class Black family. Here patterns are sometimes found that are quite different from
those in the society at large, especially the middle class. And as is the case with
much of what is found in the Black community, the form and practices of the Black
family represent adaptations to the repressive conditions imposed by American
society. Discriminatory behavior and racism have never provided a setting within
which the familiar "middle-class" type of family could develop and persist.

The reading selection by Lee Rainwater presents an excellent overview of the
lower class Black family. Many of its important characteristics are discussed: the
open nature of the household, the domination of the mother, factors that work
against the maintenence of a stable marriage relationship, and the sense of
personal inadequacy and powerlessness developed by Black youth.

Rainwater describes a type of family in which the father is seldom present.
There is an emphasis therefore on the mother's role and the mother-child relationship. The selection by Elliot Liebow focuses on the absent father and his connection with the family household. The selection is a portion of Liebow's study of a
group of lower class streetcorner men in the Washington D.C. Black ghetto.

Liebow discusses the father's idea of the child's place in the family and the way
in which children are viewed both as assets and as liabilities. Father–child relationships vary, but some of the closest and most affectionate ties may be found
between the men and children that are not their own. Many fathers apparently
establish the most stable relationships with children and with families when they
can do so on their own terms.

Although the family patterns discussed by Rainwater and Liebow are adaptations to the conditions in the ghetto, they result in a good deal of suffering and
psychological damage. As Rainwater points out, these patterns represent not so
much "strategies for living" as "strategies for survival" in a hostile environment.

ADAPTATIONS TO DISCRIMINATION

"Crucible of Identity:
The Negro Lower-Class Family"

by Lee Rainwater

But can a people . . . live and develop for over three hundred years by simply reacting? Are American Negroes simply the creation of white men, or have they at least helped create themselves out of what they found around them? Men have made a way of life in caves and upon cliffs, why can not Negroes have made a life upon the horns of the white man's dilemma? . . . American Negro life is, for the Negro who must live it, not only a burden (and not always that) but also a discipline just as any human life which has endured so long is a discipline teaching its own insights into the human conditions, its own strategies of survival . . .

For even as his life toughens the Negro, even as it brutalizes him, sensitizes him, dulls him, goads him to anger, moves him to irony, sometimes fracturing and sometimes affirming his hopes; even as it shapes his attitude towards family, sex, love, religion; even as it modulates his humor, tempers his joy—it conditions him to deal with his life and with himself. Because it is his life and no mere abstraction in someone's head. He must live it and try consciously to grasp its complexity until he can change it; must live it as he changes it. He is no mere product of his socio-political predicament. He is a product of interaction between his racial predicament, his individual will and the broader American cultural freedom in which he finds his ambiguous existence. Thus he, too, in a limited way, is his own creation.
—Ralph Ellison

As long as Negroes have been in America, their marital and family patterns have been subjects of curiosity and amusement, moral indignation and self-congratulation, puzzlement and frustration, concern and guilt, on the part of white Americans. As some Negroes have moved into middle-class status, or acquired standards of American common-man respectability, they too have shared these attitudes toward the private behavior of their fellows, sometimes with a moral punitiveness to rival that of whites, but at other times with a hard-headed interest in causes and remedies rather than moral evaluation. Moralism permeated the subject of Negro sexual, marital, and family behavior in the polemics of slavery apologists and abolitionists as much as in the Northern and Southern civil rights controversies of today. Yet, as long as the dialectic of good or bad, guilty or innocent, overshadows a concern with who, why, and what can be, it is unlikely that realistic and effective social planning to correct the clearly desperate situation of poor Negro families can begin.

This paper is concerned with a description and analysis of slum Negro family patterns as these reflect and sustain Negroes' adaptations to the economic, social, and personal situation into which they are born and in which they must live. As such it deals with facts of lower-class life that are usually forgotten or ignored in polite discussion. We have chosen not to ignore these facts in the belief that to do so can lead only to assumptions which would frustrate efforts at social reconstruction, to strategies that are unrealistic in the light of the actual day-to-day reality of slum Negro life. Further, this analysis will deal with family patterns which interfere with the efforts slum Negroes make to attain a stable way of life as working—or middle-class individuals and with the effects such failure in turn has on family life. To be sure, many Negro families live *in* the slum ghetto, but are not *of* its culture (though even they, and particularly their children, can be deeply affected by what happens there). However, it is the individuals who succumb to the distinctive family life style of the slum who experience the greatest weight of deprivation and who have the greatest difficulty responding to the few self-improvement resources that make their way into the ghetto. In short, we propose to explore in depth the family's role in the "tangle of pathology" which characterizes the ghetto. . . .

The Autonomy of the Slum Ghetto

Just as the deprivations and depredations practiced by white society have had their effect on the personalities and social life of Negroes, so also has the separation from the ongoing social life of the white community had its effect. In a curious way, Negroes have had considerable freedom to fashion their own adaptations within their separate world. The larger society provides them with few resources but also with minimal interference in the Negro community on matters which did not seem to affect white interests. Because Negroes learned early that there were a great many things they could not depend upon whites to provide they developed their own solutions to recurrent human issues. These solutions can often be seen to combine, along with the predominance of elements from white culture, elements that are distinctive to the Negro group. Even more distinctive is the *configuration* which emerges from those elements Negroes share with whites and those which are different.

It is in this sense that we may speak of a Negro subculture, a distinctive *patterning* of existential perspectives, techniques for coping with the problems of social life, views about what is desirable and undersirable in particular situations. This subculture, and particularly that of the lower-class, the slum, Negro, can be seen as his own creation out of the elements available to him in response to (1) the conditions of life set by white society and (2) the selective freedom which that society allows (or must put up with given the pattern of separateness on which it insists).

Out of this kind of "freedom" slum Negroes have built a culture which has some elements of intrinsic value and many more elements that are highly destructive to the people who must live in it. The elements that whites can value they constantly borrow. Negro arts and language have proved so popular that such commentators on American culture as Norman Mailer and Leslie Fiedler have noted processes of Negro-ization of white Americans as a minor theme of the past thirty years. A fairly large proportion of Negroes with national reputations are engaged in the occupation of diffusing to the larger culture these elements of intrinsic value.

On the negative side, this freedom has meant, as social scientists who have studied Negro communities have long commented, that many of the protections offered by white institutions stop at the edge of the Negro ghetto: there are poor police protection and enforcement of civil equities, inadequate schooling and medical service, and more informal indulgences which whites allow Negroes as a small price for feeling superior.

For our purposes, however, the most important thing about the freedom which whites have allowed Negroes within their own world is that it has required them to work out their own ways of making it from day to day, from birth to death. The subculture that Negroes have created may be imperfect but it has been viable for centuries; it behooves both white and Negro leaders and intellectuals to seek to understand it even as they hope to change it.

Negroes have created, again particularly within the lower-class slum group, a range of institutions to structure the tasks of living a victimized life and to minimize the pain it inevitably produces. In the slum ghetto these institutions include prominently those of the social network—the extended kinship system and the "street system" of buddies and broads which tie (although tenuously and unpredictably) the "members" to each other—and the institutions of entertainment (music, dance, folk tales) by which they instruct, explain, and accept themselves. Other institutions function to provide escape from the society of the victimized: the church (Hereafter!) and the civil rights movement (Now!).

The Functional Autonomy of the Negro Family

At the center of the matrix of Negro institutional life lies the family. It is in the family that individuals are trained for participation in the culture and find personal and group identity and continuity. The "freedom" allowed by white society is greatest here, and this freedom has been used to create an institutional variant more distinctive perhaps to the Negro subculture than any other. (Much of the content of Negro art and entertainment derives exactly from the distinctive characteristics of Negro family life.) At each stage in the Negro's experience of American life—slavery, segregation, *de facto* ghettoization—whites have found it less necessary to interfere in the relations between the sexes and between parents and children than in other areas of the Negro's existence. His adaptations in this area, therefore, have been less constrained by whites than in many other areas.

Now that the larger society is becoming increasingly committed to integrating Negroes into the main steam of American life, however, we can expect increasing constraint (benevolent as it may be) to be placed on the autonomy of the Negro family system. These constraints will be designed to pull Negroes into meaningful integration with the larger society, to give up ways which are inimical to successful performance in the larger society, and to adopt new ways that are functional in that society. The strategic questions of the civil rights movement and of the war on poverty are ones that have to do with how one provides functional equivalents for the existing subculture before the capacity to make a life within its confines is destroyed.

The history of the Negro family has been ably documented by historians and sociologists. In slavery, conjugal and family ties were reluctantly and ambivalently recognized by the slave holders, were often violated by them, but proved necessary to the slave system. This necessity stemmed both from the profitable offspring of slave sexual unions and the necessity for their nurture, and from the fact that the slaves' efforts to sustain patterns of sexual and parental relations mollified the men and women whose labor could not simply be commanded. From nature's promptings, the thinning memories of African heritage, and the example and guilt-ridden permission of the slave holders, slaves constructed a partial family system and sets of relations that generated conjugal and familial sentiments. The slave holder's recognition in advertisements for runaway slaves of marital and family sentiments as motivations for absconding provides one indication that strong family ties were possible, though perhaps not common, in the slave quarter. The mother-centered family with its emphasis on the primacy of the mother-child relation and only tenuous ties to a man, then, is the legacy of adaptations worked out by Negroes during slavery.

After emancipation this family design often also served well to cope with the social disorganization of Negro life in the late nineteenth century. Matrifocal families, ambivalence about the desirability of marriage, ready acceptance of illegitimacy, all sustained some kind of family life in situations which often made it difficult to maintain a full nuclear family.

Yet in the hundred years since emancipation, Negroes in rural areas have been able to maintain full nuclear families almost as well as similarly situated whites. As we will see, it is the move to the city that results in the very high proportion of mother-headed households. In the rural system the man continues to have important functions; it is difficult for a woman to make a crop by herself, or even with the help of other women. In the city, however, the women can earn wages just as a man can, and she can receive welfare payments more easily than than he can. In rural areas, although there may be high illegitimacy rates and high rates of marital disruption, men and women have an interest in getting together; families are headed by a husband-wife pair much more often than in the city. That pair may be much less stable than in the more prosperous segments of Negro and white communities but it is more likely to exist among rural Negroes than among urban ones.

The matrifocal character of the Negro lower-class family in the United States has much in common with Caribbean Negro family patterns; research in both areas has done a great deal to increase our understanding of the Negro situation. However, there are important differences in the family forms of the two areas. The impact of white European family models has been much greater in the United States than in the Caribbean both because of the relative population proportions of white and colored peoples and because equalitarian values in the United States have had a great impact on Negroes even when they have not on whites. The typical Caribbean mating pattern is that women go through several visiting and common-law unions but eventually marry; that is, they marry legally only relatively late in their sexual lives. The Caribbean marriage is the crowning of a sexual and procreative career; it is considered a serious and difficult step.

In the United States, in contrast, Negroes marry at only a slightly lower rate and slightly higher age than whites. Most Negro women marry relatively early in their careers; marriage is not regarded as the same kind of crowning choice and achievement that it is in the Caribbean. For lower-class Negroes in the United States marriage ceremonies are rather informal affairs. In the Caribbean, marriage is regarded as quite costly because of the feasting which goes along with it; ideally it is performed in church.

In the United States, unlike the Caribbean, early marriage confers a kind of permanent respectable status upon a woman which she can use to deny any subsequent accusations of immorality or promiscuity once the marriage is broken and she becomes sexually involved in visiting or common-law relation. The relevant effective status for many Negro women is that of "having been married" rather than "being married"; having the right to be called "Mrs." rather than currently being Mrs. Someone-in-Particular.

For Negro lower-class women, then, first marriage has the same kind of importance as having a first child. Both indicate that the girl has become a woman but neither one that this is the last such activity in which she will engage. It seems very likely that only a minority of Negro women in the urban slum go through their childrearing years with only one man around the house.

Table 1. Proportion of Female Heads for Families with Children by Race, Income, and Urban-Rural Categories

	Rural	*Urban*	*Total*
Negroes			
Under $3000	18%	47%	36%
$3000 and over	5	8	7
Total	14	23	21
Whites			
Under $3000	12	38	22
$3000 and over	2	4	3
Total	4	7	6

Source: U.S. Census: 1960,-PC (1) D.U.S. Volume, Table 225; State Volume, Table 140.

Among the Negro urban poor, then, a great many women have the experience of heading a family for part of their mature lives, and a great many children spend some part of their formative years in a household without a father-mother pair. From Table 1 we see that in 1960, forty-seven per cent of the Negro poor urban families with children had a female head. Unfortunately, cumulative statistics are hard to come by; but, given this very high level for a cross-sectional sample (and taking into account the fact that the median age of the children in these families is about six years), it seems very likely that as many as two-thirds of Negro urban poor children will not live in families headed by a man and a woman throughout the first eighteen years of their lives.

One of the other distinctive characteristics of Negro families, both poor and not so poor, is the fact that Negro households have a much higher proportion of relatives outside the mother-father-children triangle than is the case with whites. For example, in St. Louis, Negro families average 0.8 other relatives per household compared to only 0.4 for white families. In the case of the more prosperous Negro families this is likely to mean that an older relative lives in the home providing baby-sitting services while both the husband and wife work and thus further their climb toward stable working- or middle-class status. In the poor Negro families it is much more likely that the household is headed by an older relative who brings under her wings a daughter and that daughter's children. It is important to note that the three-generation household with the grand-mother at the head exists only when there is no husband present. Thus, despite the high proportion of female-headed households in this group and despite the high proportion of households that contain other relatives, we find that almost all married couples in the St. Louis Negro slum community have their own household. In other words, when a couple marries it establishes its own household; when that couple breaks up the mother either maintains that household or moves back to her parents or grandparents.

Finally we should note that Negro slum families have more children than do either white slum families or stable working- and middle-class Negro families. Mobile Negro families limit their fertility sharply in the interest of bringing the advantages of mobility more fully to the few children that they do have. Since the Negro slum family is both more likely to have the father absent and more likely to have more children in the family, the mother has a more demanding task with fewer resources at her disposal. When we examine the patterns of life of the stem family we shall see that even the presence of several mothers does not necessarily lighten the work load for the principal mother in charge.

The Formation and Maintenance of Families.

We will outline below the several stages and forms of Negro lower-class family life. At many points these family forms and the interpersonal relations that exist within them will be seen to have characteristics in common with the life styles of white lower-class families. At other points there are differences, or the Negro pattern will be seen to be more sharply divergent from the family life of stable working- and middle-class couples.

It is important to recognize that lower-class Negroes know that their particular family forms are different from those of the rest of the society and that, though they often see these forms as representing the only ways of behaving given their circumstances, they also think of the more stable family forms of the working class as more desirable. That is, lower-class Negroes know what the "normal American family" is supposed to be like, and they consider a stable family-centered way of life superior to the conjugal and familial situations in which they often find themselves. Their conceptions of the good American life include the notion of a father-husband who functions as an adequate provider and interested member of the family, a hard working home-bound mother who is concerned about her children's welfare and her husband's needs, and children who look up to their parents and perform well in school and other outside places to reflect credit on their families. This image of what family life can be like is very real from time to time as lower-class men and women grow up and move through adulthood. Many of them make efforts to establish such families but find it impossible to do so either because of the direct impact of economic disabilities or because they are not able to sustain in their day-to-day lives the ideals which they hold. While these ideals do serve as a meaningful guide to lower-class couples who are mobile out of the group, for a great many others the existence of such ideas about normal family life represents a recurrent source of stress within families as individuals become aware that they are failing to measure up to the ideals, or as others within the family and outside it use the ideals as an aggressive weapon for criticizing each other's performance. It is not at all uncommon for husbands or wives or children to try to hold others in the family to the norms of stable family life while they themselves engage in behaviors which violate these norms. The effect of such criticism in the end is to deepen commitment to the deviant sexual and parental norms of a slum subculture. Unless they are careful, social workers and other professionals exacerbate the tendency to use the norms of "American family life" as weapons by supporting these norms in situations where they are in reality unsupportable, thus aggravating the sense of failing and being failed by others which is chronic for lower-class people.

Going together. The initial steps toward mating and family formation in the Negro slum take place in a context of highly developed boys' and girls' peer groups. Adolescents tend to become deeply involved in their peer-group societies beginning as early as the age of twelve or thirteen and continue to be involved after first pregnancies and first marriages. Boys and girls are heavily committed both to their same sex peer groups and to the activities that those groups carry out. While classical gang activity does not necessarily characterize Negro slum communities everywhere, loosely-knit peer groups do.

The world of the Negro slum is wide open to exploration by adolescent boys and girls: "Negro communities provide a flow of common experience in which young people and their elders share, and out of which delinquent behavior emerges almost imperceptibly." More than is possible in white slum communities, Negro adolescents have an opportunity to interact with adults in various "high life" activities; their behavior more often represents an identification with the behavior of adults than an attempt to set up group standards and activities that differ from those of adults.

Boys and young men participating in the street system of peer-group activity are much caught up in games of furthering and enhancing their status as significant persons. These games are played out in small and large gatherings through various kinds of verbal contests that go under the names of "sounding," "signifying," and "working game." Very much a part of a boy's or man's status in this group is his ability to win women. The man who has several women "up tight," who is successful in "pimping off" women for sexual favors and material benefits, is much admired. In sharp contrast to white lower-class groups, there is little tendency for males to separate girls into "good" and "bad" categories. Observations of groups of Negro youths suggest that girls and women are much more readily referred to as "that bitch" or "that whore" than they are by their names, and this seems to be a universal tendency carrying no connotation that "that bitch" is morally inferior to or different from other women. Thus, all women are essentially the same, all women are legitimate targets, and no girl or woman is expected to be virginal except for reason of lack of opportunity or immaturity. From their participation in the peer group and according to standards legitimated by the total Negro slum culture, Negro boys and young men are propelled in the direction of girls to test their "strength" as seducers. They are mercilessly rated by both their peers and the opposite sex in their ability to "talk" to girls; a young man will go to great lengths to avoid the reputation of having a "weak" line.

The girls share these definitions of the nature of heterosexual relations; they take for granted that almost any male they deal with will try to seduce them and that given sufficient inducement (social not monetary) they may wish to go along with his line. Although girls have a great deal of ambivalence about participating in sexual relations, this ambivalence is minimally moral and has much more to do with a desire not to be taken advantage of or get in trouble. Girls develop defenses against the exploitative orientations of men by devaluing the significance of sexual relations ("he really didn't do anything bad to me"), and as time goes on by developing their own appreciation of the intrinsic rewards of sexual intercourse.

The informal social relations of slum Negroes begin in adolescence to be highly sexualized. Although parents have many qualms about boys and, particularly, girls entering into this system, they seldom feel there is much they can do to prevent their children's sexual involvement. They usually confine themselves to counseling somewhat hopelessly against girls becoming pregnant or boys being forced into situations where they might have to marry a girl they do not want to marry.

Girls are propelled toward boys and men in order to demonstrate their maturity and attractiveness; in the process they are constantly exposed to pressures for seduction, to boys "rapping" to them. An active girl will "go with" quite a number of boys, but she will generally try to restrict the number with whom she has intercourse to the few to whom she is attracted or (as happens not infrequently) to those whose threats of physical violence she cannot avoid. For their part, the boys move rapidly from girl to girl seeking to have intercourse with as many as they can and thus build up their "reps." The activity of seduction is itself highly cathected; there is gratification in simply "talking to" a girl as long as the boy can feel that he has acquitted himself well.

At sixteen Joan Bemias enjoys spending time with three or four very close girl friends. She tells us they follow this routine when the girls want to go out and none of the boys they have been seeing lately is available: "Every time we get ready to go someplace we look through all the telephone numbers of boys we'd have and we call them and talk so sweet to them that they'd come on around. All of them had cars you see. (I: What do you do to keep all these fellows interested?) Well nothing. We don't have to make love with all of them. Let's see, Joe, J. B., Albert, and Paul, out of all of them I've been going out with I've only had sex with four boys, that's all." She goes on to say that she and her girl friends resist boys by being unresponsive to their lines and by breaking off relations with them on the ground that they're going out with other girls. It is also clear from her comments that the girl friends support each other in resisting the boys when they are out together in groups.

Joan has had a relationship with a boy which has lasted six months, but she has managed to hold the frequency of intercourse down to four times. Initially she managed to hold this particular boy off for a month but eventually gave in.

Becoming pregnant. It is clear that the contest elements in relationships between men and women continue even in relationships that become quite steady. Despite the girls' ambivalence about sexual relations and their manifold efforts to reduce its frequency, the operation of chance often eventuates in their becoming pregnant. This was the case with Joan. With this we reach the second stage in the formation of families, that of premarital pregnancy. (We are outlining an ideal-typical sequence and not, of course, implying that all girls in the Negro slum culture become pregnant before they marry but only that a great many of them do.)

Joan was caught despite the fact that she was considerably more sophisticated about contraception than most girls or young women in the group (her mother had both instructed her in contraceptive techniques and constantly warned her to take precautions). No one was particularly surprised at her pregnancy although she, her boy friend, her mother, and others regarded it as unfortunate. For girls in the Negro slum, pregnancy before marriage is expected in much the same way that parents expect their children to catch mumps or chicken pox; if they are lucky it will not happen but if it happens people are not too surprised and everyone knows what to do about it. It was quickly decided that Joan and the baby would stay at home. It seems clear from the preparations that Joan's mother is making that she expects to have the main responsibility for caring for the infant. Joan seems quite indifferent to the baby; she shows little interest in mothering the child although she is not particularly adverse to the idea so long as the baby does not interfere too much with her continued participation in her peer group.

Establishing who the father is under these circumstances seems to be important and confers a kind of legitimacy on the birth; not to know who one's father is, on the other hand, seems the ultimate in illegitimacy. Actually Joan had a choice in the imputation of fatherhood; she chose J.B. because he is older than she, and because she may marry him if he can get a divorce from his wife. She could have chosen Paul (with whom she had also had intercourse at about the time she became pregnant), but she would have done this reluctantly since Paul is a year younger than she and somehow this does not seem fitting.

In general, when a girl becomes pregnant while still living at home it seems taken for granted that she will continue to live there and that her parents will take a major responsibility for rearing the children. Since there are usually siblings who can help out and even siblings who will be playmates for the child, the addition of a third generation to the household does not seem to place a great stress on relationships within the family. It seems common for the first pregnancy to have a liberating influence on the mother once the child is born in that she becomes socially and sexually more active than she was before. She no longer has to be concerned with preserving her status as a single girl. Since her mother is usually willing to take care of the child for a few years, the unwed mother has an opportunity to go out with girl friends and with men and thus become more deeply involved in the peer-group society of her culture. As she has more children and perhaps marries she will find it necessary to settle down and spend more time around the house fulfilling the functions of a mother herself.

It would seem that for girls pregnancy is the real measure of maturity, the dividing line between adolescence and womanhood. Perhaps because of this, as well as because of the ready resources for child care, girls in the Negro slum community show much less concern about pregnancy than do girls in the white lower-class community and are less motivated to marry the fathers of their children. When a girl becomes pregnant the question of marriage certainly arises and is considered, but the girl often decides that she would rather not marry the man either because she does not want to settle down yet or because she does not think he would make a good husband.

It is in the easy attitudes toward premarital pregnancy that the matrifocal character of the Negro lower-class family appears most clearly. In order to have and raise a family it is simply not necessary, though it may be desirable, to have a man around the house. While the AFDC program may make it easier to maintain such attitudes in the urban situation, this pattern existed long before the program was initiated and continues in families where support comes from other sources.

Finally it should be noted that fathering a child similarly confers maturity on boys and young men although perhaps it is less salient for them. If the boy has any interest in the girl he will tend to feel that the fact that he has impregnated her gives him an additional claim on her. He will be stricter in seeking to enforce his exclusive rights over her (though not exclusive loyalty to her). This exclusive right does not mean that he expects to marry her but only that there is a new and special bond between them. If the girl is not willing to accept such claims she may find it necessary to break off the relationship rather than tolerate the man's jealousy. Since others in the peer group have a vested interest in not allowing a couple to be too loyal to each other they go out of their way to question and challenge each partner about the loyalty of the other, thus contributing to the deterioration of the relationship. This same kind of questioning and challenging continues if the couple marries and represents one source of the instability of the marital relationship.

Getting married. As noted earlier, despite the high degree of premarital sexual activity and the rather high proportion of premarital pregnancies, most lower-class Negro men and women eventually do marry and stay together for a shorter or longer period of time. Marriage is an intimidating prospect and is approached ambivalently by both parties. For the girl it means giving up a familiar and comfortable home that, unlike some other lower-class subcultures, places few real restrictions on her behavior. (While marriage can appear to be an escape from interpersonal difficulties at home, these difficulties seldom seem to revolve around effective restrictions placed on her behavior by her parents.) The girl also has good reason to be suspicious of the likelihood that men will be able to perform stably in the role of husband and provider; she is reluctant to be tied down by a man who will not prove to be worth it.

From the man's point of view the fickleness of women makes marriage problematic. It is one thing to have a girl friend step out on you, but it is quite another to have a wife do so. Whereas premarital sexual relations and fatherhood carry almost no connotation of responsibility for the welfare of the partner, marriage is supposed to mean that a man behaves more responsibly, becoming a provider for his wife and children even though he may not be expected to give up all the gratifications of participation in the street system.

For all of these reasons both boys and girls tend to have rather negative views of marriage as well as a low expectation that marriage will prove a stable and gratifying existence. When marriage does take place it tends to represent a tentative commitment on the part of both parties with a strong tendency to seek greater commitment on the part of the partner than on one's own part. Marriage is regarded as a fragile arrangement held together primarily by affectional ties rather than instrumental concerns.

In general, as in white lower-class groups, the decision to marry seems to be taken rather impulsively. Since everyone knows that sooner or later he will get married, in spite of the fact that he may not be sanguine about the prospect, Negro lower-class men and women are alert for clues that the time has arrived. The time may arrive because of a pregnancy in a steady relationship that seems gratifying to both partners, or as a way of getting out of what seems to be an awkward situation, or as a self-indulgence during periods when a boy and a girl are feeling very sorry for themselves. Thus, one girl tells us that when she marries her husband will cook all of her meals for her and she will not have any housework; another girl says that when she marries it will be to a man who has plenty of money and will have to take her out often and really show her a good time.

Boys see in marriage the possibility of regular sexual intercourse without having to fight for it, or a girl safe from venereal disease, or a relationship to a nurturant figure who will fulfill the functions of a mother. For boys, marriage can also be a way of asserting their independence from the peer group if its demands become burdensome. In this case one young man seeks to have the best of both worlds.

Marriage as a way out of an unpleasant situation can be seen in the case of one of our informants, Janet Cowan:

> Janet has been going with two men, one of them married and the other single. The married man's wife took exception to their relationship and killed her husband. Within a week Janet and her single boy friend, Howard, were married. One way out of the turmoil the murder of her married boy friend stimulated (they lived in the same building) was to choose marriage as a way of "settling down." However, after marrying the new couple seemed to have little idea how to set themselves up as a family. Janet was reluctant to leave her parents' home because her parents cared for her two illegitimate children. Howard was unemployed and therefore unacceptable in his parent-in-law's home, nor were his own parents willing to have his wife move in with them. Howard was also reluctant to give up another girl friend in another part of town. Although both he and his wife maintained that it was all right for a couple to step out on each other so long as the other partner did not know about it, they were both jealous if they suspected anything of this kind. In the end they gave up on the idea of marriage and went their separate ways.

In general, then, the movement toward marriage is an uncertain and tentative one. Once the couple does settle down together in a household of their own, they have the problem of working out a mutually acceptable organization of rights and duties, expectations and performances, that will meet their needs.

Husband-wife relations. Characteristic of both the Negro and white lower class is a high degree of conjugal role segregation. That is, husbands and wives tend to think of themselves as having very separate kinds of functioning in the instrumental organization of family life, and also as pursuing recreational and outside interests separately. The husband is expected to be a provider; he resists assuming functions around the home so long as he feels he is doing his proper job of bringing home a pay check. He feels he has the right to indulge himself in little ways if he is successful at this task. The wife is expected to care for the home and children and make her husband feel welcome and comfortable. Much that is distinctive to Negro family life stems from the fact that husbands often are not stable providers. Even when a particular man is, his wife's conception of men in general is such that she is pessimistic about the likelihood that he will continue to do well in this area. A great many Negro wives work to supplement the family income. When this is so the separate incomes earned by husband and wife tend to be treated not as "family" income but as the individual property of the two persons involved. If their wives work, husbands are likely to feel that they are entitled to retain a larger share of the income they provide; the wives, in turn, feel that the husbands have no right to benefit from the purchases they make out of their own money. There is, then, "my money" and "your money." In this situation the husband may come to feel that the wife should support the children out of her income and that he can retain all of his income for himself.

While white lower-class wives often are very much intimidated by their husbands, Negro lower-class wives come to feel that they have a right to give as good as they get. If the husband indulges himself, they have the right to indulge themselves. If the husband steps out on his wife, she has the right to step out on him. The commitment of husbands and wives to each other seems often a highly instrumental one after the "honeymoon" period. Many wives feel they owe the husband nothing once he fails to perform his provider role. If the husband is unemployed the wife increasingly refuses to perform her usual duties for him. For example one woman, after mentioning that her husband had cooked four eggs for himself, commented, "I cook for him when he's working but right now he's unemployed; he can cook for himself." It is important, however, to understand that the man's status in the home depends not so much on whether he is working as on whether he brings money into the home. Thus, in several of the families we have studied in which the husband receives disability payments his status is as well-recognized as in families in which the husband is working.

Because of the high degree of conjugal role segregation, both white and Negro lower-class families tend to be matrifocal in comparison to middle-class families. Thy are matrifocal in the sense that the wife makes most of the decisions that keep the family going and has the greatest sense of responsibility to the family. In white as well as in Negro lower-class families women tend to look to their female relatives for support and counsel, and to treat their husbands as essentially uninterested in the day-to-day problems of family living. In the Negro lower-class family these tendencies are all considerably exaggerated so that the matrifocality is much clearer than in white lower-class families.

The fact that both sexes in the Negro slum culture have equal right to the various satisfactions of life (earning an income, sex, drinking, and peer-group activity which conflicts with family responsibilities) means that there is less pretense to patriarchal authority in the Negro than in the white lower class. Since men find the overt debasement of their status very threatening, the Negro family is more vulnerable to disruption when men are temporarily unable to perform their provider roles. Also, when men are unemployed the temptations for them to engage in street adventures which repercuss on the marital relationship are much greater. This fact is well-recognized by Negro lower-class wives; they often seem as concerned about what their unemployed husbands will do instead of working as they are about the fact that the husband is no longer bringing money into the home.

It is tempting to cope with the likelihood of disloyalty by denying the usual norms of fidelity, by maintaining instead that extra-marital affairs are acceptable as long as they do not interfere with family functioning. Quite a few informants tell us this, but we have yet to observe a situation in which a couple maintains a stable relationship under these circumstances without a great deal of conflict. Thus one woman in her forties who has been married for many years and has four children first outlined this deviant norm and then illustrated how it did not work out:

My husband and I, we go out alone and sometimes stay all night. But when I get back my husband doesn't ask me a thing and I don't ask him anything. . . . A couple of years ago I suspected he was going out on me. One day I came home and my daughter was here. I told her to tell me when he left the house. I went into the bedroom and got into bed and then I heard him come in. He left in about ten minutes and my daughter came in and told me he was gone. I got out of bed and put on my clothes and started following him. Soon I saw him walking with a young girl and I began walking after them. They were just laughing and joking right out loud right on the sidewalk. He was carrying a large package of hers. I walked up behind them until I was about a yard from them. I had a large dirk which I opened and had decided to take one long slash across the both of them. Just when I decided to swing at them I lost my balance—I have a bad hip. Anyway, I didn't cut them because I lost my balance. Then I called his name and he turned around and stared at me. He didn't move at all. He was shaking all over. That girl just ran away from us. He still had her package so the next day she called on the telephone and said she wanted to come pick it up. My husband washed his face, brushed his teeth, took out his false tooth and started scrubbing it and put on a clean shirt and everything, just for her. We went downstairs together and gave her the package and she left. So you see my husband does run around on me and it seems like he does it a lot. The thing about it is he's just getting too old to be pulling that kind of stuff. If a young man does it then that's not so bad—but an old man, he just looks foolish. One of these days he'll catch me but I'll just tell him, "Buddy you owe me one," and that'll be all there is to it. He hasn't caught me yet though.

In this case, as in others, the wife is not able to leave well enough alone;

her jealousy forces her to a confrontation. Actually seeing her husband with another woman stimulates her to violence.

With couples who have managed to stay married for a good many years, these peccadillos are tolerable although they generate a great deal of conflict in the marital relationship. At earlier ages the partners are likely to be both prouder and less innured to the hopelessness of maintaining stable relationships; outside involvements are therefore much more likely to be disruptive of the marriage.

Marital breakup. The precipitating causes of marital disruption seem to fall mainly into economic or sexual categories. As noted, the husband has little credit with his wife to tide him over periods of unemployment. Wives seem very willing to withdraw commitment from husbands who are not bringing money into the house. They take the point of view that he has no right to take up space around the house, to use its facilities, or to demand loyalty from her. Even where the wife is not inclined to press these claims, the husband tends to be touchy because he knows that such definitions are usual in his group, and he may, therefore, prove difficult for even a well-meaning wife to deal with. As noted above, if husbands do not work they tend to play around. Since they continue to maintain some contact with their peer groups, whenever they have time on their hands they move back into the world of the street system and are likely to get involved in activities which pose a threat to their family relationships.

Drink is a great enemy of the lower-class housewife, both white and Negro. Lower-class wives fear their husband's drinking because it costs money, because the husband may become violent and take out his frustrations on his wife, and because drinking may lead to sexual involvements with other women.

The combination of economic problems and sexual difficulties can be seen in the case of the following couple in their early twenties:

> When the field worker first came to know them, the Wilsons seemed to be working hard to establish a stable family life. The couple had been married about three years and had a two-year-old son. Their apartment was very sparsely furnished but also very clean. Within six weeks the couple had acquired several rooms of inexpensive furniture and obviously had gone to a great deal of effort to make a liveable home. Husband and wife worked on different shifts so that the husband could take care of the child while the wife worked. They looked forward to saving enough money to move out of the housing project into a more desirable neighborhood. Six weeks later, however, the husband had lost his job. He and his wife were in great conflict. She made him feel unwelcome at home and he strongly suspected her of going out with other men. A short time later they had separated. It is impossible to disentangle the varous factors involved in this separation into a sequence of cause and effect, but we can see something of the impact of the total complex.
>
> First Mr. Wilson loses his job: "I went to work one day and the man told

me that I would have to work until 1:00. I asked him if there would be any extra pay for working overtime and he said no. I asked him why and he said, 'If you don't like it you can kiss my ass.' He said that to me. I said, 'Why do I have to do all that?' He said, 'Because I said so.' I wanted to jam (fight) him but I said to myself I don't want to be that ignorant, I don't want to be as ignorant as he is, so I just cut out and left. Later his father called me (it was a family firm) and asked why I left and I told him. He said, 'If you don't want to go along with my son then your're fired.' I said O.K. They had another Negro man come into help me part time before they fired me. I think they were trying to have him work full time because he worked for them before. He has seven kids and he takes their shit."

The field worker observed that things were not as hard as they could be because his wife had a job, to which he replied, "Yeah, I know, that's just where the trouble is. My wife has become independent since she began working. If I don't get a job pretty soon I'll go crazy. We have a lot of little arguments about nothing since she got so independent." He went on to say that his wife had become a completely different person recently; she was hard to talk to because she felt that now that she was working and he was not there was nothing that he could tell her. On her last pay day his wife did not return home for three days; when she did she had only seven cents left from her pay check. He said that he loved his wife very much and had begged her to quit fooling around. He is pretty sure that she is having an affair with the man with whom she rides to work. To make matters worse his wife's sister counsels her that she does not have to stay home with him as long as he is out of work. Finally the wife moved most of their furniture out of the apartment so that he came home to find an empty apartment. He moved back to his parents' home (also in the housing project).

One interesting effect of this experience was the radical change in the husband's attitudes toward race relations. When he and his wife were doing well together and had hopes of moving up in the world he was quite critical of Negroes; "Our people are not ready for integration in many cases because they really don't know how to act. You figure if our people don't want to be bothered with whites then why in hell should the white man want to be bothered with them. There are some of us who are ready; there are others who aren't quite ready yet so I don't see why they're doing all of this hollering." A scarce eight months later he addressed white people as he spoke for two hours into a tape recorder, "If we're willing to be with you, why aren't you willing to be with us? Do our color makes us look dirty and low down and cheap? Or do you know the real meaning of 'Nigger'? Anyone can be a nigger, white, colored, orange or any other color. It's something that you labeled us with. You put us away like you put a can away on the shelf with a label on it. The can is marked 'Poison: stay away from it.' You want us to help build your country but you don't want us to live in it. . . . You give me respect; I'll give you respect. If you threaten to take my life, I'll take yours and believe me I know how to take a life. We do believe that man was put here to live together as human beings; not one that's superior and the one that's a dog, but as human beings. And if you don't want to live this way then you become the dog and we'll become the human beings. There's too much corruption, too much hate, too much one individual trying to step on another. If we don't get together in a hurry we will destroy each other." It was clear from what the respondent said that he had been much influenced by Black Muslim philosophy, yet again and again in his comments one can see the displacement into a public, race relations dialogue of the sense of rage, frustration and victimization that he had experienced in his ill-fated marriage.

Finally, it should be noted that migration plays a part in marital disruption. Sometimes marriages do not break up in the dramatic way described above but rather simply become increasingly unsatisfactory to one or both partners. In such a situation the temptation to move to another city, from South to North, or North to West, is great. Several wives told us that their first marriages were broken when they moved with their children to the North and their husbands stayed behind.

> "After we couldn't get along I left the farm and came here and stayed away three or four days. I didn't come here to stay. I came to visit but I liked it and so I said, 'I'm gonna leave!' He said, 'I'll be glad if you do.' Well, maybe he didn't mean it but I thought he did. . . . I miss him sometimes, you know. I think about him I guess. But just in a small way. That's what I can't understand about life sometimes; you know—how people can go on like that and still break up and meet somebody else. Why couldn't—oh, I don't know!"

The gains and losses in marriage and in the post-marital state often seems quite comparable. Once they have had the experience of marriage, many women in the Negro slum culture see little to recommend it in the future, important as the first marriage may have been in establishing their maturity and respectability.

The house of mothers. As we have seen, perhaps a majority of mothers in the Negro slum community spend at least part of their mature life as mothers heading a family. The Negro mother may be a working mother or she may be an AFDC mother, but in either case she has the problems of maintaining a household, socializing her children, and achieving for herself some sense of membership in relations with other women and with men. As is apparent from the earlier discussion, she often receives her training in how to run such a household by observing her own mother manage without a husband. Similarly she often learns how to run a three-generation household because she herself brought a third generation into her home with her first, premarital, pregnancy.

Because men are not expected to be much help around the house, having to be head of the household is not particularly intimidating to the Negro mother if she can feel some security about income. She knows it is a hard, hopeless, and often thankless task, but she also knows that it is possible. The maternal household in the slum is generally run with a minimum of organization. The children quickly learn to fend for themselves, to go to the store, to make small purchases, to bring change home, to watch after themselves when the mother has to be out of the home, to amuse themselves, to set their own schedules of sleeping, eating, and going to school. Housekeeping practices may be poor, furniture takes a terrific beating from the children, and emergencies constantly arise. The Negro mother in this situation copes by not setting too high standards for herself, by letting things take their course. Life is most difficult when there are babies and preschool children around because then the mother is confined to the home. If she is a grandmother and the children are her daughter's, she is often confined since it is taken as a matter of course that the mother has the right to continue her outside activities and that the grandmother has the duty to be responsible for the child.

In this culture there is little of the sense of the awesome responsibility of caring for children that is characteristic of the working and middle class. There is not the deep psychological involvement with babies which has been observed with the working-class mother. The baby's needs are cared for on a catch-as-catch-can basis. If there are other children around and they happen to like babies, the baby can be over-stimulated; if this is not the case, the baby is left alone a good deal of the time. As quickly as he can move around he learns to fend for himself.

The three-generation maternal household is a busy place. In contrast to working- and middle-class homes it tends to be open to the world, with many non-family members coming in and out at all times as the children are visited by friends, the teenagers by their boy friends and girl friends, the mother by her friends and perhaps an occasional boy friend, and the grandmother by fewer friends but still by an occasional boy friend.

The openness of the household is, among other things, a reflection of the mother's sense of impotence in the face of the street system. Negro lower-class mothers often indicate that they try very hard to keep their young children at home and away from the streets; they often seem to make the children virtual prisoners in the home. As the children grow and go to school they inevitably do become involved in peer-group activities. The mother gradually gives up, feeling that once the child is lost to this pernicious outside world there is little she can do to continue to control him and direct his development. She will try to limit the types of activities that go on in the home and to restrict the kinds of friends that her children can bring into the home, but even this she must give up as time goes on, as the children become older and less attentive to her direction.

The grandmothers in their late forties, fifties, and sixties tend increasingly to stay at home. The home becomes a kind of court at which other family members gather and to which they bring their friends for sociability, and as a by-product provide amusement and entertainment for the mother. A grandmother may provide a home for her daughters, their children, and sometimes their children's children, and yet receive very little in a material way from them; but one of the things she does receive is a sense of human involvement, a sense that although life may have passed her by she is not completely isolated from it.

The lack of control that mothers have over much that goes on in their households is most dramatically apparent in the fact that their older children seem to have the right to come home at any time once they have moved and to stay in the home without contributing to its maintenance. Though the mother may be resentful about being taken advantage of, she does not feel she can turn her children away. For example, sixty-five-year-old Mrs. Washington plays hostess for weeks or months at a time to her forty-year-old daughter and her small children, and to her twenty-three-year-old granddaughter and her children. When these daughters come home with their families the grandmother is expected to take care of the young children and must argue with her daughter and granddaughter to receive contributions to the daily household ration of food and liquor. Or, a twenty-year-old son comes home from the Air Force and feels he has the right to live at home without working and to run up an eighty-dollar long-distance telephone bill.

Even aged parents living alone in small apartments sometimes acknowledge such obligations to their children or grandchildren. Again, the only clear return they receive for their hospitality is the reduction of isolation that comes from having people around and interesting activity going on. When in the Washington home the daughter and granddaughter and their children move in with the grandmother, or when they come to visit for shorter periods of time, the occasion has a party atmosphere. The women sit around talking and reminiscing. Though boy friends may be present, they take little part; instead they sit passively, enjoying the stories and drinking along with the women. It would seem that in this kind of party activity the women are defined as the stars. Grandmother, daughter, and granddaughter in turn take the center of the stage telling a story from the family's past, talking about a particularly interesting night out on the town or just making some general observation about life. In the course of these events a good deal of liquor is consumed. In such a household as this little attention is paid to the children since the competition by adults for attention is stiff.

Boy friends, not husbands. It is with an understanding of the problems of isolation which older mothers have that we can obtain the best insight into the role and function of boy friends in the maternal household. The older mothers, surrounded by their own children and grandchildren, are not able to move freely in the outside world, to participate in the high life which they enjoyed when younger and more foot-loose. They are disillusioned with marriage as providing any more secure economic base than they can achieve on their own. They see marriage as involving just another responsibility without a concomitant reward—"It's the greatest thing in the world to come home in the afternoon and not have some curly headed twot in the house yellin' at me and askin' me where supper is, where I've been, what I've been doin', and who I've been seein'." In this situation the woman is tempted to form relationships with men that are not so demanding as marriage but still provide companionship and an opportunity for occasional sexual gratification.

There seem to be two kinds of boy friends. Some boy friends "pimp" off mothers; they extract payment in food or money for their companionship. This leads to the custom sometimes called "Mother's Day," the tenth of the month when the AFDC checks come. On this day one can observe an influx of men into the neighborhood, and much partying. But there is another kind of boy friend, perhaps more numerous than the first, who instead of being paid for his services pays for the right to be a pseudo family member. He may be the father of one of the woman's children and for this reason makes a steady contribution to the family's support, or he may simply be a man whose company the mother enjoys and who makes reasonable gifts to the family for the time he spends with them (and perhaps implicitly for the sexual favors he receives). While the boy friend does not assume fatherly authority within the family, he often is known and liked by the children. The older children appreciate the meaningfulness of their mother's relationship with him—one girl said of her mother's boy friend:

"We don't none of us (the children) want her to marry again. It's all right if she wants to live by herself and have a boy friend. It's not because we're afraid we're going to have some more sisters and brothers, which it wouldn't make us much difference, but I think she be too old."

Even when the boy friend contributes ten or twenty dollars a month to the family he is in a certain sense getting a bargain. If he is a well-accepted boy friend he spends considerable time around the house, has a chance to relax in an atmosphere less competitive than that of his peer group, is fed and cared for by the woman, yet has no responsibilities which he cannot renounce when he wishes. When women have stable relationships of this kind with boy friends they often consider marrying them but are reluctant to take such a step. Even the well-liked boy friend has some shortcomings—one woman said of her boy friend:

"Well he works; I know that. He seems to be a nice person, kind hearted. He believes in survival for me and my family. He don't much mind sharing with my youngsters. If I ask him for a helping hand he don't seem to mind that. The only part I dislike is his drinking."

The woman in this situation has worked out a reasonably stable adaptation to the problems of her life; she is fearful of upsetting this adaptation

by marrying again. It seems easier to take the "sweet" part of the relationship with a man without the complexities that marriage might involve.

It is in the light of this pattern of women living in families and men
living by themselves in rooming houses, odd rooms, here and there, that
we can understand Daniel Patrick Moynihan's observation that during
their mature years men simply disappear; that is, that census data show
a very high sex ratio of women to men. In St. Louis, starting at the age
range twenty to twenty-four there are only seventy-two men for every one
hundred women. This ratio does not climb to ninety until the age range
fifty to fifty-four. Men often do not have real homes; they move about
from one household where they have kinship or sexual ties to another;
they live in flop houses and rooming houses; they spend time in institutions. They are not household members in the only "homes" that they
have—the homes of their mothers and of their girl friends.

It is in this kind of world that boys and girls in the Negro slum community learn their sex roles. It is not just, or even mainly, that fathers are
often absent but that the male role models around boys are ones which
emphasize expressive, affectional techniques for making one's way in the
world. The female role models available to girls emphasize an exaggerated
self-sufficiency (from the point of view of the middle class) and the danger
of allowing oneself to be dependent on men for anything that is crucial.
By the time she is mature, the woman learns that she is most secure when
she herself manages the family affairs and when she dominates her men.
The man learns that he exposes himself to the least risk of failure when
he does not assume a husband's and father's responsibilities but instead
counts on his ability to court women and to ingratiate himself with them.

Identity Processes in the Family

Up to this point we have been examining the sequential development of
family stages in the Negro slum community, paying only incidental attention to the psychological responses family members make to these social
forms and not concerning ourselves with the effect the family forms have
on the psychosocial development of the children who grow up in them.
Now we want to examine the effect that growing up in this kind of a
system has in terms of socialization and personality development.

Household groups function for cultures in carrying out the initial phases
of socialization and personality formation. It is in the family that the child
learns the most primitive categories of existence and experience, and that
he develops his most deeply held beliefs about the world and about himself. From the child's point of view, the household *is* the world; his experiences as he moves out of it into the larger world are always interpreted
in terms of his particular experience within the home. The painful experiences which a child in the Negro slum culture has are, therefore, inter-

preted as in some sense a reflection of this family world. The impact of the system of victimization is transmitted through the family; the child cannot be expected to have the sophistication an outside observer has for seeing exactly where the villains are. From the child's point of view, if he is hungry it is his parents' fault; if he experiences frustrations in the streets or in the school it is his parents' fault; if that world seems incomprehensible to him it is his parents' fault; if people are aggressive or destructive toward each other it is his parents' fault, not that of a system of race relations. In another culture this might not be the case; if a subculture could exist which provided comfort and security within its limited world and the individual experienced frustration only when he moved out into the larger society, the family might not be thought so much to blame. The effect of the caste system, however, is to bring home through a chain of cause and effect all of the victimization processes, and to bring them home in such a way that it is often very difficult even for adults in the system to see the connection between the pain they feel at the moment and the structured patterns of the caste system.

Let us take as a central question that of identity formation within the Negro slum family. We are concerned with the question of who the individual believes himself to be and to be becoming. For Erikson, identity means a sense of continuity and social sameness which bridges what the individual "*was* as a child and what he is *about to become* and also reconciles his *conception of himself* and his community's recognition of him." Thus identity is a "self-realization coupled with a mutual recognition." In the early childhood years identity is family-bound since the child's identity is his identity *vis-à-vis* other members of the family. Later he incorporates into his sense of who he is and is becoming his experiences outside the family, but always influenced by the interpretations and evaluations of those experiences that the family gives. As the child tries on identities, *announces* them, the family sits as judge of his pretensions. Family members are both the most important judges and the most critical ones, since who he is allowed to become affects them in their own identity strivings more crucially than it affects anyone else. The child seeks a sense of valid identity, a sense of being a particular person with a satisfactory degree of congruence between who he feels he is, who he announces himself to be, and where he feels his society places him. He is uncomfortable when he experiences disjunction between his own needs and the kinds of needs legitimated by those around him, or when he feels a disjunction between his sense of himself and the image of himself that others play back to him.

"*Tell it like it is.*" When families become involved in important quarrels the psychosocial underpinnings of family life are laid bare. One such quarrel in a family we have been studying brings together in one place many of the themes that seem to dominate identity problems in Negro slum culture. The incident illustrates in a particularly forceful and dramatic way family processes which our field work, and some other contemporary studies of slum family life, suggests unfold more subtly in a great many families at the lower-class level. The family involved, the Johnsons, is certainly not the most disorganized one we have studied; in some respects their way of life represents a realistic adaptation to the hard living of a family nineteen years on AFDC with a monthly income of $202 for nine people. The two oldest daughters, Mary Jane (eighteen years old) and Esther (sixteen) are pregnant; Mary Jane has one illegitimate child. The adolescent sons, Bob and Richard, are much involved in the social and sexual activities of their peer group. The three other children, ranging in age from twelve to fourteen, are apparently also moving into this kind of peer-group society.

> When the argument started Bob and Esther were alone in the apartment with Mary Jane's baby. Esther took exception to Bob's playing with the baby because she had been left in charge; the argument quickly progressed to a fight in which Bob cuffed Esther around, and she tried to cut him with a knife. The police were called and subdued Bob with their nightsticks. At this point the rest of the family and the field worker arrived. As the argument continued, these themes relevant to the analysis which follows appeared:
>
> 1) The sisters said that Bob was not their brother (he is a half-brother to Esther, and Mary Jane's full brother). Indeed, they said their mother "didn't have no husband. These kids don't even know who their daddies are." The mother defended herself by saying that she had one legal husband, and one common-law husband, no more.
>
> 2) The sisters said that their fathers had never done anything for them, nor had their mother. She retorted that she had raised them "to the age of womanhood" and now would care for their babies.
>
> 3) Esther continued to threaten to cut Bob if she got a chance (a month later they fought again, and she did cut Bob, who required twenty-one stitches).
>
> 4) The sisters accused their mother of favoring their lazy brothers and asked her to put them out of the house. She retorted that the girls were as lazy, that they made no contribution to maintaining the household, could not get their boy friends to marry them or support their children, that all the support came from her AFDC check. Mary Jane retorted that "the baby has a check of her own."
>
> 5) The girls threatened to leave the house if their mother refused to put their brothers out. They said they could force their boy friends to support them by taking them to court, and Esther threatened to cut her boy friend's throat if he did not co-operate.
>
> 6) Mrs. Johnson said the girls could leave if they wished but that she would keep their babies; "I'll not have it, not knowing who's taking care of them."
>
> 7) When her thirteen-year-old sister laughed at all of this, Esther told her not to laugh because she, too, would be pregnant within a year.

8) When Bob laughed, Esther attacked him and his brother by saying that both were not man enough to make babies, as she and her sister had been able to do.

9) As the field worker left, Mrs. Johnson sought his sympathy. "You see, Joe, how hard it is for me to bring up a family. . . . They sit around and talk to me like I'm some kind of dog and not their mother."

10) Finally, it is important to note for the analysis which follows that the following labels—"black-assed," "black bastard," "bitch," and other profane terms—were liberally used by Esther and Mary Jane, and rather less liberally by their mother, to refer to each other, to the girls' boy friends, to Bob, and to the thirteen-year-old daughter.

Several of the themes outlined previously appear forcefully in the course of this argument. In the last year and a half the mother has become a grandmother and expects shortly to add two more grandchildren to her household. She takes it for granted that it is her responsibility to care for the grandchildren and that she has the right to decide what will be done with the children since her own daughters are not fully responsible. She makes this very clear to them when they threaten to move out, a threat which they do not really wish to make good nor could they if they wished to.

However, only as an act of will is Mrs. Johnson able to make this a family. She must constantly cope with the tendency of her adolescent children to disrupt the family group and to deny that they are in fact a family—"He ain't no brother of mine"; "The baby has a check of her own." Though we do not know exactly what processes communicate these facts to the children it is clear that in growing up they have learned to regard themselves as not fully part of a solidary collectivity. During the quarrel this message was reinforced for the twelve-, thirteen-, and four-teen-year-old daughters by the four-way argument among their older sisters, older brother, and their mother.

The argument represents vicious unmasking of the individual members' pretenses to being competent individuals. The efforts of the two girls to present themselves as masters of their own fate are unmasked by the mother. The girls in turn unmask the pretensions of the mother and of their two brothers. When the thirteen-year-old daughter expresses some amusement they turn on her, telling her that it won't be long before she too becomes pregnant. Each member of the family in turn is told that he can expect to be no more than a victim of his world, but that this is somehow inevitably his own fault.

In this argument masculinity is consistently demeaned. Bob has no right to play with his niece, the boys are not really masculine because at fifteen and sixteen years they have yet to father children, their own fathers were no goods who failed to do anything for their family. These notions probably come originally from the mother, who enjoys recounting the story of having her common-law husband imprisoned for nonsupport, but this comes back to haunt her as her daughters accuse her of being no better than they in ability to force support and nurturance from a man. In contrast, the girls came off somewhat better than the boys, although they must accept the label of stupid girls because they have similarly failed and inconveniently become pregnant in the first place. At least they can and have had children and therefore have some meaningful connection with the ongoing substance of life. There is something important and dramatic in which they participate, while the boys, despite their sexual activity, "can't get no babies."

In most societies, as children grow and are formed by their elders into suitable members of the society they gain increasingly a sense of competence and ability to master the behavioral environment their particular world presents. But in Negro slum culture growing up involves an ever-increasing appreciation of one's shortcomings, of the impossibility of finding a self-sufficient and gratifying way of living. It is in the family first and most devastatingly that one learns these lessons. As the child's sense of frustration builds he too can strike out and unmask the pretensions of others. The result is a peculiar strength and a pervasive weakness. The strength involves the ability to tolerate and defend against degrading verbal and physical aggressions from others and not to give up completely. The weakness involves the inability to embark hopefully on any course of action that might make things better, particularly action which involves cooperating and trusting attitudes toward others. Family members become potential enemies to each other, as the frequency of observing the police being called in to settle family quarrels brings home all too dramatically.

The conceptions parents have of their children are such that they are constantly alert as the child matures to evidence that he is as bad as everyone else. That is, in lower-class culture human nature is conceived of as essentially bad, destructive, immoral. This is the nature of things. Therefore any one child must be inherently bad unless his parents are very lucky indeed. If the mother can keep the child insulated from the outside world, she feels she may be able to prevent his inherent badness from coming out. She feels that once he is let out into the larger world the badness will come to the fore since that is his nature. This means that in the identity development of the child he is constantly exposed to identity labeling by his parents as a bad person. Since as he grows up he does not experience his world as particularly gratifying, it is very easy for him to conclude that this lack of gratification is due to the fact that something is wrong with him. This, in turn, can readily be assimilated to the definitions of being a bad person offered him by those with whom he lives. In this way the Negro slum child learns his culture's conception of being-in-the-world, a conception that emphasizes inherent evil in a chaotic, hostile, destructive world.

Blackness. To a certain extent these same processes operate in white lower-class groups, but added for the Negro is the reality of blackness. "Black-assed" is not an empty pejorative adjective. In the Negro slum culture several distinctive appellations are used to refer to oneself and others. One involves the terms, "black" or "nigger." Black is generally a negative way of naming, but nigger can be either negative or positive, depending upon the context. It is important to note that, at least in the urban North, the initial development of racial identity in these terms has very little directly to do with relations with whites. A child experiences these identity placements in the context of the family and in the neighborhood peer group; he probably very seldom hears the same terms used by whites (unlike the situation in the South). In this way, one of the effects of ghettoization is to mask the ultimate enemy so that the understanding of the fact of victimization by a caste system comes as a late acquisition laid over conceptions of self and of other Negroes derived from intimate, and to the child often traumatic, experience within the ghetto community. If, in addition, the child attends a ghetto school where his Negro teachers either overtly or by implication reinforce his community's negative conceptions of what it means to be black, then the child has little opportunity to develop a more realistic image of himself and other Negroes as being damaged by whites and not by themselves. In such a situation, an intelligent man like Mr. Wilson can say with all sincerity that he does not feel most Negroes are ready for integration—only under the experience of certain kinds of intense personal threat coupled with exposure to an ideology that places the responsibility on whites did he begin to see through the direct evidence of his daily experience.

To those living in the heart of a ghetto, black comes to mean not just "stay back," but also membership in a community of persons who think poorly of each other, who attack and manipulate each other, who give each other small comfort in a desperate world. Black comes to stand for a sense of identity as no better than these destructive others. The individual feels that he must embrace an unattractive self in order to function at all.

We can hypothesize that in those families that manage to avoid the destructive identity imputations of "black" and that manage to maintain solidarity against such assaults from the world around, it is possible for children to grow up with a sense of both Negro and personal identity that allows them to socialize themselves in an anticipatory way for participation in the larger society. This broader sense of identity, however, will remain a brittle one as long as the individual is vulnerable to attack from within the Negro community as "nothing but a nigger like everybody else" or from the white community as "just a nigger." We can hypothesize further that the vicious unmasking of essential identity as black described above is least likely to occur within families where the parents have some

stable sense of security, and where they therefore have less need to protect themselves by disavowing responsibility for their children's behavior
and denying the children their patrimony as products of a particular
family rather than of an immoral nature and an evil community.

In sum, we are suggesting that Negro slum children as they grow up in
their families and in their neighborhoods are exposed to a set of experiences—and a rhetoric which conceptualizes them—that brings home to
the child an understanding of his essence as a weak and debased person
who can expect only partial gratification of his needs, and who must seek
even this level of gratification by less than straight-forward means.

Strategies for living. In every society complex processes of socialization
inculcate in their members strategies for gratifying the needs with which
they are born and those which the society itself generates. Inextricably
linked to these strategies, both cause and effect of them, are the existential
propositions which members of a culture entertain about the nature of
their world and of effective action within the world as it is defined for
them. In most of American society two grand strategies seem to attract
the allegiance of its members and guide their day-to-day actions. I have
called these strategies those of *the good life* and of *career success.* A good
life strategy involves efforts to get along with others and not to rock the
boat, a comfortable familism grounded on a stable work career for husbands in which they perform adequately at the modest jobs that enable
them to be good providers. The strategy of career success is the choice of
ambitious men and women who see life as providing opportunities to
move from a lower to a higher status, to "accomplish something," to
achieve greater than ordinary material well-being, prestige, and social
recognition. Both of these strategies are predicated on the assumption that
the world is inherently rewarding if one behaves properly and does his
part. The rewards of the world may come easily or only at the cost of
great effort, but at least they are there.

In the white and particularly in the Negro slum worlds little in the
experience that individuals have as they grow up sustains a belief in a
rewarding world. The strategies that seem appropriate are not those of a
good, family-based life or of a career, but rather *strategies for survival.*

Much of what has been said above can be summarized as encouraging
three kinds of survival strategies. One is the strategy of the *expressive life
style* which I have described elsewhere as an effort to make yourself
interesting and attractive to others so that you are better able to manipulate their behavior along lines that will provide some immediate gratification. Negro slum culture provides many examples of techniques for
seduction, of persuading others to give you what you want in situations
where you have very little that is tangible to offer in return. In order to
get what you want you learn to "work game," a strategy which requires
a high development of a certain kind of verbal facility, a sophisticated

manipulation of promise and interim reward. When the expressive strategy fails or when it is unavailable there is, of course, the great temptation to adopt a *violent strategy* in which you force others to give you what you need once you fail to win it by verbal and other symbolic means. Finally, and increasingly as members of the Negro slum culture grow older, there is the *depressive strategy* in which goals are increasingly constricted to the bare necessities for survival (not as a social being but simply as an organism). This is the strategy of "I don't bother anybody and I hope nobody's gonna bother me; I'm simply going through the motions to keep body (but not soul) together." Most lower-class people follow mixed strategies, as Walter Miller has observed, alternating among the excitement of the expressive style, the desperation of the violent style, and the deadness of the depressed style. Some members of the Negro slum world experiment from time to time with mixed strategies that also incorporate the stable working-class model of the good American life, but this latter strategy is exceedingly vulnerable to the threats of unemployment or a less than adequate pay check, on the one hand, and the seduction and violence of the slum world around them, on the other. . . .

THE FATHER'S PERSPECTIVE

"Fathers Without Children"

by Elliot Liebow

In the springtime, on a Sunday afternoon, Richard's four-year-old son lay seriously ill in Ward E of Children's Hospital. He and the other twelve children in the ward, almost all from low-income Negro families, were being visited by some twenty-five relatives and friends. Not a single man was among the visitors.

The men had their reasons. Some had separated from their wives and children and did not know their children were hospitalized. Others knew but couldn't or wouldn't make it. Richard had intended going but something came up, he would probably go tomorrow, and anyway, he never did like being in a hospital, not even to visit someone else.

But whether the fathers were living with their children or not, the result was the same: there were no men visiting the children in Ward E. This absence of the father is one of the chief characteristics of the father-child relationship.

The father-child relationship, however, is not the same for all streetcorner fathers, nor does a given relationship necessarily remain constant over time. Some fathers are not always "absent" and some are less "absent" than others. Moreover, the same father may have relationships of different intensity with his different children at the same time. The spectrum of father-child relationships is a broad one, ranging from complete ignorance of the child's existence to continuous, day-by-day contact between father and child. The emotional content of the relationships ranges from what, to the outside observer, may seem on the father's part callous indifference or worse, all the way to hinted private intimacies whose intensity can only be guessed at.

Leaving aside, for the present, the emotional and affective content, father-child relationships can be grossly sorted out and located along a spectrum based upon the father's willingness to acknowledge paternity, his willingness to acknowledge responsibility for and to provide financial support, and the frequency and duration of contact. At the low end of the spectrum are those relationships in which the children are born of casual, short-term, even single-encounter unions; at the high end are legitimate children of married parents, all of whom live in the same household. Since the majority of streetcorner men do not live in the same households as their children, the majority of father-child relationships appear at the low and low-middle bands of the spectrum. The number falls off quickly as one approaches the other end.

At the low end of the spectrum there may be no father-child relationship at all. In some cases, the father may not know he is the father of the child; in others, even the mother may not know who the father is. Here, too, at the low end, are those fathers who acknowledge possible or actual paternity but who have had no subsequent contact with mother or child. Such seems to be the case with many of the men who, while still in their teens, had a baby "back home." Thus, Richard recalls that, before his marriage to Shirley, a girl told him he was the father of her child. He did nothing about it and neither did she "because there was nothing she could do."[1] Richard subsequently saw the mother and child on the street during a visit back home but did not speak to them. His sheepish laugh seemed a mixture of masculine pride and guilty embarrassment as he admitted that the child looked startlingly like himself.

Somewhat further along the spectrum are the relationships of Wesley and Earl with their children. Each has a child "back home" in the Carolinas and each acknowledges his paternity. Wesley has visited his hometown and has seen the mother of his child once or twice since the birth of the baby. Wesley and the child's mother are on friendly terms but Wesley gives her nothing and she asks for nothing. Earl's child also lives with its mother but Earl and the mother have remained fond of one

---

[1]He explained that "back home" a (Negro) woman in such a predicament has no legal recourse. If she files a paternity suit, the judge asks her if the putative father forced himself on her. When she admits he did not, the judge dismisses the case.

another. Earl sees her regularly and sometimes sees the child, too, on those two or three times a year he goes back home. If he has spare cash, he leaves it with her for the baby.

In the middle range of the spectrum are the father-child relationships of those once-married men who, though separated from their wives and children, remain accessible to them. These men admit to a financial responsibility for their children, provide emergency and sometimes routine financial support, and are more or less informed about their children's general well-being. Contacts between the men and their separated families are almost always initiated by the mothers, usually for the purpose of getting money for the children. Sea Cat's wife calls him on the telephone in his rooming house to tell him when she is coming. Sometimes she brings one or both of their children, sometimes not. Stoopy's wife does not usually call. She comes on Saturday mornings, brings the two children along and stays for an hour or two.

Relationships in this middle range are by no means limited to legitimate children. Tally is the father of Bess's eighteen-month-old son. For a time, at least, their relationship was indistinguishable from Sea Cat's and Stoopy's relationships with their wives and children. On Tally's pay day, Bess would sometimes call the Carry-out shop and ask that Tally be told she would be there that evening. Tally would meet her on the corner, pay her taxicab fare, then give her five or ten dollars for a doctor, a pair of shoes, or other extra expenses for the child.

In those few cases where the child is cared for by the father's mother or other members of his family, the father-child relationship seems to be closer than when the child is with the mother or member of her family. Such a child regularly carries the father's family name. The father provides at least partial financial support. He is often informed of the child's special needs and general well-being and, even where they are separated by great distances, father and child see each other one or more times during the year. Sweets, for example, has a child "back home." The child is being raised by Sweets's mother. Occasional letters are exchanged during the course of the year, and there are birthday cards and gifts for the child. Sweets manages to get down there for one or two weekends a year and, during the summer, his mother and his child come to spend a week or two with him in Washington. Tonk's relationship with his seven-year-old daughter, also "back home" where she is raised by Tonk's mother, is an even stronger one. They exchange letters and gifts and, at school's end, she comes to spend the whole summer with him. Stanton's daughter lives with his "sister"[2] only two blocks from where Stanton lives. The daughter remains his financial responsibility and, depending on circumstance or need, she moves in with him occasionally for short periods of time.

[2]Stanton and this (unrelated) woman "go for brother and sister."

At the high end of the spectrum are those relationships where father and child are regular members of the same household. In such cases, even when the father and mother are not formally married to one another, there is no question but that the child carries the father's family name. Whether his wife is working or not, and unlike the men who are separated from their children, the father who is living with his children is, in his own eyes and in the eyes of those around him, charged with the day-to-day support of his wife and children. Father and child, as members of the same household, are in more or less continuous contact.

Looking at the spectrum as a whole, the modal father-child relationship for these streetcorner men seems to be one in which the father is separated from the child, acknowledges his paternity, admits to financial responsibility but provides financial support irregularly, if at all, and then only on demand or request. His contacts with the child are infrequent, irregular, and of short (minutes or hours) duration.

When we look away from these more formal aspects of father-child relationships and turn to their quality and texture, a seeming paradox emerges. The men who do not live with their own children seem to express more affection for their children and treat them more tenderly than those who do live with them. Moreover, the men are frequently more affectionate toward other men's children than toward their own.

Fathers who live with their children, for example, seem to take no pleasure in their children and give them little of their time and attention. They seldom mention their children in casual conversation and are never seen sitting or playing with them on the steps or in the street. The fathers do not take their children to tag along while they lounge on the streetcorner or in the Carry-out, nor do they, as they see other fathers in the neighborhood do, promenade with them on Easter Sunday or take them for walks on any other Sunday or holiday. When the father walks into the home, the child may not even look up from what he is doing and the father, for his part, takes no more notice than he receives. If their eyes happen to catch one another's glances, father and child seem to look without seeing until one or the other looks elsewhere.

Perhaps this routine absence of warmth and affection accounts for the way in which an offhand gesture by the father can suddenly deepen the relationship for the child, for however brief a time. John casually distributed some change among his six children. His wife Lorena describes what happened:

> He give Buddy and the others a dime. You'd think Jesus had laid something on them. They went all around the neighborhood bragging their daddy give them a dime. I give them nickels and dimes all day long and they don't think anything about it. But John, he can give them a dime and they act like he gave them the whole world.

Since father and child are seldom together outside the home, it is in the home that casual gestures bespeaking paternal warmth and tenderness are more likely to occur. Leroy and two friends are in Leroy's house passing the time. Leroy sits on the bed and absentmindedly strokes the head of his small son lying next to him. In Richard's house, Richard distractedly rolls a ball or marble back and forth across the floor to his four-year-old son, at the same time going on with his drinking and talking; or he casually beckons to his son to come stand between his knees and, with one hand around the child's waist, the other around a can of beer, he goes on talking.

The easy manner with which the fathers manage these intimacies suggests that they have occurred before. But the child does not manage them casually. He is excited by these intimacies, and the clear delight he takes from them suggests that he assigns to them a special quality and that they are by no means routine. Indeed, physical contact between father and son seems generally to be infrequent. When it does take place, it is just as likely to be a slap as a caress.

Compared with fathers who live with their children, separated fathers who remain in touch with their children speak about them more often and show them more warmth when father and child are together. For separated fathers, the short, intermittent contacts with their children are occasions for public display of parental tenderness and affection. When Bess brought the baby along on her money-collecting visits to the Carry-out, she and Tally would sometimes remain on the corner with Tally holding the baby in his arms, cooing at or nuzzling the baby as he and Bess talked. On a Saturday morning, after a visit from his wife, Stoopy stands on the corner with three other men, watching his wife disappear down the street with their two school-age children on either side of her. "There goes my heart," says Stoopy, "those two kids, they're my heart." The other men nod understandingly. They would have felt and said the same thing had they been in his place.

These are fathers whose children are raised by the mothers. Even closer to his child is the father whose child is raised by the father's mother or members of his family. For him, too, the child is "my heart," "my life," or "the apple of my eye." Parental pride and affection are even more in public evidence when father and child are together. When Tonk's daughter arrives for her summer stay, Tonk walks around holding her hand, almost parading, stopping here and there to let bystanders testify that they didn't know Tonk had such a pretty girl, such a smart girl, or a girl who has grown so much so quickly. No, Sweets won't be at the Carry-out tomorrow afternoon, he has to take his daughter shopping for some clothes. He swears he didn't recognize her when his mother first walked up with her. It hadn't even been a year and he almost didn't know his own kid. If she hadn't called him "Daddy" he would still not have known, that's how big she got. And (with pride), she wants to be with him all the time she's here, go everywhere he goes.

But after the brief visit is over, each goes back to his own life, his own world, in which the other plays so small a part that he may be forgotten for long stretches of time. "Out of sight, out of mind" is not far off the mark—at least for the fathers—in these separated father-child relationships.

There are many ways to explain this paradox in which fathers who live with their children appear to be less warm, tender and affectionate in their face-to-face relationships with their children than separated fathers.[3] The most obvious, perhaps, is that the separated father, like the proverbial doting grandfather or favorite uncle, not charged with the day-to-day responsibility for the child, with the routine rearing and disciplining and support of this child, can afford to be attentive and effusive. Since his meetings with the child are widely spaced, he comes to them fresh and rested; since the meetings are brief, he can give freely of himself, secure in the knowledge he will soon go back to his own child-free routine.

No doubt, factors such as these are at work here and do account, in part, for the differences between fathers living with and those not living with their children. But one of the most striking things about the relationship between the streetcorner men and children is that the closest of all relationships are those where the men do live with the children, where they have accepted day-to-day responsibility for the children, but where they have done so on a voluntary basis, that is, where the children are not their own.

Not all streetcorner men who took on the role of stepfather or adoptive father were able or even attempted to establish a warm personal relationship with the children they were living with, but some of them were better able to achieve and sustain such relationships than any of the biological fathers. Thus, Robert, who had been living with Siserene and her four children for a year and a half, had become, in that time, a primary source of aid and comfort to the children. When they fell or were hit or had an object of value taken from them, they ran to Robert if he was there. He comforted them, laughed with them, and arbitrated their disputes. He painted pictures for them, made plywood cutouts of the Seven Dwarfs for them, and brought home storybooks.

Before and after Leroy and Charlene had their own child, Leroy looked after Charlene's little sisters and brother to such an extent that both their mother and the children themselves came to rely on him. Together with Calvin, a frail and ailing forty-year-old alcoholic and homosexual who

<hr>

[3]Since the attempt here is to sort out the different streetcorner father-child relationships rather than to judge them, it is not relevant that the father's willingness to remain with his children and support them, day in, day out, may be a better measure of the man as father than his expressive behavior in his face-to-face contacts with his children.

looked after the children in exchange for a place to live, Leroy bathed the children, braided the girls' hair, washed their clothes at "the Bendix" (laundromat), played with them, and on their birthdays went shoplifing to get them gifts. Even more than to Leroy, the children were attached to Calvin. When he could summon the courage, Calvin often interceded on their behalf when their mother was dealing out punishment. There was little that Calvin did not do for the children. He played with them during the day when they were well and stayed up with them at night when they were sick. During one period, when he had resolved to stop his homosexual practices (he had been married and a father), he resumed them only on those occasions when there was no food or money in the house and only long enough to "turn a trick" and get food for the children. When this did not work he raided the Safeway, despite his terror of still another jail sentence. He was proud of the part he played in their lives and he played it so well that the children took his love and support for granted.

It would seem, then, that differences in father-child relationships do not depend so much on whether the man is in continuous as against intermittent or occasional contact with the child but on whether the man voluntarily assumes the role of father or has it thrust upon him.

The man who lives with his wife and children is under legal and social constraints to provide for them, to be a husband to his wife and a father to his children. The chances are, however, that he is failing to provide for them, and failure in this primary function contaminates his performance as father in other respects as well.The more demonstrative and accepting he is of his children, the greater is his public and private commitment to the duties and responsibilities of fatherhood; and the greater his commitment, the greater and sharper his failure as the provider and head of the family. To soften this failure, and to lessen the damage to his public and self-esteem, he pushes the children away from him, saying, in effect, "I'm not even trying to be your father so now I can't be blamed for failing to accomplish what I'm not trying to do."

For the father separated from his children, there is no longer the social obligation to be their chief support. His performance as father is no longer an issue. His failure is an accomplished fact. But now that he is relatively free of the obligations of fatherhood, he can, in his intermittent contacts with his children, by giving money for their support and by being solicitous and affectionate with them, enjoy a modest success as father in precisely those same areas in which he is an established failure.

This is even more clearly seen in the man who lives with a woman who has had children by another man. For these men, obligations to the children are minor in comparison with those of fathers living with their children. Where the father lives with his own children, his occasional touch or other tender gesture is dwarfed by his unmet obligations. No matter how much he does, it is not enough. But where the man lives with children not his own, every gentleness and show of concern and affection redounds to his public and private credit; everything is profit. For him, living with children is not, as it is for the father, charged with failure and guilt. Since his own and others' expectations of him as father are minimal, he is free to enter into a close relationship with the children without fear of failure and uninhibited by guilt. It is as if living with your own children is to live with your failure, but to live with another man's children is, so far as children are concerned, to be in a fail-proof situation: you can win a little or a lot but, however small your effort or weak your performance, you can almost never lose.[4]

In addition to the very gross factors so far considered in father-child relationships, any one of a number of other factors may pull father and child closer together or push them further apart.[5]   Looking only at separated fathers, for example, who are in the majority on the streetcorner, it seems as if their relationships with their children depend to a striking degree on the father's relationships with the adult who is taking care of the child. Thus, as has been suggested earlier, fathers (e.g., Tonk and Sweets) whose children are living with the father's mother or other members of his family seem to be closer to their children than those (e.g., Sea Cat, Stoopy) whose children are living with the mother or members of her family. And when the child is with its mother, as in the great majority of cases, the frequency of contact between father and child clearly depends more on the father's relationship with the mother than on his relationship with the child himself. It is almost as if the men have no direct relationship with their children independent of their relationship with the mother. Whether in different states or in different sections of the same city, these children are never sent to spend a weekend, a Sunday, or even a few hours alone with their fathers. If, like Earl, the father does visit the child's household, it is primarily to see the

[4] Unless, of course, the man violates the ordinary decencies of everyday life and goes out of his way to abuse the child.

[5] For example, the child's sex, age or skin color; whether or not he is legitimate; number, sex and relative age and skin color of siblings; age and marital status of the father; literacy of father, child or other concerned adults (for written communications); accessibility or physical distance of separation, personality variables and so forth. The data generally are too thin to permit an assignment of relative weight to these but the evidence does suggest that no one of them is an overriding or controlling factor in the relationship. Among these factors, however, skin color appears to be one of the most important, the light-skinned child being preferred to the child with dark skin. There is also a clear preference for the legitimate child but, by itself, illegitimacy is no bar to a close father-child relationship. Sex of the child is important to some men but some seem to prefer boys, others girls. Most of the closest father-child relationships I have observed were with daughters but the total numbers are too few and the number of other variables too many to warrant even a tentative generalization. For a discussion of skin color in parent-child relationships, see St. Clair Drake and Horace Cayton, *Black Metropolis*, pp. 498ff, esp. p. 503. Morris Rosenberg's study of New York State school children offers strong evidence that lower-class fathers tend to be closer to their daughters than to their sons (*Society and the Adolescent Self-Image*, p. 42ff).

mother rather than the child. As a rule, children born of short-term unions see their fathers only if and when the father and mother maintain or reestablish a personal relationship.

The dependence of the father-child on the father-mother relationship is clearly evident in the follow-up of Tally's relationship with Bess and their son. We have here, too, a picture of the way in which the father-child relationship can change over time.

After the birth of their baby, and after she and Tally had stopped going out together, Bess came to the corner only on Tally's pay day (Wednesdays), sometimes bringing the child along, sometimes not. But as Bess and Tally rediscovered their attraction for each other, she began to bring the baby regularly, coming now on Friday or Saturday evenings and sleeping over with the baby in Tally's room until Sunday night or Monday morning. On these weekends, Tally sometimes took the boy into the Carry-out shop for a soda or, on one occasion, marched up the street with the child on his shoulder, proudly announcing that Bess had "sent the men to get a loaf of bread." But after a few weeks, Tally and Bess had a fight. Bess stayed away from the neighborhood, and Tally's contacts with his son—dependent as they were on his relationships with Bess—ended abruptly.

The incidental, derivative character of the father-child relationship is not something which arises only after the birth of the child and the separation of the parents. It is rooted in values which, even before conception, boldly and explicitly assert the primacy of the man-woman relationship over a possible father-child relationship, and this primacy continues in effect over the actual father-child relationship when a child is born.

Although the relationship with children is secondary to the man-woman relationship, streetcorner men do want children quite apart from the generalized desire to have a family and be the head of it. A man who has no children may want a child to confirm his masculinity; another may want his girl or wife to conceive in order to reduce the chances of her "cheating" or "cutting out"; and still another man may want a particular woman to have his baby because this may guarantee a continuing relationship with this woman.

Fathers and nonfathers alike also see children as liabilities. The principal liability is the financial one. On the one hand, everyone agrees that a man ought to support his children; on the other hand, money is chronically in short supply. To the men, including those who do not, in fact, contribute to their children's support, children are real, imagined, or pretended economic liabilities. Having to buy food, shoes, clothes or medicine for a child, or having to make a support payment, serve equally well as reason or excuse for asking to borrow money or refusing to lend any. Everywhere one turns, the consensus is that "Children, they'll snatch a lot of biscuits off the table [children are expensive]." So and so had a baby? "Children, they'll snatch a lot of biscuits off the table." So and so is shacking up with a woman with three kids? "Children, they'll snatch a lot of biscuits off the table."

The more the children, of course, the greater the liability. Sweets says he met a girl he likes so much that he is thinking of moving in with her "even though she's got two kids." Bernard doesn't want his girl to have any more children because "I got more than I can stand [economically] right now."

Children—one's own as well as someone else's—are also seen as liabilities in the all-important world of man-woman relationships. Where eating, sleeping, child rearing and lovemaking are frequently confined to a single room, children render privacy a scarce commodity. Not only do they constitute a standing deterrent to secrecy (so essential to the maintenance of clandestine relationships) but they may severely limit the man's freedom of action in other ways as well.

Tonk, for example, made no secret of the fact that having his seven-year-old daughter with him for the summer was not an unmixed blessing. Tonk and his wife Pearl had no children. Pearl wanted the child to remain with them permanently but Tonk insisted on her returning to his mother in the fall, complaining that he has to take care of his daughter when Pearl is not home (she worked nights), and that to do this on a year-round basis would seriously compromise his freedom.

Tonk knew whereof he spoke. A few days later, on a Saturday night while Pearl was at work, Tonk went for a ride with William and two women, taking his daughter with him. The next day, serious trouble arose when the little girl pointed to one of the women and told Pearl, "She's the one who was in my daddy's arms."

Children threaten not only exposure of illicit relationships but also active interference. Indeed, when Tonk and Earlene were kissing in the car, his daughter kept trying to pull them apart, screaming at Earlene "You're not my mother! You're not my mother!"[6]

Older children, in this respect, are bigger nuisances. Clarence lived with his wife and children but saw a great deal of Nancy. Their relationship was a stormy one. Once, when Nancy and Clarence were fighting, Nancy's twelve-year-old son hit Clarence with a baseball bat. This occasioned no surprise to the men on the street and little sympathy for Clarence. The slapstick aspects of it aside, most of the men merely shrugged their shoulders. After all, it was common knowledge that a liaison with a woman who has a half-grown son is a dangerous one. Clarence had gone into it with his eyes open.

Women are painfully aware that men see children as liabilities and that a woman who has children may find it difficult to establish a satisfactory

---

[6]Of course, Pearl was not her mother either. I assume that the child was using "mother" here to mean father's wife or stepmother. My notes do not say whether the child called Pearl "Mama." I would guess not since they were together only during the summer.

relationship with a man. Richard and Shirley are having a fight and Richard has told Shirley she is free to take the children and leave. Shirley is crying hard:

> Where can I go? To my mother's grave? To the D.C. morgue where they burned [cremated] my sister last month? You know I'm all alone, so where can I go? Nobody wants a woman with three babies.[7]

Lorena voices a sentiment widespread among women in her contemptuous assessment of men as fathers. In a kitchen discussion with Shirley and Charlene, she dismisses men's protests of love and concern for their children by citing their failure to follow through in action and concludes that, in fact, men regard children as liabilities.

> They [men] say they love them. Shit. If they love them, would they let them go hungry? In raggedy-ass clothes? They don't love them. Children are just a tie to a man.

Women are especially resentful of men's instrumental use of children, their use of children as tools for punishment or control in the man-woman relationship.[8] The mother-child relationship, generally conceded to be far closer than the bond between father and children, renders the mother especially vulnerable to such tactics. One woman dreads a fight with her husband because the children will suffer for it. She knows and he knows that he can "get" her by slapping the children around. Another woman, separated from her husband, gets only occasional financial support from him but she is afraid to take him to court for fear that, in order to get back at her, he would go to jail rather than send her money for the children. Leroy regularly uses his small son Donald as a sword of Damocles to control Charlene. Sometimes, during the course of a fight, he denies that Donald is his son and, secure in the knowledge that she has no place to go, he throws Charlene and the child, together with their belongings, out of the apartment (room). When the initiative lies with Charlene and she, in turn, threatens to leave him, Leroy forces her to remain by refusing to let her take the child. At other times he simply threatens to take Donald "back home" and give him to his grandmother to raise.

The widespread acknowledgement that the mother's attachment for the child is greater than the father's also provides the logical justification for assigning to the father (in theory) the role of principal disciplinarian. Responsibility for meting out physical punishment theoretically falls to the man because mothers are inhibited from punishing their children by virtue of being mothers.

"The man is way more important in bringing up a child," one man said,

---

[7] Other things being equal, children also compromise the market value of the working- or middle-class widow or divorcee.

[8] A practice which tends to support the argument of the primacy of the man-woman over the father-child relationship.

explaining that the father can discourage wrongdoing with a slap or a beating. Not so the woman. "The woman—well, she birthed him and she can't bring herself to hurt her baby, no matter what he does."

Men's assertions that their wives are "too easy" on the children are commonplace. "She's too easy, always kissing him and picking him up. She doesn't care if he keeps shittin' and pissin' on the floor." Tally, separated from his wife and children, continues to complain that his wife never whips them. "She's always hugging them and talking to them but sometimes they ain't going to learn [unless they are given a whipping]."

Women sometimes contend that a mother alone can raise children properly but they concede that, other things being equal, the children are better off when there's a man around to provide or threaten punishment. "I raised my three that way [alone], but it's better if there's a man. Children fear a man but they don't fear their mother. My son don't fear me at all."

Men see physical punishment as a necessary and proper part of child rearing. "A child, he needs it hard else he ain't going to learn" or "It's important [to hit children] to help them know right from wrong" are sentiments that all men subscribe to. But everyone agrees, too, that punishment ought to be meted out at the appropriate time. "You can't let them keep on doing bad things and then whip them for things they did a long time ago. You got to whip them when they done it, so they'll know what it's for." Society is seen as positively sanctioning physical punishment by specifying the way in which it is to be meted out. "You can hurt a child hitting him with a stick or in the eyes or his head. That's why it's against the law to do it like that. You're supposed to hit him on his thighs or something like that."

When one looks at the same men as sons rather than as fathers, the father-child relationship appears to be a far more distant one. In part, this may be due to the deterioration of the father-child relationship over time and to the different assessments that father and son make of their relationship, each from his own perspective. When the child is very young, the father may still be living with the family or, in any event, making an attempt to help out in some way. But after the father has left, as he usually does, the growing distance in time and space between father and family makes it increasingly difficult to sustain even a semblance of family ties between the man, on one hand, and his wife and children on the other. Just as Tally, or Stoopy, or any of the others do now, their own fathers probably spoke warmly of their children to their friends, admitted that they should be doing more for their children, and considered that, under the circumstances, they were "doing what I can." But from the child's point of view—and he sees even more from the vantage point of adulthood—the father is the man who ran out on his mother, his brothers and sisters and himself; who had, perhaps, to be taken to court to force him to pay a few dollars toward the support of his wife and children; and who, even when he was home, is perhaps best remembered with a switch or belt in his hand.

The men seldom refer to their fathers spontaneously. A group of men can reminisce for hours without the word being mentioned. Many men seem never to have known their fathers: "I don't remember him"; "He left [or died] before I was born," or simply, "Shit."

Sea Cat, who was born and raised in the neighborhood, and whose mother continued to live there, never mentioned his father at all. Leroy was raised by his grandparents. His mother and father lived in the same city, but Leroy, who remained close to his mother, mentions his father only to fix relationships or to set a scene.

Richard's father left the family while Richard was still a small child. His father operates a beer joint in Carolina and Richard has seen him on occasion, while passing through the town. His father has never seen Richard's wife or children. Richard and his father never did get along. "We just don't see eye to eye."

Tally's father also left his wife and children when Tally was a small child. "He was a racketeer, a gambler. He never worked a day in his life." When Tally was about nine or ten he was sent to stay with his father and stepmother in Birmingham. He doesn't remember why he was sent there or how long he remained. All he remembers is that his father once gave him a terrible beating.

Sometimes a brief encounter may throw light on both sides of the father-child relationship. In the episode reported below, we catch a glimpse of the man as son, husband and father. The contrast between the mother-son and father-son relationship is almost too sharp and clear, each terrifying in its own way.[9] Preston is in his middle thirties. Dressed in old army khakis, with his hands thrust in his pockets as he leans against a lamppost or the storefront, he is a regular fixture at the Downtown Cafe. Sometimes when the café is short of help, Preston is called to fill in. Such was the case this day when I took a seat at the bar. Preston brought me a beer and started the conversation.

"You know, I had a lot of trouble since I seen you last."
"What kind of trouble?"
"My mother died."
"I'm sorry to hear that."
"Yes, she died three weeks ago. I've been drinking myself to death ever since. Last week I drank up every cent I made before I got it. I don't know what to do. I've been thinking of killing myself."

[9]"Even among some of the poorest families, the mother's affectional life may be centered upon a son or daughter. . . . Her attitude often presents a *striking contrast to that of the father.*" (Emphasis added.) E. Franklin Frazier, *The Negro-Family in the United States,* p. 468.

"You just need a little more time. Three weeks isn't very long for something like this. You'll straighten out."

"Maybe I will, maybe I won't. My mother was all I had. I been thinking I'll go to the pet shop and get a cat."

"How about your father?"

"Fuck that mother. I don't even want to think about him."

"Do you have any kids?"

"What good are they? They're in Germany and Japan. I've been thinking I'll get married. But that's no good unless you get a girl who understands you."

He took a box from beneath the counter and asked me to open it. Inside was a flimsy nghtgown decorated with bright-colored flowers. With tears in his eyes, he explained that he had bought this for his mother for her stay in the hospital but never got to give it to her. On the night of the day he bought it, he got a call from the Washington Hospital Center to come immediately. He ran all the way but his mother was already dead. Preston did not remember the subsequent events very clearly. He said he began drinking very heavily that night and either that same night or the next morning he had to go to the D.C. morgue to identify his mother's body. When the morgue attendant pulled the sheet back from his mother's face, Preston smashed the attendent in the mouth. He held up the scabby knuckles of his right fist as evidence.

"Why'd you hit him?"

"Because he showed me my dead mother."

nine

Most Black Americans receive inadequate schooling. Yet education is one of the most important avenues for entry into the mainstream of American culture. What can be done to improve ghetto education? Is integration the answer? Should schools all teach standard subjects based upon middle-class values or should ghetto children, Black or White, be given a different curriculum? Why is the role of the teacher so important? Finally, why are innovative teachers usually so disliked by their superiors?

Education

The lifelong process of socialization begins in the family. In complex technological societies this process is partly carried out by formal educational organizations that have the responsibility of deliberately teaching certain elements of the culture to its members. These organizations also provide opportunities for individuals to learn the skills and knowledge and to acquire the motivation necessary to seek and fill various positions, such as occupations, at future points in time.

As a part of the socialization process, formal education performs some of the same general functions as does the family. Education transmits culture and thus helps to integrate society. Education also contributes to the formation of individual personalities and provides opportunities for personal development.

Because of its integrative function, education may be viewed as a stabilizing force in society. In complex societies however, education also serves to arouse curiosity and stimulate inquiry which may then lead to innovation and change.

In America, as in most societies, much of an individual's style of living is directly or indirectly dependent upon his occupational position. Occupation is partly determined by the quality and amount of the prior skills and information that he has learned. Because of the specialized nature of such positions in complex society, much of this learning must take place through formal education in schools.

When a group of people is denied access to good formal education, its members are severely restricted in the opportunities available to them. The group as a whole is denied any rewards, such as prestige and power, that might accrue from the collective use of such opportunities. In addition, the culture of the society at large is not effectively transmitted to the group. Thus the group is excluded from any meaningul participation in the society. This is the situation in which Black Americans find themselves today.

Blacks continue to attend segregated schools. In the South this pattern is deliberately enforced. In the North the fact that Blacks live in separate neighborhoods has lead to a "de facto" form of racial separation in schools. The crucial point is not the separation but rather inequality in education that such segregation continues to create and maintain.

Black Americans attend poor schools. Poor schools contribute to a lack of educational achievement and motivation. Poor schools help to create a feeling among ghetto youth that formal education is irrelevant to their lives. Poor schools increase the alienation and isolation felt by many Blacks toward the society at large.

The problems in the ghetto schools are enormous: curriculums are poor and outdated; teachers are unskilled, indifferent, or hostile; classes are large; counseling is inadequate; physical plants are dilapidated. General strategies proposed to alleviate the problems include integration, compensatory education and curriculum enrichment, and most recently decentralization and community control with accompanying plans for increased Black studies. Each strategy has advantages as well as serious shortcomings. Each has its advocates and detractors. It is certainly true that the problems of the schools are complex and are intertwined with the other problems in the ghetto. However, because of either deliberate intent or massive indifference, the quality of education in the Black community has not improved significantly in the past two decades.

The two reading selections focus on problems in the ghetto schools. Kenneth Clark uses materials gathered by the Harlem Youth Opportunities Unlimited project (HARYOU) to discuss some of the consequences of ghetto education on the academic achievement of young Black children in Harlem. The Harlem pupils are found to be deficient on certain measures of learning and I.Q. Clark cites teacher incompetence and attitude as being among the contributing factors. He concludes by discussing the effectiveness of programs that have partly eliminated these problems.

The two part selection by Jonathan Kozol describes some of his experiences in the ghetto schools of Boston. In the first part, Kozol dscusses the physical conditions in the schools and the effect of such conditions on the educational process. He tragically notes the unwillingness on the part of many, including himself, to point out the need for change.

In the second part, Kozol points out the need for new and imaginative teaching techniques in the ghetto classroom. He also touches upon a different aspect of the teaching problem: Where concerned and skillful teachers do attempt to use new styles of teaching they often encounter resistance or lack of support on the part of the educational system. Schools not only need new kinds of teachers and techniques but the school environment must also be changed to provide encouragement and stimulation for the teacher as well as the student.

PROBLEMS

"Ghetto Schools: Separate and Unequal"

by Kenneth B. Clark

Educational Inequality

The basic story of academic achievement in Harlem is one of inefficiency, inferiority, and massive deterioration. The further these students progress in school, the larger the proportion who are retarded and the greater is the discrepancy between their achievement and the achievement of other children in the city. This is also true for their intelligence test scores. This deterioration can be traced in sequence, beginning with the elementary schools and following through the junior high schools to the high schools.[1]

In reading comprehension, the ability to understand what one is reading, 30 percent of the Harlem third grade pupils are reading below grade level, compared to 21.6 percent who are reading above. For sixth grade pupils, the story is even more dismal; there 80.9 percent of the pupils score below grade level in reading, while 11.7 percent score above, indicating a rather rapid relative deterioration in reading comprehension within three school years.

Between grades three and six, word knowledge falters also; in third grade, 38.9 percent score below grade level, 18.7 percent score above; in sixth grade, 77.5 percent are below, 10.6 percent above. Arithmetic shows a similar pattern of underachievement, though figures are only available for the sixth grade (57.6 percent are below grade level in "computation," 66.6 below in "problems and concepts"). By eighth grade, three-quarters

[1]The data, summarized in the following pages and discussed in considerable detail in *Youth In the Ghetto, A Study of the Consequences of Powerlessness and a Blueprint for Change* (Harlem Youth Opportunities Unlimited, Inc., New York, 1964), are drawn from standard tests applied in the third, sixth, and eighth grades throughout the New York City school system and from I.Q. tests given at the same time. These data were made available to the Haryou research staff by the New York City Board of Education. The standard tests given during the third, sixth, and eighth grades, include: *Third grade:* intelligence—Otis Quick Scoring Alpha Test; reading—Metropolitan Achievement Reading Test. *Sixth grade:* intelligence—Otis Beta; reading—Metropolitan Achievement Intermediate A; arithmetic—Metropolitan Intermediate A. *Eighth grade:* intelligence—Pintner General Ability and Intermediate Test, Form A; reading—Metropolitan Achievement Advanced; arithmetic—New York City Computation.

of the Harlem junior high school students score below grade level in reading comprehension and word knowledge; in arithmetic, their perform- ance is even more discouraging—83.8 percent are now below.[2]

The academic performance of Harlem pupils in reading and arithmetic is still more depressing when compared to the performance of other chil- dren in New York City and in the nation as a whole (see Charts 1, 2, 3[3]). In the third grade, New York City pupils, on the average, are about equal to those elsewhere. By the eighth grade they have slipped almost a half grade behind. During those same grades, the pupils in Harlem slip further and further behind the achievement levels of both the city and the nation. In the third grade, Harlem pupils are one year behind the achievement levels of New York City pupils. By the sixth grade they have fallen nearly two years behind; and by the eighth grade they are about two and one-half years behind New York City levels and three years behind students in the nation as a whole.

In I.Q. the picture is just as alarming; a sharp drop for ghetto children between third and sixth grades, with a slight improvement by the eighth grade, but still behind where they were in the third grade.

Although the ghetto's pupils show a decrease in mean I.Q. scores from the third to the sixth grade and a slight recovery by the eighth, New York City pupils as a whole show a slight, but steady, increase in I.Q., until by the eighth grade they match national norms (see Chart 4[3]). These findings strongly suggest that for Harlem pupils I.Q. tests reflect the quality of teaching and the resulting educational achievement more than intellectual potential, since I.Q. as an index of intellectual potential was at one time thought to be constant, and still is considered generally to be more con- stant than achievement fluctuations. Only 2.8 percent of Central Harlem junior high school pupils are in "special progress" (SP) or "special pro- gress enrichment" (SPE) classes for the academically alert youngster, while 13.4 percent of all New York City junior high school pupils are in these classes. At present, students who excel are skimmed off into pitiably few classes for the "Intellectually Gifted Child," special progress classes, and special progress enrichment classes, where great things are expected of them. Those who fail are shunted into classes for "children with men- tally retarded development" and "opportunity" classes. Most stay in their regular classes that "meet their ability." Little is expected of them; they are rewarded for mediocre performance, and consequently accomplish increasingly less than pupils at their grade level should accomplish.

It is an ironic and tragic inversion of the purpose of education that

[2] These figures probably present a more positive figure than the realities of academic performance of these children in the Junior High School would warrant since it is the custom for some school officials to withhold the scores of those students who score too low on these standardized tests in Elementary and Junior High Schools because these very low scores would "distort" the averages.

[3] These charts were prepared for *Youth in the Ghetto.*

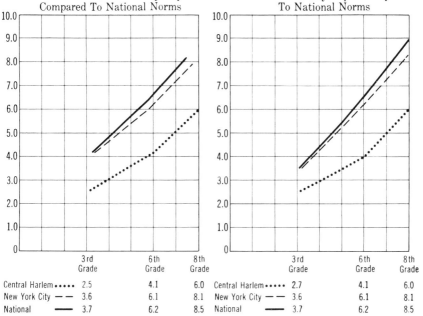

Chart 1. Median Equivalent Grades In Reading Comprehension For Central Harlem And New York City Pupils Compared To National Norms

Chart 2. Median Equivalent Grades In Word Knowledge For Central Harlem And New York City Pupils Compared To National Norms

	3rd Grade	6th Grade	8th Grade
Central Harlem •••••	2.5	4.1	6.0
New York City — —	3.6	6.1	8.1
National ———	3.7	6.2	8.5

	3rd Grade	6th Grade	8th Grade
Central Harlem •••••	2.7	4.1	6.0
New York City — —	3.6	6.1	8.1
National ———	3.7	6.2	8.5

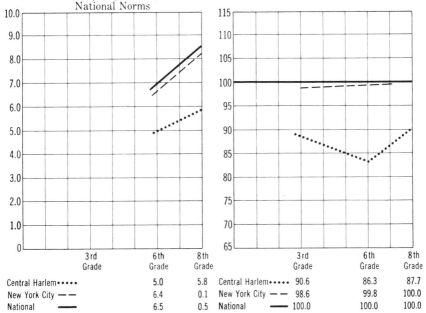

Chart 3. Median Equivalent Grades In Arithmetic For Central Harlem And New York City Pupils Compared To National Norms

Chart 4. Median I.Q. Scores For Central Harlem And New York City Pupils Compared To National Norms

	3rd Grade	6th Grade	8th Grade
Central Harlem •••••		5.0	5.8
New York City — —		6.4	0.1
National ———		6.5	0.5

	3rd Grade	6th Grade	8th Grade
Central Harlem •••••	90.6	86.3	87.7
New York City — —	98.6	99.8	100.0
National ———	100.0	100.0	100.0

Negro children in ghetto schools tend to lose ground in I.Q. as they proceed through the schools and to fall further and further behind the standard for their grade level in academic performance. The schools are presently damaging the children they exist to help.

Scarcely surprising then are the high figures for school dropouts—one out of ten from Harlem schools. Four out of five of the pupils from Harlem's junior high schools who do go on to high school, go to academic high schools; but this reflects not a plan to enter college or to seek a white-collar job, but the fact that the city's vocational schools now have higher entrance requirements; the "academic" high schools, in a reversal of the earlier situation, have become the "dumping ground" for inferior students.

Of the 1,276 students from four Harlem junior high schools who started high school in 1959–1960, less than half were graduated in 1962 (records were located for 1,012; 117 others transferred to other schools. Of the 1,-012, 44.6 percent were graduated). The Board of Education of the City of New York awards "general" diplomas to any student who stayed in school for the required period of time but who is not prepared for any further education; an "academic" diploma indicates that a student satisfactorily completed a college preparatory curriculum. Of the academic high school graduates from Harlem, only one-seventh received "academic" diplomas—compared to about half of the academic school pupils for the city as a whole. More than three-fourths of the academic high school diplomas that went to Harlem students were "general" diplomas. But even this picture of the relatively small proportion of Harlem's young people who graduate from high school with "diplomas" does not reflect the full negative picture of the educational wastage which afflicts this community.

Thousands of students drop out of school before graduation, thereby increasing the chances that they will end up unemployed or with a menial job. Harlem has far more than its share of such alienated teen-agers. A survey by the New York State Division of Youth showed that in 1960–1961, about 10 percent of Harlem's pupils attending high school in Manhattan left that year. Of the students from Harlem who entered academic high schools in 1959, 53 percent became dropouts; 61 percent who entered vocational schools that year left before graduating. Even though attendance at school is compulsory until sixteen, more than a fifth of the boys and more than half of the girls leaving junior high (during 1960–1961, 3.8 percent of these pupils left school) were under sixteen. A number of these boys were sent to correctional institutions, a number of the girls were pregnant—but the schools do not mention reform schools in their own records and far underestimate the number of pregnancies; they generally refer instead to "over-age."[4] Nor do the schools mention discouragement over academic failure as a cause, though the dropouts themselves do, and their records show the

[4]According to a study of ninety-six school dropouts serviced by the Urban League of Greater New York, *Youth in the Ghetto, op, cit.,* p. 185.

evidence: 88.1 percent of the boys and 68.5 percent of the girls leaving high school were inferior in reading; in mathematics, 89.5 percent of the boys and 84.6 percent of the girls were inferior. One cannot avoid the question whether it was the inability of these young people to learn or the failure of the schools to teach that led to this pattern of deterioration in learning skills, decline in I.Q. and eventual dropout. Fewer than half of the ghetto youth seem likely, as matters now stand, to graduate from high school. And few of them are prepared for any job; fewer still will go on to college.

The Debate on the Causes of Inferiority

The fact of the academic inferiority of Negro students in ghetto schools is no longer in dispute. Some Negroes resent this and consider it a key problem of the civil rights struggle; some whites argue that this justifies the continued segregation of these children—or at best, the acceptance of only the few superior Negro children in predominantly white schools. What remains in dispute is: How does one explain the continued inferiority of Negro students? How much validity is there to the hypotheses used as a basis for explaining and dealing with this persistent problem? Among the most tempting of these assumptions now in vogue are:

1. That each child should be educated in terms of his own needs and his capacities. On the surface this seems like a perfectly logical position and has been offered by individuals whose humanitarian and democratic instincts should certainly not be questioned. But it has led to a great deal of confusion, misunderstanding, and injustice in the educational process.

2.That children from workingclass cultures (and this second assumption necessarily follows from the first) need not only a different approach in the educational process, but a different type of education from that provided for children from middle-class families.

3. That one cannot expect from culturally deprived children adequate educational performance in the classroom because they come from homes in which there is no stimulation for educational achievement. This generalization is usually supported by such specifics as the absence of books from the home and of discussions that would stimulate intellectual curiosity. (It is assumed that in homes in which there are books, these books are read or that the presence of books in some other manner influences the child in a way relevant to his ability to learn to read in the primary grades.) Every child has to be taught how to read, however, and, as present evidence indicates, a child whose parents have no books can learn to read in school as quickly as a child whose home is well equipped.

4. That children from deprived communities bring into the classroom

certain psychological problems that are peculiar to their low socio-economic status and that interfere with the educational process in the classroom.

5. That one can predict the future academic success of the child by knowing his I.Q. score, which is obtained early in the elementary grades. Some educational systems begin to give children I.Q. tests by the first or second grade, and classify them and relegate them to various types of educational procedures on this basis. The test scores will follow them for the rest of their lives. This is considered efficient and economic: Time is not wasted trying to teach children who cannot learn. This is related to the first assumption, that a child should be educated according to his needs, his status in life, and his capacities.

A second group of assumptions can be categorically recognized as subtle forms of social class and racial snobbery and ignorance, arguing, for example, that it is not really worth it to put time and effort into teaching Negroes because, after all "they" will only become frustrated. There is no point in "their" having high academic aspirations since "their" lives will be restricted to menial jobs. In the late 1950s a number of teachers in the New York public school system told white student interviewers assigned by the author that Negro children are inherently inferior in intelligence and therefore cannot be expected to learn as much or as readily as white children; and that all one would do, if one tried to teach them as if they could learn, would be to develop in them serious emotional disturbances, frustrations and anxieties. The humanitarian thing to do for these children, the proponents of such theories maintain, is to provide schools that are essentially custodial, rather than educational institutions.

Each of the above assumptions is primarily an alibi for educational neglect, and in no way is a reflection of the nature of the educational process. Each of these assumptions—the well-intentioned as well as those that reflect clear prejudice and ignorance—contributes to the perpetuation of inferior education for lower-status children, whether their lower status is socio-economic or racial. Each intensifies racial and class cleavages in schools and therefore perpetuates and extends such cleavages in society. Each, when implemented in an educational procedure, makes the public schools and public education not instruments in facilitating social mobility, but very effective instruments in widening socio-economic and racial cleavages in our society and in imposing class and caste rigidities.

Educational Atrophy: The Self-Fulfilling Prophecy

The most insidious consequence of these assumptions is that they are self-fulfilling prophecies. The fallacy in the assumptions does not mean that a system based upon them will be demonstrated to be ineffective; for once one organizes an educational system where children are placed in tracks or where certain judgments about their ability determine what is done for them or how much they are taught or not taught, the horror is that the results seem to justify the assumptions. The use of intelligence test scores to brand children for life, to determine education based upon tracks and homogeneous groupings of children, impose on our public school system an intolerable and undemocratic social hierarchy, and defeat the initial purposes of public education. They induce and perpetuate the very pathology which they claim to remedy. Children who are treated as if they are uneducable almost invariably become uneducable. This is educational atrophy. It is generally known that if an arm or a leg is bound so that it cannot be used, eventually it becomes unusable. The same is true of intelligence.

Children themselves are not fooled by the various euphemisms educators use to disguise educational snobbery. From the earliest grades a child knows when he has been assigned to a level that is considered less than adequate. Whether letters, numbers, or dog or animal names are used to describe these groups, within days after these procedures are imposed the children know exactly what they mean. Those children who are relegated to the inferior groups suffer a sense of self-doubt and deep feelings of inferiority which stamp their entire attitude toward school and the learning process. Many children are now systematically categorized, classified in groups labeled slow learners, trainables, untrainables, Track A, Track B, the "Pussycats," the "Bunnies," etc. But it all adds up to the fact that they are not being taught; and not being taught, they fail. They have a sense of personal humiliation and unworthiness. They react negatively and hostilely and aggressively to the educational process. They hate teachers, they hate schools, they hate anything that seems to impose upon them this denigration, because they are not being respected as human beings, because they are sacrificed in a machinery of efficiency and expendability, because their dignity and potential as human beings are being obscured and ignored in terms of educationally irrelevant factors—their manners, their speech, their dress, or their apparent disinterest.

The contempt of these children for school is clearly related to the high dropout statistics, the hostility, aggression, and the seeming unmanageability of children in such schools. They are in a sense revolting against a deep and pervasive attack upon their dignity and integrity as human beings.

Educators, parents, and others really concerned with the human aspects of American public education should dare to look the I.Q. straight in the eye, and reject it or relegate it to the place where it belongs. The I.Q. cannot be considered sacred or even relevant in decisions about the future of the child. It should not be used to shackle children. An I.Q. so misused contributes to the wastage of human potential. The I.Q. can be a valuable educational tool within the limits of its utility, namely, as an index of what needs to be done for a particular child. The I.Q. used as the Russians use it, namely, to determine where one must start, to determine what a particular child needs to bring him up to maximum effectiveness, is a valuable educational aid. But the I.Q. as an end product or an end decision for children is criminally neglectful. The I.Q. should not be used as a basis for segregating children and for predicting—and, therefore, determining—the child's educational future.[5]

"The clash of cultures in the classroom" is essentially a class war, a socio-economic and racial warfare being waged on the battleground of our schools, with middle-class and middle-class-aspiring teachers provided with a powerful arsenal of half-truths, prejudices, and rationalizations, arrayed against hopelessly outclassed workingclass youngsters. This is an uneven balance, particularly since, like most battles, it comes under the guise of righteousness.

The Cult of "Cultural Deprivation"

Among the earliest explanations of the educational inferiority of Negro children was that the poor average performance was to be accounted for in terms of inherent racial inferiority. After the research findings of Otto Klineberg and others in the 1930s came a serious re-examination among social scientists of the racial inferiority explanation.

More recently, it has become fashionable to attempt to explain the persistent fact of the academic retardation of Negro children in terms of general environmental disabilities. Taking their lead from the Klineberg type of research, these explanations tend to emphasize the pattern of environmental conditions as the cause which depresses the ability of these children to learn—economic and job discrimination, substandard housing, poor nutrition, parental apathy. The most recent version of the environmentalistic approach comes under the general heading of "cultural deprivation." The literature on this topic has used a variety of synonyms for this concept. Among them are: culturally disadvantaged, the disadvantaged, minority groups, socially neglected, socially rejected, socially deprived, school retarded, educationally disadvantaged, lower socio-economic groups, socio-economically deprived, culturally impoverished, culturally different, rural disadvantaged, the deprived slum children.

The cultural deprivation approach is seductive. It is both reasonable and consistent with contemporary environmentalistic thought, which seems to dominate social science thinking. Indeed, it is presented as a rejection of

[5]In 1963, on the initiative of top staff of the New York City Board of Education, a policy was adopted to de-emphasize the use of I.Q. scores in placing of pupils in the elementary grades.

the inherent racial inferiority theories of the nineteenth and early twentieth centuries. The recent rash of cultural deprivation theories, however, should be subjected to intensive scrutiny to see whether they do, in fact, account for the pervasive academic retardation of Negro children. Specifically, in what way does a low economic status or absence of books in the home or "cognitive deficit," referred to constantly by proponents of this point of view, actually interfere with the ability of a child to learn to read or to do arithmetic in the elementary grades?

What is meant by "cognitive deficit?" How remediable or unremediable is it? If it is remediable, how? Is it merely a jargon tautology which says only what everyone knows: that these children are not learning? In what way does it explain difficulties in learning to read? What are the implications of these cultural deprivation theories for educational prognosis and methods? What is the relationship between the methodology for educating these children suggested by proponents of these theories and the theories themselves? A rigorously objective study vof these problems and attempts to answer these questions might provide answers which will not only increase our understanding of problems of education of lower status groups but might contribute to our understanding of problems of education in general—the teaching and learning phenomena. Cultural deprivation theories might also be crucial to the important problem of determining the reasonable expectations and limits of education.

To what extent are the contemporary social deprivation theories merely substituting notions of environmental immutability and fatalism for earlier notions of biologically determined educational unmodifiability? To what extent do these theories obscure more basic reasons for the educational retardation of lower-status children? To what extent do they offer acceptable and desired alibis for the educational default: the fact that these children, by and large, do not learn because they are not being taught effectively and they are not being taught because those who are charged with the responsibility of teaching them do not believe that they can learn, do not expect that they can learn, and do not act toward them in ways which help them to learn.

The answers to these and related questions cannot be found in rhetoric or continued speculative discourse. Speculation appears to reflect primarily the status of those who speculate. Just as those who proposed the earlier racial inferiority theories were invariably members of the dominant racial groups who presumed themselves and their groups to be superior, those who at present propose the cultural deprivation theory, are, in fact, members of the privileged group who inevitably associate their privileged status with their own innate intellect and its related educational success. Such association neither proves nor disproves the theory in itself, but the implicit caste and class factors in this controversy cannot and should not be ignored. Many of today's scholars and teachers came from "culturally deprived" backgrounds. Many of these same individuals, however, when confronted with students whose present economic and social predicament is not unlike their own was, tend to react negatively to them, possibly to escape the painful memory of their own prior lower status. It is easy for one's own image of self to be reinforced and made total by the convenient device of a protective forgetting—a refusal to remember the specific educational factor, such as a sympathetic and understanding teacher or the tutorial supports which made academic success and upward mobility possible in spite of cultural deprivation. The role of empathy, the understanding and identification of a teacher with his students in eliciting maximum academic performance from them, is an important educational question which should be studied systematically. The problems of empathy and identification between Negro students and their teachers are complex in an essentially racist society. It is significant that this relationship, as a systematic examination of the cultural deprivation literature reveals, has been so far totally ignored.

Looked at one way, it seems the epitome of common sense—and certainly compassion—to be convinced that a child who never has had toys to play with, or books to read, who has never visited a museum or a zoo or attended a concert, who has no room of his own, or even a pencil he can call his own, ought not to be expected to achieve in school on a level to match a more fortunate child. His image of himself is certain to be poor, his motivation weak, his vision of the world outside the ghetto distorted. But common sense and compassion may not tell the whole story. The evidence of the pilot projects in "deprived" schools—odd though it may appear to many—seems to indicate that a child who is expected by the school to learn does so; the child of whom little is expected produces little. Stimulation and teaching based upon positive expectation seem to play an even more important role in a child's performance in school than does the community environment from which he comes.

A key component of the deprivation which afflicts ghetto children is that generally their teachers do not expect them to learn. This is certainly one possible interpretation of the fact that ghetto children in Harlem *decline* in relative performance and in I.Q. the longer they are in school. Furthermore, other evidence supports this conclusion: Statistical studies of the relationship between social factors such as broken homes, crowded housing, low income with performance in Harlem schools show a very tenuous link between environment and performance.[6] Depth interviews and questionnaires with Harlem teachers and school supervisors sustain the same observation. There are some school personnel who feel that the learning potential of the children is adequate. Though the majority be-

---

[6] *Youth in the Ghetto, op. cit.,* pp. 212–13.

lieved one-fourth or less had potential for college, they did believe the majority could finish high school. One suspects that the children's level of motivation is, to some extent, set by their teachers. One guidance counselor said: "The children have a poor self-image and unrealistic aspirations. If you ask them what they want to be, they will say 'a doctor,' or something like that." When asked, "What would you say to a child who wanted to be a doctor?" she replied, "I would present the situation to him as it really is; show him how little possibility he has for that. I would tell him about the related fields, technicians, etc." One suspects, from this type of guidance reinforced by poor teaching and academic retardation, that the poor motivation and absence of a dignified self-image stem from the negative influence of such teachers more than from the influence of home and community.

The majority of teachers and administrators interviewed, nevertheless, talked of lowering standards to meet what they considered the intellectual level of their students. Assistant principals, who expressed this view with particular frequency, are in a position to influence curriculum. If they view the ghetto students as unteachable, one could scarcely blame the teachers they supervise for adopting a similar skepticism. When schools do not have confidence in their job, they gradually shift their concept of their function from teaching to custodial care and discipline.

Defeatism in Ghetto Schools

As Haryou [Harlem Youth Opportunities Unlimited Project] gathered data on the schools, it became increasingly clear that the attitude of the teachers toward their students was emerging as a most important factor in attempting to understand the massive retardation of these children. It was necessary to find out what they really felt, and so the schools were asked to recommend teachers to discuss the problems of teachers in slum schools. Interviews were held; group discussions were conducted; questionnaires were distributed. They tended to make clear what a crucial role the teachers really played in the success or failure of their students. The problems of identifying with children of different backgrounds—especially for persons from the white middle class—the problems of rejection of children deemed unappealing or alien, and the problems of achieving empathy are multiple. Courses in educational philosophy and psychology as presently taught do not prepare these teachers for the challenge of their job.

The pattern of teaching in Harlem is one of short tenure and inexperience. Many white teachers are afraid to work in Harlem; some Negroes consider a post outside of Harlem to be a sign of status. Discipline problems pervade a number of schools, as students show contempt for teachers and principals they do not respect; and, in turn, the emphasis on "good discipline" displaces an emphasis on learning, both in evaluating a teacher's record and in a teacher's estimate of his own effectiveness. Apathy seems pervasive.

A pattern of violence expected from students and counterforce from the teachers creates a brutalizing atmosphere in which any learning would be hard. One teacher reported: "The children are not taught anything; they are just slapped around and nobody bothers to do anything about it."

Some teachers say or imply that Harlem children expect to be beaten:

> When I came to school "X," I had never seen anything like that school. I cried, they behaved so badly. I soon learned that the boys like to be beaten; like to be spoken to in the way in which they are accustomed, and when I learned to say things to them that, to me, would be absolutely insulting and to hit them when they needed it, I got along all right and they began to like me. Somehow that made them feel that I liked them. I talked to them in the terms and in the way to which they are accustomed, and they like it.

Another white teacher said:

> Here, both the Negro and white teachers feel completely free to beat up the children, and the principal knows it. They know he knows it and that nothing will be done about it. The principal is prejudiced. Because he knows he is prejudiced, he covers it by giving the Negro teachers the best classes. The Negro teachers are the best teachers because they are more stable. Some colored and white teachers ask for the worst classes because they don't want to work. In the worst classes they don't have to work because whatever happens, they can just say, "It is the children." The white teachers are largely inexperienced—the principal does not expect very much from the teachers. He often says, openly, "Why did they put me here?" The Board of Education should have put an experienced principal there. There is a lot of brutality—brutal beatings, and nobody cares—nothing is done about it. The parents, the principal and the teachers don't care.

One teacher told of a teacher who exploited his students:

> The teacher should set a good example; not a teacher who comes to class to shave, clean his teeth, and sleep—as does one of the teachers in my school. Then, so that he will be free of responsibility, he tells one of the bullies of the class to strong-arm the class and keep order.

One teacher of some sensitivity commented on the reaction of Negro children to the often severe, even brutal punishment inflicted upon them:

> A child won't respond to minor discipline and will more often only respond to a more brutal form of discipline. There is inconsistent discipline and a lot of brutality in the Harlem schools. Many children are immature and, therefore, are extremely hurt by being disciplined. I have had the experience of children running out of the room after they had been yelled at—there seems to be a very low frustration point at which they can take discipline.

It is only in a context of utter apathy that such behavior could be tolerated. If only *one* teacher could talk of children expecting to be beaten, this
would be evidence of inhumanity. The fact is that in the ghetto schools
many teachers believe that such discipline is necessary for children who
come from ghetto homes. In such an atmosphere where the priority is not
on superior teaching, it is not surprising to discover that nearly half of the
school personnel report that they find their work in the ghetto "more
demanding and less satisfying" than work in other parts of the city.

Negro teachers tended to feel that the Negroes in Harlem are better
teachers than the whites, in part because they stayed longer and could
keep better discipline. One Negro woman teacher said that a white male
teacher constantly asked her to restore order in his classroom. Whites, in
turn, often feel a Harlem post is a step down. A Negro teacher said
Harlem schools are "a dumping ground for condemned white teachers."
Some white teachers report that they feel uneasy with Negroes. One
white teacher interviewed said, "When I walk through the streets here I
feel conspicuous; I would like to be able to blend into the scenery." Yet
there are a number of dedicated men and women for whom the job of
teaching the many neglected children of Harlem brings satisfaction and
reward.

White teachers who feel they are in hostile territory and Negro teachers
who resent their presence can hardly be expected to work together without friction. Much of the feeling is repressed, however, and only emerges
in depth interviews conducted in confidence. Negroes express the feeling
that whites feel and act superior and "cold" even when they are less well
educated. Many of the white teachers are Jewish; for some of them this
fact brings a sense of identification with another oppressed minority; for
others, an impatience with an ethnic group, unlike their own, where the
tradition of eager learning has not yet been firmly established. One Negro
teacher expressed her view on the subject in these words:

> I find that the Jewish people, in particular, will protect their own and are
> protected by their own. In our school, this young teacher says that the
> children "just can't be taught" and even when the method used to teach is
> not a good one, she blames the children for not having the mentality to
> learn.
>
> Unless she is a lackey, the Negro teacher has a hard road to travel.
> Mostly, they are doing a good job, but I don't think that there are enough
> Negroes in the teaching field with the guts to fight against the things that
> should not be. Negro teachers are too often trying to placate and please the
> white teachers. Most of the white teachers are Jewish. They respect the
> Negro who will fight, but if they find that they will not fight, they will walk
> all over them.

Negro teachers generally prefer not to associate with white teachers. As
one said:

I, by choice, try not to socialize with them because I get sick and tired of hearing how our children will never amount to anything, our children are ignorant, the homes they come from are so deprived, these children are nothing, and so forth, and so on. I get tired of hearing this conversation even though I realize there is a problem.

Another Negro implied that friendliness to white teachers was taboo, and would be frowned upon or punished by her Negro colleagues:

I am a person who has been around and I get tired of "Oh, you feel white today, you're eating with the white teachers." "Oh, ha, she's joining their gang, she's turning on us." I won't eat with any of them. You know what, I'd rather go down to the Harlem Embers and eat by myself.

The dominant and disturbing fact about the ghetto schools is that the teachers and the students regard each other as adversaries. Under these conditions the teachers are reluctant to teach and the students retaliate and resist learning.

Negroes seldom move up the ladder of promotion in urban school systems. There are only six Negroes out of more than 1,200 top-level administrators in New York City, and only three Negroes out of 800 are full principals. Practically all of the Negroes are to be found quite far down in the organizational hierarchy—a fact discouraging in the extreme to Negro teachers and indirectly damaging to the self-image of Negro children who rarely see Negroes in posts of authority.

In past attempts to obtain experienced and qualified teachers for the schools in deprived communities, the Board of Education of the City of New York has not used its statutory power to assign teachers to these schools. The implicit and explicit reasons for not doing so were based upon the assumption that, given the "teacher shortage," teachers would refuse to accept such assignments and would leave the New York City school system if the board insisted upon exercising its power to make such assignments. The board, therefore, sought "volunteers" for these schools and flirted with proposals for providing extra bonuses for teachers who sought assignments in them. These methods have not been successful. The Allen Report declared that:

A spurious "reward structure" exists within the staffing pattern of the New York schools. Through it, less experienced and less competent teachers are assigned to the least "desirable" yet professionally most demanding depressed area schools. As the teacher gains experience and demonstrated competence, his mobility upward usually means mobility away from the pupils with the greatest need for skilled help. The classrooms that most urgently need the best teachers are thus often deprived of them.

Schools in deprived communities have a disproportionately high number of substitute and unlicensed teachers. Some of the classes in these schools have as many as ten or more different teachers in a single school year. Although precise figures are unavailable, nearly half of the teachers answering a Haryou questionnaire said they had held their posts for three years or less—far more than the citywide average (20 percent in present post three years or less).

The persistent failure on the part of the New York Board of Education to solve the problem of the adequate staffing of these schools points to the need for a new approach to this problem. It is suggested that teachers be selected for assignment in these schools in terms of their special qualifications, training, and human understanding. Rather than seek to entice, cajole, or bribe teachers into serving in such "hardship or ghetto outposts," the board should set up rather rigorous standards and qualifications for the teachers who would be invited or accepted for this type of service. These teachers should be motivated and recognized as *master teachers* or individuals working toward such professional recognitiion. Realistic professional and financial incentives must be provided if this professional status is to be other than perfunctory or nominal. Extra pay should be specifically tied to superior skill and more challenging responsibilities. A high-level professional atmosphere of competent and understanding supervision, a system of accountability—objective appraisal of professional performance—and a general atmosphere conducive to high-quality teaching and clear standards for differentiation of inferior, mediocre, and superior teaching with appropriate corrections and rewards must be maintained.

Excellent teaching can be obtained and sustained only under conditions of excellent supervision. The roles of field assistant superintendents, principals, and assistant principals must be re-examined. Those individuals who are assigned to schools in deprived communities must be selected in terms of special competence and in terms of the highest professional and personal standards. It should be understood that they would be judged primarily, if not exclusively, in terms of objective evidence.

Evidence of Effective Learning

The schools in the ghetto have lost faith in the ability of their students to learn and the ghetto has lost faith in the ability of the schools to lead. There are two conflicting points of view—one, that the pupils do not learn because they cannot; the other, that they do not learn because they are not taught. The fact is they are not learning. The problem is to see that they do, and only when the attempt is made with enthusiasm and competence will the answer be clear. As the Haryou report said:

> Children do enter school with individual differences in experience, skills, and attitudes which make teaching more or less difficult. It is not unreasona-

ble to expect that some of these differences will stem from differences in cultural or economic background. What has not been demonstrated, however, is that these differences constitute a permanent barrier to learning.

How long does it take to learn the colors of the spectrum, or develop the manipulative skills needed in order to do first grade work?

The studies cited by school administrators are silent on this point. Further, the data here presented show that the major deterioration in learning takes place between the third and sixth grades, not in the first and second grades. This leads to the inference that underachievement is the result of an accumulation of deficiencies while in school, rather than the result of deficiencies prior to school.[7]

Given no evidence to the contrary, the assumption can be made that cultural and economic backgrounds of pupils do not constitute a barrier to the type of learning which can reasonably be expected of normal children in the elementary grades—however much of a barrier such backgrounds are in respect to social problems such as delinquency, emotional stability, and the like. Only when it is permitted to be a barrier does it become a cumulative deteriorating force.

What are the facts that are presently available that would substantiate this point of view? A few examples follow:

1. A "crash program" of remedial reading for one summer month starting in 1955 and continuing until the summer of 1964 (the data available, however, cover only 1955-1959) at Northside Center for Child Development in New York discovered that a child who has one month of extra daily instruction can gain on the average of almost one school year in reading. The children with the least retardation gained the most—those with I.Q.'s of above 110 gained more than two years in reading achievement, but the most retarded gained at least five months. The 104 children helped came eagerly and voluntarily to the program. Attendance never was less than 85 percent. Those who came more learned more.

This study of large numbers of woefully retarded, economically inferior Negro and Puerto Rican students reveals that such children can learn if taught. Nothing was done to change their "cultural deprivation." The only thing that was done was that they were being taught to read by individuals who believed that they could learn to read and who related to them with warmth and acceptance. Under these conditions they learned. And what is more, they sustained what they had learned during the school year. It is ironic, however, that when they returned to school they sustained their summer gains but they did not advance further.

All studies of the problem of education in deprived communities agree in concluding that the central problem in ghetto schools is the fact that the children are woefully deficient in reading. It has been suggested by the

[7] *Youth in the Ghetto, op cit.,* pp. 239–40.

remedial reading staff of Northside Center that as a necessary first step in the development of a program to attain educational excellence in the Harlem schools, the Board of Education drop its normal curriculum in these schools for a period of half a school year, or perhaps a full school year, and immediately mobilize all of its resources toward the goal of raising the reading level of all children in the Harlem schools, especially those from the third to the eighth grades. During this *Reading Mobilization Year* the total school program in these schools would be geared toward the improvement of reading. All other school work would be temporarily postponed for those children who are retarded until they are brought up to grade level.

There is general agreement also, supported by Haryou's research findings and by the Board of Education itself, that there is a desperate need for afterschool remedial centers. Space is available in churches, renovated store fronts and lofts, social agencies, and community centers. What is not agreed upon, however, is the most effective type of remedial program. There is serious question whether submitting the child who has already experienced defeat in school to the same teachers, techniques, classroom settings, and general atmosphere is likely to result in any great educational achievement. An effective remedial program would require a revised curriculum, advanced teaching techniques and materials, a stimulating atmosphere, and generally increased motivation.

2. "Culturally deprived" children have learned in those public schools in which they are expected to learn and in which they are taught. Children attending Harlem schools in the 1920s and 1930s had average academic achievement close to, if not equal to, the white norms. Klineberg's study of the performance of Negro children migrating from the South to the North and those already in Northern schools during the thirties can be used as evidence that at that time the discrepancy between norms of white students and those of Negro students was minimal compared with the present gap.[8] It would be difficult to argue and to prove the contention that Negroes at that time were less culturally deprived than they were in the 1950s or than they are now.

3. Junior High School 43 on the periphery of Harlem, like most Harlem schools, was holding largely a custodial program for the "culturally deprived." In 1956, before the pilot project began, the teachers felt helpless to teach. Their students seemed then to be hopeless, and considered themselves failures, their teachers as enemies. Then the school became a pilot demonstration guidance program and what looked like a miracle occurred. Six times as many students went to college (25 percent) than had earlier (4 percent). The dropout rate fell one-half, from 50 percent to 25 percent. Eighty-one percent were judged to have greater intellectual

[8]Otto Klineberg, *Negro Intelligence and Selective Migration,* New York, Columbia University Press, 1935.

capacity than their earlier I.Q. and achievement scores would have predicted—their I.Q.'s in the eleventh grade went up an average of eight to
nine points. In the more than two years during which the tests were made,
the average student gained 4.3 years in reading scores compared with 1.7
years during a similar earlier period. When one studies this pilot project,
one does not find any revolutionary educational methods. Most of the
New York City schools had both curriculum and individual counseling,
trips and programs for parents, as did JHS 43, prior to the project.

The "miracle" seemed due primarily to an implementation of the belief
that such children can learn.

School personnel were told to adopt affirmative view of their students
and give up their earlier negative views. Therefore, certain educational
methods previously considered questionable for lower-class children were
now used. Those who had openly blocked changes before became less
influential in the wake of the prestige of the new project. Most of the
emphasis on discipline was toned down. Teacher responsibility for maintaining order was relaxed. Students felt that they were "special," and that
they were expected to achieve and learn. Teachers were evaluated more
on their teaching skill than on their discipline. Because the school administration was eager for the success of the experiment, it opened many
previously clogged channels of communication between itself and teachers, parents, and pupils. Originally this was meant to win their support,
but also, the administration was unconsciously stimulated to solve some
of the problems and attend to some of the grievances not necessarily
related to all to the question of race. Teachers began to consider themselves competent and their students capable. Pupils were told that they
were trustworthy and that their teachers were committed to helping them
succeed. Parents were advised that they could help in their children's
education and progress. There was no attempt, because the task was too
formidable, to reverse the environment of cultural deprivation of the community's children.

The cyclic relationship between educational effectiveness and heightened morale is indicated by the fact that a serious program designed to
increase educational effectiveness invariably heightens the morale of
pupils, teachers, and supervisors; the heightened morale increases the
chances of success of the educational program. Conversely, inferior education in a school decreases morale of teachers, pupils, and supervisors,
and the decreased morale tends to reinforce the educational inefficiency.

4. The Banneker Project in St. Louis, Missouri, showed similar striking
results.

In 1957, St. Louis high schools inaugurated a three-track system of
ability grouping based upon standardized I.Q. and achievement scores.
Students scoring high on both tests were placed in Track I and given
college preparatory courses. Those scoring below average were placed in

Track III and given vocational and technical courses. Average students fell into Track II.

The Banneker School District is one of five elementary school groups in St. Louis and is one of two having the largest proportion of Negroes. The neighborhood is characterized by old housing, slums, high crime rate, high unemployment, etc. Of the 16,000 pupils in the Banneker schools, 9,590 are Negro.

The initial test scores for students in the Banneker District showed that only 7 percent had Track I scores, whereas 47 percent went into Track III. The median scores for reading, arithmetic, and language achievement were consistently below grade level. Otis Intelligence Test scores for 1958-1959 showed Banneker children with an I.Q. median of 90.5, with 12.1 percent below I.Q. 79.

The district director, Dr. Samual Shepard, immediately moved to improve performance, suggesting that the children had not been properly prepared for the testing experience and for that reason did not measure up as well as they might have if well motivated. Shepard initiated a program designed to stimulate teachers to teach students to learn, and parents to facilitate learning. The initial scores were graphically and comparatively represented to teachers, principals, students, and parents. It was made quite clear, however, that the low standing of Banneker children relative to children in other parts of the city was not to be ignored or explained away as the inevitable consequence of underprivilege. Rather, it was to be used to bring about improvement.

Principals were asked to help teachers have a more positive attitude toward the children and their chances for success. Teachers were to visit the homes of their pupils to familiarize themselves with the social and familial situation. In addition, teachers were asked to ignore I.Q. scores and to treat all children as if they had superior ability. As a result of this intensive, yet inexpensive and relatively uncomplicated approach, eighth graders went from 7.7 years in reading to 8.8 in two and one-half years; from 7.6 in language to 9.1; and 7.9 to 8.7 in arithmetic. Children assigned to Track I increased from 7 percent to 22 percent, while Track III assignments fell from 47.1 percent to 10.9 percent. Attendance in one school reached an unprecedented 97.1 percent. The median I.Q. was raised almost ten points.

In spite of the fact that there had been no drastic change in curriculum, instructional technique, or the basic "underprivileged" social situation, improvements were definitely evident. What had changed was the attitude and perspective of teachers which influenced the way in which the students were taught and learned.

5. Baltimore, Maryland, has tried another interesting program—this one a preschool year for sixty children of four years of age in two of the city's most depressed neighborhoods, both Negro, where crime and delinquency

rates have been so high that teachers hesitated to make home visits alone or at night. Francis Keppel, U.S. Commissioner of Education, reports that the school administrator in charge, Mrs. Catherine Brunner, has found that: Every child who entered in 1963 began kindergarten the following year, a record their older brothers and sisters had not matched. In kindergarten they did as well as children from middle- or upper-class families. In first grade, they showed better use of language, superior understanding of ideas and problem solving than other children from the same depressed neighborhoods. In the first grade, two-thirds of the original sixty were in the top half of their class; ten in the top quarter. Keppel quotes one kindergarten teacher's "candid and heartwarming judgment" of the project:

> I've always been in the habit of dividing my kindergarten classes into two sections—those who come from poor neighborhoods and lack much background for learning, and those who come from better homes and are accustomed to books and cultural experiences in their families. In a sense, this has also seemed a logical division between the dull children, the ones who need help, and the bright ones, who go along very quickly.
>
> But what seemed so logical before the project started now doesn't seem logical to me today. The youngsters who have this new preschool experience, I'm finding, belong among the highest achieving children in my classes and this is where I place them. It makes me wonder now whether many of us in teaching haven't a great deal to learn ouselves.

Despite the evidence of the effectiveness of early childhood education for the growth and development of children, public schools have not made adequate provision for extensive preprimary education. For children who live in disadvantaged circumstances, well-organized centers for early childhood educations can partially compensate for lack of opportunities for wholesome development in these formative years.

There are more than 12,000 children between three and six years of age in Harlem. All of the twenty elementary schools in the area have kindergartens which children may enter at the age of five, but there are at least 4,000 children under five who should have preschool education if community pathology is to be resisted. Haryou proposed that in each school zone, two preschool academies be established, each serving 100 children three through five years old. At first, preference would be to the four- and five-year olds. But preschool experience, however desirable for its own sake, will not lead children to learn basic skills in the primary grades if, when they reach these grades, the schools react to them as though they cannot learn.

One variable held constant in each of these programs is the nature and extent of the cultural deprivation found in the particular group before the program began. The programs' success then would have to be due either to the unlikely fact that the culturally deprived are particularly responsive to a program of education or that their deprivation is less important in their success than other factors—such as the faith of the teachers, the quality of the education. The common denominator in all these successful programs was more efficient teaching—these children can be taught if they are accepted and respected. But how does one transform an apathetic teacher into an empathic, accepting, and enthusiastic one?

If it were assumed on the other hand that teachers could only teach children who came from homes where learning is respected and encouraged, it would be analogous to physicians asserting that they could only help patients who are not too ill, or who are not ill at all.

If the cultural deprivation theories are valid and relevant explanations of the widespread problem, then it would follow that the extent and degree of academic retardation would be constant, that is, the same, under different conditions and at varying periods of time as long as the social, economic, and cultural conditions of the Negro group remained the same. A related hypothesis would be that the degree of retardation would increase or decrease in proportion to similar changes in the status of the Negro. Any evidence showing constancy in the degree of retardation in spite of changes in the economic and social status of the Negro would seem to raise serious questions about the cultural deprivation theories, and it would then be necessary to seek explanations of the academic retardation of Negro children in terms of variables directly related to the educational processes: What is happening in the classroom? Are these children being taught or are they being ignored? What is the attitude of their teachers toward them? Are they seen as primitive, unmanageable discipline problems and burdens, rather than as modifiable human beings who will respond positively if they are reacted to positively? In short, are these children seen as essentially uneducable because they are racially or culturally inferior? In the 1930s, Otto Klineberg, as noted earlier, succeeded in demonstrating that the academic performance of Negro youngsters in the New York City public schools was nearly equal to that of whites. The economic conditions of Negroes at that time were significantly lower than today. To assume that Negro children are inherently inferior or that environmental inferiority is responsible for poor school performance is educationally irrelevant—and even false. The assumption of inferiority might be the controlling fact which restricts the educational responsiveness of children to the alleged educational experience. In this regard, racial inferiority and cultural inferiority have identical practical educational consequences. This might, therefore, be the chief obstacle—the subtle, insidious human obstacle—which must be overcome if lower-status children are to be educated up to a level of efficiency necessary to bring them within a useful and creative role in society.

There is considerable evidence that this can be done. It has been done. The resistance to accepting this evidence and implementing it, the insistence upon labeling these children with euphemistically derogatory terms, might be the key human and educational problems to be studied if our society is to obtain the benefits of the trained intelligence of these children.

This is not to say that a teacher's affirmative attitude toward children is the only relevant factor influencing the performance of children in ghetto schools and that overcrowded classrooms, inadequate plants and facilities, unimaginative curricula, and the like, are irrelevant. All of these influence a child's educational growth. The point is rather that these factors cannot be given equal importance; in the light of available evidence the controlling factor which determines the academic performance of pupils and which establishes the level of educational efficiency and the over-all quality of the schools is the competence of the teachers and their attitude of acceptance or rejection of their students. Competent teachers who have confidence in children strive to achieve the other dimensions of good education also. But without such competence and confidence, children do not learn even if the textbooks are new and the classes small. There are ghetto schools which are brand new. There are some ghetto schools with comparatively small classes and with adequate facilities. But there are few ghetto schools where the morale of teachers and pupils is high and where the teachers truly believe in the humanity and capacity of the children to learn. In those few schools the children learn.

The pilot experiments in St. Louis, New York, and elsewhere are encouraging evidence that children can learn when they are expected to learn. The Negro child, like the Negro teacher, must be held to the same high standards of academic performance as their white counterparts in white schools. Obviously some Negroes, like some whites, will not have the innate capacity to respond. But many will, and each deserves the chance. Negro students cannot be excused for shoddy performance because they are Negro. To do so makes more rigid and intolerable the pathology, injustices, and distinctions of racism. There can be no double standards in education, no easy alibi. Schools are institutions designed to compensate for "cultural deprivation." If this were not true there would be no need for schools.

The schools are crucial to any positive resolution of the problems of the ghetto. As long as these ghetto schools continue to turn out thousands and thousands of functional illiterates yearly, Negro youth will not be prepared for anything other than menial jobs or unemployment and dependency; they will continue the cycle of broken homes, unstable family life, and neglected and uneducated children. The tragic waste of human resources will go on unabated.

GHETTO SCHOOLS IN BOSTON

Death at an Early Age

by Jonathan Kozol

Part One

The room in which I taught my Fourth Grade was not a room at all, but the corner of an auditorium. The first time I approached that corner, I noticed only a huge torn stage curtain, a couple of broken windows, a badly listing blackboard and about thirty-five bewildered-looking children, most of whom were Negro. White was overcome in black among them, but white and black together were overcome in chaos. They had desks and a teacher, but they did not really have a class. What they had was about one quarter of the auditorium. Three or four blackboards, two of them broken, made them seem a little bit set apart. Over at the other end of the auditorium there was another Fourth Grade class. Not much was happening at the other side at that minute so that for the moment the noise did not seem so bad. But it became a real nightmare of conflicting noises a little later on. Generally it was not until ten o'clock that the bad crossfire started. By ten-thirty it would have attained such a crescendo that the children in the back rows of my section often couldn't hear my questions and I could not hear their answers. There were no carpetings or sound-absorbers of any kind. The room, being large, and echoing, and wooden, added resonance to every sound. Sometimes the other teacher and I would stagger the lessons in which our classes would have to speak aloud, but this was a makeshift method and it also meant that our classes had to be induced to maintain an unnatural and otherwise unnecessary rule of silence during the rest of the time. We couldn't always do it anyway, and usually the only way out was to try to outshout each other so that both of us often left school hoarse or wheezing. While her class was reciting in unison you could not hear very much in mine. When she was talking alone I could be heard above her but the trouble then was that little bits of her talk got overheard by my class. Suddenly in the middle of our geography you could hear her saying:

"AFTER YOU COMPARE, YOU HAVE GOT TO BRING DOWN."
Or "PLEASE GIVE THAT PENCIL BACK TO HENRIETTA!"

Neither my class nor I could help but be distracted for a moment of sudden curiosity about exactly what was going on. Hours were lost in this way. Yet that was not the worst. More troublesome still was the fact that we did not ever *feel* apart. We were tucked in the corner and anybody who wanted could peek in or walk in or walk past. I never minded an intruder or observer, but to notice and to stare at any casual passer-by grew to be an irresistible temptation for the class. On repeated occasions I had to say to the children: "The class is still going. Let them have their discussion. Let them walk by if they have to. You should still be paying attention over here."

Soon after I came into that auditorium, I discovered that it was not only our two Fourth Grades that were going to have their classes here. We were to share the space also with the glee club, with play rehearsals, special reading, special arithmetic, and also at certain times a Third or Fourth Grade phonics class. I began to make head-counts of numbers of pupils and I started jotting them down:

Seventy children from the two regular Fourth Grades before the invasion.

Then ninety one day with the glee club and remedial arithmetic.

One hundred and seven with the play rehearsal.

One day the sewing class came in with their sewing machines and then that seemed to become a regular practice in the hall. Once I counted one hundred and twenty people. All in the one room. All talking, singing, yelling, laughing, reciting—and all at the same time. Before the Christmas break it became apocalyptic. Not more than one half of the classroom lessons I had planned took place throughout that time.

"Mr. Kozol—I can't hear you."

"Mr. Kozol—what's going on out there?"

"Mr. Kozol—couldn't we sing with them?"

One day something happened to dramatize to me, even more power-fully than anything yet, just what a desperate situation we were really in. What happened was that a window whose frame had rotted was blown right out of its sashes by a strong gust of wind and began to fall into the auditorium, just above my children's heads. I had noticed that window several times before and I had seen that its frame was rotting, but there were so many other things equally rotted or broken in the school building that it didn't occur to me to say anything about it. The feeling I had was that the Principal and custodians and Reading Teacher and other people had been in that building for a long time before me and they must have seen the condition of the windows. If anything could be done, if there were any way to get it corrected, I assumed they would have done it by this time. Thus, by not complaining and by not pointing it out to anyone, in a sense I went along with the rest of them and accepted it as something inevitable. One of the most grim things about teaching in such a school and such a system is that you do not like to be an incessant barb and irritation to everybody else, so you come under a rather strong compulsion to keep quiet. But after you have been quiet for a while there is an equally strong temptation to begin to accept the conditions of your work or of the children's plight as natural. This, in a sense, is what had happened to me during that period and that, I suppose, is why I didn't say anything about the rotting window. Now one day it caved in.

First there was a cracking sound, then a burst of icy air. The next thing I knew, a child was saying: "Mr. Kozol—look at the window!" I turned and looked and saw that it was starting to fall in. It was maybe four or five feet tall and it came straight inward out of its sashes toward the heads of the children. I was standing, by coincidence, only about four or five feet off and was able to catch it with my hand. But the wind was so strong that it nearly blew right out of my hands. A couple of seconds of good luck —for it was a matter of chance that I was standing there—kept glass from the desks of six or seven children and very possibly preserved the orginal shape of half a dozen of their heads. The ones who had been under the glass were terrified but the thing that I noticed with most wonder was that they tried very hard to hide their fear in order to help me get over my own sense of embarrassment and guilt. I soon realized I was not going to be able to hold the thing up by myself and I was obliged to ask one of the stronger boys in the class to come over and give me a hand. Meanwhile, as the children beneath us shivered with the icy wind and as the two of us now shivered also since it was a day when the mercury was hovering all morning close to freezing, I asked one of the children in the front row to run down and fetch the janitor.

When he asked me what he should tell him, I said: "Tell him the house is falling in." The children laughed. It was the first time I had ever come out and said anything like that when the children could hear me. I am sure my reluctance to speak out like that more often must seem odd to many readers, for at this perspective it seems odd to me as well. Certainly there were plenty of things wrong within that school building and there was enough we could have joked about. The truth, however, is that I did not often talk like that, nor did many of the other teachers, and there was a practical reason for this. Unless you were ready to buck the system utterly, it would become far too difficult to teach in an atmosphere of that kind of honesty. It generally seemed a great deal easier to pretend as well as you could that everything was normal and okay. Some teachers carried out this posture with so much eagerness, in fact, that their defense of the school ended up as something like a hymn of praise and adoration. "You children should thank God and feel blessed with good luck for all you've got. There are so many little children in thw world who have been given so much less." The books are junk, the paint peels, the cellar stinks, the teachers call you nigger, and the windows fall in on your heads. "Thank

God that you don't live in Russia or Africa! Thank God for all the blessings that you've got!" Once, finally, the day after the window blew in, I said to a friend of mine in the evening after school: "I guess that the building, I teach in is not in very good condition." But to state a condition of dilapidation and ugliness and physical danger in words as mild and indirect as those is almost worse than not saying anything at all. I had a hard time with that problem—the problem of being honest and of confronting openly the extent to which I was compromised by going along with things that were abhorrent and by accepting as moderately reasonable or unavoidably troublesome things which, if they were inflicted on children of my own, I would have condemned savagely.

A friend of mine to whom I have confided some of these things has not been able to keep from criticizing me for what he thinks of as a kind of quiet collusion. When I said to him, for example, that the Reading Teacher was trying to do the right thing and that she was a very forceful teacher, he replied to me that from what I had described to him she might have been a very forceful teacher but she was not a good teacher but a very dangerous one and that whether she was *trying* to do the right thing or not did not impress him since what she *did* do was the wrong thing. Other people I know have said the same thing to me about this and I am certain, looking back, that it is only the sheer accident of the unexpected events which took place in my school during the last weeks of the spring that prompted me suddenly to speak out and to take some forthright action. I am also convinced that it is that, and that alone, that has spared me the highly specialized and generally richly deserved contempt which is otherwise reserved by Negro people for their well-intending but inconsistent liberal friends.

After the window blew in on us that time, the janitor finally came up and hammered it shut with nails so that it would not fall in again but also so that it could not open. It was a month before anything was done about the large gap left by a missing pane. Children shivered a few feet away from it. The Principal walked by frequently and saw us. So did supervisors from the School Department. So of course did the various lady experts who traveled all day from room to room within our school. No one can say that dozens of people did not know that children were sitting within the range of freezing air. At last one day the janitor came up with a piece of cardboard or pasteboard and covered over about a quarter of that lower window so that there was no more wind coming in but just that much less sunshine too. I remember wondering what a piece of glass could cost in Boston and I had the idea of going out and buying some and trying to put it in myself. That rectangle of cardboard over our nailed-shut window was not removed for a quarter of the year. When it was removed, it was only because a television station was going to come and visit in the building and the School Department wanted to make the room look more attractive. But it was winter when the window broke, and the repairs did not take place until the middle of the spring.

In case a reader imagines that my school may have been unusual and that some of the other schools in Roxbury must have been in better shape, I think it's worthwhile to point out that the exact opposite seems to have been the case. The conditions in my school were said by many people to be considerably better than those in several of the other ghetto schools. One of the worst, according to those who made comparisons, was the Endicott, also situated in the Negro neighborhood and, like my own school, heavily imbalanced. At Endicott, I learned, it had become so overcrowded that there were actually some classes in which the number of pupils exceeded the number of desks and in which the extra pupils had to sit in chairs behind the teacher. A child absent one day commonly came back the next day and found someone else sitting at his desk. These facts had been brought out in the newspapers, pretty well documented, and they were not denied by the School Department. Despite this, however, as in most cases like this, nothing had been done. When the parents of the Endicott children pressed the School Department to do something about it, a series of events transpired which told a large part of the story of segregation in a very few words.

The School Department offered, in order to resolve the problem, to buy a deserted forty-year-old Hebrew school and then allot about seven thousand dollars to furnish it with desks and chairs. Aside from the indignity of getting everybody else's castoffs (the Negroes already lived in former Jewish tenements and bought in former Jewish stores), there also was the telling fact that to buy and staff this old Hebrew school with about a dozen teachers was going to cost quite a lot of money and that to send the children down the street a couple of miles to a white school which had space would have saved quite a lot. The Hebrew school was going to cost over $180,000. To staff it, supply it with books and so forth would cost about $100,000 more. To send the children into available seats in nearby white classrooms (no new teachers needed) would have cost $40,000 to $60,000 for the year. The School Department, it seemed, was willing to spend something in the area of an extra $240,000 in order to put the Negro children into another segregated school. It was hard for me to believe, even after all I had seen and heard, that it could really be worth a quarter of a million dollars to anyone to keep the Negro children separate. As it happened, the School Committee dragged its heels so long and debated the issue in so many directions that most of the school year passed before anything of a final nature was decided. Meanwhile the real children in the real Endicott classrooms had lost another real year from their real lives.

In my own school, there was another bad situation in a Fourth Grade class across the stair-landing. Here in a room in which one window was nailed to the window sill and in which words could not be read clearly on the blackboard because that old blackboard was so scratchy and so worn, there was a gentle soul on the apparent verge of mental breakdown and of whom it was said that he had had a mental collapse not long before. He had been dismissed, I was told, from a previous position in the Boston system after it had grown evident that he could not effectively handle the problems posed by an ordinary crowded class. Instead of being either retired or else given the type of specialized work in which he might have been effective, the man had simply been shunted along into another over-crowded ghetto school. The assignment was unjust both to him and to the children. The classroom to which he had been assigned was filled with chaos, screams and shouting all day long. The man gave his class mixed-up instructions. He was the sort of mild, nervous person who gives in-structions in a tone that makes it clear in advance that he does not really expect to be either believed or obeyed. He screamed often but his screams contained generally not force but fear. Bright children got confused; all children grew exhausted. There was very little calm or order. Going in there on an errand during the middle of the morning, it was not always immediately possible to find him. You would not be able to make out where he was in the midst of the movements of the shouting, jumping class. On rare occasions, the children, having no one else to blame for this except their teacher, would rise up in an angry instant and strike back. I remember a day in the middle of January, in quite cold weather, when the teacher went out onto the metal fire escape for a moment for some pur-pose—perhaps just to regain his composure and try to calm himself down —and one of the children jumped up and slammed the door. It locked behind him. "Let me in!" the man started screaming. It was unjust to him but he must have seemed like Rumpelstiltskin, and the children, not ever having had a chance at revenge before, must have been filled with sudden joy. "Let me in! How dare you," etc. At last they relented. Someone opened up the door and let the man back in.

After I went in there the first time in November, I began to find my attention being drawn repeatedly by two of the children. One of them was a bright and attractive and impatient Negro girl who showed her hatred for school and teacher by sitting all day with a slow and smoldering look of cynical resentment in her eyes. Not only was she bright but she also worked extremely hard, and she seemed to me remarkably sophisticated, even though she was still very much a little child. I thought that she would easily have been the sure candidate for Girls' Latin School or for one of the other local girls' schools of distinction had she not been Negro and not been a victim of this segregated school. For two years now she had had substitute teachers, and this year a permanent teacher in a state of perpetual breakdown. Her eyes, beautiful and sarcastic, told that she understood exactly what was going on. Enough shrewdness and sense of dignity belonged to her that she made no mistake about where to place the blame. She was one of thousands who gave the lie, merely by her silent eloquence, to the utterances of the Boston School Committee. She was a child who, in her insight and calm anger, gave the lie to every myth of a slow and sleepy Negro timidly creeping up and creeping along. Five years from now, if my guess was correct, she would be fourteen and she would be out on picket lines. She would stand there and she would protest because there alone, after so much wasting of her years, would be the one place where her pride and hope would still have a chance. But how could a child like her, with all of her awareness and all of her intelligence, ever in her lifetime find a way to forgive society and the public school system for what it had done to her?

The other child whom I noticed in that Fourth Grade room was in an obvious way less fortunate. In this case it was the situation of a boy who was retarded. For this child, whom I call Edward, there was no chance at all of surviving inwardly within this miserable classroom, still less of figuring out where the blame ought to be applied. The combination of low intelligence with a state of emotional confusion resulted, in him, in behavior which, while never violent, was unmistakably peculiar. No one could have missed it—unless he wanted to, or needed to. The boy walked upstairs on the stairway backward, singing. Many teachers managed not to notice. He walked with his coat pulled up and zippered over his face and inside he roared with laughter, until a teacher grabbed him and slammed him at the wall. Nobody said, "Something is wrong." He hopped like a frog and made frog-noises. Occasionally a teacher would not be able to help himself and would come right out and say, "Jesus, that kid's odd." But I never did hear anyone say that maybe also, in regard to the disposition of this one child at least, something in the stystem of the school itself was wrong or odd. This was his situation, repeated hundreds of times in other public schools of Boston:

The boy was designated a "special student," categorized in this way because of his measured I.Q. and hence, by the expectation of most teachers, not teachable within a normal crowded room. On the other hand, owing to the overcrowding of the school and the lack of special teachers, there was no room for him in our one special class. Again, because of the school system's unwillingness to bus Negro children into other neighborhoods, he could not attend class in any other school which might have room. The consequence of all of this, as it came down through the channels of the system, was that he was to remain a full year mostly unseen and virtually forgotten, with nothing to do except to vegetate, cause trouble, daydream or just silently decay. He was unwell. His sickness was obvious, and it was impossible to miss it. He laughed to near crying over unimaginable details. If you didn't look closely it seemed often that he was laughing over nothing at all. Sometimes he smiled wonderfully with a look of sheer ecstasy. Usually it was over something tiny: a little dot on his finger or an imaginary bug upon the floor. The boy had a large olive head and very glassy rolling eyes. One day I brought him a book about a little French boy who was followed to school by a red balloon. He sat and swung his head back and forth over it and smiled. More often he was likely to sulk, or whimper or cry. He cried in reading because he could not learn to read. He cried in writing because he could not be taught to write. He cried because he couldn't pronounce words of many syllables. He didn't know his tables. He didn't know how to subtract. He didn't know how to divide. He was in this Fourth Grade class, as I kept on thinking, by an administrative error so huge that it seemed at times as if it must have been an administrative joke. The joke of HIM was so obvious it was hard not to find it funny. The children in the class found it funny. They laughed at him all day. Sometimes he laughed with them since it's quite possible, when we have few choices, to look upon even our own misery as some kind of desperate joke. Or else he started to shout. His teacher once turned to me and said very honestly and openly: "It's just impossible to teach him." And the truth, of course, in this case, is that teacher *didn't* teach him; nor had he really been taught since the day he came into this school.

In November I started doing special work in reading with a number of the slowest readers out of all of the Fourth Grades. It was not easy to pick them, for few children at our school read near grade-level. Only six or seven in my own class were Fourth Grade readers. Many were at least a year, frequently two years, behind. Those who had had so many substitutes in the previous two years tended to be in the worst shape. In selecting this special group of children, it seemed to me that Edward deserved the extra help as much as anyone. He wanted it too—he made that apparent. For he came along with excitement and with a great and optimistic smile and he began by being attentive to me and appeared happy for a while. The smiling stopped soon, however, because he could not follow even the extremely moderate pace that we were keeping. The other children, backward as they had seemed, were far ahead of him. He soon began to cry. At this point the Reading Teacher came rushing on the scene. Her reaction was not unusual, or unexpected. Rather than getting angry in any way at all at either the school or the city or the system for this one child's sake, her anger was all for him and her outrage and her capacity for onslaught all came down upon his head. "I will not have it!" she said of him and of his misery and then, virtually seething with her decision-making power, she instructed me that I was not to teach him any longer. Not taught by me and not by his regular teacher. I asked her, in that case, by whom he would be taught from now on, and the answer in effect was nobody. The real decision, spoken or unspoken, was that he would not be taught at all. In this, as in many of the other things I have described, I was reluctant at that time to argue forcefully. Instead, I acquiesced in her authority and I quietly did as I was told. For the duration of the fall and for the major portion of the winter, the little boy with the olive smile would ask me, it seemed, almost every morning: "Mr. Kozol—can I come to reading with you?" And almost every morning I pretended that his exclusion was only temporary and I lied to him and told him: "I'm sorry, Edward. Just not for today."

After a while he got the point that it was permanent. . . .

Part Two

Perhaps a reader would like to know what it is like to go into a new classroom in the same way that I did and to see before you suddenly, and in terms you cannot avoid recognizing, the dreadful consequences of a year's wastage of real lives.

You walk into a narrow and old wood-smelling classroom and you see before you thirty-five curious, cautious and untrusting children, aged eight to thirteen, of whom about two-thirds are Negro. Three of the children are designated to you as special students. Thirty per cent of the class is reading at the Second Grade level in a year and in a month in which they should be reading at the height of Fourth Grade performance or at the beginning of the Fifth. Seven children out of the class are up to par. Ten substitutes or teacher changes. Or twelve changes. Or eight. Or eleven. Nobody seems to know how many teachers they have had. Seven of their lifetime records are missing: symptomatic and emblematic at once of the chaos that has been with them all year long. Many more lives than just seven have already been wasted but the seven missing records become an embittering symbol of the lives behind them which, equally, have been lost or mislaid. (You have to spend the first three nights staying up until dawn trying to reconstruct these records out of notes and scraps.) On the first math test you give, the class average comes out to 36. The children tell you with embarrassment that it has been like that since fall.

You check around the classroom. Of forty desks, five have tops with no hinges. You lift a desk-top to fetch a paper and you find that the top has fallen off. There are three windows. One cannot be opened. A sign on it written in the messy scribble of a hurried teacher or some custodial person warns you: DO NOT UNLOCK THIS WINDOW IT IS BROKEN. The general look of the room is as of a bleak-light photograph of a mental hospital. Above the one poor blackboard, gray rather than really black, and hard to write on, hangs from one tack, lopsided, a motto attributed to Benjamin Franklin: "*Well begun is half done.*" Everything, or almost everything like that, seems a mockery of itself.

Into this grim scenario, drawing on your own pleasures and memories, you do what you can to bring some kind of life. You bring in some cheerful and colorful paintings by Joan Miro and Paul Klee. While the paintings by Miro do not arouse much interest, the ones by Klee become an instantaneous success. One picture in particular, a watercolor titled "Bird Garden," catches the fascination of the entire class. You slip it out of the book and tack it up on the wall beside the doorway and it creates a traffic jam every time the children have to file in or file out. You discuss with your students some of the reasons why Klee may have painted the way he did and you talk about the things that can be accomplished in a painting which could not be accomplished in a photograph. None of this seems to be above the children's heads. Despite this, you are advised flatly by the Art Teacher that your naïveté has gotten the best of you and that the children cannot possibly appreciate this. Klee is too difficult. Children will not enjoy it. You are unable to escape the idea that the Art Teacher means herself instead.

For poetry, in place of the recommended memory gems, going back again into your own college days, you make up your mind to introduce a poem of William Butler Yeats. It is about a lake isle called Innisfree, about birds that have the funny name of "linnets" and about a "bee-loud glade." The children do not all go crazy about it but a number of them seem to like it as much as you do and you tell them how once, three years before, you were living in England and you helped a man in the country to make his home from wattles and clay. The children become intrigued. They pay good attention and many of them grow more curious about the poem than they appeared at first. Here again, however, you are advised by older teachers that you are making a mistake: Yeats is too difficult for children. They can't enjoy it, won't appreciate it, wouldn't like it. You are aiming way above their heads . . . Another idea comes to mind and you decide to try out an easy and rather well-known and not very complicated poem of Robert Frost. The poem is called "Stopping By Woods on a Snowy Evening." This time, your supervisor happens to drop in from the School Department. He looks over the mimeograph, agrees with you that it's a nice poem, then points out to you—tolerantly, but strictly—that you have made another mistake. "Stopping By Woods" is scheduled for Sixth Grade. It is not "a Fourth Grade poem," and it is not to be read or looked at during the Fourth Grade. Bewildered as you are by what appears to be a kind of idiocy, you still feel reproved and criticized and muted and set back and you feel that you have been caught in the commission of a serious mistake.

On a series of other occasions, the situation is repeated. The children are offered something new and something lively. They respond to it energetically and they are attentive and their attention does not waver. For the first time in a long while perhaps there is actually some real excitement and some growing and some thinking going on within that one small room. In each case, however, you are advised sooner or later that you are making a mistake. Your mistake, in fact, is to have impinged upon the standardized condescension on which the entire administration of the school is based. To hand Paul Klee's pictures to the children of this classroom, and particularly in a twenty-dollar volume, constitutes a threat to this school system. It is not different from sending a little girl from the Negro ghetto into an art class near Harvard Yard. Transcending the field of familiarity of the administration, you are endangering its authority and casting a blow at its selfconfidence. The way the threat is handled is by a continual and standardized underrating of the children: They can't do it, couldn't do it, wouldn't like it, don't deserve it . . . In such a manner, many children are tragically and unjustifiably held back from a great many of the good things that they might come to like or admire and are pinned down instead to books the teacher knows and to easy tastes that she can handle. This includes, above all, of course, the kind of material that is contained in the Course of Study.

Try to imagine, for a child, how great the gap between the outside world and the world conveyed within this kind of school must seem: A little girl, maybe Negro, comes in from a street that is lined with car-carcasses. Old purple Hudsons and one-wheel-missing Cadillacs represent her horizon and mark the edges of her dreams. In the kitchen of her house roaches creep and large rats crawl. On the way to school a wino totters. Some teenage white boys slow down their car to insult her, and speed on. At school, she stands frozen for fifteen minutes in a yard of cracked cement that overlooks a hillside on which trash has been unloaded and at the bottom of which the New York, New Haven and Hartford Railroad rumbles past. In the basement, she sits upon broken or splintery seats in filthy toilets and she is yelled at in the halls. Upstairs, when something has been stolen, she is told that she is the one who stole it and is called a liar and forced abjectly to apologize before a teacher who has not the slightest idea in the world of who the culprit truly was. The same teacher, behind the child's back, ponders audibly with imagined compassion: "What can you do with this kind of material? How can you begin to teach this kind of child?"

Gradually going crazy, the child is sent after two years of misery to a pupil adjustment counselor who arranges for her to have some tests and considers the entire situation and discusses it with the teacher and finally files a long report. She is, some monthes later, put onto a waiting-list some place for once-a-week therapy but another year passes before she has gotten anywhere near to the front of a long line. By now she is fourteen, has lost whatever innocence she still had in the back seat of the old Cadillac and, within two additional years, she will be ready and eager for dropping out of school.

Once at school, when she was eight or nine, she drew a picture of a rich-looking lady in an evening gown with a handsome man bowing before her but she was told by an insensate and wild-eyed teacher that what she had done was junk and garbage and the picture was torn up and thrown away before her eyes. The rock and roll music that she hears on the Negro station is considered "primitive" by her teachers but she prefers its insistent rhythms to the dreary monotony of school. Once, in Fourth Grade, she got excited at school about some writing she had never heard about before. A handsome green book, brand new, was held up before her and then put into her hands. Out of this book her teacher read a poem. The poem was about a Negro—a woman who was a maid in the house of a white person—and she liked it. It remained in her memory. Somehow without meaning to, she found that she had done the impossible for her: she had memorized that poem. Perhaps, horribly, in the heart of her already she was aware that it was telling about her future: fifty dollars a week to scrub floors and bathe little white babies in the suburbs after an hour's streetcar ride. The poem made her want to cry. The white lady, the lady for whom the maid was working, told the maid she loved her. But the maid in the poem wasn't going to tell any lies in return. She knew she didn't feel any love for the white lady and she told the lady so. The poem was shocking to her, but it seemed bitter, strong and true. Another poem in the same green book was about a little boy on a merry-go-round. She laughed with the class at the question he asked about a Jim Crow section on a merry-go-round, but she also was old enough to know that it was not a funny poem really and it made her, valuably, sad. She wanted to know how she could get hold of that poem, and maybe that whole book. The poems were moving to her . . .

This was a child in my class. Details are changed somewhat but it is essentially one child. The girl was one of the three unplaced special students in that Fourth Grade room. She was not an easy girl to teach and it was hard even to keep her at her seat on many mornings, but I do not remember that there was any difficulty at all in gaining and holding onto her attention on the day that I brought in that green book of Langston Hughes.

Of all of the poems of Langston Hughes that I read to my Fourth Graders, the one that the children liked most was a poem that has the title "Ballad of the Landlord."* . . . This poem may not satisfy the taste of every critic, and I am not making any claims to immortality for a poem just because I happen to like it a great deal. But the reason this poem did have so much value and meaning for me and, I believe, for many of my students, is that it not only seems moving in an obvious and immediate human way but that it *finds* its emotion in something ordinary. It is a poem which really does allow both heroism and pathos to poor people, sees strength in awkwardness and attributes to a poor person standing on

---

*Editor's note: The poem appears at the end of this selection.

the stoop of his slum house every bit as much significance as William Wordsworth saw in daffodils, waterfalls and clouds. At the request of the children later on I mimeographed that poem and, although nobody in the classroom was asked to do this, several of the children took it home and memorized it on their own. I did not assign it for memory, because I do not think that memorizing a poem has any special value. Some of the children just came in and asked if they could recite it. Before long, almost every child in the room had asked to have a turn.

All of the poems that you read to Negro children obviously are not going to be by or about Negro people. Nor would anyone expect that all poems which are read to a class of poor children ought to be grim or gloomy or heart-breaking or sad. But when, among the works of many different authors, you do have the will to read children a poem by a man so highly renowned as Langston Hughes, then I think it is important not to try to pick a poem that is innocuous, being like any other poet's kind of poem, but I think you ought to choose a poem that is genuinely representative and then try to make it real to the children in front of you in the way that I tried. I also think it ought to be taken seriously by a teacher when a group of young children come in to him one morning and announce that they have liked something so much that they have memorized it voluntarily. It surprised me and impressed me when that happened. It was all I needed to know to confirm for me the value of reading that poem to children which will build upon, and not attempt to break down, the most important observations and very deepest foundations of their lives.

"Ballad of the Landlord"

by Langston Hughes

Landlord, landlord,
My roof has sprung a leak.
Don't you 'member I told you about it
Way last week?

Landlord, landlord,
These steps is broken down.
When you come up yourself
It's a wonder you don't fall down.

Ten bucks you say I owe you?
Ten bucks you say is due?
Well, that's ten bucks more'n I'll pay you
Till you fix this house up new.

What? You gonna get eviction orders?
You gonna cut off my heat?
You gonna take my furniture and
Throw it in the street?

Um-huh! You talking high and mighty.
Talk on—till you get through.
You ain't gonna be able to say a word
If I land my fist on you.

Police! Police!
Come and get this man!
He's trying to ruin the government
and overturn the land!

Copper's whistle!
Patrol bell!
Arrest.

Precinct station.
Iron cell.
Headlines in press:

MAN THREATENS LANDLORD

TENANT HELD NO BAIL

JUDGE GIVES NEGRO 90 DAYS IN COUNTY JAIL

Special interest groups, such as big business, often exert powerful forces upon representatives of government. Groups with limited power find it difficult to affect political change. Can Black Americans, starting with limited resources, influence local, state, and national government? What kinds of leadership emerge within the ghetto? What is the likelihood of an independent Black community succeeding?

Political Organization

Every society must maintain some degree of internal order. Its members must behave in the expected manner and must perform certain tasks. A certain amount of control is achieved through the processes of socialization which result in the internalization of norms and through informal pressures that are exerted during the course of interaction in groups. To supplement these control mechanisms societies have developed organized means of formulating formal rules or laws. These rules are implemented and enforced through the exercise of power that has been delegated for this purpose. Such organized arrangements in complex societies are manifested in specialized governmental bodies.

To maintain order governmental bodies often have additional responsibilities beyond the enactment and enforcement of laws. Through a legal system they must resolve disputes and administer justice. Governmental bodies must also handle and coordinate relationships with other societies. Such relationships may be cooperative, as in the case of economic trade, or they may involve conflict. Governmental bodies also administer numerous activities, such as formal education and social welfare that affect the well-being of the entire society. The scope of governmental activity can vary and it often becomes problematic as to which areas are seen as being appropriate for control and regulation. In America every individual falls within the jurisdiction of numerous governmental agencies and it is readily apparent that government touches upon almost every aspect of social life.

The exercise of power is a prerogative of governmental bodies. The use of power is considered legitimate by some criteria and is referred to as authority. In America as in all democratic societies the use of power is legitimated through the consent of its members. The will of the people is expressed through periodic elections in which issues are decided and lawmaking representatives are selected. In actual practice, however, the political system sometimes departs from this ideal.

For example legislators do not always represent a consensus of the views of their constituents.

In the American political system groups exert varying degrees of control over governmental bodies. Groups can exert control by affecting the process through which officials are selected. For example they may actively support their own candidates in an election or those individuals with views similar to their own. Groups can also exert control by influencing the formulation and enforcement of governmental laws and policies. Thus groups such as organized labor may actively lobby for or against specific pieces of legislation.

Politically active groups tend to differ widely. Some are not organized in any fashion but are merely composed of individuals that are working more or less independently for similar goals. Most groups are concerned only with issues in a particular area of interest and attempt to influence certain specific governmental agencies. The amount of influence exerted varies and depends in part upon the amount and quality of resources available. Groups often compete with one another, and the amount of influence exerted may also depend upon the nature of the opposition encountered.

Black Americans lack many of the resources necessary for effective political participation. Such resources often include large amounts of money, widespread knowledge about political processes, access to communication media, and specialists in legal and political fields. Extensive opposition by outside groups, and value differences and disputes over strategy also serve to limit participation. In addition, ghetto residents must spend most of their time attending to personal and social problems.

As a result Black involvement in the more conventional modes of political activity has usually been limited. Blacks have tended to rely more upon direct protest activity such as demonstrations and boycotts. Many organizations employ some form of this strategy. However, in recent years dramatic increases have occurred in the number of Blacks voting and holding public office, and numerous organizations are now working with governmental agencies. Some attempts are also being made to set up types of political organization based entirely within the Black community.

Michael Lipsky discusses the use of protest as a political device. Such a strategy has limitations because of the demands that must be met by a protest leader and because of opposition that can be mounted by target groups with resources of their own. Blacks may have to turn to other strategies in order to generate influence and power.

Daniel Thompson points out that styles of leadership vary among the Blacks and Whites in New Orleans. Men from one group are most apt to negotiate with those holding similar attitudes in the other. It is easy to realize why conflicts occur when the leadership of both groups differs.

Thompson's patterns can probably be generalized to comment on biracial situations in other areas of the South and in the North. Some of his observations, however, might be modified in light of recent political trends and events. For *example, it might be argued that a more militant fourth type of Black leader has recently emerged, one who is concerned with the development of a more independent form of Black community. Such a leader may be reluctant to cooperate or work with White leaders. And it might also be argued that since Black leaders are increasingly being elected and appointed to important political positions in both large cities and small communities, this minority group is often no longer powerless. Black leaders may therefore have more influence in determining patterns of intergroup leadership. Thompson's observation that such patterns are determined by White leaders may not always be appropriate.*

PROTEST AS A POLITICAL TACTIC

"Rent Strikes: Poor Man's Weapon"

by Michael Lipsky

The poor lack not only money, but power. Low-income political groups may be thought of as politically impoverished. In the bargaining arena of city politics the poor have little to trade.

Protest has come to be an important part of the politics of low-income minorities. By attempting to enlarge the conflict, and bring outside pressures to bear on their concerns, protest has developed as one tactic the poor can use to exert power and gain greater control over their lives. Since the sit-in movement of 1960, Negro civil-rights strategists have used protest to bring about political change, and so have groups associated with the war on poverty. Saul Alinsky's Industrial Areas Foundation continues to receive invitations to help organize low-income communities because it has demonstrated that it can mobilize poor people around the tactics of protest.

The Harlem rent strikes of 1963 and 1964, organized by Jesse Gray, a dynamic black leader who has been agitating about slum housing for more than 15 years, affected some tenants in approximately 150 Harlem tenements. Following the March on Washington in August, 1963, the rent strikes played on the liberal sympathies of New Yorkers who were just beginning to re-examine the conditions of New York City slums. Through a combination of appeal and threat, Jesse Gray mounted a movement that succeeded in changing the orientation of some city services, obtained greater *legal* rights for organized tenants, and resulted in obtaining repairs in a minority of the buildings in which tenants struck. Along with rent strikes conducted by Mobilization for Youth, a pre-war poverty program, the rent strikes managed to project images of thousands of aroused tenants to a concerned public, and to somewhat anxious reform-oriented city officials.

The rent strikes did not succeed in obtaining fundamental goals. Most buildings in which tenants struck remained in disrepair, or deteriorated even further. City housing officials became more responsive to housing problems, but general programs to repair slum housing remained as remote as ever. Perhaps most significant, the rent strike movement, after a hectic initial winter, quickly petered out when cold weather again swept the Harlem streets. Focusing upon the rent strikes may help explain why this protest failed, and why protest in general is not a reliable political weapon.

Protest Has Long-Range Limits

Protest as a political tactic is limited because protest leaders must appeal to four constituencies at the same time. A protest leader must:

1. nurture and sustain an organization composed of people who may not always agree with his program or style;

2. adapt to the mass media—choose strategies and voice goals that will give him as much favorable exposure as possible;

3. try to develop and sustain the protest's impact on third parties—the general public, sympathetic liberals, or anyone who can put pressure on those with power; and

4. try to influence directly the targets of the protest—those who have the power to give him what he wants.

The tensions that result from the leader's need to manipulate four constituencies at once are the basic reason why protest is an unreliable political tactic, unlikely to prove successful in the long run.

Protest activity may be defined as a political activity designed to dramatize an objection to some policies or conditions, using unconventional showmanship or display and aimed at obtaining rewards from the political system while working within that system. The problem of the powerless is that they have little to bargain with, and must acquire resources. Fifteen people sitting in the Mayor's Office cannot, of themselves, hope to move City Hall. But through the publicity they get, or the reaction they evoke, they may politically activate a wider public to which the city administration is sensitive.

The tactic of activating third parties to enter the political process is most important to relatively powerless groups, although it is available to all. Obviously any organization which can call upon a large membership to engage in political activity—a trade union on strike, for example—has some degree of power. But the poor in individual neighborhoods frequently cannot exert such power. Neighborhood political groups may not have mass followings, or may not be able to rely on membership participation in political struggles. In such cases they may be able to activate other political forces in the city to enter the conflict on their behalf. However, the contradictions of the protest process suggest that even this tactic— now widely employed by various low-income groups—cannot be relied upon.

Take, for example, the problem of protest leaders and their constituents. If poor people are to be organized for protest activities, their involvement must be sustained by the symbolic and intangible rewards of participation in protest action, and by the promises of material rewards that protest leaders extend. Yet a leadership style suited to providing protesters with the intangible rewards of participating in rebellious political movements is sometimes incompatible with a style designed to secure tangible benefits for protest group members.

Furthermore, the need of protest leaders to develop a distinctive style in order to overcome the lack of involvement of potential group members diffuses as well as consolidates support. People who want psychological gratification (such as revenge or public notice and acknowledgment), but have little hope of material rewards, will be attracted to a militant leader. They want angry rhetoric and denunciation. On the other hand, those people who depend on the political system for tangible benefits, and there-fore believe in it and cooperate with it to some extent, are likely to want moderate leadership. Groups that materially profit from participating in the system will not accept men who question the whole system. Yet the cohesion of relatively powerless groups may be strengthened by militant, ideological leadership that questions the rules of the game, that challenges their morality and legitimacy.

On the other hand, the fact that the sympathies and support of third parties are essential to the success of protesters may make the protesters' fear of retribution, where justified, an asset. For when people put them-selves in danger by complaining, they are more likely to gain widespread sympathy. The cattle-prod and police-dog tactics of Alabama police in breaking up demonstrations a few years ago brought immediate response and support from around the country.

In short, the nature of protesters curtails the flexibility of protest leader-ship. Leaders must limit their public actions to preserve their basis of support. They must also limit protest in line with what they can reasona-bly expect of their followers. The poor cannot be expected to engage in activities that require much money. The anxieties developed throughout their lives—such as loss of job, fear of police, or danger of eviction—also limit the scope of protest. Negro protest in the South was limited by such retributions or anxieties about facing reprisals.

Jesse Gray was able to gain sympathy for the rent strikers because he was able to project an image of people willing to risk eviction in order to protest against the (rarely identified) slumlords, who exploited them, or the city, whose iceberg pace aided landlords rather than forced them to make repairs. In fact, Gray used an underutilized provision of the law which protected tenants against eviction if they paid their rent to court. It was one of the great strengths of the rent strikes that the image of danger to tenants was projected, while the tenants remained somewhat secure and within the legal process. This fortunate combination is not readily transferable to other cases in which protest activity is contemplated.

Apart from problems relating to manipulation of protest group members, protest leaders must command at least some resources. For instance, skilled professionals must be made available to protest organizations. Lawyers are needed to help protesters use the judicial process, and to handle court cases. The effectiveness of a protest organization may depend upon a combination of an ability to threaten the political system and an ability to exercise legal rights. The organization may either pay lawyers or depend on volunteers. In the case of the rent strikes, dependence on volunteer lawyers was finally abandoned—there were not enough available, and those who were willing could not survive long without payment.

Other professionals may be needed in other protest circumstances. A group trying to protest against an urban renewal project, for example, will need architects and city planners to present a viable alternative to the city's plan.

Financial resources not only pay lawyers, but allow a minimum program of political activity. In the Harlem rent strikes, dues assessed aginst the protesters were low and were not collected systematically. Lawyers often complained that tenants were unwilling to pay incidental and minor fees, such at the $2 charge to subpoena departmental records. Obtaining money for mimeo flyers, supplies, rent, telephones, and a small payroll became major problems. The fact that Jesse Gray spent a great deal of time trying to organize new groups, and speaking all over the city, prevented him from paying attention to organizational details. Furthermore, he did not or could not develop assistants who could assume the organizational burden.

Lack of money can sometimes be made up for by passionate support. Lawyers, office help, and block organizers did come forth to work voluntarily for the rent strike. But such help is unreliable and usually transient. When spring came, volunteers vanished rapidly and did not return the following winter. Volunteer assistance usually comes from the more educated and skilled who can get other jobs, at good salaries. The diehards of *ad hoc* political groups are usually those who have no place else to go, nothing else to do.

Lack of money also can be overcome with skilled nonprofessionals; but usually they are scarce. The college students, Negro and white, who staffed the rent-strike offices, handled paper work and press releases, and served as neighborhood organizers, were vital to the strike's success. Not only could they communicate with tenants, but they were relatively sophisticated about the operations of the city government and the communications media. They could help tenants with city agencies, and tell reporters that they wanted to hear. They also maintained contacts with other civil rights and liberal organizations. Other workers might have eventually acquired these skills and contacts, but these student organizers allowed the movement to go into action quickly, on a city-wide scale, and with a large volume of cases. One of the casualities of "black power" has been the exclusion of skilled white college students from potentially useful roles of this kind.

Like the proverbial tree that falls unheard in the forest, protest, politically speaking, does not exist unless it is projected and perceived. To the extent that a successful protest depends on appealing to, or perhaps also threatening, other groups in the community, publicity through the public media will set the limits of how far that protest activity will go toward success. (A number of writers, in fact, have noticed that the success of a protest seems directly related to publicity outside the immediate protest area.) If the communications media either ignore the protest or play it down, it will not succeed.

When the protest *is* covered, the way it is given publicity will influence all participants including the protesters themselves. Therefore, it is vital that a leader know what the media consider newsworthy, and be familiar with the prejudices and desires of those who determine what is to be covered and how much.

Media's Demands May Be Destructive

But media requirements are often contradictory and hard to meet. TV wants spot news, perhaps 30 seconds' worth; newspapers want somewhat more than that, and long stories may appear only in weekly neighborhood or ethnic papers. Reporters want topical newsworthiness in the short run —the more exciting the better. They will even stretch to get it. But after that they want evidence, accuracy, and reliability. The leader who was too accommodating in the beginning may come to be portrayed as an irresponsible liar.

This conflict was well illustrated in the rent strike. Jesse Gray and the reporters developed an almost symbiotic relationship. They wanted fresh, dramatic news on the growth of the strike—and Gray was happy to give them progress reports he did not, and could not, substantiate.

Actually, just keeping the strikes going in a limited number of buildings would have been a considerable feat. Yet reporters wanted more than that —they wanted growth. Gray, of course, had other reasons for reporting that the strike was spreading—he knew that such reports, if believed, would help pressure city officials. In misrepresenting the facts, Gray was encouraged by sympathetic reporters—in the long run actually undermining his case. As a *New York Times* reporter explained, "We had an interest in keeping it going."

Having encouraged Gray to go out on a limb and overstate the support he had, the reporters later were just as eager for documentation. It was not forthcoming. Gray consistently failed to produce a reliable list of rent-strike buildings that could withstand independent verification. He took the reporters only to those buildings he considered "safe." And the newspapers that had themselves strongly contributed to the inflation of Gray's claims then helped deflate them and denied him press coverage.

The clash between the needs of these two constituencies—the media and the protesters—often puts great strain on leaders. The old-line leader who appeals to his followers because of his apparent responsibility, integrity, and restraint will not capture the necessary headlines. On the other hand, the leader who finds militant rhetoric a useful weapon for organizing some people will find the media only too eager to carry his more inflammatory statements. But this portrayal of him as an uncompromising firebrand (often meant for a limited audience and as a limited tactic) will alienate him from people he may need for broad support, and may work toward excluding him from bargaining with city officials.

If a leader takes strong or extreme positions, he may win followers and newspaper space, but alienate the protest's target. Exclusion from the councils of bargaining or decision-making can have serious consequences for protest leaders, since the targets can then concentrate on satisfying the aroused public and civic groups, while ignoring the demands of the protesters.

What a protest leader must do to get support from third parties will also often conflict with what he must do to retain the interest and support of his followers. For instance, when Negro leaders actually engage in direct bargaining with politicians, they may find their supporters outraged or discouraged, and slipping away. They need militancy to arouse support; they need support to bargain; but if they bargain, they may seem to betray that militancy, and lose support. Yet bargaining at some point may be necessary to obtain objectives from city politicians. These tensions can be minimized to some extent by a protest organization's having divided leadership. One leader may bargain with city officials, while another continues rhetorical guerilla warfare.

Divided leadership may also prove useful in solving the problem that James Q. Wilson has noted: "The militant displays an unwillingness to perform those administrative tasks which are necessary to operate an organization." The nuts and bolts of administrative detail are vital. If protest depends primarily on a leader's charisma, as the rent strikes did some extent, allocating responsibility (already difficult because of lack of

skilled personnel) can become a major problem. In the rent strike, somebody had to coordinate court appearances for tenants and lawyers; somebody had to subpoena Building and Health Department records and
collect money to pay for them; and somebody had to be alert to the fact,
through landlord duplicity or tenant neglect, tenants might face immediate eviction and require emergency legal assistance. Jesse Gray was often
unable, or unwilling, to concentrate on these details. In part failures of
these kinds are forced on the protest leader, who must give higher priority
to publicity and arousing support than to administrative detail. However,
divided leadership can help separate responsibility for administration from
responsibility for mobilization.

Strain between militancy to gain and maintain support and reasonable-
ness to obtain concessions can also be diminished by successful "public
relations." Protest groups may understand the same words differently
than city officials. Imperatives to march or burn are usually not the com-
mands frightened whites sometimes think they are.

Bargaining Is for Insiders

Protest success depends partly upon enlarging the number of groups and
individuals who are concerned about the issues. It also depends upon
ability to influence the shape of the decision, not merely whether or not
there will be a decision. This is one reason why protest is more likely to
succeed when groups are trying to veto a decision (say, to stop construction of an expressway), than when they try to initiate projects (say, to
establish low-cost transportation systems for a neighborhood).

Protest groups are often excluded from the bargaining arena because
the civic groups and city officials who make decisions in various policy
areas have developed relationships over long periods of time, for mutual
benefit. Interlopers are not admitted to these councils easily. Men in
power do not like to sit down with people they consider rogues. They do
not seek the dubious pleasure of being denounced, and are uneasy in the
presence of people whose class, race, or manners are unfamiliar. They
may make opportunities available for "consultation," or even "confrontation," but decisions will be made behind closed doors where the nature of
the decision is not open to discussion by "outsiders."

As noted before, relatively powerless protest groups seldom have
enough people of high status to work for their proposals. Good causes
sometimes attract such people, but seldom for long. Therefore protest
groups hardly ever have the expertise and experience they need, including
professionals in such fields as law, architecture, accounting, education,
and how to get government money. This is one area in which the "political impoverishment" of low-income groups is most clearly observed. Protest groups may learn how to dramatize issues, but they cannot present

data or proposals that public officials consider "objective" or "reasonable." Few men can be both passionate advocate and persuasive arbiter at the same time.

Ultimately the success of a protest depends on the targets.

Many of the forces that inhibit protest leaders from influencing target groups have already been mentioned: the protesters' lack of status, experience, and resources in bargaining; the conflict between rhetoric that will inspire and hold supporters, and what will open the door to meaningful bargaining; conflicting press demands, and so on.

But there is an additional factor that constrains protest organizations that deal with public agencies. As many students of organizations have pointed out, public agencies and the men who run them are concerned with maintaining and enhancing the agency's position. This means protecting the agency from criticism and budget cuts, and attempting to increase the agency's status and scope. This piece of conventional wisdom has great importance for a protest group which can only succeed by getting others to apply pressure on public policy. Public agencies are most responsive to their regular critics and immediate organizational allies. Thus if they can deflect pressure from these, their reference groups, they can ease the pressure brought by protest *without meeting any of the protest demands.*

At least six tactics are available to targets that are inclined to respond in some way to protests. They may respond with symbolic satisfactions. Typical, in city politics, is the ribbon-cutting, street-corner ceremony, or the Mayor's walking press conference. When tension builds up in Harlem, Mayor Lindsay walks the streets and talks to the people. Such occasions are not only used to build support, but to persuade the residents that attention is being directed to their problems.

City agencies establish special machinery and procedures to prepare symbolic means for handling protest crises. For instance, in those New York departments having to do with housing, top officials, a press secretary, and one or two others will devote whatever time is necessary to collecting information and responding quickly to reporters' inquiries about a developing crisis. This is useful for tenants: It means that if they can create enough concern, they can cut through red tape. It is also useful for officials who want to appear ready to take action.

During the New York rent strikes, city officials responded by: initiating an anti-rat campaign; proposing ways to "legalize" rent strikes (already legal under certain conditions); starting a program to permit the city to make repairs; and contracting for a costly university study to review housing code enforcement procedures. Some of these steps were of distinct advantage to tenants, although none was directed at the overall slum problem. It is important to note, however, that the announcement of these programs served to deflect pressure by reassuring civic groups and a liberal public that something was being done. Regardless of how well-meaning public officials are, real changes in conditions are secondary to the general agency need to develop a response to protest that will "take the heat off."

Another tactic available to public officials is to give token satisfaction. When city officials respond, with much publicity, to a few cases brought to them, they can appear to be meeting protest demands, while actually meeting only those few cases. If a child is bitten by a rat, and enough hue and cry is raised, the rats in that apartment or building may be exterminated, with much fanfare. The building next door remains infested.

Such tokenism may give the appearance of great improvement, while actually impeding real overall progress by alleviating public concern. Tokenism is particularly attractive to reporters and television news directors, who are able to dramatize individual cases convincingly. General situations are notoriously hard to dramatize.

To blunt protest drives, protest targets may also work to change their internal procedures and organization. This tactic is similar to the preceding one. By developing means to concentrate on those cases that are most dramatic, or seem to pose the greatest threats, city officials can effectively wear down the cutting-edges of protest.

As noted, all New York City agencies have informal arrangements to deal with such crisis cases. During the rent strikes two new programs were developed by the city whereby officials could enter buildings to make repairs and exterminate rats on an emergency basis. Previously, officials had been confined to trying to find the landlords and to taking them to court (a time-consuming, ineffective process that has been almost universally criticized by knowledgeable observers). These new programs were highly significant developments because they expanded the scope of governmental responsibility. They acknowledged, in a sense, that slum conditions are a social disease requiring public intervention.

At the same time, these innovations served the purposes of administrators who needed the power to make repairs in the worst housing cases. If public officials can act quickly in the most desperate situations that come to their attention, pressure for more general attacks on housing problems can be deflected.

The new programs could never significantly affect the 800,000 deteriorating apartments in New York City. The new programs can operate only so long as the number of crises are relatively limited. Crisis treatment for everyone would mean shifting resources from routine services. If all cases receive priority, then none can.

The new programs, however welcomed by some individual tenants, help agencies to "cool off" crises quicker. This also may be the function of police review boards and internal complaint bureaus. Problems can be handled more expeditiously with such mechanisms while agency personnel behavior remains unaffected.

Target groups may plead that their hands are tied—because of laws or stubborn superiors, or lack of resources or authority. They may be sympathetic, but what can they do? Besides, "If-I-give-it-to-you-I-have-to-give-it-to-everyone."

Illustratively, at various times during the rent strike, city officials claimed they did not have funds for emergency repairs (although they found funds later), and lacked authority to enter buildings to make emergency repairs (although the city later acted to make emergency repairs under provisions of a law available for over 60 years). This tactic is persuasive; everyone knows that cities are broke, and limited by state law. But if pressure rises, funds for specific, relatively inexpensive programs, or expansion of existing programs can often be found.

Targets may use their extensive resources and contacts to discredit protest leaders and organizations: "They don't really have the people behind them"; they are acting "criminally"; they are "left-wing." These allegations can cool the sympathies of the vital third parties, whether or not there is any truth behind them. City officials, especially, can use this device in their contacts with civic groups and communication media, with which they are mutually dependent for support and assistance. Some city officials can downgrade protesters while others appear sympathetic to the protesters' demands.

Finally, target groups may postpone action—time is on their side. Public sympathy cools quickly, and issues are soon forgotten. Moreover, because low-income protest groups have difficulty sustaining organization (for reasons suggested above), they are particularly affected by delays. The threat represented by protest dissipates with time, the difficulty of managing for constituencies increases as more and more information circulates, and the inherent instability of protest groups makes it unlikely that they will be able to take effective action when decisions are finally announced.

Survey Research as Procrastination

The best way to procrastinate is to commit the subject to "study." By the time the study is ready, if ever, the protest group will probably not be around to criticize or press for implementation of proposals. The higher the status of the study group, the less capable low-status protest groups will be able to effectively challenge the final product. Furthermore, officials retain the option of rejecting or failing to accept the reports of study groups, a practice developed to an art by the Johnson administration.

This is not to say that surveys, research and study groups are to be identified soley as delaying tactics. They are often desirable, even necessary, to document need and mobilize public and pressure group support.

But postponement, for whatever reason, will always change the pressures on policy-makers, usually in directions unfavorable to protest results.

Groups without power can attempt to gain influence through protest. I have argued that protest will be successful to the extent that the protesters can get third parties to put pressure on the targets. But protest leaders have severe problems in trying to meet the needs and desires of four separate and often conflicting constituencies—their supporters, the mass media, the interested and vital third parties, and the targets of the protest.

By definition, relatively powerless groups have few resources, and therefore little probability of success. But to survive at all and to arouse the third parties, they need at least some resources. Even to get these minimal resources, conflicting demands limit the leader's effectiveness. And when, finally, public officials are forced to recognize protest activity, it is not to meet the demands, but to satisfy other groups that have influence.

Edelman has written that, in pratice, regulatory policy consists of reassuring mass publics symbolically while at the same time dispensing tangible concessions only to narrow interest groups. Complementing Edelman, I have suggested that public officials give symbolic reassurance to protest groups, rather than real concessions, because those on whom they most depend will be satisfied with appearances of action. Rent strikers wanted to see repairs in their apartments and dramatic improvements in slum housing; but the wider publics that most influence city officials could be satisfied simply by the appearance of reform. And when city officials had satisfied the publics this way, they could then resist or ignore the protesters' demands for other or more profound changes.

Kenneth Clark, in *Dark Ghetto,* has observed that the illusion of having power, when unaccompanied by material rewards, leads to feelings of helplessness and reinforces political apathy in the ghetto. If the poor and politically weak protest to acquire influence that will help change their lives and conditions, only to find that little comes from all that risk and trouble, then apathy or hostility toward conventional political methods may result.

If the arguments presented in this article are convincing, then those militant civil-rights leaders who insist that protest is a shallow foundation on which to build longterm, concrete gains are essentially correct. But their accompanying arguments—the fickleness of the white liberal, the difficulty of changing discriminatory institutions as opposed to discriminatory laws—are only part of the explanation for the essential failure of protest. An analysis of the politics involved strongly suggests that protest is best understood by concentrating on problems of managing diverse protest constituencies.

It may be, therefore, that Saul Alinsky is on soundest ground when he recommends protest as a tactic to build an organization, which can then command its own power. Protest also may be recommended to increase or change the political consciousness of people, or to gain short run goals in a potentially sympathetic political environment. This may be the most significant contribution of the black power movement—the development of group consciousness which provides a more cohesive political base. But ultimately relatively powerless groups cannot rely on the protest process alone to help them obtain long-run goals, or general improvements in conditions. What they need for long-run success are stable political resources—in a word, power. The American political system is theoretically open; but it is closed, for many reasons suggested here, to politically impoverished groups. While politicians continue to affirm the right to dissent or protest within reason, the political process in which protest takes place remains highly restricted.

BLACK LEADERSHIP

"Patterns of Race Relations Leadership"

by Daniel Thompson

Race relations constitute an aspect of every social issue in New Orleans. The problem has for generations "disturbed the religious moralists, the political philosophers, the statesmen, the philanthropists, the social scientists, the politicians, the businessmen, and the plain citizens."[1] Practically every recognized leader, both white and Negro, is called upon sooner or later to declare his stand on some question involving the citizenship status of Negroes. The Negro problem is so central to the ethos of the culture that all community leaders are disposed to view all other social issues from the perspective of race. And what is even more fundamental, white "men of power" who would remain neutral in regard to the Negro problem find that almost all of their duties, responsibilities, and actions are enmeshed in it.

Community decisions in New Orleans usually have some serious implication for the citizenship status of Negroes. For example, a certain amount of tax funds will be set aside for a project such as the paving of streets. Obviously, all streets that need paving cannot be included in the budget. What streets, then, will be selected? Experience tells us that unpaved streets in predominantly white neighborhoods are likely to be first on the priority list. Unpaved streets in Negro neighborhoods are likely to

[1] Gunnar Myrdal, *An American Dilemma* (New York: Harper & Row, 1944), p. 27.

recieve secondary consideration, or to be overlooked altogether. Thus, what on its face might appear to be a budget decision turns out to be a decision that reflects a basic philosophy of race relations.

We may say, then, that both Negro and white leaders in New Orleans are inescapably ensnared in this problem. "The white South," observed Myrdal, "is virtually obsessed by the Negro problem. It has allowed the Negro problem to rule its politics and its business, fetter its intelligence and human liberties, and hamper its progress in all directions."[2]

Because whites, in the biracial New Orleans social system, have a near monopoly of social power, it would be meaningless to discuss Negro leadership as though it were isolated from white influence. Actually, in any biracial system composed of a relatively powerless minority and a powerful majority, the patterns of intergroup leadership are determined very largely by the majority group. This is so because the prime role of the leader is to get things done. Impotent leaders must depend upon the favors or concessions voluntarily granted by the powerful.

So it is in a biracial social system that certain *complementary patterns* of race relations leadership develop, wherein each social type of leader among white men of power will choose a complementary type of Negro leader with whom he is willing to negotiate. Consequently, the achievements of Negro leaders cannot be understood except within the total context of the social reality in which they operate.[3]

This chapter will deal with some of the most typical of leaders who form the characteristic patterns of race relations leadership in New Orleans. A leader's type will be determined by three interrelated criteria: one, his conception of the Negro race and race relations; two, his attitudes toward race and race relations; and, three, his own behavior and actions in the field of race relations. On the basis of these three criteria, we may distinguish the following ideal types. Each type of white leader will be paired with the type of Negro leader with whom he normally has contact.[4]

Segregationist—Uncle Tom

As conceived here, a segrationist is one who expresses belief in the morality, legality, and workability of a biracial social system. He is essentially a reactionary, who dreams of a society in which there is complete separation of the races. He would reject all changes that might lead to social intercourse on a basis of equality between Negroes and whites. He would revert to a social situation akin to slavery in which all Negroes would be

[2]*Op. cit.,* p. 30.
[3]The dependency of northern Negro leaders on white leaders was noted by James Q. Wilson, *Negro Politics* (Chicago: The University of Chicago Press, 1960), p. 100.
[4]Leaders of the Black Muslim movement are not included in this study because they constitute a very small and, so far, uninfluential segment of the Negro leadership class in New Orleans.

socially inferior to all whites. According to the best available evidence (political elections, legislative actions, administrative policies, referendums, polls, "letters to the editor," public and "private" statements, and the editorial policies of mass media) the majority of white people in New Orleans appear to be segregationists. We find that segregationists differ in terms of the rationales they give for their beliefs, attitudes, and actions in regard to race and race relations. Accordingly, there are three distinct, though overlapping, subtypes of segregationists.

The white supremacists. White supremacists are those who hold that all Negroes, regardless of how worthy their achievement, should be permanently relegated to the bottom rung of the social ladder. They categorically deny the validity of the principles of equal citizenship, the central tenet of the Negro uplift ideology. They tend to rationalize the doctrine of white supremacy in terms of the alleged "inherent inequality of races."

Perhaps the main characteristic of this group is *closed-mindedness.* They refuse to accept any scientific finding, logical interpretation, or concrete achievement on the part of Negroes as in any way a contradiction to their belief in white supremacy. Thus, they seek to revive and perpetuate scientifically rejected Negro stereotypes. They persistently hold that the Negro is biologically and psychologically inferior to whites, and that "racial integration would be a fatal blow to civilization as we know it." A highly vocal woman segregationist in New Orleans, for example, insists that "it is just as sinful to integrate racially as it is to commit murder or adultery. . . . The New Testament clearly established that the Law of Segregation is immutable and that it is therefore just as binding upon man today as it was before the incarnation and the redemption."

In short, white supremacists defend the biracial system in New Orleans because they claim to be convinced that the Negro is biologically and psychologically inferior to whites. This position has been reiterated in one way or another by all of them. Perhaps the best summary of it was given in a leaflet passed out to the public by an anti-Negro group. The author of this pamphlet contended that

> There must be no defilement of race. . . . Blood mixture and the resultant drop in racial level is the sole cause of the dying out of old cultures. . . . It is the quintessence of folly to suppose that the nigger can emulate the white in progressive civilization. . . . We will never accept equality with these animals.

In the eyes of the white supremacist, therefore, the Negro cannot achieve the equality of citizenship that is inherent in the American Creed and the Negro's uplift ideology.

The states' righters. The main argument of the states' righters is legalistic. They rely mainly upon the Tenth Amendment to the Constitution for their authority. According to their interpretation of the Amendment, each individual state is a sovereign power, and as such it has the right to make any laws its state legislators deem necessary in regard to civil rights. The only criterion by which a given legislature can be limited in this respect is by the will of the majority of its white citizens. Thus, certain high-ranking officials in Louisiana have actually held that the state has the right to deny Negroes civil privileges which the federal courts insist that the Constitution guarantees in the Fourteenth Amendment. This group relies strongly upon the belief that the only limitation of a state's power should be a referendum in which its own white citizens register their desires.

It was this relatively small, but powerful, group of states' righters in Louisiana that led the movement for that state to interpose itself between the "people" and the federal government in November 1960. The Interposition Bill that passed the State Legislature unanimously cited the Tenth Amendment to the United States Constitution as authorizing the state to prevent any

> government agency, judge, marshal or other officer, agent or employee of the United States (from) undertaking or attempting the enforcement of any judgement, decree or order of any federal court, nor make or attempt to make service of any citation, summons, warrant or process in connection therewith predicated upon the United States Supreme Court's decision and decree in the case of *Brown vs. Topeka Board of Education* upon any officer of the State of Louisiana or any of its subdivisions, agencies or school boards, or upon any of their agents, employees or representatives in the maintenance of the public schools of the state, or who may be engaged in carrying out the provisions of this act, or other law, right or power of the State of Louisiana.

Carried to its logical conclusion the states' rights doctrine, as interpreted by segregationists in Louisiana, would set up a confederation of fifty sovereign states. Each individual state would have the exclusive right to establish any system of race relations deemed desirable by the majority of its white citizens. It would regard *state citizenship* as *primary* and *national citizenship* as *secondary*. And, despite the fact that the United States Supreme Court unanimously held that the doctrine of interposition is "without substance," some segregationists still persist in the right of Louisiana to determine its own racial policies without regard to their constitutionality.

A few states' righters will even admit that there is a serious racial problem in New Orleans and that Negroes are often treated unjustly. Yet they insist that white New Orleanians understand this problem better than outsiders, and should be left alone to solve it in their own way.

The culturists. The basic position of the culturists is that Negroes are not yet ready for full citizenship. They base their contention primarily upon alleged immorality and a high crime rate among Negroes. This argument is expressed in every meeting of the white Citizens' Councils, by many state and local officials, and by numerous individuals in other public meetings, and in "letters to the editor." The fact is, this seems to be the unstated race relations editorial policy of the daily newspapers in New Orleans. Every effort is made by these papers to emphasize Negro crimes and all negative Negro news, and frequently even editorial space is given over to propagandizing the views of the segregationists. On the other hand, Negro achievements and progress are either ignored or given the most superficial attention.

The outstanding trait of the culturists is their deliberately overlooking the fact that many white people do not measure up to the social and cultural standards that they assume to be basic in "our great white civilization," and that many Negroes could be given the highest ranking according to these standards. In other words, they tend to judge all white people according to the highest achievements of which that race can boast, while all Negroes are judged according to the lowest achievement level of their race, usually the criminal element among them. They make no distinction among Negroes. They propagandize exaggerated stereotypes of Negroes as if they were actual physical, social, and psychological realities.

Even allegedly "liberal" whites often cite the cultural backwardness of the Negro masses as an apology for their segregationist stands. Thus, one of the most respected writers in the South, who achieved the reputation of being "another liberal voice," held in an interview with a *Life* reporter that "Negroes in this area are still not ready for integration because of the cultural disparity that still exists, largely through economic causes . . . as evidenced by the vast differences by race, in such cultural indices as crime commission, illegitimacy, illiteracy, venereal disease, and general social standards."[5]

We may conclude that, though the rationales differ, segregationists are dedicated to the proposition that the biracial system in New Orleans is moral, legal, and workable. With what type of Negro leaders will white segregationists, who have a virtual monopoly of social power, negotiate?

The Uncle Toms. According to the most reliable evidence in history and in contemporary social life, white supremacists are willing to do business with Negro leaders who are disposed to accept their "place" in the biracial system. The "place" of Negroes in New Orleans society is defined by segregationists in terms of what might be called a parasite-host relationship. According to this pattern of race relations, white men of power regard themselves as hosts and Negroes as parasites. Put in another way, the relationship segregationists accept with Negroes is paternalistic. Consequently, the Negro leaders with whom white segregationists will do business may be described as "Uncle Toms."

[5]September 17, 1956, p. 120.

The most characteristic trait of the Uncle Tom is his acceptance of the parasitic status assigned him by white supremacists. He never demands on the basis of the Negro's rights, but instead begs for favors. Always underlying his requests is the assumption that something not necessarily deserved may be given. A vivid example of this type was related by a white lawyer describing what he regarded as a great Negro leader: He came "hat in hand, stood at my desk, waiting for an invitation to be seated, as was his custom . . . as an humble, but great supplicant for the friendship of the white man for his race."

Not only does the role of Uncle Tom prescribe that he should be a supplicant, but it also entails his bringing other Negroes to appreciate what some white authority has done for "our people." For example, a white schoolboard authority may accede to a Negro educator's request for funds to expand a program in his school. A similar program might already be in effect in all of the white schools, yet when such funds are granted to the Negro educator's school, he will try to find some occasion at which the white official responsible can be recognized publicly as "our friend." On such an occasion, the white authority will also play a familiar role by declaring himself a "friend of the Negro people." As a matter of fact, the most avid segregationist interviewed for this study likes to picture himself as the "best friend Negroes have." Among white segregationist tremendous prestige seems to be attached to "the friend of the Negro" role. They actually compete among themselves, at least verbally, at being a friend of the Negro. This, then, is the most effective technique employed by Uncle Toms: white men of power are challenged to qualify as the "friend of Negroes." It is expected that the highest prestige in this regard will go to the wealthier, more established, and most powerful among the white supremacists. We can see then why Uncle Toms almost always "go to the top men, don't bother about straw bosses," as one such leader put it.

Myrdal saw Negro leaders of this type as functioning primarily as instruments in the hands of white people. In this capacity they were used, he concluded, to keep other Negroes in line. This, of course, is one of their major functions. Yet, it must not be overlooked that they do get things done. Just as white people use Negro leaders of this type to control the Negro masses, so the Uncle Toms manipulate white authorities to serve their own purposes. Thus the Uncle Toms have often been responsible for persuading Negroes not to join labor unions or to engage in mass protest, and generally they are able to stifle Negro radicals. However, through the Uncle Toms Negro workers may receive also some benefits, such as somewhat higher salaries or better working conditions. Uncle Toms are also frequently granted certain personal favors in return for their role as liaison between the Negro and the white communities.

Most of the favors the Uncle Toms receive are due to the fact that in order to be serviceable to the white community, they must maintain prestige among Negroes. They must, therefore, evince some influence with white authorities. This the white community understands. As a result, the trusted Negro liaison leader is often allowed to "get away with murder." That is, he is permitted, so to speak, to engage in what sometimes appears to be almost radical social action. Yet such radical behavior is really a kind of social catharsis, without which a leadership vacuum would be created that might be filled by a really radical Negro leader, who is not under the control of white authorities. So, even in an apparently radical role, the Uncle Tom proves to be an invaluable preserver of a biracial system which perpetuates white paternalistic men of power in their status as hosts and Negroes as parasites.

Moderate—Racial Diplomat

There are two distinctly opposite points of view or philosophies toward the biracial system in New Orleans. On the one hand, segregationists hold that the best, certainly the most desirable, social system is one that adheres religiously to the principles of racial segregation. On the other hand, integrationists insist that the basic principle inherent in our republican form of government is equal citizenship. Accordingly, racial segregation is logically untenable and a legal contradiction.

Ideally, the moderate occupies a postion somewhere between the segregationist and the integrationist. He may be described as a "middle-of-the-roader," a kind of eclectic. Actually he has no definite, defensible philosophy of race relations. Sometimes his racial views on certain issues are similar to those of the avowed segregationist. At other times, even on the same issues, the moderate may take a stand very much like that of the integrationist. Therefore, the moderate is usually indefinite and vacillating when it comes to the question of equal citizenship rights.

Most moderates create the impression that they try to hold fast to a belief in equal citizenship, while "realistically" hanging onto the conviction that individual differences and inequalities are important. They seem never to resolve this conflict in their basic ideology. This ideological contradiction often leads them into a kind of legal legerdemain. Thus, while acknowledging certain "unalienable" rights inherent in American citizenship, they manifest at the same time a willingness to entrust the securing of these rights to the uncertain will of city and state authorities who have repeatedly pledged to maintain segregation and inequal citizenship at all costs.

A few moderates attempt to resolve their ideological dilemma through education and persuasion. That is, they gather, interpret, and disseminate facts designed to encourage local men of power to formulate plans and to map out courses of action "best suited to local needs," whereby "certain racial injustices" might be eliminated.

There are perhaps three distinctly different degrees of moderation insofar as race relations are concerned:

The lukewarm. Those who fall into this classification are ostensibly neutral in regard to the racial segregation-integration controversy. This is the traditional stand of most white businessmen, independent professionals, and acedemicians. When possible, they avoid making any statement about "the problem." They can seldom be persuaded to take any public stand on the race issue, and they almost never join racially militant organizations, either those advocating racial uplift or those advocating racial segregation.

When asked to express his views on race relations in New Orleans a high-ranking public official made the following statement:

> I have made a policy of saying nothing. I know your work is confidential [meaning the interview], but this is a rule which admits no exceptions and that's why I've been able to stay out of trouble. . . . Some people accuse me of being stupid and having no guts, but I don't see it that way at all. I think it is my duty to do my job [naming his profession] and keep away from emotional disturbances. I'm hired to administer under established policies and this sets the limits upon my activity.

When circumstance makes the need to respond to some racial issue inevitable, the lukewarm moderate is likely to respond "objectively." As a rule, the question of equal citizenship rights will be equated with some other value, such as good business, a good civic reputation, or high academic standards. Thus, when an outstanding businessman was pressed to express himself on the school-desegregation crisis in New Orleans, he finally stated, "One thing I am sure of, we simply cannot afford to let our city become another Little Rock. Look what happened to business after the riots and everything. They may never get over the mess they made of the school business." Again, a college professor expressed this fear—

> I think that the politicians are making far too big an issue about four little girls [referring to the four Negro girls in New Orleans who were admitted to the first grade in two formerly all-white schools]. If this keeps up recognized scholars will begin to avoid the South. Already I know of a few professors who plan to leave southern colleges. I hope our leaders will soon show a little more sanity.

Because some of the lukewarm moderates are persons of great influence, their opinions on race issues are diligently sought and highly valued. Therefore, in New Orleans, where a white person is assumed to be a segregationist unless he indicates otherwise, persons in this category are often unwittingly included among "the vast majority of white people who regard racial segregation as a sacred heritage," in the often-repeated phraseology of segregationist leaders. In this way their lukewarm attitudes on race relations give tacit sanction to the biracial social system as it now exists.

The gradualists. The characteristic trait of the gradualists is their insistence that Negroes must "qualify" for equal citizenship status. In some respects they are similar to the segregationists who hold that "Negroes are not yet ready for equality." They differ from the segregationists, however, in that they are much more willing to acknowledge that *some* Negroes are "ready" for equality with white people. They are less likely than the segregationists to participate in movements designed to impede the progress of "qualified" Negroes, because other Negroes happen to have a high crime rate or behave in an unseemly fashion. In fact, some gradualists seek out opportunities to promote or enhance the prestige of certain qualified Negroes.

Sometimes gradualists make important and far-reaching contributions to Negro advancement. They have been known to donate substantial sums to segregated Negro institutions. One Negro leader expressed the belief that "practically all white people on boards of directors of Negro institutions, or who are assigned special duties in the Negro community as representatives of white authorities in the field of public education and 'Negro affairs,' are gradualists."

Much of the progress Negroes have been able to make during the last twenty years in New Orleans has been due directly or indirectly to gradualists. This is so primarily because gradualists tend to view race relations more or less in terms of enlightened self-interest. That is, they are much more likely than the segregationists to understand the ubiquitous nature of disease, crime, and poverty, and to attempt to eradicate them without regard to race. As one gradualist labor leader put it:

> I have always insisted that Negro workers should be treated the same as white workers, because after all we need them to help us raise the general standard of living in our community. Nothing gives us a stronger argument in our own ranks than demonstrating that organized labor is interested in all of its workers. Do you know that the most loyal members we had during [our last strike] were our Negroes?

A favorite technique used by the gradualists to get things done in the Negro community is the threat of "total integration." The argument, for example, that a high city official gave for expanding certain recreational facilities for Negroes was that if improved facilities for Negroes were not provided, Negroes would seek to break down segregation patterns "protecting" white facilities. He insisted that when Negroes have adequate public facilities "of their own" only a few of them attempt to use facilities set aside for whites, even when all legal barriers have been removd. He even boasted that certain "white" public facilities had been legally desegregated for a considerable length of time, yet only a "token" number of Negroes had ever sought to use them.

Perhaps the best illustration of the gradualists' position is the stand taken on the desegregation of the public schools. Gradualists tend to accept "limited integration," such as was attempted through a program of "pupil placement." According to this placement program in New Orleans, Negro first graders had to qualify for white schools by passing a long comprehensive examination intended to test their mental aptitudes, cultural achievements, and social adjustment. This test was admittedly designed to "eliminate all but a few of the Negro pupils who might apply" to attend hitherto white schools.

The rate of change in race relations acceptable to gradualists was pointed up by a Negro attorney representing some Negro children seeking to attend nonsegregated schools. The lawyer for the Negro plaintiffs filed a motion that held that pupil placement effectively limits the number of Negro children who should be receiving nonsegregated education. He contended that "the plaintiffs and the class they represent—approximately 50,000 Negro students, save four—are still effectively denied their constitutional rights to nonsegregated education."[6] ("Pupil placement" in New Orleans was eventually declared unconstitutional by a federal court.)

Gradualists were asked, "How long do you think it will be before Negroes are generally admitted to participate in civic organizations, such as the Chamber of Commerce, Rotary, and the Lions Clubs?" They usually predicted that it would be "a long time." When pressed for a definite answer they mentioned fifteen, twenty, twenty-five years.

The borderline liberals. The most stable element among the moderates is composed of well-to-do white people, generally women, who make a career out of helping Negroes. Some of them are convinced that they are absolutely indispensable to Negro progress. These are the ones who serve on important welfare boards where "Negro interests" are of major concern. They are called upon by Negro leaders to plan fund-raising campaigns, and to negotiate with white men of power, from whom certain favors are sought and whose offices are necessary for the success of some project. As one outstanding woman leader phrased it, "I walk in two worlds."

Persons in this category, more than any other type of white leader, manifest a strong sense of community pride. This may be the main reason why they would prefer to have "local problems solved by local people," as one of them said. She maintains that if she could get the Negro community and the white community to work together on common projects, "then there would be no race relations problem. We could cut through the lines to get some things done." She gave as a specific example a project on which she had worked in the Negro community. It was successful, she said, because "we had teamwork. If this had been an all-Negro project, then we could not have gone to the [white] papers with our publicity and had it accepted the way it was."

[6]The four referred to in this Brief applies to the four Negro children admitted to formerly all-white schools in November 1960.

Their strong sense of community pride leads most of them to take the position that New Orleans should be left alone to solve its own problems of equal citizenship for Negroes. One leader said, "I am optimistic about this. I know that if a few of the truly respected men in this city could be convinced that our public schools must be kept open, and Negroes generally should be accorded more respect, then it would be done." This statement revealed two important basic attitudes held by individuals who are classified in this category.

First, they have an almost child-like faith in the integrity of "truly respected" authorities. In all of their public pronouncements, as well as in private interviews, they tend to project their own sense of community pride onto others. They refuse to believe that a responsible authority would allow racial discord or injustices to exist, "if he understands their nature and counsequences." Thus, they see themselves as "advisors" to city officials on Negro affairs.

Second, they manifest optimistic faith in the leadership of powerful authorities. During every discussion of possible racial strife, they reiterate that certain city officials must be apprised of the seriousness of the situation so that they can "tell the people what to do." Thus, as we shall see later, this attitude of trust on the part of these race relations leaders was primarily the reason why almost no preparation was made to meet the public-school-desegregation deadline ordered by the federal courts. These leaders simply could not visualize a situation in which the mayor would be unwilling or unable to "handle the situation in the best interests of everyone." They felt that whatever line of action the mayor proposed would be followed without question by the vast majority of citizens.

To them, "The Embarrassment of Louisiana," as characterized by the *Saturday Evening Post* (May 27,1961) and popularly referred to as the "Shame of New Orleans," was not due basically to what the *Post* writer described as "the integration conflicts [that] broke out in all their ugliness," but rather to the fact that local authorities refused to handle their own problems and the federal government found it necessary to intervene. Sympathizing with this point of view, Helen Fuller, writing in *The New Republic* (February 16, 1959), prophetically lamented: "New Orleans Knows Better."

Segregationists and moderates have at least one basic attitude in common: both strongly resent outsiders. Consequently, when it comes to the problem of equal citizenship, they are likely to invoke the doctrine of "home rule," or local autonomy. This doctrine springs from confidence and faith in the ability of people, on a local level, to work together in the solution of their own common problems. There is, of course, one important fallacy in this belief: it presupposes that men of power are also men of good will, who are willing to sacrific personal, political, and economic gain for the welfare of the total community.

Moderates tend to place too much faith in the doctrine of community autonomy. They manifest a willingness, they even prefer to entrust the securing of equal citizenship rights to local authorities who, in the name of "law and order," are ironically, pledged to maintain the same biracial system that the segregationists consider sacred.

Again, with what kind of Negro leader will moderates negotiate?

The racial diplomat. The racial diplomat is usually class-oriented. He is highly skilled in dealing with white leaders. However, unlike the Uncle Tom, he does not accept segregation as right, but as an effective diplomat, he does manifest an astute understanding of the "ways of the South." Like the white moderate, he has a strong feeling of belonging in the local community and a keen sense of community pride. He identifies with the problems of the total community and he talks about the welfare of human beings, as one racial diplomat put it, and not just about "what is good for the Negro." This leader emphasized one point he always makes when working with white people on some committee or project: "I let them know to begin with," he said, "that I am not just concerned about doing things for Negroes, but rather, about how I can benefit mankind. I refuse to serve on any committee where they regard me as simply a Negro representative."

This, then, is the primary role of the racial diplomat. He essays to interpret the peculiar needs of Negroes in terms of general community well being. For example, on this basis one Negro leader appealed for funds to support a Community Fund agency. "I did not ask to have this [institution] supported simply because Negroes needed it," he said. "I went on record as supporting three such projects, only one of which would be for Negro youth."

Another familiar role played by the racial diplomat is that of advising moderates on the "best way" of promoting uplift in some specific area of life. A powerful white labor union leader said that when he first came to New Orleans he wanted to bring drastic pressure to bear on white businessmen who refused to employ Negro members in positions for which they qualified or to pay them salaries commensurate with their work. In the most positive "union language" he said that he would have followed through with actions calculated to "break the backs of the employers" in regard to the rights of Negro members, but a Negro official of the union "taught me better." The Negro official had advised a diplomatic approach rather than pressure tactics. Therefore, instead of the union's taking direct action in regard to equal membership status to Negroes, it adopted a diplomatic approach calculated to minimize resistance on the part of white employers.

The racial diplomat can always be depended upon to *protect* white race relations leaders from being embarrassed by other Negroes. For instance, a white moderate will hardly accept an invitation to speak before a Negro group, or to serve on an interracial committee, unless he is invited by a well-known racial diplomat. The later will, first of all, select the Negroes to be present and then serve throughout the meeting as a buffer or "friend" when untoward situations develop. In some instances, the racial diplomat will simply explain away embarrassing questions which might be put to the white moderate. In other instances, he will deliberately select the kind of questions that should be answered regarding some specific action engaged in, or position taken by, the moderate present. In other words, regardless of his personal feelings in the matter, his most important function in a group the membership of which is predominantly Negro is to protect the white moderate (the visitor) from any unpleasantness.

A few of the most skilled racial diplomats can be trusted to participate in traditionally all-white groups. This is occasionally arranged by moderates in order to achieve two interrelated ends:

1. To demonstrate to segregationists (whom they would like to persuade) that some Negroes do, in fact, "qualify" for equal citizenship. Needless to say, when their "exhibit number one" measures up, they are gratified and happy. One white leader described a racial diplomat in these glowing terms: "A great Negro leader," "perennial optimist," "skilled in getting things out of others," "unusual capacity for understanding," "patience like unto a saint," "in touch with reality," "always alert," and a "great capacity for work."

2. To enhance the prestige of the racial diplomat in the eyes of other Negro leaders and in the community at large. This is, indeed, an important reward for his "understanding service" in helping them to accomplish racial uplift in the framework of a biracial system. Furthermore, such an assignment functions to advise other types of Negro leaders that this is the kind of Negro with whom influential white moderates are willing to do business.

It is very probable that if the actual achievements of Negro leaders in race relations were compared, those of the racial diplomat would rank highest. Unlike the Uncle Tom, who is not respected by either the white or the Negro community, the racial diplomat is respected by both because he fits well into the success pattern inherent in our national ideology. And, in the true Machiavellian tradition, he chooses respect in preference to love. Actually, the racial diplomat is often hated by other Negro leaders because there is always a feeling of suspicion on their part that he "sells out to white people." Nevertheless, he does get things done.

One of the best insights into the philosophy of the racial diplomat was provided by a Negro leader who ranks high in that category. He said

> It is my belief that the main job of race relations organizations is keeping race relations on an even keel. Therefore, my organization surrounds itself with white leaders who are willing to support this approach to race relations. We believe in the scientific approach. We first gather facts . . . then we sit

around a table and on the basis of these facts we seek to secure change. Undue sentiment and emotion should not be involved in our deliberations.

Another prominent racial diplomat gave a projected appraisal of a colleague in these words

> A good leader should have genuine concern for the group, should be active rather than offering mere lip service, should have racial consciousness, and a keen sense of social change. I know of no one who measures up to this standard better than [Mr.———]. He approaches white people in the right manner. He can discuss issues intelligently with moderation, tact, and poise with them. The prestige of his position helps him out. He demonstrates social graces, culture and refinement. He is on big boards.

We may conclude that racial diplomats are generally *middle-class oriented*. To them, a successful Negro leader is one who possesses all of the traditional middle-class traits. These traits were summarized by one such leader in this way: "The essential qualities of a leader should be: . . . altruism, humanitarianism, appreciation for the principles upon which our government was founded, the ability to do long-range planning, economic independence and security, and high social status."

Liberal—Race Man

The concept of the liberal as used here is intended to classify individuals who would rank national citizenship above state or local citizenship. The most characteristic attitude held by liberals is that inherent in American citizenship is equality of status. They insist that second-class citizenship is in fundamental contradiction with the principles of equality and freedom upon which our government is founded.

Liberals maintain that all persons, regardless of race, religion, or national origin, should have equal opportunities to develop to the fullest extent of their individual capacities unhampered by laws and traditions. Therefore, no matter how difficult or unpleasant a given situation may be, the liberal insists that the basic principle of the American Creed—equality of citizenship—should never be compromised.

Generally, liberals in American society have favored movements to expand the electorate, to get stronger civil rights legislation, and to equalize economic and educational opportunities. Specifically, liberals renounce the biracial social system. They take the position that racial discrimination in any area of our national life is "undemocratic, unjust, and undermines our national strength and international prestige."

Basically, the liberals' argument against a biracial system is this: Every individual citizen has a heritage bequeathed to him by a republican form of government. This heritage includes equal rights and opportunities. They point out that when the majority sanctions political or social techniques designed to abridge these rights for a minority in any way (no matter how despised the minority in question might be), they also sanction the techniques that will eventually destroy the equal rights and opportunities of the majority as well.

One liberal explained his conception of equal citizenship in this way:

> I feel that all laws restricting Negroes from enjoying full citizenship privileges should be abolished. Just removing restrictions, however, is not enough. It should also mean employing Negro personnel in public facilities without discrimination. Also, I think that there should be laws passed, like in New York, to make it illegal to discriminate in public facilities, such as hotels, restaurants, parks, and so forth. Complete desegregation of the school should only be a first step.

Very few white people in New Orleans may be classified as liberals. There are no manifest liberals, at the moment, in positions of authority in the city. Why are there so few liberals in the area of race relations in New Orleans? This is a difficult question to answer, because the reasons white persons offer as answers to this question usually stem from complex psychological sources. However, if we were to give the single most pervasive reason it would be *fear*. This emotion has been expressed by practically every white leader or official who has been called upon to face up publicly to problems in race relations. Three examples illustrate this.

1. A wealthy realtor opposes "open occupancy" in housing because he is *afraid* that certain bussinesses that traditionally cater to white patrons would be seriously hurt if the predominantly white community were to become a mixed neighborhood. He is particularly concerned about an old, well-established mortuary. This business has catered to moderately wealthy white people in his neighborhood for several decades, and he wondered "what would happen to this business if the neighborhood becomes black? I tell you what I am afraid would happen—this business would just fold up."

The fear expressed here is typical of a large number of white businessmen. In one way or another, all of them when pressed indicated that they were afraid to take a liberal stand on race relations. A wealthy department store manager, when asked to employ Negroes in sales positions, expressed his fear in this way:

> I am sure that there are Negroes who would do an adequate job as sales people, or on any other job they had a chance to learn. I would like to be able to employ people for what they could do, not because of race, yet, I feel that I would lose more white customers if I employed Negroes as sales people than I would gain Negro customers. I am not in business for my health.

2. Some of the younger politicians who would like to function as liberals confide that they are *afraid* that if they are reputed to be liberals (or integrationists) they would be committing "political suicide." When,

therefore, the Louisiana State Legislature was passing scores of bills, reso-
lutions, and amendments designed to maintain racial segregation despite
federal court orders to the contrary the illegal liberals in the legislature
from New Orleans voted for almost every "anti-Negro" measure presented. When explaining their contradictory behavior as legislators, they
all agreed that they took the stand they did because they were *afraid* to
do otherwise.

3. A prominent head of a wealthy law firm was entreated to make a
public statement warning the state legislature against the passing of obviously unconstitutional laws aimed at preserving segregation. This lawyer
agreed that "most of this current legislation is not even legal on its face."
He further acknowledged that such laws tend to heighten negative race
relations and "will serve to bring us national and international disgrace."
He refused, however, to make the public statement some citizens desired
of him because, he said, "most of my law partners are young, ambitious,
capable lawyers. Whereas I am a wealthy man, I don't think it would be
fair for me to jeopardize their future on such a controversial issue as race
relations is at present in New Orleans."

The examples given above are only a few of the many that might have
been selected from interview materials, newspaper reports, and public
statements by leading white citizens. All of these indicate a fear of taking
a positive stand on the question of equal citizenship status for Negroes.
When we tried, painstakingly, to ferret out the sources of this fear, we
encountered great difficulties. Individually, a large proportion of the men
of power expressed their belief in equal citizenship, and the reason they
gave for not expressing these beliefs publicly were seldom logical, consistent, or sound. Their responses tended to remind the researchers of the
much-quoted statement of the late President Franklin D. Roosevelt sum-
marizing the psychological condition of the American businessman after
experiencing years of depression. He said, "We have nothing to fear, but
fear itself."

On numerous occasions representatives of powerful political, economic,
civic, social, and religious groups meet together to consider, among other
things, the question of race relations. Personally, almost to the man, they
express concern about the "race problem." They generally agree as individuals that something should be done. But, when the question arises
regarding what specifically is to be done and who is to do it, fear takes
over. It is at this point that such expressions are heard as, "If this course
of action is taken, we might have violent reaction from *them*"; "If I stick
my neck out, *they* will promptly cut it off"; "I just don't think New
Orleans is ready for that action yet"; "Members of my organization
wouldn't go along with this, because *they* would be afraid of losing business"; or, "*They* just wouldn't stand for it."

One significant thing stands out in the quotations above: there is seldom any attempt made to define who "they" are. Thus, after listening to a long discussion as to whether or not an Interracial Human Relations Council should be appointed by or legitimitized by the city government and certain powerful city organizations, a white liberal summarized his impression in this way—

> I got the idea that these hard-headed businessmen and politicians all agreed in their minds and in their hearts that we need such a committee operating in our community. Yet, each one who spoke continued to use the word fear over and over again. Then it occurred to me that there were no real people they feared because they, among themselves, had the power to control or even outlaw any group in the community that would dare challenge them. I also knew that even if they were prejudiced that they would not be so stupid as to allow their personal prejudices to ruin their businesses or disgrace our city. So I had to conclude that their fear was based upon ghost-like images of their own creation.

There is, of course, some basis in reality for this fear syndrome so frequently expressed by "men of power." After individuals have made liberal statements or participated in liberal action, a few have actually lost business, been harassed by cranks who called on the telephones at all hours of the night or been forced to endure public criticism by segregationists. Yet, even this is often instigated more by fear than by any other consideration. One business man suggested this in a statement to a white interviewer. He said—

> Mr.[———] lost all of his business when he got on the wrong side of the school desegregation issue. Before this, I was one of his main customers myself. I cancelled my orders with him, not because I disagreed with his stand, I think that he was a perfectly honest man and did what he thought was right, but if I had not cancelled my orders with him, with the climate of opinion what it is now, I am sure I would have lost business myself.

It seems, then, that fear is compounded by fear so that "a perfectly honest" man is persecuted, not for what he has done, but because his persecutors are afraid not to persecute.

Whatever may be the reasons, or imagined reasons, there are very few white persons in New Orleans who are acknowledged liberals. Those who are publicly regarded as liberals must endure persecution, ostracism, and "investigations." The systematic harassment to which they are subject is apparently calculated to make them anathema. The most effective technique is to declare them "Communists" or "fellow travelers." When this is done, other liberals, who actually know of their staunch Americanism, often refuse to associate with them personally, in groups, or on committees. One liberal, in analyzing the reasons why an interracial committee disbanded in New Orleans, cited as the main cause the fact that a member of the committee had been investigated by the House Committee on Un-American Activities. He said that the accused was never "proven to be a Communist, but a shadow was cast over him. This man knew that the members of the group wanted him to resign, but he refused to do so." This informer concluded, "I am inclined to believe that it was because he was naïve. He believes that each man has a right to his own beliefs. I would say that men can believe as they please, but that they do not have the right to jeopardize the rights of the others. All rights are thus conditioned." According to him, the committee disbanded, not because one of its members was a *proven* Communist, but because he had been *accused* of being a Communist. This is only one example of how insidiously effective the technique of name-calling is in limiting the number and influence of militant liberals.

Although there are no acknowledged liberals in municipal or state government posts in the city, there are a few white liberals who represent wealthy respected families with entree to city and state authorities. Using this advantage, some have been able to make significant contributions to the changing status of Negroes. In most cases, liberals negotiate with local authorities as preliminary steps in accomplishing some definite goal in race relations. The ultimate, most reliable, and certainly the most frequently used strategy is appeal to the federal government—that is, to Congress, the President, or the federal courts. These appeals generally come after a long period of skillful propaganda based upon evidences of discrimination and injustice. These evidences are compiled and analyzed in terms of the basic principle of equality of citizenship.

With what type of Negro leader will white liberals do business?

The race man. Perhaps the best insight into the personality of the race man is offered by Robert Johnson. According to him

> The "Race Man" is generally the spearhead of militant race leadership.
> . . . He has achieved a measure of personality adjustment on racial matters,
> but sees the world through race colored glasses and interprets most events
> in their racial context—how they will affect the Negro. . . . The "Race Man"
> is bitter not only at whites, but also at more accommodating Negro leader-
> ship, at the indifferent Negro masses who won't support him, at the more
> disorganized areas of Negro life, and at all persons who are able or qualified
> to help in the struggle for Negro rights, but refuse to do so.
> On the other hand, "Race Men" are favorably disposed toward all liberal
> elements in the community. . . .[7]

There has been no period in the history of Negroes in American society when there was not recognized militant Negro leadership, such as characterized here by the race man. In order to appreciate and properly evaluate the role of the race man in history, it is necessary to see him in his proper social context.

One of the distinguishing traits of the race man during the Negro's

[7]"Negro Reactions to Minority Group Status," in Milton L. Barron, Editor, *American Minorities* (New York: Alfred A. Knopf, 1957), p. 207

struggle for equal citizenship has been his unwillingness to compromise the basic principles of freedom and equality inherent in our American Creed. Historically, he has disagreed with such celebrated compromises as the all-Negro army unit, the "separate but equal" doctrine of race relations, and "token" integration. Though he realistically worked within the biracial framework, he has prophetically looked forward to total participation in American life. His greatest contribution is likely to have been his insistence that Negroes should unceasingly prepare to accept first-class citizenship, wherever it might be secured. Thus, in the most fundamental sense the race man never accepted racial segregation as a proper or workable way of life. He has always insisted that a biracial society is ethically and legally inconsistent with our democratic commitment.

One race man averred that he felt that the main purpose of all Negro organizations—colleges, churches, and particularly the NAACP—is to "improve race relations to the extent that they will no longer be necessary in American society." The fact is, this is the position formally taken by Negro lawyers in New Orleans who found it necessary to organize the all-Negro Martinet Legal Society, because they could not participate in the Louisiana Bar Association.[8] One of the stated objectives of this society is—

> To encourage and promote the full and complete integration of all lawyers irrespective of race, creed or color in the professional life and activities of the Louisiana Bar Association.

From this Guillory concluded that—

> As these objectives clearly suggest Negro lawyers regarded this segregated institution as first a temporary organization designed primarily to foster the integration of Negro lawyers into the professional life and activities of the Louisiana Bar Association.[9]

The race man differs significantly from both the Uncle Tom and the racial diplomat. The Uncle Tom, through his actions and public pronouncements, tends to accept the biracial system in the South as right. Therefore, he begs for the crumbs that fall from the tables of the dominant white majority. He is apparently satisfied to accept second-class citizenship if it is made at all tolerable. The Negro diplomat never quite accepts the biracial system as right or just. He has learned, however, to *work well* within the framework of the "separate but equal" doctrine. Accordingly, he has been successful in founding and maintaining influential institutions through which members of his race have greatly benefited. As a rule, however, his pronounced class prejudices have functioned to separate him from the masses and mass movements.

[8]The Louisiana Bar Association accepts only dues from Negro lawyers. They are not permitted to attend its meetings or otherwise participate.
[9]*Op. cit.,* pp. 66–67.

The race man, on the other hand, *has been a perennial enemy of the biracial system.* He has insisted that racial segregation of any kind is psychologically harmful, socially unworkable, and a legal contradiction. He has constantly voiced his protest in literature, music, public utterances, and organizational objectives. At all times he expresses a restlessness and declares his impatience with second-class citizenship. Examples of this attitude are legion. The following are typical:

A Negro minister expressed a militant "charisma"[10] at a "loyalty rally" just prior to the desegregation of buses in New Orleans. He said—

> God has given me a mission and I cannot be content until that mission is accomplished. I cannot sit idly by and see my people oppressed on every side and remain silent. I would rather be dead than to spend the balance of my days on my knees begging for what rightfully belongs to me and my people as human beings and as citizens of the United States of America. As soon as this cup passes, we will strive to register every eligible man and woman, so that we may boast of a citizenry of first-class citizens.

The ideology of the race man is well stated in the editorial platform of *The Louisiana Weekly:*

> *The Louisiana Weekly* shall work relentlessly for human and civil rights for all citizens and will expose those who appeal to prejudices rather than reason in their approach to problems concerning human relations. *The Louisiana Weekly* shall strive to mold public opinion in the interest of all things constructive.

When asked what he thought Negro uplift organizations should endeavor to achieve, an official of the NAACP answered—

> The first step should be to abolish all laws designed to discriminate against Negroes. Laws may not change the hearts of men, but they do affect what they will do. If there were no segregation laws, communication between the races could take place on a different plane—a plane of mutual respect. What Negroes want is not necessarily social equality—they want this too—but more than that they want human dignity.

In a prepared speech before a conference of Negro leaders, the chairman of an influential Negro organization summarized what he regarded as a creative approach to racial uplift. His statement also summarizes the ideology of the race man.

> The historical experiences through which the Negro has come are unparalleled in regard to deprivation and success; pain and pleasure; degradation and respect. This multitude of varied, unmatched experiences have uniquely prepared us for the kind of intelligent, courageous, understanding leadership our community, our nation and the free world so desperately needs. We have been conditioned by our own struggle for survival to the point that we

[10]According to Talcott Parsons, *The Social System* (Glencoe, Ill.: The Free Press, 1951), p. 402, "The charismatic leader plays an expressive leadership role where moral authority is claimed."

are able to identify with the universal struggle now going on for freedom and dignity. Perhaps no other race or ethnic group in history, not even the Jews, has ever been so inextricably involved in man's struggle for freedom and dignity as is the Negro race today.

At this moment in time, Negro leaders have two interrelated challenges:

1. We must recognize, first of all, that as Negro people we have a common goal and a common destiny. History, experience, and our enemies have made us one people. This we cannot escape. This we should not want to escape. Consequently, the success or failure, the suffering or joy of any one Negro anywhere on the face of the globe affects me and you because we are one with him.

2. As Negro leaders we are also challenged to transcend the narrow confines of race and realize our involvement in mankind. Therefore, Negro leadership must raise its sights above the issues and problems of Negro people only. It must come to realize that the Negro's struggle for full citizenship, though the most dramatic and perennial in modern history, is only one phase of the social revolution of our time. This revolution will continue until freedom and dignity can be claimed by all men regardless of race.
. . . Therefore, we must have a solidly organized Negro leadership class whose primary goal will be the complete abolition of racial segregation in our community.

The quotations cited indicate that the race man has a vital concern for the welfare of Negro people. He insists upon equality of citizenship. His ideology is based fundamentally on the American Creed. He constantly reminds America that it "must either live up to its democratic commitments or continue to be shamed before the world." More and more, he is coming to equate the Negro's efforts to attain first-class citizenship with the perennial struggles of mankind for freedom and dignity.

A clear statement of this position was made by Dr. Ralph J. Bunche, the Undersecretary for Special Political Affairs of the United Nations and winner of the Nobel laureate as mediator in the 1948–49 Palestine conflict. Speaking before the National Convention of the NAACP which met in Atlanta, Georgia in July, 1962, he said that he granted to anyone

the right to find me unacceptable as a person, as an individual; but never to indict my group and slur my ancestry as the reason for rejecting me.

The point is that no individual Negro can be free from the degradation of racial discrimination until every Negro is free of it.

There is no emancipation and no escape for the individual Negro American until the entire group is emancipated, there can be no dignity for one without dignity for all; no Negro can ever walk down any American street with full security and serenity until all Negroes can do so in every town; old or young, black, brown, or high yellow, the axiom applies to all alike.

Until all racial discrimination is ended here [Atlanta], the progress can never be fast enough and every deprived underprivileged Negro will be immensely impatient or he isn't worthy of the rights to which he is entitled and wishes to exercise.

The race man is *not a racist.* He is *not chauvinistic.* Instead, he sees himself as the Negro symbol of mankind's struggle for dignity. He does not apologize for his Negro-ness, yet he continues to insist that he is an American and feels that being Negro should not in any way limit the rights, duties, and opportunities inherent in American citizenship. He is, therefore, at ease when working with white liberals, to whom he is a natural complement.

It is true, of course, that most of his energy has been devoted to the Negro problem.[11] This has been a deliberate choice and race men often express guilt feelings because they would like to concern themselves with the broader problems of mankind. Some have felt compelled to spend practically all of their time in the unmasking of Negro stereotypes, fitting Negroes for full citizenship, and defending the Negro cause in courts and before a critical public opinion. This compulsion to dedicate himself to his people was dramatically expressed by an outstanding Negro writer. He said that he had devoted about twenty years to writing on Negro life and problems. During that time he had several widely read books published. In the last of these books, he lamented that he had felt compelled to dedicate himself to the Negro cause. He vowed that he would make no further statement about the problem because he had earned the right to a commitment to something outside himself which is necessary to human and humanistic development.[12]

We may conclude, then, that in the biracial society of New Orleans, the type of Negro leader who can get things done is determined very largely by the type of white leader with whom he must do business. Consequently, if we would properly understand and evaluate the changing status of Negroes we must take into consideration at least three basic race relations leadership patterns: Segregationists who prefer to work through *Uncle Toms, moderates* who work well with *racial diplomats,* and *liberals* who find ideological kinship with the *race man.*

We do not imply that only one of these patterns operates in race relations at a given time. Actually, in New Orleans, and perhaps throughout the South, all of these patterns can be detected, especially when racial crises are imminent or present. It is true, however, that in different social contexts one pattern may be more prominent and effective than other patterns.

It should be clear that the patterns of race relations leadership discussed above, in a strict sociological sense, involve complementary roles certain leaders elect to play. These patterns are not meant to describe the personalities or character of the leaders. Though personality factors do tend to limit the different roles an individual may play, theoretically an in-

[11]This has been true, also, of southern white liberals.
[12]J. Saunders Redding, *On Being A Negro in America* (Indianapolis: Bobbs-Merrill Co., 1951), pp. 25–27.

dividual may, at one time or another, play the appropriate complementary role in each of the three major race relations patterns analyzed. For example, the race man is occasionally pressured into playing the role of the racial diplomat because the Negro community needs things done, and there are no liberals in authority with whom he can do business. Therefore, out of expediency, he is sometimes led into negotiations and compromises that fall short of his desired goals. Thus, for example, some race men in New Orleans accepted the "pupil placement" plan for school desegregation and tried to make it work, though their goal was still total integration. It is in this regard that the race man is often absorbed by the racial diplomats in order that he may do business with influential moderates.

It should be pointed out that the race man is seldom flexible enough to adjust to the Uncle Tom role. This is an important reason why there have been several crises in race relations in New Orleans since 1956. Specifically, segregationists in positions of authority have had no reliable Negro complements with whom they were willing to negotiate because their natural complements, the Uncle Toms, are generally discredited. More and more the Negro community rejects the Uncle Tom, and since white men of power tend to refuse to do business with Negro diplomats and race men, an impasse in race relations has developed. This impasse can only be countered by what Dr. Mays refers to as "straight talk" between Negro and white leaders.[13] This communication must not be based upon wishful thinking or half-truths, as has been characteristic of the segregationists and the Uncle Toms in the past, but must be honest communication based upon mutual respect.

---

[13]Benjamin E. Mays, "A Plea for Straight Talk Between the Races," *The Atlantic,* December 1960.

eleven

Why are Blacks poor? What does it mean to be poor in a materialistic society? As Black Americans attempt to close the income gap between themselves and White Americans, we can expect strong efforts to end job and union discrimination. In the meantime, what patterns emerge within the ghetto among those attempting to increase their own personal economic positions?

Economic System

In order to subsist men must provide themselves with certain basic items such as food, clothing, and shelter. Beyond these essentials, men also come to desire other things. The nature of such additional wants, as well as the manner in which basic needs are fulfilled, are primarily determined by culture. Needs and wants involve material goods but may also include services such as transportation or education. Because available resources are usually scarce and because men must work together to produce the required goods and services, some forms of organization are necessary. The economy of a society is the sum of the processes by which goods and services are produced, distributed, and consumed.

Societies differ greatly in the size and complexity of their economies. The economy of a given society may also change over time, as when an agricultural society undergoes industrialization. The actual form of an economy depends upon many factors. Among the most important are: the nature of available resources, the state of technology, the values and goals of the society, and the prevailing economic ideology or philosophy.

In the production and distribution of goods and services the American economy might be characterized as having an advanced industrial technology and a high degree of specialization and coordination among its unit parts. Within this system money is used as the medium of exchange. Distribution and trade take place in the competitive setting of an open market, although political agencies increasingly regulate economic activity. Because of the growth of large corporations there is an increasing tendency for people to work for others, to be employees rather than entrepreneurs. Such growth also means that economic power is becoming concentrated in the hands of a few, though labor unions and governmental bodies are able to restrict the power of owners and managers. Ideally all economic activity is highly rational, efficient, and designed to maximize profit. In practice, however, values, customs, obligations, and the complex interrelationship between the economy and other parts of society serve as limiting factors.

Consumption patterns differ within American society and are primarily determined by level of income. So, for example, the poor spend a high proportion of their income on food and housing. Consumption is also influenced by level of education, prior experiences, social and marital status, ethnicity, area of residence, age, and sex. Differences in consumption patterns between groups in society are usually seen as differences in styles of living. A large proportion of Black Americans are unable to find jobs with good incomes, and, as a result, many have consumption patterns and a style of life characteristic of the lower class.

Most Black Americans do not acquire the skills and knowledge necessary to fill meaningful and important jobs. Discrimination in hiring, placement, promotions, and training programs, and the exclusionary practices of labor unions often prevent those with adequate preparation from attaining occupations that are equal to their qualifications. As a result Blacks are predominately found in the lower layers of the occupational structure and are often working in marginal positions where employment is only temporary. This condition is reflected in extremely high rates of unemployment and in the wide and increasing income gap between Blacks and other members of society. This level of occupational attainment is also reflected in a style of living that so often includes inadequate housing and diet, little or no health protection or insurance, family instability, a high rate of deviance, and welfare dependency.

In recent years efforts have been made to help alleviate these problems. Some organizations and unions have sought to remove their discriminatory practices and have made attempts to recruit more Black employees. Federal, state, and local governments have passed fair employment legislation and have allocated funds for job training programs. However, these and other efforts have largely been ineffective.

One small but important source of employment is the jobs within the Black community. Though many of the commercial and business establishments in the ghetto are not owned or operated by Blacks, the community has often found it necessary to provide some services for itself. Black entrepreneurs have established small businesses such as grocery stores, luncheonettes, bars and taverns, funeral homes, cleaning establishments, barbershops, and beauty parlors. In a few areas Blacks operate banks, insurance firms, and community newspapers. But the level of Black business activity has always been low because of the lack of available capital and business knowledge within the community. In addition many services have always been provided by others. Recent efforts by governmental agencies and banks to make capital available coupled with an increasing desire among some Blacks to control the services in the ghetto have resulted in some increases in Black capitalism. It remains to be seen whether such commercial ventures will become a significant source of employment.

Rashi Fein discusses unemployment, occupations, and income level, comparing statistics for whites and nonwhites. The Black American is more likely to be unemployed and for a longer period of time than his white counterpart. It is significant that the highest rates of unemployment appear in a highly discontented and volatile segment of the Black community, the young males. As expected, Blacks are found in the lowest portions of the occupational structure. This is reflected in their income levels. Although Black incomes are rising, so are those of the rest of society, and the gap remains. Though much of the Black's economic situation can be attributed to a lack of formal education, Fein notes that outright discrimination is also an important determinant. Thus " . . . the Negro who has attended (but not completed) college earns less than the white with only 8 years of elementary school . . . ."

John Horton presents a description of street life in the ghetto. In order to supplement other sources of income many of the young men turn to "hustling" activities such as stealing, gambling, pimping, and drug peddling. Much of street life revolves around hustling, which represents, in part, an adaptation by one segment of the ghetto to an oppressive economic situation. It is unfortunate that the personal qualities necessary to successfully adapt and survive in such a setting do not readily lend themselves to participation in the world of work outside the ghetto. The activities of street life give some indication of the obstacles that must be met by any solutions to the economic problem. They are also evidence of the immense differences that exist between Blacks and the rest of society.

THE SITUATION

"An Economic and Social Profile of the Negro American"

by Rashi Fein

In the author's preface to *An American Dilemma,* [1] Gunnar Myrdal wrote that he was a "stranger" to the American scene and that "Things look different, depending upon 'where you stand.' " It is also true that things look different, depending upon where you look. The profile of the Negro American is a changing profile. What one sees depends on what one looks at, on the period that one examines, and on the comparisons one makes. Our profile will not "look." It will "look different" or "look similar." Without comparisons its significance would be limited.

In this essay I examine a variety of socioeconomic indicators. I do so for various points in time in order to compare the world in which the

[1]Gunnar Myrdal, *An American Dilemma* (New York, 1944), p. xviii.

Negro American lives with the world in which he lived and with the world (both past and present) of the white American. Always we shall compare. For, as indicated, the data have meaning only as they are compared. They may be compared with an American ideal; they may be compared with a potential; they may be compared with the past; but compared they must be. Roosevelt's "one-third of a nation" could be contrasted with the remaining two-thirds and Martin Luther King's dream with a present reality. To understand where the Negro American stands today requires a frame of reference. . . .

Let us examine unemployment. Today the Negro faces an unemployment situation unknown to the white for almost two and one-half decades —and the Negro has been facing it for a number of years. What is recession for the white (say, an unemployment rate of 6 per cent) is prosperity for the nonwhite. He last saw an unemployment rate below 7.5 per cent in 1953—a full decade ago. In 1964, when the total unemployment rate for white males twenty years old and over was 3.4 per cent, the nonwhite rate was over twice as high—7.7 per cent. The rate for Negro females aged twenty and over was almost twice as high as for whites, and this was also the case for males and females combined (aged fourteen to nineteen). In 1964—a prosperity year—the Negro confronted an unemployment rate (9.8 per cent) more than 50 per cent higher than the highest rate faced by whites at any time since the great depression. Surely, the Negro must feel wry as he considers the debate about the level of unemployment that shall be considered full employment. His employment rate has not reached the "interim target" of 4.0 per cent a single time in the postwar period.

Let me make it clear that I do not say that the Negro fails to share in upward movements of the economy. He does share in prosperity—just as he is hurt by recessions. There *are* differences between unemployment rates for Negro males of 4.4 per cent in 1953, 13.7 per cent in 1958, and 9.1 per cent in 1964. It is a fact, however, that Negro unemployment rates are higher than white rates at the same moment in time and that the Negro *frequently* faces unemployment rates which—if faced by all workers—would be considered a national scandal. The fact is that the unemployment rate for Negroes in 1964, a year of general prosperity, was over one and one-half times as large as that for whites in *any* of the postwar recessions. Therefore, perhaps, it is appropriate to say that whites fluctuate between prosperity and recession but Negroes fluctuate between depression and great depression.

The difference in over-all white and Negro unemployment rates is not explained entirely by a different age-sex structure. Negro unemployment rates for every age-sex grouping (except for women over fifty-five) are higher—sometimes far higher—than the highest postwar rate for whites in the same age-sex group. We spoke of *fluctuations* between depression and great or deep depression. But for some of the age-sex groups—particularly, but not exclusively, among teen-agers—unemployment rates appear perpetually high: the unemployment rate for male Negroes aged sixteen and seventeen was last below 20 per cent in 1957 (it reached 31 per cent in 1961); it was last below 20 per cent for males aged eighteen and nineteen in 1956; and it was last below 10 per cent for males aged twenty to twenty-four in 1953. In only five of the seventeen years since 1948 has the rate for Negro females aged eighteen and nineteen been below 15 per cent and it has not been below 20 per cent in the last eleven years.

The differential in unemployment rates presents a real and severe problem. It is a problem requiring special attention and strong specific (as well as general) measures. Indeed, it may require relatively stronger action than would have been necessary fifteen years ago. At that time (in 1950) the white unemployment rate was 4.6 per cent and the nonwhite was 8.5 per cent (1.6 times the white). In 1964, with a white rate again at 4.6 per cent, the nonwhite rate was up to 9.8 per cent (2.1 times the white).

And when the Negro is unemployed, it is for a longer period of time. In 1964, nonwhites represented 11 per cent of the labor force and 21 per cent of the unemployed, but they accounted for 23 per cent of those unemployed fifteen weeks or longer and 25 per cent of those unemployed for over half a year. In 1963, 27 per cent of white, but 35 per cent of nonwhite unemployed males were unemployed fifteen weeks or more and 14 per cent of white but 20 per cent of nonwhite unemployed males were unemployed twenty-seven weeks or more. The average duration of unemployment for white males was slightly under fifteen weeks, for nonwhites slightly over nineteen.

Finally, it should be noted that Negroes, when employed, are more likely to be working only part time. In 1963, for example, while 81 per cent of whites at work in nonagricultural industries worked full time, this was true of only 74 per cent of nonwhites. Only 3.1 per cent of whites worked part time for economic reasons—slack work, inability to find full-time work—but this was the case for 9.6 per cent of employed nonwhites. The average number of hours worked by those employed was 8 per cent higher for white males than for nonwhite males.

The Negro faces higher unemployment rates, more frequent periods of unemployment in a given year, longer duration of unemployment, more part-time rather than full-time work—and all this is true even when occupation is held constant. The often-heard comment that the differentials result from the fact that nonwhites have a disadvantageous occupational structure is only partly true. Thus, for example, 6 per cent of white professional and technical workers with work experience in 1962 were unemployed for some time during the year, but this was true of 11 per cent of nonwhites (and while 6 per cent of white male professionals had worked at part-time jobs, 12 per cent of nonwhites had done so). Twelve per cent of white but 18 per cent of nonwhite clerical workers were unemployed in 1962 (and while 25 per cent of the white unemployed clerical workers were unemployed for fifteen or more weeks, this was the case for 38 per cent of the nonwhite unemployed). Thirty-two per cent of white laborers had some unemployment in 1962 but 45 per cent of nonwhites did (and while 50 per cent of whites had two or more spells of unemployment, 69 per cent of nonwhites did).

We have indicated that the unemployment situation is worse for Negroes than for whites even if we correct for occupational structure of the Negro labor force. But it is also true that the unfavorable occupational structure does contribute to the problem. In addition, it affects more than unemployment rates (and income). The sharply different occupational structure among Negroes surely has an impact on the child and narrows his horizons. In 1963—as in earlier years—the white child, for example, had a far greater opportunity to meet white-collar workers than did the Negro child: 47 per cent of whites were so employed, but only 18 per cent of Negroes. While the data are rough, it would appear that already in 1900, when we were still a heavily agricultural country, the percentage of white-collar workers in the white population was 18 per cent—a lag of some sixty years. Similarly, in 1963 about 13 per cent of employed Negroes were laborers (except farm and mine)—the same percentage as in the white population of 1900 (a percentage which for whites had gradually declined to 4 per cent by 1963).

Thus our Negro child grows up in a world in which opportunity seems closed. And surely his aspirations are in part influenced by the achievements of other Negroes. In 1960, when 10 per cent of the male experienced labor force was nonwhite, only 3.5 per cent of male professionals, technical, and kindred workers were nonwhite (and perhaps one-quarter of these were not Negro). Only 1.4 per cent of accountants and auditors were nonwhite, 1.7 per cent of engineers, 1.3 per cent of lawyers and judges, 1.3 per cent of salaried managers, officials, and proprietors, 2.0 per cent of bookkeepers (and 6.8 per cent of clerical and kindred workers), 2.1 per cent of sales workers, and 4.9 per cent of craftsmen, foremen, and kindred workers (all data for males only). But the 10 per cent proportion of the labor force was exceeded in some occupations: 48.4 per cent of private household workers are nonwhite, 26.1 per cent of laborers, and we find large percentages for other occupations at the bottom rungs of the occupational ladder. When a nonwhite child met an employed nonwhite, the chances that he was meeting a janitor were six times as great and the chances that he was meeting an engineer were only one-sixth as great as when a white child met a white employee. There are thirty-one times as many nonwhite male janitors as nonwhite engineers but more white engineers than white janitors. Almost twice as many nonwhite males are professional and technical workers, but only one-tenth as many whites are janitors as are professionals. Over four times as many nonwhite males are janitors as are sales workers, but almost seven times as many whites are sales workers as are janitors. And the situation among females, where nonwhites represent 13 per cent of the experienced labor force, is similar: 55 per cent of the private household workers are non-white. Surely our Negro child aspires to a higher occupational achievement than nonwhites now have, but how difficult the road ahead appears (and is) when he confronts today's nonwhite occupational distribution.

The difference in educational attainment accounts for much, but not all, of the difference found in occupational structure. In 1962, for example, 20 per cent of nonwhite male high-school graduates were laborers. This was true of only 4 per cent of white male high-school graduates. Even among white males with an elementary education or less, the equivalent percentage was only 9 per cent. Nineteen per cent of nonwhite females with some college were private household workers but this was virtually unknown (1 per cent) among white females who had attended college. It was not even as high as 19 per cent (only 13 per cent) for white females with zero to eight years of elementary school.

The interrelation of the various parts of our description is depressing— the relative disadvantage in one area causes and is caused by disadvantages in another area. Relatively high unemployment and a disadvantageous occupational structure, for example, both contribute to lower incomes for Negroes than for whites. We now examine income patterns. What are our child's chances in that area?

In 1964 the Negro family with income had a median income of $3839 —only 56 per cent of that for white families. White families had reached a $3800 income level back in 1951, but the situation is worse than is implied by this thirteen-year gap. Negroes in 1964 purchased commodities at 1964 prices, while whites in 1951 purchased at substantially lower 1951 prices. If we correct for price changes and compare income in dollars with 1964 purchasing power, we find that white income, even as far back as 1947, exceeded present Negro income by, perhaps, 10 to 15 per cent. Census data permit more detailed analysis. Using constant 1959 dollars (dollars with the same purchasing power), we find that in 1960 13.7 per cent of all Negro families had annual total money income of under $1,000 and 32.1 per cent had incomes of under $2,000. Even as long ago as 1947 this was true of only 6.5 per cent and 19.1 per cent of all white families. The lag is found among urban, rural nonfarm, and rural farm families (Table 1).

In 1960 the urban nonwhite caught up to the 1947 level for rural nonfarm whites. The urban white had, of course, achieved this level many years before 1947. To say that in 1960 the *urban* Negro family had the same real money income that the white *rural nonfarm* family had in 1947, to say that in 1960 the median Negro family had an income equal to the

Table 1. Median Annual Money Income and Percentage of Families Below
Specified Income Levels, by Residence and Color, 1947 and 1960

		(Income levels expressed in dollars with 1959 purchasing power)	
	Median income	*Per Cent of Families*	
		Below $1,000	*Below $2,000*
Urban nonwhite 1960	$3,844	7.0	21.8
Urban white 1947	4,544	3.6	10.8
Rural nonfarm nonwhite 1960	2,000	24.8	50.0
Rural nonfarm white 1947	3,809	6.6	17.0
Rural farm nonwhite 1960	1,155	44.0	77.3
Rural farm white 1947	2,827	16.4	34.9

median white *farm* family is to point up the substantial lag and gap in income.

In 1964 the relative situation was only slightly better: 7.7 per cent of Negro families had incomes below $1,000 (measured in 1964 dollars) but this was true for only 2.7 per cent of whites. Our child had a twenty-two in one hundred chance (unadjusted for differential birth rates by income) of being born to a family with an income below $2,000. A white child would have an eight in one hundred chance. Our child has only a two in one hundred chance of being born in a family with income over $15,000 (eight in one hundred for income of over $10,000). For a white child the chances are seven and twenty-four in one hundred respectively.

If we use a poverty standard—families with incomes under $3,000—the chances in 1963 were forty-three in one hundred that our child was born into a family in poverty (by 1964 the chances were down to thirty-seven in one hundred). It is of course true, as many have pointed out, that the large majority of poor families are white (after all, an even greater majority of all families are white). A program to eliminate poverty cannot, therefore, be successful if it addresses itself only to Negroes. However, the Negro has a far greater chance (almost three times as great) of being in poverty than does the white. Even as late as 1963 the percentage of Negro families in poverty was 50 per cent higher than the white level had been sixteen years earlier in 1947 (measured in 1963 constant dollars). To whom can we ask the Negro to compare himself if he is to have some degree of hope? Apparently only to himself at some earlier period—in 1947 two-thirds of Negro families were poor—but not to the rest of America which already in 1947 was better off than the Negro was in 1963 and which, since 1947, had a decline of 30 per cent in the number of poor families while the number of poor Negro families (in part as a result of the increase in the absolute number of families) *increased* by 2 per cent.

In discussions of income data, the point is often, and validly, made that the worker's educational attainment is an important determinant of income. It is surely small comfort for the Negro to be told that his present low income status is due to his lack of education. Explanations do not assist in making purchases; only money does. Analysis is not a substitute for cash. Perhaps the analysis does make the income determination process a less personal one—things were "determined" at some earlier period, and we are all now acting out our roles. But there is a difficulty with this—even aside from the fact that the Negro's low educational attainment itself is the result of discrimination. The difficulty is that low education does not provide the total explanation for low income. As with a number of variables already discussed, simply being Negro also makes a difference. For in 1963 our Negro child's family had a median income of $4,530 if the family head completed high school. But the white family with the same years of education for the head had an income of $6,997 —almost 55 per cent more. Indeed, if the white had but eight years of schooling, his income was $5,454, 20 per cent more than for the Negro high-school graduate. Nor are these unfavorable comparisons isolated cases: The Negro family whose head had some high school earned less than the white with fewer than eight years of schooling; *the Negro who has attended (but not completed) college earns less than the white with only eight years of elementary school,* the Negro college graduate earns but slightly more than does the white high-school graduate. Surely there are differences in the quality of education. In parts of the nation a year of Negro education was not (and is not) equal to a year of white education. Nevertheless, to argue that there is no discrimination in employment and income requires that we argue that the Negro with some college knows no more than does the white with only eight years of elementary school. This is hard to accept. And, surely, the value of an education is less clear when, for those who attended college, Negro male income is only 60 per cent of white male income, but is 68 per cent for those who only completed high school and 73 per cent for those who only attended elementary school. In a survey conducted in February 1963, it was found that 73 per cent of males aged sixteen to twenty-one who had completed less than four years of high school earned $40 a week or more on their first full-time job. This was true for only 41 per cent of nonwhite males. Conversely, 27 per cent of all males, but only 11 per cent of nonwhite males earned more than $60 a week.

It is important to realize the story these data tell. It is true that we cannot correct for quality of education—that the data measure only years of education not amount taught or learned. But even taking this into account, and even taking into account the fact that Negroes reside disproportionately in the South (a low income region), it is clear that, important as education may be, it does not offer a complete explanation of low

Negro incomes. It is a simple fact that the Negro is *qualified* for higher occupational levels and for higher incomes than he attains. The data document a story of discrimination. Some may pessimistically conclude that it is harder to eliminate discrimination than to raise levels of education. I would respond that, painful as is the story the data reveal, there are grounds for optimism. We need not wait until today's and tomorrow's (better educated) youths become adults to increase incomes and raise occupational levels. Discrimination may be harder to combat than poor education—though even this is not certain. But it can be combated *in the short run.* To raise education and reap its rewards must take time—considerable time. But if discrimination accounts for much (though not all) of the income disparity—and I conclude that it does—we can make more rapid, more immediate progress. Perhaps as little as one-third of the total disparity between white and nonwhite incomes is due to less years of education.[2] Corrections for quality of education and geographic distribution of population would lower the proportion that can be accounted for by discrimination. Nevertheless, substantial income increases could result —even with today's educational levels—as a consequence of the elimination of discrimination. Surely we favor better and more education, but we need not wait for the effects of today's better education to take hold a decade hence.

Perhaps the discrimination that exists can be illustrated by comparing 1959 median nonwhite and white earnings for a series of occupations. We also present data for median years of school completed for nonwhites and for the total population in the particular occupation, thus pointing up the fact that differences in income exist even in occupations where high levels of education are not a requisite. Of course, in many of the occupations, experience on the job has had an opportunity to overcome the influence of poor education. Yet, even so, differentials remain.

How low the family's income is will depend, in part, on the region in which the family resides. But the differences between white and nonwhite income are large in all regions. First, income is reduced because, while almost two-thirds of white families are headed by a year-round full-time worker, only one-half of Negro families are so headed. These differences are found in all regions except the West. Furthermore, family income— even if the head is fully employed—is lower for the nonwhite (again in all regions): In the Northeast it is 70 per cent of white, in the North Central 83 per cent, in the South 51 per cent, and in the West 86 per cent. If account is taken of lower full-time employment as well as lower earnings, the percentage that nonwhite family income is of white family income drops significantly to 65, 73, 45, and 76 per cent respectively for the four regions. Clearly, there are large differences among regions. Equally

[2] Derived from data released by the Council of Economic Advisers, "Economic Costs of Racial Discrimination in Employment" (Washington, D. C., September 24, 1962).

Table 2. *Median Income and Median Years of School Completed, Total Population and Nonwhite, by Occupation, 1959*

Occupation	Median Income		Median Years of School Completed	
	Nonwhite	Total	Nonwhite	Total
Bakers	$3354	$4633	8.9	9.2
Carpenters	2320	4271	8.1	9.3
Welders and flame-cutters	4454	5116	9.6	9.7
Elevator operators	3122	3487	8.7	8.6
Automobile mechanics	3173	4372	8.9	9.9
Tinsmiths, coppersmiths, and sheet metal workers	4710	5542	11.1	10.8

clearly, the situation is an unhappy one in all regions.

Our Negro child has been born into a family that is substantially poorer than the average white family. In part, this is because the Negro family head has less education than the white, earns less even at the same levels of education, has less chance of year-round full-time employment. All this most of us know. But startling is the fact that there has been very little change in the ratio of nonwhite family income to white family income over the last decade and a half (there had been extremely rapid progress in the first half of the decade of the 1940's). In 1947 the ratio of nonwhite to white family income was .51 and, though it reached .57 in 1952 (with progress from 1950 to 1952), it had fallen back to .51 in 1958 and stood at .56 in 1964. This was true in spite of the considerable outmigration during the 1950's of Negroes from the South to higher income regions. As has been shown,[3] the ratio of Negro to white income for males fell during the period 1949 to 1959 in every region of the country. Thus, even despite outmigration, the ratio of nonwhite to white male income in the nation fell in the decade of the 1950's. Progress in reducing the disparity in income ratios has been concentrated in periods of tight labor markets (parts of the 1940's and the early 1950's) but it is unfortunate for all of us and most unfortunate for Negroes that many years have passed since the United States has faced tight labor markets. . . .

Sources

Data from the following general sources: U. S. Bureau of the Census, *Statistical Abstract of the United States: 1964* (85th edn.: Washington, D. C., 1964) and earlier *Abstracts;* U. S. Bureau of the Census, *Historical Statistics of the United States, Colonial Times to 1957* (Washington, D. C.,

[3] Alan Batchelder, "Decline in the Relative Income of Negro Men," *Quarterly Journal of Economics,* Vol. 78, No. 4 (November 1964), 525–48.

1960); Donald J. Bogue, *The Population of the United States* (Glencoe, Ill., 1959).

Employment, unemployment, and occupation data from: U. S. Department of Labor, *A Report on Manpower Requirements, Resources, Utilization, and Training* (Washington, D. C., March 1965), and reports issued in 1964 and 1963; U. S. Department of Labor, Bureau of Labor Statistics, *Special Labor Force Report,* No. 43, "Labor Force and Employment in 1963" and *Special Labor Force Report,* No. 38, "Work Experience of the Population in 1962"; U. S. Bureau of the Census, *U. S. Census of Population: 1960, Subject Reports, Occupational Characteristics,* Final Report PC(2)-7A, (Washington, D. C., 1963).

Income data from: U. S. Bureau of the Census, *Current Population Reports: Income of Families and Persons in the United States, 1963,* Series P-60 No. 43 (Washington, D. C., September 29, 1964); U. S. Bureau of the Census, *Trends in the Income of Families and Persons in the United States: 1947 to 1960,* Technical Paper No. 8 (Washington, D. C., 1963); Council of Economic Advisers, *Annual Report of the Council of Economic Advisers,* (Washington, D. C., 1964); U. S. Department of Labor, Bureau of Labor Statistics, *Special Labor Force Report,* No. 46, "Out of School Youth, February, 1963"; U. S. Bureau of the Census, *Current Population Reports, Average Family Income up 5 Percent in 1964,* Series P-60, No. 44, (Washington, D. C., May 27, 1965); U. S. Bureau of the Census, *Current Population Reports, Low-Income Families and Unrelated Individuals in the United States: 1963,* Series P-60, No. 45 (Washington, D. C., June 18, 1965).

Housing data from: U. S. Bureau of the Census, U. S. Census of Housing: 1960, Vol. 1, *States and Small Areas, United States Summary,* Final Report HC(1)-1, (Washington, D. C., 1963).

The interested reader will also find useful a variety of U. S. government publications which frequently present white-nonwhite data. The Bureau of the Census, Bureau of Labor Statistics, and Social Security Administration are among the agencies which publish occasional reports and articles of interest.

"Time and Cool People"

by John Horton

Street culture exists in every low income ghetto. It is shared by the hustling elements of the poor, whatever their nationality or color. In Los Angeles, members of such street groups sometimes call themselves "street people," "cool people," or simply "regulars." Whatever the label, they are known the world over by outsiders as hoods or hoodlums, persons who live on and off the street. They are recognizable by their own fashions in dress, hair, gestures, and speech. The particular fashion varies with time, place, and nationality. For example, in 1963 a really sharp Los Angeles street Negro would be "conked to the bone" (have processed hair) and "togged-out" in "continentals." Today "natural" hair and variations of mod clothes are coming in style.

Street people are known also by their activities—"duking" (fighting or at least looking tough), "hustling" (any way of making money outside the "legitimate" world of work), "gigging" (partying)—and by their apparent nonactivity, "hanging" on the corner. Their individual roles are defined concretely by their success or failure in these activities. One either knows "what's happening" on the street, or he is a "lame," "out of it," "not ready" (lacks his diploma in street knowledge), a "square."

There are, of course, many variations. Negroes, in particular, have contributed much to the street tongue which has diffused into both the more hip areas of the middle class and the broader society. Such expressions as "a lame," "taking care of righteous business," "getting down to the nitty-gritty," and "soul" can be retraced to Negro street life.

The more or less organized center of street life is the "set"—meaning both the peer group and the places where it hangs out. It is the stage and central market place for activity, where to find out what's happening. My set of Negro street types contained a revolving and sometimes disappearing (when the "heat," or police pressure, was on) population of about 45 members ranging in age from 18 to 25. These were the local "dudes," their term meaning not the fancy city slickers but simply "the boys," "fellas," the "cool people." They represented the hard core of street culture, the role models for younger teenagers. The dudes could be found when they were "laying dead"—hanging on the corner, or shooting pool and "jiving" ("goofing" or kidding around) in a local community project. Isolated from "the man" (in this context the man in power—the police, and by extension, the white man), they lived in a small section of Venice outside the central Los Angeles ghetto and were surrounded by a predominantly Mexican and Anglo population. They called their black "turf" "Ghost-town"—home of the "Ghostmen," their former gang. Whatever the origin of the word, Ghost-town was certainly the home of socially "invisible" men.

The Street Set

In 1965 and 1966 I had intensive interviews with 25 set members. My methods emerged in day to day observations. Identified as white, a lame, and square, I had to build up an image of being at least "legit" (not working for police). Without actually living in the area, this would have been impossible without the aid of a key fieldworker, in this case an outsider who could be accepted inside. This field worker, Cowboy, was a white dude of 25. He had run with "Paddy" (white), "Chicano" (Mexican), and "Blood" (Negro) sets since the age of 12 and was highly respected for having been president of a tough gang. He knew the street, how to duke, move with style, and speak the tongue. He made my entry possible. I was the underprivileged child who had to be taught slowly and sympathetically the common-sense features of street life.

Cowboy had the respect and I the toleration of several set leaders. After that, we simply waited for the opportunity to "rap." Although sometimes used synonymously with street conversation, "rap" is really a special way of talking—repartee. Street repartee at its best is a lively way of "running it down," or of "jiving" (attempting to put someone on), of trying "to blow another person's mind," forcing him "to lose his cool," to give in or give up something. For example, one needs to throw a lively rap when he is "putting the make on a broad."

Sometimes we taped individuals, sometimes "soul sessions." We asked for life histories, especially their stories about school, job, and family. We watched and asked about the details of daily surviving and attempted to construct street time schedules. We probed beyond the past and present into the future in two directions—individual plans for tomorrow and a lifetime, and individual dreams of a more decent world for whites and Negroes.

The set can be described by the social and attitudinal characteristics of its members. To the observer, these are expressed in certain realities of day to day living: not enough skill for good jobs, and the inevitable trouble brought by the problem of surviving. Of the 25 interviewed, only four had graduated from high school. Except for a younger set member who was still in school, all were dropouts, or perhaps more accurately kicked-outs. None was really able to use or write formal language. However, many were highly verbal, both facile and effective in their use of the street tongue. Perhaps the art of conversation is most highly developed here where there is much time to talk, perhaps too much—an advantage of the *lumpen*-leisure class.

Their incomes were difficult to estimate, as "bread" or "coins" (money) came in on a very irregular basis. Of the 17 for whom I have figures, half reported that they made less than $1,400 in the last year, and the rest claimed income from $2,000-$4,000 annually. Two-thirds were living with and partially dependent on their parents, often a mother. The financial strain was intensified by the fact that although 15 of 17 were single, eight had one or more children living in the area. (Having children, legitimate or not, was not a stigma but proof of masculinity.)

At the time of the interview, two-thirds of them had some full- or part-time employment—unskilled and low-paid jobs. The overall pattern was one of sporadic and—from their viewpoint—often unsatisfactory work, followed by a period of unemployment compensation, and petty hustling whenever possible and whenever necessary.

When I asked the question, "When a dude needs bread, how does he get it?" the universal response was "the hustle." Hustling is, of course, illegitimate from society's viewpoint. Street people know it is illegal, but they view it in no way as immoral or wrong. It is justified by the necessity of surviving. As might be expected, the unemployed admitted that they hustled and went so far as to say that a dude could make it better on the street than on the job: "There is a lot of money on the street, and there are many ways of getting it," or simply, "This has always been my way of life." On the other hand, the employed, the part-time hustlers, usually said, "A dude could make it better on the job than on the street." Their reasons for disapproving of hustling were not moral. Hustling meant trouble. "I don't hustle because there's no security. You eventually get busted." Others said there was not enough money on the street or that it was too difficult to "run a game" on people.

Nevertheless, hustling is the central street activity. It is the economic foundation for everyday life. Hustling and the fruit of hustling set the rhythm of social activities.

What are the major forms of hustling in Ghost-town? The best hustles were conning, stealing, gambling, and selling dope. By gambling, these street people meant dice; by dope, peddling "pills" and "pot." Pills are "reds" and "whites"—barbiturates and benzedrine or dexedrine. Pot is, of course, marijuana—"grass" or "weed." To "con" means to put "the bump" on a "cat," to "run a game" on somebody, to work on his mind for goods and services.

The "woman game" was common. As one dude put it, "If I have a good lady and she's on County, there's always some money to get." In fact, there is a local expression for getting county money. When the checks come in for child support, it's "mother's day." So the hustler "burns" people for money, but he also "rips off" goods for money; he thieves, and petty thieving is always a familiar hustle. Pimping is often the hustler's dream of the good life, but it was almost unknown here among the small-time hustlers. That was the game of the real professional and required a higher level of organization and wealth.

Hustling means bread and security but also trouble, and trouble is a major theme in street life. The dudes had a "world of trouble" (a popular song about a hustler is "I'm in a World of Trouble")—with school, jobs, women, and the police. The intensity of street life could be gauged in part by the intensity of the "heat" (police trouble). The hotter the street, the fewer the people visible on the street. On some days the set was empty. One would soon learn that there had been a "bust" (an arrest). Freddy had run amok and thrown rocks at a police car. There had been a leadership struggle; "Big Moe" had been cut up, and the "fuzz" had descended. Life was a succession of being picked up on suspicion of assault, theft, possession, "suspicion of suspicion" (an expression used by a respondent in describing his life). This was an ordinary experience for the street dude and often did lead to serious trouble. Over half of those interviewed claimed they had felony convictions.

The Structure of Street Time

Keeping cool and out of trouble, hustling bread, and looking for something interesting and exciting to do created the structure of time on the street. The rhythm of time is expressed in the high and low points in the day and week of an unemployed dude. I stress the pattern of the unemployed and full-time hustler because he is on the street all day and night and is the prototype in my interviews. The sometimes employed will also know the pattern, and he will be able to hit the street whenever released from the bondage of jail, work, and the clock. Here I describe a typical time schedule gleaned through interviews and field observation.

Characteristically the street person gets up late, hits the street in the late morning or early afternoon, and works his way to the set. This is a place for relaxed social activity. Hanging on the set with the boys is the major way of passing time and waiting until some necessary or desirable action occurs. Nevertheless, things do happen on the set. The dudes "rap" and "jive" (talk), gamble, and drink their "pluck" (usually a cheap, sweet wine). They find out what happened yesterday, what is happening today, and what will hopefully happen on the weekend—the perpetual search for the "gig," the party. Here peer socialization and reinforcement also take place. The younger dude feels a sense of pride when he can be on the set and throw a rap to an older dude. He is learning how to handle himself, show respect, take care of business, and establish his own "rep."

On the set, yesterday merges into today, and tomorrow is an emptiness to be filled in through the pursuit of bread and excitement. Bread makes possible the excitement—the high (getting loaded with wine, pills, or pot), the sharp clothes, the "broad," the fight, and all those good things which show that one knows what's happening and has "something going" for himself. The rhythm of time—of the day and of the week—is patterned by the flow of money and people.

Time is "dead" when money is tight, when people are occupied elsewhere—working or in school. Time is dead when one is in jail. One is "doing dead time" when nothing is happening, and he's got nothing going for himself.

Time is alive when and where there is action. It picks up in the evening when everyone moves on the street. During the regular school year it may pick up for an hour in the afternoon when the "broads" leave school and meet with the set at a corner taco joint. Time may pick up when a familiar car cruises by and a few dudes drive down to Johnny's for a "process" (hair straightening and styling). Time is low on Monday (as described in the popular song, "Stormy Monday"), Tuesday, Wednesday, when money is tight. Time is high on Friday nights when the "eagle flies" and the "gig" begins. On the street, time has a personal meaning only when something is happening, and something is most likely to happen at night—especially on Friday and Saturday nights. Then people are together, and there may be bread—bread to take and bread to use.

Human behavior is rational if it helps the individual to get what he wants whether it is success in school or happiness in the street. Street people sometimes get what they want. They act rationally in those situations where they are able to plan and choose because they have control, knowledge, and concern, irrationally where there are barriers to their wants and desires.

When the street dude lacks knowledge and power to manipulate time, he is indeed irrational. For the most part, he lacks the skills and power to plan a move up and out of the ghetto. He is "a lame" in the middle class world of school and work; he is not ready to operate effectively in unfamiliar organizations where his street strengths are his visible weaknesses. Though irrational in moving up and out of the street, he can be rational in day to day survival in the street. No one survives there unless he knows what's happening (that is, unless he knows what is available, where to get what he can without being burned or busted). More euphemistically, this is "taking advantage of opportunities," exactly what the rational member of the middle class does in his own setting.

To know what's happening is to know the goods and the bads, the securities, the opportunities, and the dangers of the street. Survival requires that a hustling dude know who is cool and uncool (who can be trusted); who is in power (the people who control narcotics, fences, etc.); who is the "duker" or the fighter (someone to be avoided or someone who can provide protection). When one knows what's happening he can operate in many scenes, providing that he can "hold his mud," keep cool, and out of trouble.

With his diploma in street knowledge, a dude can use time efficiently and with cunning in the pursuit of goods and services—in hustling to eat and yet have enough bread left over for the pleasures of pot, the chicks, and the gig. As one respondent put it, "The good hustler has the know-how, the ambition to better himself. He conditions his mind and must never put his guard too far down, to relax, or he'll be taken." This is street rationality. The problem is not a deficient sense of time but deficient knowledge and control to make a fantasy future and a really better life possible.

The petty hustler more fully realizes the middle class ideal of individualistic rationality than does the middle class itself. When rationality operates in hustling, it is often on an individual basis. In a world of complex organization, the hustler defines himself as an entrepreneur; and indeed, he is the last of the competitive entrepreneurs.

The degree of organization in hustling depends frequently on the kind of hustling. Regular pimping and pushing require many trusted contacts and organization. Regular stealing requires regular fences for hot goods. But in Ghost-town when the hustler moved, he usually moved alone and on a small scale. His success was on him. He could not depend on the support of some benevolent organization. Alone, without a sure way of running the same game twice, he must continually recalculate conditions and people and find new ways of taking or be taken himself. The phrase "free enterprise for the poor and socialism for the rich" applies only too well in the streets. The political conservative should applaud all that individual initiative.

Clock Time vs. Personal Time

Negro street time is built around the irrelevance of clock time, white man's time, and the relevance of street values and activities. Like anyone else, a street dude is on time by the standard clock whenever he wants to be, not on time when he does not want to be and does not have to be.

When the women in school hit the street at the lunch hour and he wants to throw them a rap, he will be there then and not one hour after they have left. But he may be kicked out of high school for truancy or lose his job for being late and unreliable. He learned at an early age that school and job were neither interesting nor salient to his way of life. A regular on the set will readily admit being crippled by a lack of formal education.

Yet school was a "bum kick." It was not his school. The teachers put him down for his dress, hair, and manners. As a human being he has feelings of pride and autonomy, the very things most threatened in those institutional situations where he was or is the underdeveloped, unrespected, illiterate, and undeserving outsider. Thus whatever "respectable" society says will help him, he knows oppresses him, and he retreats to the streets for security and a larger degree of personal freedom. Here his control reaches a maximum, and he has the kind of autonomy which many middle class males might envy.

In the street, watches have a special and specific meaning. Watches are for pawning and not for telling time. When they are worn, they are decorations and ornaments of status. The street clock is informal, personal, and relaxed. It is not standardized nor easily synchronized to other clocks. In fact, a street dude may have almost infinite toleration for individual time schedules. To be on time is often meaningless, to be late an unconsciously accepted way of life. "I'll catch you later," or simply "later," are the street phrases that mean business will be taken care of, but not necessarily now.

Large areas of street life run on late time. For example, parties are not cut off by some built-in alarm clock of appointments and schedules. At least for the unemployed, standard time neither precedes nor follows the gig. Consequently, the action can take its course. It can last as long as interest is sustained and die by exhaustion or by the intrusion of some more interesting event. A gig may endure all night and well into another day. One of the reasons for the party assuming such time dimensions is purely economic. There are not enough cars and enough money for individual dates, so everyone converges in one place and takes care of as much business as possible there, that is, doing whatever is important at the time—sex, presentation of self, hustling.

Colored People's Time

Events starting late and lasting indefinitely are clearly street and class phenomena, not some special trait of Afro-Americans. Middle class Negroes who must deal with the organization and coordination of activities in church and elsewhere will jokingly and critically refer to a lack of standard time sense when they say that Mr. Jones arrived "CPT" (colored people's time). They have a word for it, because being late is a problem for people caught between two worlds and confronted with the task of meshing standard and street time. In contrast, the street dudes had no self-consciousness about being late; with few exceptions they had not heard the expression CPT. (When I questioned members of a middle class Negro fraternity, a sample matched by age to the street set, only three of the 25 interviewed could not define CPT. Some argued vehemently that CPT was the problem to be overcome.)

Personal time as expressed in parties and other street activities is not simply deficient knowledge and use of standard time. It is a positive adaption to generations of living whenever and wherever possible outside of the sound and control of the white man's clock. The personal clock is an adaptation to the chance and accidental character of events on the street and to the very positive value placed on emotion and feeling. (For a discussion of CPT which is close to some of the ideas presented here, see Jules Henry, "White People's Time, Colored People's Time," *Transaction,* March/April 1965.)

Chance reinforces personal time. A dude must be ready on short notice to move "where the action is." His internal clock may not be running at all when he is hanging on the corner and waiting for something to do. It may suddenly speed up by chance: Someone cruises by in a car and brings a nice "stash" of "weed," a gig is organized and he looks forward to being well togged-out and throwing a rap to some "boss chick," or a lame appears and opens himself to a quick "con." Chance as a determinant of personal time can be called more accurately *uncertain predictability.* Street life is an aggregate of relatively independent events. A dude may not know exactly what or when something will happen, but from past experience he can predict a range of possibilities, and he will be ready, in position, and waiting.

In white middle class stereotypes and fears—and in reality—street action is highly expressive. A forthright yet stylized expression of emotion is positively evaluated and most useful. Street control and communication are based on personal power and the direct impingement of one individual on another. Where there is little property, status in the set is determined by personal qualities of mind and brawn.

The importance of emotion and expression appears again and again in street tongue and ideology. When asked, "How does a dude make a rep on the set?" over half of the sample mentioned "style," and all could discuss the concept. Style is difficult to define as it has so many referents. It means to carry one's self well, dress well, to show class. In the ideology of the street, it may be a way of behaving. One has style if he is able to dig people as they are. He doesn't put them down for what they do. He shows toleration. But a person with style must also show respect. That means respect for a person as he is, and since there is power in the street, respect for another's superior power. Yet one must show respect in such a way that he is able to look tough and inviolate, fearless, secure, "cool."

Style may also refer to the use of gestures in conversation or in dance. It may be expressed in the loose walk, the jivey or dancing walk, the slow cool walk, the way one "chops" or "makes it" down the street. It may be the loose, relaxed hand rap or hand slap, the swinger's greeting which is used also in the hip middle class teen sets. There are many refined variations of the hand rap. As a greeting, one may simply extend his hand, palm up. Another slaps it loosely with his finger. Or, one person may be standing with his hand behind and palm up. Another taps the hand in passing, and also pays his respect verbally with the conventional greeting "What's happening, Brother." Or, in conversation, the hand may be slapped when an individual has "scored," has been "digging," has made a point, has got through to the person.

Style is a comparatively neutral value compared to "soul." Soul can be many things—a type of food (good food is "soul food," a "bowl of soul"), music, a quality of mind, a total way of acting (in eating, drinking, dancing, walking, talking, relating to others, etc.). The person who acts with soul acts directly and honestly from his heart. He feels it and tells it "like it is." One respondent identified soul with ambition and drive. He said the person with soul, once he makes up his mind, goes directly to the goal, doesn't change his mind, doesn't wait and worry about messing up a little. Another said soul was getting down to the nitty-gritty, that is, moving directly to what is basic without guise and disguise. Thus soul is the opposite of hypocrisy, deceit, and phoniness, the opposite of "affective neutrality," and "instrumentality." Soul is simply whatever is considered beautiful, honest, and virtuous in men.

Most definitions tied soul directly to Negro experience. As one hustler put it, "It is the ability to survive. We've made it with so much less. Soul is the Negro who has the spirit to sing in slavery to overcome the monotony." With very few exceptions, the men interviewed argued that soul was what Negroes had and whites did not. Negroes were "soul brothers," warm and emotional—whites cold as ice. Like other oppressed minorities these street Negroes believed they had nothing except their soul and their humanity, and that this made them better than their oppressors.

The Personal Dream

Soul is anchored in a past and present of exploitation and deprivation, but are there any street values and activities which relate to the future? The regular in the street set has no providential mission; he lives personally and instrumentally in the present, yet he dreams about the day when he will get himself together and move ahead to the rewards of a good job, money, and a family. Moreover, the personal dream coexists with a nascent political nationalism, the belief that Negroes can and will make it as Negroes. His present-future time is a combination of contradictions and developing possibilities. Here I will be content to document without weighing two aspects of his orientation: *fantasy personal future* and *fantasy collective future*. I use the word fantasy because street people have not yet the knowledge and means and perhaps the will to fulfill their dreams. It is hard enough to survive by the day.

When the members of the set were asked, "What do you really want out of life?" their responses were conventional, concrete, seemingly realistic, and—given their skills—rather hopeless. Two-thirds of the sample mentioned material aspirations—the finer things in life, a home, security, a family. For example, one said, in honest street language, "I want to get things for my kids and to make sure they have a father." Another said, jokingly, "a good future, a home, two or three girls living with me." Only one person didn't know, and the others deviated a little from the material response. They said such things as "for everyone to be on friendly terms —a better world . . . then I could get all I wish," "to be free," "to help people."

But if most of the set wanted money and security, they wanted it on their own terms. As one put it, "I don't want to be in a middle class bag, but I would like a nice car, home, and food in the icebox." He wanted the things and the comforts of middle class life, but not the hypocrisy, the venality, the coldness, the being forced to do what one does not want to do. All that was in the middle class bag. Thus the home and the money may be ends in themselves, but also fronts, security for carrying on the usual street values. Street people believed that they already had something that was valuable and looked down upon the person who made it and moved away into the middle class world. For the observer, the myths are difficult to separate from the truths—here where the truths are so bitter. One can only say safely that street people dream of a high status, and they really do not know how to get it.

The Collective Future

The Negro dudes are political outsiders by the usual poll questions. They do not vote. They do not seek out civil rights demonstrations. They have very rudimentary knowledge of political organization. However, about the age of 18, when fighting and being tough are less important than before, street people begin to discuss their position in society. Verbally they care very much about the politics of race and the future of the Negro. The topic is always a ready catalyst for a soul session.

The political consciousness of the street can be summarized by noting those interview questions which attracted at least a 75 percent rate of agreement. The typical respondent was angry. He approves of the Watts incident, although from his isolated corner of the city he did not actively participate. He knows something about the history of discrimination and believes that if something isn't done soon America can expect violence: "What this country needs is a revolutionary change." He is more likely to praise the leadership of Malcolm X than Lyndon Johnson, and he is definitely opposed to the Vietnam war. The reason for his opposition is clear: Why fight for a country which is not mine, when the fight is here?

Thus his racial consciousness looks to the future and a world where he will not have to stand in the shadow of the white man. But his consciousness has neither clear plan nor political commitment. He has listened to the Muslims, and he is not a black nationalist. True, the Negro generally has more soul than the white. He thinks differently, his women may be different, yet integration is preferable to separatism. Or, more accurately, he doesn't quite understand what all these terms mean. His nationalism is real as a folk nationalism based on experience with other Negroes and isolation from whites.

The significance of a racial future in the day to day consciousness of street people cannot be assessed. It is a developing possibility dependent on unforeseen conditions beyond the scope of their skill and imagination. But bring up the topic of race and tomorrow, and the dreams come rushing in—dreams of superiority, dreams of destruction, dreams of human equality. These dreams of the future are salient. They are not the imagination of authoritarian personalities, except from the viewpoint of those who see spite lurking behind every demand for social change. They are certainly not the fantasies of the hipster living philosophically in the present without hope and ambition. One hustler summarized the Negro street concept of ambition and future time when he said:

> The Negro has more ambition than the whites. He's got farther to go. "The man" is already there. But we're on your trail, daddy. You still have smoke in our eyes, but we're catching up.

twelve

Why do societies develop systems of religious belief? What functions does the church serve within the Black community? Are such functions different from those traditionally performed by churches in White communities? Is religion a stabilizing influence in the Black community or is it a force for social change?

Religion

Some form of religion may be found within every known human society. Most religions may be characterized by a system of beliefs and an accompanying set of practices and rituals. Often the religion is maintained by a separate organizational structure and religious activities are conducted only by certain individuals. The actual forms that religion can take vary widely. However its apparent universality can be attributed to the numerous social functions that it fulfills.

Men in every society live in a state of uncertainty, surrounded by things they cannot explain and over which they exert little control. Many social scientists argue that because of this situation men develop systems of belief to make their world understandable and more meaningful. Such systems of belief help explain mysterious natural phenomena. They also provide answers to "ultimate questions" such as the purpose of man's existence and strivings, and the origin and meaning of the universe. Religion provides a sense of security or certainty and a justification for human activities.

Systems of religious belief provide standards for appropriate behavior. Human conduct may therefore be judged as "good" or "bad," "right" or "wrong" in some moral and ethical sense. Religion and culture greatly influence one another and religious standards include many of the basic norms and values of a culture. Because of this religion may be viewed as an integrative or stabilizing mechanism in society. In complex societies, however, religious organizations are concerned with the improvement of social conditions and often contribute to constructive change. In societies with a number of religious faiths, religion may become a source of disruption and conflict.

Religion performs additional functions such as serving as an expressive and emotional outlet, providing opportunities for recreation and social interaction, and even serving as a basis for educational, political, or economic organization. Different forms of religion may emphasize one or more of the above functions. It should also be noted that religion may be only one of a number of alternative means by which certain kinds of things be achieved. For example, other institutions in a society may provide explanations of phenomena and serve to help men overcome their fears.

In America organized religion has played a major role in shaping basic values such as freedom, equality, and brotherhood. Most religious groups have been deeply concerned with human suffering. This is apparent, for example, in their charitable endeavors and the involvement of religious leaders in the civil rights movement. It is therefore ironic that organized religion is one of the most segregated features of American society.

In response to this separation Blacks have developed their own churches. Black religious organizations vary widely in their size and practices. In the rural South, churches are small and the services have an emotional other-worldly content. In the urban centers of the North many cults and sects have a similar orientation. However, many Northern Blacks attend the more conventional, though segregated, Methodist and Baptist churches. A small minority participate in integrated Protestant and Roman Catholic churches.

In the Black community the church often serves as a place of refuge, a place where individuals may express their feelings and emotions. Because it is one of the few organizations in the community, the church is also a center for social, recreational, and charitable activity. It also functions as an important meeting place and as a source of information. In times of crisis or change it serves as a basis for community organization. The church provides an important source of opportunity for individuals to develop leadership ability. Therefore, ministers and clergymen make up a substantial portion of the leadership in the community. A small minority of religious organizations also have highly developed political concerns, such as the Black Muslims with their Black nationalist ideology.

Historically Black churches have been a stabilizing influence, counseling their adherents to accomodate themselves to the existing social conditions. On rare occasions they have also been a source of protest. Many of the major slave rebellions were led by Black ministers such as Nat Turner. In recent years Black churches have been an important basis for civil rights activity, and Black ministers such as Martin Luther King have been among the leaders in the Movement. Gary Marx examines the relationship between religious activity and civil rights protest. These two factors tend to be inversely related, although the type of religious involvement must be taken into consideration.

The late E. Franklin Frazier describes various types of Black churches and their religious practices. Though he wrote more than a decade ago, his observations and insights remain valid. Unfortunately Frazier did not live long enough to fully appreciate the leading role assumed by Black churches and their ministers in the struggle for equal rights and opportunity.

FUNCTIONS OF RELIGIOUS BELIEF

"Religion: Opiate or Inspiration
of Civil Rights Militancy Among Negroes?"[1]

by Gary T. Marx

The relationship between religion and political radicalism is a confusing one. On the one hand, established religious institutions have generally had a stake in the status quo and hence have supported conservatism. Furthermore, with the masses having an otherworldly orientation, religious zeal, particularly as expressed in the more fundamentalist branches of Christianity, has been seen as an alternative to the development of political radicalism. On the other hand, as the source of universal humanistic values and the strength that can come from believing one is carrying out God's will in political matters, religion has occasionally played a strong positive role in movements for radical social change.

This dual role of religion is clearly indicated in the case of the American Negro and race protest. Slaves are said to have been first brought to this country on the "good ship Jesus Christ."[2] While there was occasional controversy over the effect that religion had on them it appears that most slave-owners eventually came to view supervised religion as an effective means of social control. Stampp, in commenting on the effect of religion notes:

> . . . through religious instruction the bondsmen learned that slavery had divine sanction, that insolence was as much an offense against God as against the temporal master. They received the Biblical command that servants should obey their masters, and they heard of the punishments awaiting the disobedient slave in the hereafter. They heard, too, that

[1]Revision of paper read at the annual meeting of the American Sociological Association, August, 1966. This paper may be identified as publication A-72 of the Survey Research Center, University of California, Berkeley. I am grateful to Gertrude J. Selznick and Stephen Steinberg for their work on the early phase of this project, and to the Anti-Defamation League for support.

[2]Louis Lomax, *When the Word is Given,* New York: New American Library, 1964, p. 34. It has often been noted that when the missionaries came to Africa they had the Bible and the people had the land. When the missionaries left, they had the land and the Africans had the Bible.

eternal salvation would be their reward for faithful service . . . [3]

In discussing the period after the Civil War, Myrdal states that " . . . under the pressure of political reaction, the Negro church in the South came to have much the same role as it did before the Civil War. Negro frustration was sublimated into emotionalism, and Negro hopes were fixed on the after world."[4] Many other analysts, in considering the consequences of Negro religion from the end of slavery until the early 1950's reached similar conclusions about the conservatizing effect of religion on race protests.[5]

However, the effect of religion on race protest throughout American history has by no means been exclusively in one direction. While many Negroes were no doubt seriously singing about chariots in the sky, Negro preachers such as Denmark Vesey and Nat Turner and the religiously inspired abolitionists were actively fighting slavery in their own way. All Negro churches first came into being as protest organizations and later some served as meeting places where protest strategy was planned, or as stations on the underground railroad. The richness of protest symbolism in Negro spirituals and sermons has often been noted. Beyond this symbolic role, as a totally Negro institution, the church brought together in privacy people with a shared problem. It was from the church experience that many leaders were exposed to a broad range of ideas legitimizing protest and obtained the savoir faire, self-confidence, and organizational experience needed to challenge an oppressive system. A recent commentator states that the slave churches were "the nucleus of the Negro protest" and another that "in religion Negro leaders had begun to find sanction and support for their movements of protest more than 150 years ago."[6]

[3] Kenneth Stampp, *The Peculiar Institution,* New York: Alfred A. Knopf, 1956, p. 158.
[4] Gunnar Myrdal *et al., An American Dilemma,* New York: Harper, 1944, pp. 851–853. About the North he notes that the church remained far more independent "but on the whole even the Northern Negro church has remained a conservative institution with its interests directly upon other-worldly matters and has largely ignored the practical problems of the Negro's fate in this world."
[5] For example Dollard reports that "religion can be seen as a mechanism for the social control of Negroes" and that planters have always welcomed the building of a Negro church on the plantation but looked with less favor upon the building of a school. John Dollard, *Caste and Class in a Southern Town,* Garden City: Doubleday Anchor, 1957, p. 248. A few of the many others reaching similar conclusions are, Benjamin E. Mays and J. W. Nicholson, *The Negro's Church,* New York: Institute of Social and Religious Research, 1933; Hortense Powdermaker, *After Freedom,* New York: Viking Press, 1939, p. 285; Charles Johnson, *Growing Up in the Black Belt,* Washington, D.C.: American Council of Education, 1941, pp. 135–136; Horace Cayton and St. Clair Drake, *Black Metropolis,* New York: Harper and Row, 1962, pp. 424–429; George Simpson and Milton Yinger, *Racial and Cultural Minorities,* New York: Harper, rev. ed., 1958, pp. 582–587. In a more general context this social control consequence of religion has of course been noted throughout history from Plato to Montesquieu to Marx to Nietzsche to Freud to contemporary social theorists.
[6] Daniel Thompson, "The Rise of Negro Protest," *Annals of the American Academy of Political and Social Science,* 357 (January, 1965).

Differing perceptions of the varied consequences religion may have on protest have continued to the present time. While there has been very little in the way of empirical research on the effect of the Negro church on protest,[7] the literature of race relations is rich with impressionistic statements which generally contradict each other about how the church either encourages and is the source of race protest or inhibits and retards its development. For example, two observers note, "as primitive evangelism gave way to a more sophisticated social consciousness, the church became the spearhead of Negro protest in the deep South,"[8] while another indicates "the Negro church is a sleeping giant. In civil rights participation its feet are hardly wet."[9] A civil rights activist, himself a clergyman, states: " . . . the church today is central to the movement . . . if there had been no Negro church, there would have been no civil rights movement today."[10] On the other hand, a sociologist, commenting on the more involved higher status ministers, notes: " . . . middle class Negro clergymen in the cities of the South generally advocated cautious gradualism in race activities until the mid-1950's when there was an upsurge of protest sentiment among urban Negroes . . . but most of them [ministers] did not embrace the more vigorous techniques of protest until other leaders took the initiative and gained widespread support."[11] Another sociologist states, "Whatever their previous conservative stance has been, the churches have now become 'spearheads of reform.' "[12] Still another indi-

[7]The empirical evidence is quite limited. The few studies that have been done have focused on the Negro minister. Thompson notes that in New Orleans Negro ministers constitute the largest segment of the Negro leadership class (a grouping which is not necessarily the same as "protest leaders") but that "The vast majority of ministers are primarily interested in their pastoral role . . . their sermons are essentially biblical, dealing only tangentially with social issues." Daniel Thompson, *The Negro Leadership Class*, Englewood Cliffs, New Jersey: Prentice-Hall, 1963, pp. 34–35. Studies of the Negro ministry in Detroit and Richmond, California also stress that only a small fraction of Negro clergymen show any active concern with the civil rights struggle. R. L. Johnstone, *Militant and Conservative Community Leadership Among Negro Clergymen*, Ph.D. dissertation, University of Michigan, Ann Arbor, 1963, and J. Bloom, *The Negro Church and the Movement for Equality*, M.A. thesis, University of California, Berkeley, Department of Sociology, 1966.

It is worthy of mention that, although the number of cases was small, the Negro ministers in our sample had the lowest percentage militant of any occupational group. With respect to the sons of clergymen, the situation seems somewhat different. While the myth of the preacher's son gone bad is almost a part of American folklore, one would think that a comparable myth might develop within the Negro community—that of the preacher's son gone radical. Malcolm X, James Baldwin, A. Philip Randolph, Martin Luther King, James Farmer, Adam Clayton Powell, Elijah Muhammad, and a number of others had clergymen as fathers. To be taken into consideration is that clergymen make up a relatively larger segment of the Negro middle class than of the white middle class.

[8]Jane Record and Wilson Record, "Ideological Forces and the Negro Protest," *Annals, op. cit.,* p. 92.

[9]G. Booker, *Black Man's America*, Englewood Cliffs, N.J.: Prentice-Hall, 1964, p. 111.

[10]Rev. W. T. Walker, as quoted in William Brink and Louis Harris, *The Negro Revolution in America*, New York: Simon and Schuster, 1964, p. 103.

[11]N. Glenn, "Negro Religion in the U.S." in L. Schneider, *Religion, Culture and Society*, New York: John Wiley, 1964.

[12]Joseph Fichter, "American Religion and the Negro," *Daedalus* (Fall, 1965), p. 1087.

cates: " . . . the Negro church is particularly culpable for its general lack of concern for the moral and social problems of the community . . . it has been accommodating. Fostering indulgence in religious sentimentality, and riveting the attention of the masses on the bounties of a hereafter, the Negro church remains a refuge, and escape from the cruel realities of the here and now."[13]

Thus one faces opposing views, or at best ambiguity, in contemplating the current effect of religion. The opiating consequences of religion are all too well known as is the fact that the segregated church is durable and offers some advantages to clergy and members that might be denied them in a more integrated society. On the other hand, the prominent role of the Negro church in supplying much of the ideology of the movement, many of its foremost leaders, and an institution around which struggle might be organized—particularly in the South—can hardly be denied. It would appear from the bombings of churches and the writings of Martin Luther King and other religiously inspired activists that for many, religion and protest are closely linked.

Part of this dilemma may lie in the distinction between the church as an institution in its totality and particular individual churches within it, and the further distinctions among different types of individual religious concern. This paper is concerned with the latter subject; it is an inquiry into the relationship between religiosity and response to the civil rights struggle. It first considers how religious denomination affects militancy, and then how various measures of religiosity, taken separately and together, are related to civil rights concern. The question is then asked of those classified as "very religious" and "quite religious," how an "otherworldly orientation"—as opposed to a "temporal" one—affects militancy.

In a nationwide study of Negroes living in metropolitan areas of the United States, a number of questions were asked about religious behavior and beliefs as well as about the civil rights struggle.[14] Seven of the questions dealing with civil rights protest have been combined into an index

[13] E. U. Essien-Udom, *Black Nationalism,* New York: Dell Publishing Co., 1962, p. 358. Many other examples of contradictory statements could be offered, sometimes even in the same volume. For example, Carleton Lee stresses the importance of religion for protest while Rayford Logan sees the Negro pastor as an instrument of the white power structure (in a book published to commemorate 100 years of emancipation). Carleton Lee, "Religious Roots of Negro Protest," and Rayford Logan, "Educational Changes Affecting American Negroes," both in Arnold Rose, *Assuring Freedom to the Free,* Detroit: Wayne University Press, 1964.

[14] This survey was carried out in 1964 by the Survey Research Center, University of California, Berkeley. A non-Southern metropolitan area probability sample was drawn as well as special area samples of Negroes living in New York City, Chicago, Atlanta and Birmingham. Since the results reported here are essentially the same for each of these areas, they are treated together. More than 90% of the interviews were done with Negro interviewers. Additional methodological details may be found in Gary Marx, *Protest and Prejudice: A Study of Belief in the Black Community,* New York: Harper & Row, forthcoming.

of conventional militancy.[15] Built into this index are a number of dimensions of racial protest such as impatience over the speed of integration, opposition to discrimination in public facilities and the sale of property, perception of barriers to Negro advancement, support of civil rights demonstrations, and expressed willingness to take part in a demonstration. Those giving the militant response to five or more of the questions are considered militant, those giving such a response to three or four of the questions, moderate, and fewer than three, conservative.[16]

Denomination

It has long been known that the more fundamentalist sects such as the Holiness groups and the Jehovah's Witnesses are relatively uninterested in movements for secular political change.[17] Such transvaluational movements with their otherworldly orientation and their promise that the last shall be first in the great beyond, are said to solace the individual for his lowly status in ths world and to divert concern away from efforts at collective social change which might be brought about by man. While only a minority of Negroes actually belong to such groups, the proportion is higher than among whites. Negro literature is rich in descriptions of these churches and their position on race protest.

In Table 1 it can be seen that those belonging to sects are the least likely to be militant; they are followed by those in predominantly Negro denominations. Ironically those individuals in largely white denominations (Episcopalian, Presbyterian, United Church of Christ, and Roman Catholic) are those most likely to be militant, in spite of the perhaps greater civil rights activism of the Negro denominations. This pattern emerged even when social class was held constant.

In their comments members of the less conventional religious groups clearly expressed the classical attitude of their sects toward participation in the politics of the secular world. For example, an Evangelist in the Midwest said, "I don't believe in participating in politics. My church don't vote—they just depends on the plans of God." And an automobile

[15]Attention is directed to conventional militancy rather than to that of the Black Nationalist variety because a very small percentage of the sample offered strong and consistent support for Black Nationalism. As in studying support for the KKK, the Birch Society or the Communist Party, a representative sample of normal size is inadequate.

[16]Each of the items in the index was positively related to every other and the index showed a high degree of internal validity. The index also received external validation from a number of additional questions. For example, the percentage belonging to a civil rights organization went from zero among those lowest in militancy to 38 percent for those who were highest, and the percenage thinking that civil rights demonstrations had helped a great deal increased from 23 percent to 58 percent. Those thinking that the police treated Negroes very well decreased from 35 percent to only 2 percent among those highest in militancy.

[17]Liston Pope, *Millhands and Preachers,* New Haven: Yale University Press, 1942, p. 137. J. Milton Yinger, *Religion, Society, and the Individual,* New York: The Macmillan Company, 1957, pp. 170–173.

Table 1. *Proportion Militant (%) by Denomination**

Denomination	% Militant
Episcopalian	46 (24)
United Church of Christ	42 (12)
Presbyterian	40 (25)
Catholic	40 (109)
Methodist	34 (142)
Baptist	32 (658)
Sects and Cults	20 (106)

*25 respondents are not shown in this table because they did not specify a denomination, or belonged to a non-Christian religious group, or other small Christian group.

serviceman in Philadelphia stated, "I, as a Jehovah's Witness, cannot express things involving the race issue." A housewife in the Far West ventured, "In my religion we do not approve of anything except living like it says in the Bible; demonstrations mean calling attention to you and it's sinful."

Table 2. *Militancy by Subjective Importance Assigned to Religion**

Importance	% Militant
Extremely important	29 (668)
Somewhat important	39 (195)
Fairly important	48 (96)
Not too important	56 (18)
Not at all important	62 (13)

*Sects are excluded here and in all subsequent tables.

The finding that persons who belong to sects are less likely to be militant than the non-sect members is to be expected; clearly this type of religious involvement seems an alternative for most people to the development of radicalism. But what of the religious style of those in the more conventional churches which may put relatively less stress on the after-life and encourage various forms of secular participation? Are the more religiously inclined within these groups also less likely to be militant?

Religiosity

The present study measured several dimensions of religious involvement. Those interviewed were asked how important religion was to them, several questions about orthodoxy of belief, and how frequently they attended worship service.[18] Even with the sects excluded, irrespective of the dimension of religiosity considered, the greater the religiosity the lower the percentage militant. (See Tables 2, 3, and 4.) For example, militancy increases consistently from a low of only 29 percent among those who said religion was "extremely important" to a high of 62 percent for those who indicated that religion was "not at all important" to them. For those very high in orthodoxy (having no doubt about the existence of God or the devil) 27 percent were militant while for those totally rejecting these ideas 54 percent indicated great concern over civil rights. Militancy, also varies inversely with frequency of attendance at worship service.[19]

Table 3.   Militancy by Orthodoxy

Orthodoxy	% Militant
Very high	27 (414)
High	34 (333)
Medium	39 (144)
Low	47 (68)
Very low	54 (35)

Each of these items was strongly related to every other; when taken together they help us to better characterize religiosity. Accordingly they have been combined into an overall measure of religiosity. Those scored as "very religious" in terms of this index attended church at least once a

[18]These dimensions and several others are suggested by Charles Y. Glock in "On the Study of Religious Commitment," *Religious Education Research Supplement,* 57 (July–August, 1962), pp. 98–100. For another measure of religious involvement, the number of church organizations belonged to, the same inverse relationship was noted.

[19]There is a popular stereotype that Negroes are a "religious people." Social science research has shown that they are "over-churched" relative to whites, i.e., the ratio of Negro churches to the size of the Negro population is greater than the same ratio for whites. Using data from a nationwide survey of whites, by Gertrude Selznick and Stephen Steinberg, some comparison of the religiosity of Negroes and whites was possible. When these various dimensions of religiosity were examined, with the effect of education and region held constant, Negroes appeared as significantly more religious *only* with respect to the subjective importance assigned to religion. In the North, whites were more likely to attend church at least once a week than were Negroes; while in the South rates of attendance were the same. About the same percentage of both groups had no doubts about the existence of God. While Negroes were more likely to be sure about the existence of a devil, whites, surprisingly, were more likely to be sure about a life beyond death. Clearly, then, any assertions about the greater religiosity of Negroes relative to whites are unwarranted unless one specifies the dimension of religiosity.

week, felt that religion was extremely important to them, and had no doubts about the existence of God and the devil. For progressively lower values of the index, frequency of church attendance, the importance of religion, and acceptance of the belief items decline consistently until, for those scored "not at all religious," church is rarely if ever attended, religion is not considered personally important and the belief items are rejected.

Table 4. Militancy by Frequency of Attendance at Worship Services

Frequency	% Militant
More than once a week	27 (81)
Once a week	32 (311)
Once a month or more but less than once a week	34 (354)
Less than once a month	38 (240)

Using this measure for non-sect members, civil rights militancy increases from a low of 26 percent for those labeled "very religious" to 30 percent for the "somewhat religious" to 45 percent for those "not very religious" and up to a high of 70 percent for those "not at all religious."[20] (Table 5.)

Table 5. Militancy by Religiosity

Religiosity	Very Religious	Somewhat Religious	Not Very Religious	Not at All Religious
% Militant	26	30	45	70
N	(230)	(523)	(195)	(36)

Religiosity and militancy are also related to age, sex, education, religious denomination and region of the country. The older, the less educated, women, Southerners and those in Negro denominations are more likely to be religious and to have lower percentages scoring as militant. Thus it is possible that the relationship observed is simply a consequence of the fact that both religiosity and militancy are related to some third factor. In Table 6 it can be seen, however, that even when these variables are controlled the relationship is maintained. That is, even among those

[20]When the sects are included in these tables the results are the same. The sects have been excluded because they offer almost no variation to be analyzed with respect to the independent variable. Since virtually all of the sect members scored as either "very religious" or "somewhat religious," it is hardly possible to measure the effect of their religious involvement on protest attitudes. In addition the import of the relationships shown in these tables is considerably strengthened when it is demonstrated that religious involvement inhibits militancy even when the most religious and least militant group, the sects, are excluded.

in the North, the younger, male, more educated and those affiliated with predominantly white denominations, the greater the religiosity the less the militancy.

Table 6. Proportion Militant (%) by Religiosity, for Education, Age, Region, Sex, and Denomination

	Very Religious	Somewhat Religious	Not Very Religious	Not at All Religious
Education				
Grammar school	17 (108)	22 (201)	31 (42)	50 (2)
High school	34 (96)	32 (270)	45 (119)	58 (19)
College	38 (26)	48 (61)	59 (34)	87 (15)
Age				
18-29	33 (30)	37 (126)	44 (62)	62 (13)
30-44	30 (53)	34 (180)	48 (83)	74 (19)
45-59	25 (71)	27 (131)	45 (33)	50 (2)
60+	22 (76)	18 (95)	33 (15)	100 (2)
Region				
Non-South	30 (123)	34 (331)	47 (159)	70 (33)
South	22 (107)	23 (202)	33 (36)	66 (3)
Sex				
Men	28 (83)	33 (220)	44 (123)	72 (29)
Women	26 (147)	28 (313)	46 (72)	57 (7)
Denomination				
Episcopalian, Presbyterian, United Church of Christ	20 (15)	27 (26)	33 (15)	60 (5)
Catholic	13 (15)	39 (56)	36 (25)	77 (13)
Methodist	46 (24)	22 (83)	50 (32)	100 (2)
Baptist	25 (172)	29 (354)	45 (117)	53 (15)

The incompatibility between piety and protest shown in these data becomes even more evident when considered in light of comments offered by the respondents. Many religious people hold beliefs which clearly inhibit race protest. For a few there was the notion that segregation and a lowly status for Negroes was somehow God's will and not for man to question. Thus a housewife in South Bend, Indiana, in saying that civil rights demonstrations had hurt Negroes, added: "God is the Creator of everything. We don't know why we all dark-skinned. We should try to put forth the effort to do what God wants and not question."[21]

A Negro spiritual contains the lines "I'm gonna wait upon the Lord till my change comes." For our respondents a more frequently stated belief stressed that God as the absolute controller of the universe would bring

[21]Albert Cardinal Meyer notes that the Catholic Bishops of the U.S. said in their statement of 1958: "The heart of the race question is moral and religious." "Interracial Justice and Love," in M. Ahmann, ed., *Race Challenge to Religion,* Chicago: H. Regnery, 1963, p. 126. These data, viewed from the perspective of the activist seeking to motivate Negroes on behalf of the civil rights struggle, suggest that this statement has a meaning which Their Excellencies no doubt did not intend.

about the change in his own way and at his own time, rather than expressing segregation as God's will. In indicating her unwillingness to take part in a civil rights demonstration, a Detroit housewife said, "I don't go for demonstrations. I believe that God created all men equal and at His appointed time He will give every man his portion, no one can hinder it." And in response to a question about whether or not the government in Washington was pushing integration too slowly, a retired clerk in Atlanta said: "You can't hurry God. He has a certain time for this to take place. I don't know about Washington."

Others who desired integration more strongly and wanted immediate social change felt that (as Bob Dylan sings) God was on their side. Hence man need do nothing to help bring about change. Thus a worker in Cleveland, who was against having more civil rights demonstrations, said: "With God helping to fight our battle, I believe we can do with fewer demonstrations." And in response to a question about whether Negroes should spend more time praying and less time demonstrating, an Atlanta clergyman, who said "more time praying," added "praying is demonstrating."[22]

Religion Among the Militants

Although the net effect of religion is clearly to inhibit attitudes of protest it is interesting to consider this relationship in the opposite direction, i.e., observe religiosity among those characterized as militant, moderate, and conservative with respect to the civil rights struggle. As civil rights concern increases, religiosity decreases. (Table 7). Militants were twice as likely to be scored "not very religious" or "not at all religious" as were conservatives. This table is also of interest because it shows that, even for the militants, a majority were scored either "very religious" or "somewhat religious." A study of Southern Negro CORE activists reports that less than one person in ten never attends church while almost six out of ten attended church weekly.[23] Clearly, for many, a religious orientation and a concern with racial protest are not mutually exclusive.

Given the active involvement of some churches, the singing of protest spirituals, and the ideology of the movement as it relates to Christian principles of love, equality, passive suffering,[24] and the appeal to a higher

[22]A study of ministers in Richmond, California notes that, although almost all questioned were opposed to discrimination, very few had taken concrete action, in part because of their belief that God would take care of them. One minister noted, "I believe that if we all was as pure . . . as we ought to be, there would be no struggle. God will answer my prayer. If we just stay with God and have faith. *When Peter was up, did the people march to free him? No. He prayed, and God did something about it.*" (Bloom, *op. cit.,* italics added.)

[23]Ingeborg B. Powall, *Ideology and Strategy of Direct Action: A Study of the Congress of Racial Equality* (Unpublished Ph. D. dissertation, University of California, Berkeley, 1965), p. 207. In the North the same figure, four out of ten, report never attending as indicate that they go to church weekly.

[24]Non-violent resistance as it relates to Christianity's emphasis on suffering, sacrifice, and

moral law, it would be surprising if there were only a few religious people among the militants.

Table 7. Religiosity by Civil Rights Militancy

	Militants	Moderates	Conservatives
Very religious	18%	24%	28%
Somewhat religious	48	57	55
Not very religious	26	17	16
Not at all religious	8	2	1
Total	100	100	100
N	332	419	242

A relevant question accordingly is: Among the religious, what are the intervening links which determine whether religion is related to an active concern with racial matters or has an opiating effect?[25] From the comments reported above it seemed that, for some, belief in a highly deterministic God inhibited race protest. Unfortunately the study did not measure beliefs about the role of God as against the role of men in the structuring of human affairs. However, a related variable was measured which would seem to have much relevance—the extent to which these religious people were concerned with the here and now as opposed to the after-life.

Table 8. Proportion (%) with Temporal (as Against Otherworldly) Concern, by Religiosity

Religiosity	% with Temporal Concern
Very religious	42 (225)
Somewhat religious	61 (531)
Not very religious	82 (193)
Not at all religious	98 (34)

The classical indictment of religion from the Marxist perspective is that by focusing concern on a glorious after-life the evils of this life are ignored. Of course there are important differences among religious institutions and among individuals with respect to the importance given to other worldly concerns. Christianity, as with most ideologies, contains within it,

---

privation, is discussed by James W. Vander Zanden, "The Non-Violent Resistance Movement Against Segregation," *American Journal of Sociology,* 68 (March, 1963), pp. 544–550.

[25] Of course, a most relevant factor here is the position of the particular church that an individual is involved in. Unfortunately, it was difficult to obtain such information in a nationwide survey.

if not out-and-out contradictory themes, then certainly themes which are likely to be in tension with one another. In this fact, no doubt, lies part of the explanation of religion's varied consequences for protest. One important strand of Christianity stresses acceptance of one's lot and glorifies the after-life;[26] another is more concerned with the realization of Judeo-Christian values in the current life. King and his followers clearly represent this latter "social gospel" tradition.[27] Those with the type of temporal concern that King represents would be expected to be higher in militancy. A measure of temporal vs. otherworldly concern has been constructed. On the basis of two questions, those interviewed have been classified as having either an otherworldly or a temporal orientation.[28] The evidence is that religiosity and otherworldly concern increase together. For example, almost 100 percent of the "not at all religious" group were considered to have a temporal orientation, but only 42 percent of the "very religious." (Table 8). Those in predominantly white denominations were more likely to have a temporal orientation than those in all-black denominations.

Among the religious groups, if concern with the here and now is a relevant factor in overcoming the opiating effect of religion then it is to be anticipated that those considered to have a temporal religious orientation would be much higher in militancy than those scored as other-

[26]The Muslims have also made much of this theme within Christianity, and their militancy is certainly tied to a rejection of otherworldly religiosity. The Bible is referred to as a "poison book" and the leader of the Muslims states, "No one after death has ever gone any place but where they were carried. There is no heaven or hell other than on earth for you and me, and Jesus was no exception. His body is still . . . in Palestine and will remain there." (As quoted in C. Eric Lincoln, *The Black Muslims in America,* Boston: Beacon Press, 1961, p. 123).

However, while they reject the otherworldly theme, they nevertheless rely heavily on a deterministic Allah; according to E. U. Essien-Udom, this fact leads to political inactivity. He notes, "The attainment of black power is relegated to the intervention of "Almighty Allah" sometime in the future. . . . Not unlike other religionists, the Muslims too may wait for all eternity for the coming of the Messiah, the predicted apocalypse in 1970 notwithstanding." E. U. Essien-Udom, *Black Nationalism, op. cit.,* pp. 313–314.

[27]He states: "Any religion that professes to be concerned with the souls of men and is not concerned with the slums that damn them, the economic conditions that strangle them, and the social conditions that cripple them is a dry-as-dust religion." He further adds, perhaps in a concession, that "such a religion is the kind the Marxists like to see—an opiate of the people." Martin Luther King, *Stride Toward Freedom,* New York: Ballantine Books, 1958, pp. 28–29.

John Lewis, a former SNCC leader and once a Baptist Divinity student, is said to have peered through the bars of a Southern jail and said, "Think not that I am come to send peace on earth. I came not to send peace, but a sword." (Matthew 10:34.)

[28]The two items used in this index were: "How sure are you that there is a life beyond death?"; and "Negroes should spend more time praying and less time demonstrating." The latter item may seem somewhat circular when observed in relation to civil rights concern. However, this is precisely what militancy is all about. Still it would have been better to measure otherworldly vs. temporal concern in a less direct fashion; unfortunately, no other items were available. Because of this the data shown here must be interpreted with caution. However it does seem almost self-evident that civil rights protest which is religiously inspired is related to a temporal religious outlook.

Table 9. Proportion Militant (%) by Religiosity and Temporal or Otherworldly Concern

Concern	Very Religious	Somewhat Religious
Temporal	39 (95)	38 (325)
Otherworldly	15 (130)	17 (206)

worldly. This is in fact the case. Among the otherworldly religious, only 16 percent were militant; this proportion increases to almost 40 percent among those considered "very religious" and "somewhat religious" who have a temporal religious outlook. (Table 9). Thus it would seem that an important factor in determining the effect of religion on protest attitudes is the nature of an individual's religious commitment. It is quite possible, for those with a temporal religious orientation, that—rather than the effect of religion being somehow neutralized (as in the case of militancy among the "not religious" groups)—their religious concern serves to inspire and sustain race protest. This religious inspiration can, of course, be clearly noted among some active civil rights participants.

Conclusion

The effect of religiosity on race protest depends on the type of religiosity involved. Past literature is rich in suggestions that the religiosity of the fundamentalist sects is an alternative to the development of political radicalism. This seems true in the case of race protest as well. However, in an overall sense even for those who belong to the more conventional churches, the greater the religious involvement, whether measured in terms of ritual activity, orthodoxy of religious belief, subjective importance of religion, or the three taken together, the lower the degree of militancy.

Among sect members and religious people with an otherworldly orientation, religion and race protest appear to be, if not mutually exclusive, then certainly what one observer has referred to as "mutually corrosive kinds of commitments."[29] Until such time as religion loosens its hold over these people or comes to embody to a greater extent the belief that man as well as God can bring about secular change, and focuses more on the here and now, religious involvement may be seen as an important factor working against the widespread radicalization of the Negro public.

However, it has also been noted that many militant people are never-

[29]Rodney Stark, "Class, Radicalism, and Religious Involvement," *American Sociological Review,* 29 (October, 1964), p. 703.

theless religious. When a distinction is made among the religious between the "otherworldly" and the "temporal," for many of the latter group, religion seems to facilitate or at least not to inhibit protest. For these people religion and race protest may be mutually supportive.

Thirty years ago Donald Young wrote: "One function which a minority religion may serve is that of reconciliation with inferior status and its discriminatory consequences . . . on the other hand, religious institutions may also develop in such a way as to be an incitement and support of revolt against inferior status."[30] The current civil rights struggle and the data observed here certainly suggest that this is the case. These contradictory consequences of religion are somewhat reconciled when one distinguishes among different segments of the Negro church and types of religious concern among individuals.

OVERVIEW

"The Negro Church"

by E. Franklin Frazier

Negro Churches in the South

The church is the one outstanding institution of the community over which the Negroes themselves exercise control, and because it stands so alone in administering to their own conception of their needs, its function is varied. The religious emotions of the people demand some channel of formal expression, and find it in the church. But more than this, the church is the most important center for face-to-face relations. It is in a very real sense a social institution. It provides a large measure of the recreation and relaxation from the physical stress of life. It is the agency looked to for aid when misfortune overtakes a person. It offers the medium for community feeling, singing together, eating together, praying together, and indulging in the formal expression of fellowship. Above this it holds out a world of escape from the hard experiences of life common to all. It is the agency which holds together the subcommunities and families physically scattered over a wide area. It exercises some influence over social relations, setting up certain regulations for behavior, passing

---

[30]Donald Young, *American Minority Peoples,* New York: Harper, 1937, p. 204.

These data are also consistent with Merton's statement that it is premature to conclude that "all religion everywhere has only the one consequence of making for mass apathy" and his insistence on recognizing the "multiple consequences" and "net balance of aggregate consequences" of a given institution such as religion. Robert Merton, *Social Theory and Social Structure,* Glencoe: Free Press, 1957, revised edition, p. 44.

judgements which represent community opinion, censuring and penalizing improper conduct by expulsion.[1]

The majority of the Negro churches in the South are small, unpretentious wooden structures. The following description of the Damascus Baptist Church in Macon County, Alabama, is typical of the rural churches in the plantation South:

> The church is a small, painfully conventional boxlike structure with gabled roof and a small bell tower over the entrance. It has once or twice been whitewashed but it is now gray under the long assault of time and the elements. Two giant oaks at the rear, dripping with a Spanish trailing moss, give shelter for the horses and mules of the communicants. Back of the schoolhouse with its broken windows and sagging shutters is a small cemetery with boards and short tombstones jutting up at odd angles to mark the mounds of departed members. . . . Inside the church there are three rows of plain wooden benches. The walls of the interior are of white, painted, horizontal boards, and the ceiling, as far up as could be reached, is painted a vivid green. At the end of the room is a very cluttered rostrum. The inclined pedestal has the center; the pastor's seat is directly behind. Then there are three small benches for the choir, two hat racks, and an old clock which is out of order. On the wall back of the rostrum is a large calendar with a picture of Lincoln, an even larger placard announcing a "drive" for $225,000 on behalf of Selma University in 1927, a framed crayon portrait of a former pastor, a placard warning in red letters of the danger of malaria, and two framed certificates. Beside the rostrum is a coal stove.[2]

The services in the rural churches are characterized by general participation on the part of the congregation.[3] After the congregation has assembled, someone—usually a deacon or prominent member—"raises a hymn," that is, begins singing. The noise dies down and as the singer's voice grows in volume, the congregation joins in the singing. The singing is followed by a prayer by a deacon, which is approved by "Amens" on the part of the congregation. Then follows more spontaneous singing and a prayer. After this comes the sermon, which is characterized by much dramatization on the part of the minister. Members in the audience express their approval by "Amens," groans and such expressions as "Preach it," and "Yes, Lord." As the minister reaches the climax, "shouting" or a form of ecstatic dancing begins. The contagion often spreads until most of the congregation is "shouting." As the "shouting" dies down, someone —very likely the minister, who has not lost control of the services— "raises a hymn." Afterward the minister turns to such practical matters as the collection and announcements concerning future services.

[1]*Shadow of the Plantation* by Charles S. Johnson, p. 150. Copyright 1934 by The University of Chicago Press.
[2]*Shadow of the Plantation* by Charles S. Johnson, pp. 153–54. Copyright 1934 by The University of Chicago Press.
[3]See *ibid.*, pp. 154–62 for a description of a service.

The ministers in these rural churches are older men with a meager education. Scarcely more than two-fifths of them have more than a grammar school education.[4] Moreover, there is much turnover among the rural ministers, especially among the Baptists, where their tenure depends upon their personal inclinations and the extent to which they satisfy the demands of their congregations. The ministers are generally men who have been "called" to preach and therefore they tend to emphasize the mystical aspects of religion and their sermons are otherworldly. Since they themselves "got religion," they place great emphasis upon "getting religion" as prerequisite to church membership.[5] Consequently, the revival continues to play an important rôle in the church services, though there are indications that the revival is not as important as formerly.

The pattern of religious services in the towns and smaller cities of the South is similar to that in the rural communities.[6] In southern cities as in the rural areas, the Negro population is "overchurched." A study in 1933 of Negro churches in seven southern cities revealed that there were 1,075 churches with a combined adult membership of 263,122 or 245 per church.[7] In this study it was pointed out that, "If the white people of Atlanta had proportionately as many churches as the Negroes have, white Atlanta would have 386 churches rather than 136. If the Negroes of Atlanta had proportionately as few churches as the whites, they would have 68 instead of 184."[8] However, in Atlanta and other larger cities of the South, there are differences in the character of the religious services in the Baptist and Methodist churches corresponding to the class differences in the Negro population. In the smaller churches of these denominations and those in which the lower classes are concentrated, the services are similar to those in the rural areas. On the other hand, the solid members of the middle class and a small number of upper-class Negroes are found chiefly in the churches with a more dignified form of religious service. Moreover, in the larger cities of the South, Congregational, Episcopal, and Presbyterian churches become more important in the religious life of the Negro. The relatively small congregations affiliated with these denominations are comprised largely of upper-class Negroes.

[4]Benjamin E. Mays and Joseph W. Nicholson, *The Negro's Church* (New York, 1933) pp. 238–41. See W. A. Daniel, *The Education of Negro Ministers* (New York, 1925) concerning schools for the education of Negro ministers.
[5]See Hortense Powdermaker, *After Freedom* (New York, 1939), pp. 253–73 on "Getting Religion."
[6]See *ibid.,* pp. 232–52.
[7]*Ibid.,* p. 210.
[8]Mays and Nicholson, *op. cit.,* p. 204.

The Impact of the North on the Religion of Negro Migrants

The migrations of Negroes to northern cities affected the character of their churches as well as other phases of their life. . . .

In northern cities, as in the South, most upper-class persons form the majority of the comparatively small congregations of the Episcopal, Presbyterian, and Congregational churches. The ministers in these churches are educated men and their sermons are generally of a scholarly character. Usually there are a few large Baptist and Methodist churches in which the more solid members of the middle class are concentrated. But in the numerous smaller Baptist and Methodist churches the church-centered elements of the lower class are concentrated. According to Drake and Cayton,

> It has been estimated that of the approximately 30,000 lower-class persons who were actually affiliated with churches, about a sixth belonged to three very large lower-class churches (each having more than 1,500 members); another sixth were distributed among a score of medium-sized lower-class churches (each with 200 to 500 members); about one-third of the total group were worshiping in remodeled stores, garages, theaters, houses, and halls; and another third were members of churches in which higher-status members predominated. Lower-class neighborhoods were plentifully supplied with small Baptist and Holiness churches.[9]

The lower-class people carry over into the northern city their traditional attitudes in regard to religion. There is great emphasis upon "Sin" and the "Devil." The chief sin against which the preachers constantly carry on warfare is loose sex behavior. The emphasis upon sex is, of course, a reflection of the sex pattern among the lower class. Since the lower-class churches are attended largely by women, many of whom are deserted or have other irregular marital relations, the church helps to accommodate the women of this class to their fate. The sermons in the lower-class churches reflect the Negro's naïve conception of the strange world about him. The complex and puzzling world of the city is usually pictured as a "wicked world," which will be destroyed by God. Therefore, the faithful should keep themselves uncontaminated by the wickedness of the world. The wickedness of the world consists largely of dancing, card playing, and drinking. The first step toward salvation involves conversion. The conversion experiences are losing much of their dramatic qualities in the city, though the services in these churches are characterized by much of the same emotionalisms found in the small rural churches of the South.

The emergence of the "storefront" church in the urban environment is of peculiar interest because it represents, on the whole, the adaptation of the small rural church to city life. Consequently, it is not surprising that

[9] *Black Metropolis* by St. Clair Drake and Horace R. Cayton, pp. 612–13. Copyright 1945 by Harcourt, Brace and Company, Inc.

the "storefront" church is more characteristic of the northern than of the southern city. In Chicago 75 per cent of the nearly 500 churches in the Negro community were "storefront" churches. Moreover, the location of these churches in relation to the spatial pattern of the Negro community indicates their relation to the economic and cultural organization of the community. The "storefront" churches are clustered in the poorer areas of the Negro community in which the newcomers from the South are concentrated.[10] The existence of these churches is due partly to the poverty of their members and the fact that the members may participate more freely—in praying as well as "shouting"—in the services. There is, however, a more important reason why "storefront" churches flourish in the northern city. In the large churches the Negro from the South, being lost in the mass of members, has no status and longs for the warmth and sympathetic relationship which is provided in the face-to-face association in the small church. Some of the ministers are, of course, charlatans, who take advantage of the ignorance and simple faith of their followers.[11] Then there are the so-called "jack-leg" preachers—untrained and seeking an escape from manual labor—who find in the "storefront" church a chance for employment or a chance to supplement their regular income. The regularly established churches have failed to provide the type of church or the trained ministry required by recently urbanized Negroes. But, on the whole, the "storefront" church owes its existence to the fact that it provides an opportunity for self-expression and social contacts.

The Increase in Negro Sects and Cults in Northern Cities

The most radical transformation in the religious life of the folk Negro is revealed in the various sectarian churches which have sprung up in the northern city. In Chicago over a fifth of the Negro churches are affiliated with various "holiness" denominations and another tenth with "spiritualist" churches. There are in addition to the various "holiness" and "spiritualist" churches other cults or sects which are nationalistic in their orientation. In his study of these cults in the northern cities, Fauset gives four compulsions, "the supernatural being, the personality of the leader, relief from physical and mental illness, and race consciousness," which appear to be responsible for the attraction of Negroes to the cults. In the case of the first compulsion, which is characteristic of all the cults, there is the desire to get closer to "some supernatural power, be it God, the Holy Spirit, or Allah."[12] The

[10]Mays and Nicholson, *op. cit.,* p. 219. See also Drake and Cayton, *op. cit.,* pp. 632–36; E. Franklin Frazier, *The Negro Family in Chicago* (Chicago, 1939), p. 276.

[11]In Chicago over 700 preachers were competing for 500 churches. Many of these preachers were "jack-leg" preachers or men without any formal training who had received the "call" to preach. Drake and Cayton, *op. cit.,* pp. 629–30.

[12]Arthur H. Fauset, *Black Gods of the Metropolis* (Philadelphia, 1944), p. 76. Raymond J. Jones, *A Comparative Study of Cult Behavior among Negroes with Special Reference to Emo-*

influence of the personality of the leader is likewise a common characteristic of the cults. The other two compulsions—physical and mental illness and race consciousness—are of greater importance because they have a peculiar relation to the Negro's adjustment to the northern environment.

The migration of the folk Negro to the northern metropolis often produces a severe crisis in his life. It often results in the disruption of family relations which provided emotional as well as a certain degree of economic security in the South. Generally it means the loss of friends and neighbors who gave the Negro the sense of "belonging" to a social group. Moreover, in the large city church, as we have pointed out, the folk Negro does not enjoy the face-to-face contacts and the status which the church in the South afforded. The folk knowledge and folk practices which provided a guide to life in the South lose their meaning especially in time of crises involving sickness and death. Consequently, the folk Negro seeks new ways to meet these crises and attempts to find a new meaning for his existence in the world of the city. In the cults in which "faith healing" plays an important rôle he finds a "cure" for both physical and mental ills. "Faith healing" appeals to him because it combines elements similar to the folk beliefs of the southern Negro with an "intellectual" element acquired through the reflection which is forced upon the Negro in the city. In the cults in which "holiness" or sanctification is important, he is able to resolve the moral conflicts created by the conflict between the simple mores of the South and free and easy ways of the city.

The most important cult to appear among Negroes in the northern city has been the Father Divine Peace Mission movement. This movement, which involves "faith healing" and "holiness" or sanctification, began in an obscure town on Long Island. It attracted Negroes from Harlem who disturbed the peace with their noisy religious behavior and thereby caused its leader, Father Divine, to run afoul of the law. As the result of the prosecution of Father Divine and the death of the judge who tried him, which his followers regarded as an act of divine displeasure, he became a Messiah. When he entered the impoverished Harlem community during the depth of the Depression in 1932, the Negroes were in a state of hopelessness.[13] Father Divine thus became the embodiment of a deliverer who had appeared to heal the physically and mentally sick and feed the hungry. Physical ailments were redefined as the result of straying from the "faith" in Father Divine and death became a weakness which the faithful had to overcome. Mental illness or doubt and conflicts were to be resolved

---

tional Group Conditioning Factors (Washington, 1939), classifies the various cults in five types: Faith Healing, Holiness, Islamic, Pentecostal, and Spiritualist. Fauset, *op. cit.,* has shown that in the various cults there is much overlapping of the types presented in Jones' study.

[13]See Robert A. Parker, *The Incredible Messiah* (Boston, 1937) for a thorough study of the development of the movement in relation to the psychological, social, and economic backgrounds of Negroes in Harlem.

simply by thinking of Father Divine and saying "Thank you, Father."[14] At the same time, "one must refrain from stealing, refusing to pay just debts, indulging in liquor in any form, smoking, obscene language, gambling, playing numbers, racial prejudice or hate of any kind, greed, bigotry, selfishness, and lusting after the opposite sex.[15]

One may discover in this cult a number of elements which reveal a new orientation of the Negro to life in the city. There is a sacred text, so to speak, which reflects the growing literacy of the Negro in the city. This sacred text is the *New Day,* a weekly newspaper which contains the advertisements of nationally known firms as well as local stores. The absence of the Bible is indicative of a certain sophistication or emancipation from traditional modes of thought and behavior. The *New Day* deals with the current issues of the day as interpreted by Father Divine to his followers. There are fourteen planks in the "Righteous Government" platform which serves as a guide to the faithful in their daily contacts. At the same time, the faithful are given an opportunity to indulge in ecstatic forms of religious behavior. These sporadic expressions of religious behavior are a part of living "evangelically," which involves communion with Father Divine. In their day to day existence, the faithful are encouraged to engage in business enterprises which have been, on the whole, successful.

In the Father Divine Peace movement, there are also whites among the faithful and any form of racial prejudice is strictly forbidden. By teaching amity in race relations this movement represents one form of adjustment of the Negro to whites in the urban environment of the North. Thus it stands in marked contrast to those cults which have fostered racial chauvinism and racial exclusiveness. The latter type of adjustment to race relations in the northern city has achieved its most extreme expression in the Moorish Science Temple of America. This cult was founded in 1913 by a twenty-seven-year-old Negro with little formal education, who was born in North Carolina.[16] After becoming acquainted with some phases of oriental philosophy, "he became obsessed with the idea that the salvation for the Negro people lay in the discovery by them of their national origin, i.e., they must know whence they came, and refuse longer to be called Negroes, black folk, colored people, or Ethiopians. They must henceforth call themselves Asiatics, to use the generic term, or, more specifically, Moors or Moorish Americans."[17] The reflections of the leader of this cult have been set down in a secret text, Holy Koran, which is not, of course, the Mohammedan Koran.

This movement with its "temples" spread from Newark to Chicago where hundreds of Negroes flocked to the new teacher. Those who

[14]Fauset, *op. cit.,* p. 63.
[15]*Ibid.,* p. 64.
[16]See Fauset, *op. cit.,* pp. 41–51.
[17]*Ibid.,* p. 41.

became full members of the cult were changed from Negroes to Asiatics. One of the important beliefs inculcated by the leader was that "a star within a crescent moon had been seen in the heavens" and that this sign was a portent of the coming dominance of the Asiatics and the destruction of the whites. The members wore fezzes and publicly exhibited their contempt toward the whites. Because of the increasing conflicts with whites, including the police, it was necessary for the prophet, Noble Drew Ali, to warn his followers to restrain themselves. As the movement grew, conflicts within the organization resulted in the murder of one of the leaders. The prophet was arrested for the murder but was never brought to trial because he died while free on bond. Despite the death of the leader, the movement continued to grow for awhile and spread to other metropolitan areas. Although the movement is still in existence, it has ceased to attract large numbers of Negroes.

This movement, like the Divine movement, combined certain elements in the history of the Negro with new definitions of the Negro's experiences in the city. Although the members of the cult were taught that Christianity is the white man's religion and that Islam was the religion of Asiatics (Negroes are regarded as Asiatics), in their service Christian hymns were set to words which embodied Moslem instruction. A striking feature of the religious services was that the emotionalism characteristic of Negro churches was lacking. In fact, there was little singing except in the form of chants. Members of the cult were required to pray three times a day turning their faces to the East, and to observe dietary restrictions and keep the body clean. The most important feature of the cult was that while it forbade "radicalism" and enjoined loyalty to the country, it offered a transformation of the Negro's personality which enabled him to adjust to the racial discriminations in the northern city.

Changes in the Orthodox Denominations

In the northern city the orthodox Baptist and Methodist churches have undergone changes which, though less dramatic, have been important in the adjustment of the Negro church to the urban environment. These changes have been brought about by changes in the mental outlook of the Negro in the city. Because of the greater literacy and experience of the northern Negro it has been necessary for their ministers to have more education.[18] Then, too, the sophisticated Negro in the northern city has a more secular attitude toward the problems which he faces. Consequently, the ministers in the orthodox Baptist and Methodist churches have been forced to direct their sermons to mundane affairs as well as otherworldly matters. The urbanized Negro has increasingly sought in the church an answer to the problems of making a living and a guide for the

[18]Cf. Mays and Nicholson, *op. cit.,* pp. 47–48.

exercise of his newly acquired political rights. In some of the orthodox churches, the ministers have attempted to continue to stress the super-natural aspects of religion and have taken a conservative attitude toward unions and the political affiliations of the Negro. This attitude has not been always unrelated to the fact that they have received contributions from wealthy white industrialists. But the pressing economic needs of Negroes, especially during the Depression, and their growing knowledge of the relation of economics and politics, have forced the majority of Negro ministers to relate their churches more or less to the social and economic problems of the Negro.[19]

The changes in the character of Negro Baptist and Methodist churches have been most striking in those churches under the dynamic leadership of outstanding ministers. The development of the Abyssinian Baptist Church in Harlem provides an example of the extent to which the ortho-dox Negro church in the northern city may become secularized in its outlook and in its function.[20] This church began as an orthodox Baptist Church in which many "respectable" Negroes of the day worshiped. After the church moved to Harlem, it began to cater to the needs of the thou-sands of Negroes who migrated from the South during and following World War I. A large structure costing nearly $400,000 was erected with three auditoriums and a community house. The father of the present minister, Adam Clayton Powell, Jr., had to fight the more conservatively religious elements in the church but by the time the membership had reached 11,000 the conservatives had been submerged. This new "social gospel institution," as the young minister who succeeded his father calls it, was equipped to serve the recreational and other needs of young and old. Moreover, the church has been the meeting place for organizations fighting to break down prejudice and secure employment for Negroes in the stores of Harlem. Because of his leadership in the secular interests of the people of Harlem, the minister of this church was the first Negro from Harlem to be elected to the Congress of the United States.

The changes in the character of the orthodox Baptist and Methodist churches in the northern cities are due principally to changes in the religious outlook of the middle class in the Negro community. There have also been changes in the character of the churches attended largely by upper-class Negroes which are indicative of the adjustment which these churches are making to the urban environment of the North. In Harlem, the Negro Presbyterian Church, probably the largest of this denomination in the country, under the leadership of a prominent minister, William Lloyd Imes, carried on a fight for the economic, political, and civil rights of Negroes. Its church activities have included many social features which

[19]See *Whither The Negro Church?* Seminar held at Yale Divinity School, New Haven, Conn. April 13–15, 1931. See also Drake and Cayton, *op. cit.,* pp. 424–29.
[20]See Adam Clayton Powell, Jr., *Marching Blacks* (New York, 1945), pp. 93ff.

were designed to help the Negro in his adjustment to urban life. Likewise, the Negro Protestant Episcopal Church, one of the oldest in the country, has maintained a community house and provided social services for the Negroes of Harlem.

There have been other changes in the religious affiliation of Negroes in the northern city which have been the result of more radical changes in the religious outlook of Negroes. There have appeared in northern cities a few institutional churches which attract Negro churchgoers with a broad humanistic as opposed to a strictly religious outlook on life. There is an increasing number of ministers with university education who are concerned with economic and social problems. The churches are the meeting place for clubs with various interests and Sunday forums for the discussion of social and economic problems. For some Negroes who have become emancipated from the orthodox Negro churches, the institutional churches are too secular in their outlook. Consequently, these people are likely to become affiliated with Christian Science churches and the Bahaist movement. While affiliation with these churches offers the means of resolving mental and moral conflicts, it is also related to the status of the Negro. In joining these churches, some Negroes have sought a church which does not practice segregation and in which they might feel at home. Then, too, Negroes and whites who have intermarried have often sought a congenial group in the Bahaist Church. These same motivations have often prompted Negroes to join the Catholic Church.

In its relations with the Negro the Catholic Church has faced a number of obstacles, both outside and within the Negro group.[21] One of the "external" obstacles has been the fact that the masses of Negroes have been concentrated in the South, where there has been much prejudice against the Catholic Church. Then, too, the Church has been forced to set up separate churches, for which there were no trained priests. Even more important than these "external" obstacles have been those "internal" obstacles or conditions existing within the Negro group. The most important of the "internal" obstacles has been the existence of Baptist and Methodist Negro church organizations, which remain one of the chief organized expressions of the race consciousness of the Negro masses. Moreover, the Negro has become accustomed to a type of church service which is opposed to the restraint characteristic of the worship in the Catholic churches. Despite these "external" and "internal" obstacles, and until recent years the belief of Catholics concerning the emotional nature of the Negro and his lack of moral restraint, the Catholic Church has given more attention to the evangelization of Negroes since their migrations to cities.

It appears that the immediate effect of the migration of Negroes to cities was a decline in the number of Negro members of the Catholic

[21]See Gillard, *The Catholic Church and the Negro,* pp. 212–57. This book contains a history of the relation of the Negro to the Catholic Church up to 1929.

Church.[22] This resulted from the disruption of missions in the South and the border states and the general disorganization of the Negro population as the result of the migrations. Around 1930, the Catholic Church began to give serious attention to the migrants. In some cities the Church directed its attention to the economic needs of the Negroes during the depression years. In fact, it seems that many urban Negroes were attracted to the Catholic Church during this period of economic stress. But the efforts of the Church have not been confined to giving aid to Negroes. It has undertaken to provide recreational and educational facilities for Negro youth in cities. For example, in Chicago the Catholic Church has opened parochial schools which provide a full-time program while many of the public schools in Negro neighborhoods are run on double shifts.[23] Only recently the Church has provided a first-class high school in Montgomery, Alabama, for Negroes. The archbishop of St. Louis has instructed the parochial schools to admit Negroes and has at the same time censured the whites who opposed the ruling.

From all indications the efforts of the Catholic Church to attract Negroes are proving successful. This success has been the result primarily of its attention to the problems of Negro youth in cities. The disruption of the Negro folk culture together with family disorganization has tended to alienate Negro youth from their traditional religious heritage. The Catholic Church through its systematic approach to the educational and recreational problems of Negro youth, a program involving the personal relations of the priest to these activities, has created a new religious orientation of the Negro in the city. Moreover, the Catholic Church has come out in recent years in the defense of the Negro's right to full participation in American culture. The general position of the Church has been set forth in recommendations developed in a four-day Seminar on Negro Problems, called by the National Catholic Welfare Conference in July 1946.[24] The recommendations included an endorsement of a permanent federal Fair Employment Practices Committee, a condemnation of unions excluding Negroes and of segregation in housing, and a strong defense of the civil rights of the Negro.

The new interest of the Catholic Church in the Negro during the past two decades has been paralleled by a new attitude on the part of white Protestantism toward the Negro. This new attitude has been manifested in the pronouncements of national organizations rather than in changes in the policies of local churches in regard to admitting Negroes to membership. When the three branches of the Methodist Church were united in 1939, the plan for the incorporation of the Negro members of the *Metho-*

---

[22]See *ibid.,* pp. 263–64.
[23]See Drake and Cayton, *op. cit.,* footnote, pp. 412, 415.
[24]See *Seminar on Negro Problems in the Field of Social Action,* National Catholic Welfare Conference, November, 1946, Washington 5, D. C.

dist Episcopal Church represented a concession to the *Methodist Episcopal Church, South,* which had split from the parent body in 1844 over the question of slavery. A central jurisdiction was set up which included Negro churches and over which Negro bishops elected by the Negro constituency presided.[25] The Negro membership is opposed, it appears, to this form of segregation but, according to one of their bishops, will accept the un-Christian arrangement "on account of the Christian childness of some American Methodists who need a little coddling until they can grow into full manhood and womanhood in Jesus Christ."[26] The need for "coddling," it was pointed out, existed among the local Methodist churches in the North as well as in the South.

On the other hand, the Federal Council of Churches in Christ took an unusual step at its meeting in Columbus, Ohio, in 1946 when it pledged to end racial discrimination and urged member churches to work toward the goal of racially mixed churches.[27] The General Assembly of the Presbyterian Church (Northern) has come out against racial segregation as un-Christian. The General Council of Congregational Christian Churches accepted a report condemning racial discrimination within the churches. Despite these pronouncements by national church organizations, Negroes have not been integrated to any significant extent into the white churches. The present situation in regard to the Congregational Christian churches was brought out in a recent survey. In 1944 about 5 per cent of the Congregational churches were "special" Negro churches.[28] Responses to inquiries sent to 3,800 ministers of Congregational Christian churches revealed that 388 churches had both white and nonwhite members. In 123 of the 388 churches there were white and Negro members in the same church; and in 75 churches there were Negroes and other nonwhite peoples and whites. The Negro membership of these churches consisted in most cases of one to four persons. Among the Congregational churches in New England there is a general disposition to set up separate churches for Negroes or to admit one or two in exceptional cases. There is less resistance to the participation of Negroes in such activities as Sunday School and Vacation Bible School than to full adult membership in the churches.

In considering the relationship of the Negro to white churches, it should be pointed out that in recent years small interracial churches have sprung up over the country. As a rule these churches have two pastors,

[25]See *Doctrines and Discipline of The Methodist Church* (New York and Cincinnati, 1912).

[26]See article by Joshua C. Williams, "Shall We Continue the Control Jurisdiction?" *The Central Christian Advocate,* November 13, 1947.

[27]See "The New Social Rôle of American Churches," *A Monthly Summary of Events and Trends in Race Relations,* December, 1946.

[28]See L. Maynard Catchings, "The Participation of Racial and Nationality Minority Peoples in Congregational-Christian Churches," *The Journal of Negro Education,* Vol. XV, pp. 681–89.

one Negro and the other white, with the membership including nonwhite members other than Negroes.

The development of the religious life of the Negro and his church organizations in the United States has paralleled other phases of his adjustment to American life and his gradual integration into American society. Whatever remained of his African religious heritage was rapidly lost and the Negro assimilated the forms of religious life found in the American environment. The process of assimilation was determined by the extent to which the Negro was integrated into the religious life of his masters. In the South, the Baptist and Methodist churches because of their appeal and their type of services enabled Negroes under favorable conditions to share largely in the religious life of the masters. However, the Negro church as an institution had its birth among the free Negroes in the North who seceded from white Methodist churches. The growth of the Negro Methodist Church as an independent organization was restricted in the South, though independent Methodist and Baptist churches sprang up among the free Negroes. After Emancipation the independent Negro church organizations, the Baptist churches and the various Methodist denominations, experienced a rapid growth since the thousands of Negroes who were only nominal Christians became affiliated with these churches. The rapid growth of Negro church organizations was a part of their emancipation from white dominance, though the Negro church became one of the most effective agencies in accommodating the Negro to his subordinate status in the South.

With the migration of Negroes to nothern cities, the Negro church has lost much of its former influence. At the same time the Negro church has undergone certain transformations in adapting itself to the urban environment. The "storefront" church, in which the simple folk from the South find a congenial form of worship, has made its appearance in the northern city. Various cults and sects have sprung up in answer to the mental and moral conflicts of the frustrated and disillusioned migrants. The orthodox churches have added secular interests in order to hold the urbanized Negro who has acquired a new attitude toward his problems. During the crisis produced by World War II both Protestant and Catholic churches recognized the segregated Negro church as a violation of the spirit of Christianity but practically no progress has been made in admitting Negroes to membership in local white churches. Yet, it is probable that as the result of rivalry between the Protestant and Catholic churches, the Negro will be increasingly admitted to membership in local churches.

DATE DUE